Issues in Contemporary Legal Philosophy

Issues in Contemporary Legal Philosophy

The Influence of H. L. A. Hart

Edited by
RUTH GAVISON

CLARENDON PRESS · OXFORD
1987

Oxford University Press, Walton Street, Oxford OX2 6DP

Oxford New York Toronto
Delhi Bombay Calcutta Madras Karachi
Petaling Jaya Singapore Hong Kong Tokyo
Nairobi Dar es Salaam Cape Town
Melbourne Auckland

and associated companies in
Beirut Berlin Ibadan Nicosia

Oxford is a trade mark of Oxford University Press

Published in the United States
by Oxford University Press, New York

British Library Cataloguing in Publication Data
Issues in Contemporary legal philosophy : the
influence of H.L.A. Hart.
1. Hart, H.L.A.
I. Gavison, Ruth
340'.109   KD632.H/
ISBN 0–19–825517–9

Library of Congress Cataloging-in-Publication Data
Jerusalem : issues in contemporary legal philosophy.
Papers from a conference held in Jerusalem in
Mar. 1984.
Bibliography: p.
Includes index.
1. Law—Philosophy—Congresses.   2. Hart, H. L. A.
(Herbert Lionel Adolphus), 1907–   —Congresses.
I. Hart, H. L. A. (Herbert Lionel Adolphus), 1907–   .
II. Gavison, Ruth.
K225.J47 1986   340'.1   86–31200
ISBN 0–19–825517–9

Set by Wyvern Typesetting, Bristol
Printed in Great Britain
at Oxford University Printing House, Oxford
by David Stanford
Printer to the University

Contents

List of Contributors

Hanina Ben-Menachem is Senior Researcher in the Jewish Law Research Institute, Faculty of Law, Hebrew University.

Ronald Dworkin is the Professor of Jurisprudence, Oxford University.

John Finnis is Praelector in Jurisprudence at University College and Reader in Law, Oxford University.

Chaim Gans is Lecturer in Legal Philosophy, Faculty of Law, Tel Aviv University.

Ruth Gavison is an Associate Professor and the incumbent of the Haim Cohn Chair of Human Rights, Faculty of Law, Hebrew University.

Kent Greenawalt is Cardozo Professor of Jurisprudence at the School of Law, Columbia University.

Miriam Gur-Arye is Senior Lecturer in Criminal Law, Faculty of Law, Hebrew University.

H. L. A. Hart is Emeritus Professor of Jurisprudence, Oxford University.

David Heyd is Senior Lecturer, Department of Philosophy, Hebrew University.

Sanford Kadish is Alexander and May T. Morrison Professor of Law, Boalt Hall School of Law, University of California, Berkeley.

Mordechai Kremnitzer is Senior Lecturer in Criminal Law, Faculty of Law, Hebrew University.

David Lyons is member of the Philosophy and Law faculties at Cornell University.

Neil MacCormick is Regius Professor of Public Law and Dean of the Faculty of Law at Edinburgh University.

Michael Moore is Robert Kingsley Professor of Law at the University of Southern California.

Thomas Morawetz is Professor of Law at the University of Connecticut School of Law.

Gerald J. Postema is Associate Professor of Philosophy at the University of North Carolina at Chapel Hill.

Igor Primoratz is Senior Lecturer, Department of Philosophy, the Hebrew University.

Joseph Raz is Professor of the Philosophy of Law at Oxford University and a fellow of Balliol College.

Rolf Sartorius is Professor of Philosophy in Minneapolis, Minnesota.

Yoram Shachar is Senior Lecturer, Faculty of Law, Tel Aviv University.

Leon Sheleff is Associate Professor of Criminology, Faculty of Law, Tel Aviv University.

Philip Soper is Professor of Law in the University of Michigan.

C. L. Ten is Reader in Philosophy at Monash University.

Introduction

This is neither a book about Hart's legal philosophy, nor a comprehensive survey of contemporary legal philosophy. Rather, it is a contribution to legal philosophy as we find it *after* Hart has transformed it. The book (and the conference on which it is based) was conceived as a tribute to Hart and is founded on the belief that the best tribute one could give a teacher and mentor is to take the lead he has given us, to pursue further the many avenues that he has opened up. With Hart, starting from the many works that now belong to the classics of jurisprudence, the task has been an easy one. Hart himself, through his never-ending curiosity and alertness, made this choice almost mandatory: he has never been interested in more commentaries on his own work. He has always preferred a new challenge, a promise of a new insight, something that he could incorporate into his thought rather than an introduction to a new polemic. The book is thus a very partial illustration of the ways in which Hart's thought has affected contemporary trends in legal philosophy and inspired its development. It is an original contribution to legal philosophy building on Hart, not a critical exposition of his views.

The structure of this book is less coherent and comprehensive than it might have been since we opted for giving the contributors their choice of subject (within a general framework). Thus there are important themes of Hart's work that are not even touched upon (such as his position on definitions in jurisprudence;[1] his developing theories of rights and powers;[2] the relationships between utilitarianism and rights;[3] and his theory of adjudication). Similarly, no one took up the implications of Hart's positions for legal education, a theme Hart himself debated with Bodenheimer.[4] It would have been rewarding to have papers on these topics as well, but I do not regret the choice made. The

---

[1] See Hart's inaugural lecture, 'Definition and Theory in Jurisprudence', *Law Quarterly Review*, vol. 70 (1954), reprinted in *Essays in Jurisprudence and Philosophy*, Oxford (1983) (hereafter *Essays*) 19.

[2] See essays 4, 6, 7, 8 in *Essays on Bentham*, Oxford (1982).

[3] See essays 8, 9 in *Essays*.

[4] Bodenheimer, 'Modern Analytical Jurisprudence and the Limits of its Usefulness', *University of Pennsylvania Law Review*, vol. 104 (1956), 1080–6; and H. L. A. Hart, 'Analytical Jurisprudence in Mid-Twentieth Century', *U Pa. L Rev.* vol. 105 (1957), 953–75.

quality of contributions is usually much higher when people write of what intrigues them at the time rather than on 'commissioned' subjects. Furthermore, the volume reflects the variety and breadth of Hart's legal philosophy, on a number of levels; and it has the advantage that it takes up issues that are at the forefront of debate at the time of publication. Neither do I regret the occasional overlap in the volume. I see it as one of its virtues that all those dealing with legal theory have something to say about the normative basis of obedience to the law. This is not a mere overlap stemming from bad organization. It is the salutary reflection of the fact that today no one can deal with questions about the nature of law without addressing the question of the law's claim to authority. It is usually hard to talk of 'progress' in a humanistic field. In legal philo-sophy this growing awareness that legal theory is linked, in ways to be specified, to moral and political authority, is clearly an instance of progress in legal philosophy, progress to which Hart has contributed a number of crucial steps.

One of the unique features of Hart's legal thought is its versatility. There is hardly a subject or issue in legal philosophy on which it is not natural, almost inevitable, to start with his views. On some issues, we have not managed to go much further than he did. Most legal philo-sopher; are content to take most of their field 'on faith', and make particular contributions to one or two subjects. This has not been the case with Hart. In some fields he has defined the questions which we are all trying to answer, and has provided an answer of his own. In others he has revolutionized the 'state of the art' by changing the level and quality of public and professional debate. Consequently, it was impossible to do partial justice even to Hart's work within a single cluster of questions. The three clusters represented here—legal theory, criminal responsi-bility, and the enforcement of morals—have interested Hart for most of his career as a legal philosopher, but are far from exhausting this interest.

Four of the contributions, those by Dworkin, Sartorius, Postema, and Soper, concern legal theory. Hart's own interest in this cluster of questions has been, perhaps, the most enduring.[5] This is demonstrated in the span of years covered by his works cited in these four contribu-tions. It should be noted that today we take for granted that there is a connection between the articulation of criteria for identifying the law (Sartorius's enterprise, following Hart's *Concept of Law*), the nature of

---

[5] See the overview Hart himself gives of his work in the introduction to *Essays*.

the theory of law we endorse (Postema's paper), the obligation to obey the law (Soper's issue) and the general nature of law and of judicial reasoning. All these themes are reflected in Dworkin's paper and in Hart's response. It is proper to recall, therefore, that this presentation of the issues as interrelated was first dramatized by the Hart–Fuller debate in 1958.[6] Sartorius provides a further elaboration of the rule of recognition as the prime identifier of the law. Postema returns to the old question of the adequacy of positivism as a theory of law, in view of more recent and more sophisticated versions of such theories. Soper seeks to develop an alternative basis for the general moral obligation to obey the law. Dworkin, finally, presents an integrated view of law as a certain kind of interpretive concept, and explores the implications of such a description for questions such as judicial reasoning, the relationships between law and morality, the universality of conceptions of law, and the problem of unjust legal systems.

The second cluster of subjects addressed by Hart which is reflected in this volume is principles of legal responsibility in general, and criminal responsibility in particular. Hart's own work in this field covers treatment of conceptual questions such as the presuppositions of ascription of liability[7] and the nature of punishment,[8] the nature and function of causation in the law,[9] and substantive questions relating to the nature and desirable scope of defences.[10] Primoratz's paper puts Hart's contribution to the nature of punishment in the broader context of the continuing debate between retributivist and consequentialist theories of punishment. Kadish constructs a theory of complicity, invoking Hart's notions of causation in the law. Moore seeks to analyse the paradigmatic 'mental element' of intention, and to explore the implication of such philosophical analysis for the requirement of *mens rea* in criminal law.

Last but not least of Hart's concerns reflected in this book is that with liberty, tolerance, and the enforcement of morals by the law. Underlying

[6] See Hart, 'Positivism and the Separation of Law and Morals', *Harvard Law Review*, vol. 71 (1958) reprinted in *Essays*, 49; and Fuller, 'Positivism and Fidelity to Law: a reply to Professor Hart', *Harvard Law Review*, vol. 71 (1958), 630.

[7] See e.g. one of Hart's first pieces: 'The Ascription of Responsibility and Rights', *Proceedings of the Aristotelian Society*, vol. 49 (1949), 171.

[8] For a discussion of Hart's theory of punishment see essay 5 and the comments in this volume.

[9] The main source is still Hart and Honoré, *Causation in the Law*, Oxford (1959) (hereafter *Causation*).

[10] See essays 2, 5, 6 in *Punishment and Responsibility*, Oxford (1968).

Hart's critique of Devlin and Stephen[11] is a concern with the value of liberty and autonomy. Acceptance that enforcement of positive morality by the law is undesirable, as Mill and Hart argue, entails regarding tolerance as a value. Raz gives us a much-needed exploration of the conditions of seeing tolerance as a value, thus pushing further the debate on this crucial question of public morality.

All these papers taken together, and the fact that we have among the participants philosophers, lawyers, and sociologists, demonstrates another important contribution of Hart's work. It is well known that interdisciplinary work is not easy, since different disciplines tend to develop their own jargon and their distinctive concerns. Specialization and the structure of university departments have not helped. Yet it is equally well known that especially in some branches of knowledge this division of labour and interest is unfortunate and can lead to inadequate understanding of phenomena whose reach goes beyond one discipline. Hart is undoubtedly largely responsible for the ease with which scholars in legal philosophy rely on general philosophical, and to some lesser extent, sociological and psychological literature. Indeed, we now think that not to bring to legal thought the insights gained by these other disciplines is to impoverish the attempt to understand the law. This claim is not original to Hart. Yet he has done much to persuade practitioners in the field to do so by showing us, through his own example, how illuminating and inspiring these insights can be.[12]

In addition to participating in this tribute to Hart the contributors had the bonus of presenting their work at a conference entitled 'The Legal Philosophy of H. L. A. Hart', held in Jerusalem on 13–15 March 1984. The idea originated with and was efficiently carried out by the Van Leer Jerusalem Foundation (VLJF). The conference was sponsored by the Israel Academy of Arts and Sciences, the VLJF and the Faculties of Law of the Hebrew University in Jerusalem and of Tel Aviv University. I thank them all for their support. The structure of the book reflects its origins, with a few minor changes.

The conference was an exciting event, not least because of Hart's presence and comments on all issues. In addition, anyone familiar with

[11]   *Law, Liberty and Morality*, London (1965); 'Social Solidarity and the Enforcement of Morality', *University of Chicago Law Review*, vol. 35 (1967), 1, reprinted in *Essays*, 248.

[12]   Hart himself draws attention to the extent of his indebtedness to philosophy, and especially linguistic philosophy, in the introduction to *Essays*. In the article cited in note 11 above he analyses solidarity in expressly sociological terms. It is a well-known observation that his rule of recognition, and his analysis of social obligation, have proved very powerful contacts between legal philosophy and sociology.

the literature on legal philosophy may guess that most of the participants had a lot to say on subjects other than those to which they contributed in writing. In consequence the meeting was an exchange within a community of scholars of the highest standard.

In his closing remarks at the conference Professor Ronald Dworkin, Hart's successor to the Oxford chair in Jurisprudence, told a large audience how Hart has 'made' the field for us today. Before him, Dworkin said, legal philosophy consisted of asking questions such as what the concept of possession meant. These are, of course, interesting and important questions. But they are very different from the questions discussed in this book, questions that are now at the centre of work in legal philosophy. There can be no doubt that the questions Hart has revived so effectively are central to our understanding of the law and its social functions. Thus Hart has more than earned the rare compliment, that, had we not had his presence and contribution the field would not have looked the same.

In addition, we are all grateful to Hart for the many things he gave us: his profound insights, clear and elegant formulations, commitment to rational debate and to intellectual integrity, his generosity to students, and fairness towards critics. Many of the contributors have had the pleasure of studying under Hart. All the others, and the many people in the field who could not join us, are students of his written work. It is a great honour and pleasure to give him this book.

PART I
LEGAL THEORY

1.1   Legal Theory and the Problem of Sense*

RONALD DWORKIN

I spoke at the conference in Jerusalem without a text, but I had given commentators excerpts from an early draft of the beginning of a book since published, *Law's Empire*.[1] These excerpts were too long to publish in full here but, at the editor's request, I have tried to summarize them in a fresh statement so that readers might have at least some idea of the material Ruth Gavison and H. L. A. Hart used to prepare their comments. Interested readers should nevertheless consult the full and final version of my arguments, in the first three chapters of *Law's Empire*, particularly since some of the remarks these commentators made presuppose a more detailed account of my argument than this summary provides. I have taken the opportunity to add, at the end, some brief observations about what Gavison and Hart said at the conference.

I   THE PROBLEM

I spoke about the general character of jurisprudence: about the proper aims of that discipline and its proper methods. I was concerned with one central issue of jurisprudence: analysing or accounting for what might be called the *sense* of propositions of law. Lawyers and laymen accept and assert (or disbelieve and deny) propositions about what the law of their nation or state 'says'. These propositions are sometimes very general (the law forbids states to deny anyone the equal protection of the laws within the meaning of the 14th Amendment), sometimes much less general (the law does not allow murderers to inherit from their victims), and sometimes very concrete (the law requires Mr O'Brien to compensate Mrs McLoughlin for the emotional injury she suffered on 19 October 1973).

The question of sense asks what these propositions of law should be understood to mean, and in what circumstances they should be taken to be true or false or neither. (Or, if you object to using 'true' or 'false'

---

[1]   *Law's Empire*, Cambridge, Mass., and London (1986).

about propositions of law, in what circumstances it is proper and improper to assert them.) These must always be central problems of jurisprudence. Since the use of propositions of law and debate over their truth or soundness are pervasive features of legal practice, no competent account of that practice can ignore the issue of what kind of claims these propositions are used to make. We can no more grasp what legal practice is like without some understanding of the sense of propositions of law than we could understand the institution of mathematics with no grasp of the sense of mathematical propositions. That is why successful theories of law will always have or entail what might seem a merely linguistic aspect or component.

II   THE ORTHODOX ANSWER

Orthodox legal theories (I shall mention some examples in a moment) each contain some general thesis about what propositions of law mean and when they are true, although this must sometimes be dug out from beneath the surface. I believe they share a common and mistaken assumption: that lawyers all use roughly the same factual criteria for deciding when propositions of law are true or false, and that a correct statement of the criteria they use constitutes a statement of the sense these propositions have. So a philosopher answers the question of sense by an accurate report of these shared criteria, which must be a neutral, descriptive report quite independent of any moral or political convictions the philosopher might have.

This story supposes that lawyers follow common rules—I shall call these semantic rules—which stipulate necessary and sufficient factual conditions for the truth of any particular proposition of law. It does not follow that lawyers know what rules these are, in the sense of being able to state them in some crisp and comprehensive form. For we all follow rules, in using our language, of which we are not fully aware. It falls to legal philosophy, on this account, to explicate the conceptual rules lawyers have been following unawares. This may be a matter of some difficulty and legal philosophers may well disagree.

Legal positivism, as a school of jurisprudence, argues that the rules lawyers follow unawares stipulate exclusively historical grounds for law, stipulate, that is, criteria that make the truth of propositions of law turn on whether certain specified social and psychological events have actually occurred. Positivists differ about the exact characterization of these historical criteria. Austin, for example, said that a proposition of law is true, within a particular political society, if it correctly reports the past command of some person or group occupying the position of sovereign in that society, and he defined a sovereign as someone whose commands are habitually obeyed and who is not himself or itself in the habit of obeying anyone else.

Hart rejected Austin's account of legal authority as a brute fact of habitual command and obedience. He said that the true grounds of law lie in the acceptance, by the community as a whole, of a fundamental master rule (he called this a 'rule of recognition') that assigns to particular people or groups the authority to create law. So propositions of law are true, when they are true, not just in virtue of the commands of people who happen to enjoy habitual obedience, but more fundamentally in virtue of social conventions which represent the community's acceptance of a scheme of rules empowering such people or groups to create, by their decisions from time to time, valid law.

All forms of legal positivism must meet a formidable challenge, which we can describe most quickly by noticing a distinction between two kinds of disagreement lawyers can have about any particular proposition of law. They might agree about what I called the grounds of law—about which non-legal facts can make a particular proposition of law true or false—but disagree about whether those grounds are in fact available in a particular case. They might agree, for example, that the speed limit is 55 if the appropriate legislature has passed such a law, but disagree about whether it has because they have not yet consulted the statute books. Call this an empirical disagreement. Or they might disagree about what really are the grounds of law, about which non-legal facts make a proposition of law true or false. Call that a theoretical disagreement about the law.

If the positivist's general solution to the problem of sense is sound, then theoretical disagreement would be impossible or at least very rare. How can lawyers and judges disagree about the grounds of law if they all follow the same rules (whether or not they are able to articulate these rules) for deciding what grounds make a proposition of law true? The positivist's reply, so far as it appears in the literature, is a bold claim. Theoretical disagreement is, in some sense or another, an illusion. There are two versions of this bold claim. The first is the cruder: it holds that when lawyers and judges appear to disagree about whether some proposition of law is true they are actually agreed that it is not because there is in fact no law at all on the question it purports to answer. They are actually debating about whether the proposition *should* be true, about whether judges should use their power to fill gaps in the law in the way that would make the proposition true after they act. Why then do they all pretend that there is law and that they are disagreeing about what the law is? Because the public believes that there always is law and that judges should always follow it. On this view lawyers and judges connive to keep the truth from the public so as not to disillusion it or arouse its ignorant anger.

This crude answer is unpersuasive, because it is unclear why the pretence should be necessary, or how it could be successful. If lawyers all agree that there is no decisive law in hard cases, then why has this view not become part of our popular political culture long ago? Why do losing as well as winning lawyers co-operate in the deception? In any case, there is no evidence, in actual judicial opinions, that when lawyers and judges seem to be disagreeing about the law they are really keeping their fingers crossed. Most of their arguments would be entirely inappropriate as arguments for either the repair or improvement of law; they make sense only as arguments about what judges must do in virtue of their responsibility to enforce the law as it is.

The second version of the claim that theoretical disagreement is a kind of illusion is more sophisticated. It stresses the importance of distinguishing between standard or core uses of the word 'law' on the one hand and border-line or penumbral uses of that word on the other. Rules for using words (it points out) are not precise and exact; they create penumbral or borderline cases in which people speak somewhat differently from one another. So lawyers may use the word 'law' differently in marginal cases when some but not all of the grounds specified in the main rule are satisfied. This explains, according to the present argument, why they disagree in hard cases. Each uses a slightly different version of the main rule, and the differences become manifest in these special cases.

According to this more sophisticated defence of positivism lawyers are in no way pretending or trying to deceive the public. They really do believe they disagree about the state of the law, but their disagreement is spurious. From our standpoint, as critics, it is better to think of their argument as one about repair, about what the law should be, because we will understand the legal process better if we use 'law' only to describe what lies within the core of that concept. If we use it, that is, to cover only propositions of law true according to the central or main rule for using 'law' that everyone accepts, like the propositions of the highway code. So legal positivism, defended in this different way, has a reforming as well as a descriptive character, but the reform is in the interests of clarity not any particular vision of political morality.

This new story is in one way like the fingers-crossed story, however: it leaves wholly unexplained why the legal profession should have acted for so long in the way the story claims it has. How could they think that important decisions about the use of state power should turn on an arbitrary decision to use a word one way rather than another at its borders? The crossed-fingers defence shows judges as well-meaning liars; the borderline case defence shows them as simpletons instead.

The borderline defence is worse than insulting, moreover, because its diagnosis ignores an important distinction between two kinds of disagreements. I mean the distinction between borderline cases and testing or pivotal cases. People sometimes do speak at cross-purposes in the way that defence describes. They agree about the correct tests for applying some word in what they consider normal cases—they all agree about what ordinarily makes a house a house—but they happen to use the word somewhat differently in what they all recognize to be marginal cases like the case of a palace. Sometimes, however, they argue about the appropriateness of some word or description not for that reason but because they disagree about the correct tests for using the word or phrase on *any* occasion, including occasions on which they agree the word applies. The arguments judges and lawyers have about propositions of law in hard cases are arguments of this second kind, pivotal arguments testing fundamental principles, not borderline arguments about where some concededly arbitrary line should be drawn. Arguments about the proper way to read a statute, for example, are deep arguments that reflect different sets of assumptions about the character and point of legislation not just when statutes are unclear but when they are clear as well.

III   LAW AS AN INTERPRETIVE CONCEPT

I said that orthodox theories go wrong in this way because they fail to realize that propositions of law make *interpretive* claims, and that any useful account of the truth conditions of such propositions must therefore be normative rather than simply descriptive. This claim assumes a particular account of what interpretation, most abstractly described, really is. In the context I have in mind, it is the activity of trying to impose coherence on the behaviour that makes up a social practice, and imposing coherence means proposing some consistent point or meaning the behaviour can be taken to express or exemplify. Very often—perhaps even typically—the data will under-determine the point. In that event normal interpretation aims to make, of the material being interpreted, the best it can be of the enterprise to which it is taken to belong. So an interpretation of something assumed to be a work of art seeks to make it the best it can be artistically, and an interpretation of all or some part of legal practice seeks to make this the best it can be from the point of view of political morality.

Propositions of law, I argued, make interpretive claims of that general character. They claim that some part of legal practice is seen in its best light if it is understood as deploying and enforcing the principle or rule the proposition reports. Judges develop, over their careers and in response to their own convictions and instincts, working theories about the best interpretation of various levels and parts of the legal practices of their jurisdiction. They expand and rely on these theories when they are confronted with new and difficult issues; they try to decide hard cases consistently, so far as they can, with what they take to be the best interpretation of the general practice of deciding hard cases. When they disagree about the law their disagreements are interpretive. If two judges disagree about how statutes should be read, or about what force should be given to precedent decisions not directly in point, this will ordinarily reflect a deeper disagreement over the best general interpretation of their community's practices of adjudication, that is, a disagreement about which account of that practice shows it in its best light from the point of view of political morality. Interpretations struggle side by side with litigants before the bar.

Legal philosophers cannot produce useful semantic theories of law. They cannot expose the common ground rules lawyers follow for fixing legal labels onto facts, for there are no such rules. General theories about the circumstances in which propositions of law are true are abstract interpretations. They are abstract because they aim to interpret the main point and structure of legal practice not some particular part or department of it. But for all their abstraction they remain interpretations: they try to show legal practice as a whole in the best light it can bear. So no firm line divides jurisprudence from adjudication or any other aspect of legal practice. Legal philosophers debate about the general part, the interpretive foundation any legal argument must have. We may turn that coin over. Any practical legal argument, no matter how detailed and limited, assumes a general foundation of exactly the kind jurisprudence offers, and when rival foundations compete it assumes one of these and rejects others. Jurisprudence is the general part of adjudication.

An abstract interpretation of legal practice—a 'conception' of law— will deploy, as its organizing idea, some account of how the familiar practices and procedures of modern legal systems contribute to the justification of collective coercive force. Legislation—the practice of recognizing as law the explicit decisions of special bodies widely assumed to have that power—is a prominent part of our legal landscape, and precedent also has a prominent place. So any competent conception must provide some answer to the question why statutes enacted through particular procedures and past judicial decisions should in themselves provide a justification for the later use of state power. No conception need justify every feature of the practice it offers to interpret: like any interpretation it can condemn some of its data as a mistake, as inconsistent with the justification it offers for the rest, and perhaps propose that this mistake be abandoned. A conception of law might try to show, for example, that the general explanation of legislation that provides overall the best justification of that institution requires, con- trary to now prevailing practice, that old and out-of-date statutes should be treated as no longer law. Conceptions of law are controversial just because they differ in this way in their post-interpretive accounts of legal practice, in their opinions about the right way to expand or extend the practice in topics or areas or procedures at present controversial. These controversial opinions are the cutting edge of a conception of law, and that is why hard cases provide the best theatre for their power.

IV SCEPTICAL THEORIES AND WICKED LAW

There is plainly room, in this general picture of what legal theory should be like, for sceptical or nihilistic conceptions of law. It must be open to a philosopher of law to conclude that the practice he sets out to interpret has no decent justification that fits even most of what is done or demanded in its name, and to recommend that the practice therefore be abandoned or ignored. Some of the more extreme examples of legal realist theories have that flavour, when they are understood as interpret- ations instead of semantic theories of law, as do some theories that call themselves Marxist. The question whether a particular conception of law is a negative or sceptical conception, however, is sometimes a matter of perspective. An interpretation that emphasizes one point or purpose is sceptical about others, and if the latter appear more ambitious or profound the theory will have an overall sceptical cast.

In the heyday of semantic theories legal philosophers worried about whether wicked places really had law. Semantic rules were meant to capture the use of 'law' generally, and therefore to cover statements people make not only about their own legal system, in which they participate as members of a continuing practice, but about very different historical and foreign legal systems as well. It was, for example, a common argument against strong 'natural law' theories, which claim that a scheme of political organization must satisfy certain minimal standards of justice in order to count as a legal system at all, that our linguistic practice does not deny the title of law to obviously immoral schemes. We say the Nazis had law though it was very bad law. This fact about our linguistic practice was widely thought to argue for positivism, with its axiom that the existence of law is independent of the value of that law, in preference to any 'natural law' theory.

If useful theories of law are not semantic theories of this kind, but are instead interpretive of a particular stage of an historically developing practice, then the problem of immoral legal systems appears in a very different light. Interpretive theories are in their nature addressed to a particular legal culture, generally the culture to which their authors belong. Unless these theories are deeply sceptical they will treat that legal system as a flourishing example of law, one that calls for and rewards the interpretive attitude. They will offer to find, in its general structure of their practice, a political justification of its role in licensing political coercion. They should therefore not be supportive, but in some way sceptical, about legal systems that lack features essential to that justification.

But it does not follow that a lawyer who finds the best interpretation of Anglo-American law in some feature the Nazi regime wholly lacked must then deny that the Nazis had law. His theory is not a semantic theory about all uses of the word 'law', but an interpretive theory about the consequences of taking the interpretive attitude towards his own legal system. He may, with perfect linguistic propriety, insist that the Nazis did have law. We would know what he meant. He would mean that the Nazi system can be recognized as one historical realization of the general practices and institutions from which our own legal culture also developed. It is law, that is, in what we might call the pre-interpretive sense.

We need not deny that the Nazi system was an example of law, no matter which interpretation we favour of our own law, because, as I have just said, there is an available sense in which it plainly was. But we have no difficulty in understanding someone who does say that Nazi law was not really law, or was law in a degenerate sense, or was less than fully law. For he is not then using 'law' in that sense; he is not making a pre-interpretive judgement of that character, but a sceptical interpretive judgement that Nazi law lacked features crucial to flourishing legal systems whose rules and procedures do justify coercion. His judgement is now a special kind of political judgement for which his language, if the context makes this clear, is entirely appropriate. We do not understand him fully, of course, unless we know which interpretation of the point of flourishing legal systems he favours. But we catch his drift; we know the direction in which he will argue if he continues.

It is perfectly true that the lawyer just mentioned, who says that Nazi law was no law, might have put the very same point in the different way favoured by positivists. He might have said that the Nazis had law but very bad law lacking the features of a minimally decent system. But that would have told us less of what he thinks, revealed less of his overall jurisprudential position, because it would not have signalled his view about the consequences of lacking those features. On the other hand, on some occasions, this curtailment might be an advantage. It might be unnecessary and even diversionary—productive of argument unnecess-ary to his present purpose—for him to reveal more. In that case the alternative positivist formulation of his point would be preferable, and there is no reason why we should artificially limit our language to make context-sensitive choices of this kind impossible.

Context sensitivity will be even more important when the question in play is sharper, more specialized, more practical than simply one of general classification or critique of a foreign and very different legal system. Suppose the question somehow arises, for example, how a judge in the foreign system we disapprove—Judge Siegfried, for example—should decide some hard case arising there. The focus has changed, because this question requires, not merely a general comparison of the foreign system with our own, but an independent interpretation of that system in some detail.

Suppose we think that Siegfried's legal system is so wicked that it can never provide any justification at all, even a weak one, for state coercion, so that in every case Siegfried, if he can get away with it, should simply ignore legislation and precedent altogether. Once again we might, but need not, put that opinion in the dramatic language that denies that there is any law in Siegfried's nation at all. That choice of words, which relies on the post-interpretive sense of 'law', would enforce the premiss that interpretation proposes a justification, so that when no justification at all is provided by what is law in the pre-interpretive sense, the right interpretive judgement is the sceptical one that denies the title of law. But we could make the same complex point by using 'law' in the pre-interpretive rather than the post-interpretive sense, and then adding that in this case what is law provides no warrant for a judicial decision. Whichever language we choose the important point, for us, would be the point of political morality, that nothing just in the fact that this nation has law in the pre-interpretive sense provides any litigant with any right to win what he seeks in its courts.

Suppose, however, that on further reflection this is not exactly our view. For we might find something in the history of the legal practices of Siegfried's community that we think justifies *some* claim of right by some litigant in some case before him, in spite of the general wickedness of the political system, and in spite of the fact that we believe these practices as a whole are so defective that no supportive general interpretation is possible. Suppose, for example, that the case in question is an ordinary contract case that seems to involve no issue of racial or political discrimination or otherwise any piece of tyranny. We might think that the plaintiff in this case has an overall right to win just because the statutes and precedents of his jurisdiction grant him that right. Our opinion might, in another case, be more guarded. Suppose the case does in some way involve discriminatory or otherwise unjust legislation. Suppose the defendant is a Jew and the plaintiff has appealed to some statute denying Jews defences available to Aryans in contract cases. We might still think that the facts just cited justify a *weak* right in the plaintiff to win, although we would want to add that this weak right is overriden, all things considered, by a competing moral right in the defendant so that Siegfried should nevertheless do all in his power—even lie about the law if this would help—to dismiss the claim.

We can make the political issues more difficult still by improving the complexity of our example in various ways. The underlying moral issues would then change, and more distinctions and discriminations would become necessary. Even so the question of which words we used— whether we wished to report our conclusions in an interpretive judge- ment and what standards of interpretation would then be appropriate— would be secondary to the moral convictions we used these words to report, and the resources of legal language are sufficiently flexible so that much the same convictions could be reported in rather different language. The question of wicked legal systems is not, in the sense jurisprudence has long assumed it is, a conceptual question about the right way to use the word 'law'. It is not one but many questions, and they all arise at the level where political convictions, not semantic rules, are in play. Of course, all these various discriminations can be made within the positivist vocabulary. But the problem of wicked legal systems hardly forces positivism upon us.

V COMMENTS

Ruth Gavison said I had attacked a straw man. She said the positivists were interested in discovering semantic rules for the use of 'law' not out of interest in definition for its own sake but in order to discover the distinctive character of law as a social phenomenon. I agree; but they were wise enough to see (as some other legal theorists have not been) that what is distinctive to law, as a social phenomenon, is largely a matter of asserting and debating propositions of law, and that we cannot describe law as social practice in a revealing and illuminating way without facing what I called the question of sense, the question of what these propositions mean to those who make them and of what disagreement over them is disagreement about. I do not criticize positivists for their concern with the question of sense. On the contrary. But I criticize, for the reasons I have given, their answer to that question.

Hart urged two critical points. He was worried, first, about an imperialist claim he detected in my remarks: the claim that the interpretive issues I discussed were the only proper issues for legal theory. He listed a variety of issues he had himself explored in *The Concept of Law* and suggested that these were both important and descriptive rather than evaluative in the interpretive way. I had said that jurisprudence was the general part of adjudication, which gave him ample grounds for his suspicion of imperialism, but I meant, and should have made plainer, that this was true of jurisprudence about the question of sense. But it is worth stressing how pervasive that question is in the issues that general legal theories, like Hart's, have mainly discussed. The issues he listed drawn from his own book, for example, included the problem of distinguishing claims of law, on the one hand, from both moral appeals and naked commands on the other, and the book as a whole aims to acount for the distinctive character of law as a social phenomenon different from both moral institutions and brute force. These fundamental issues about the distinctive character of law cannot be attacked successfully except through the partly evaluative techniques of interpretation. They are issues at stake in the contest between competing conceptions of law, and they are continuous with the more limited issues at stake in adjudication.

His second point was, I think, the more important, and continues a discussion we have had before. I argued that in normal cases, when philosophers and lawyers and laymen take the interpretive attitude to a legal practice they in general approve, the interpretations they construct to present the practice in its best light serve both to identify and to justify the discrete requirements of that practice. Hart rightly pointed out that in some circumstances—when the legal practice is wicked—an interpretation that identifies the implications of the practice by showing it in the best possible light is nevertheless unable to justify it because the best light is still a very poor light. That is one of the problems I meant to address in my remarks about sceptical interpretations. In these circumstances the questions of identification and justification come apart: the sceptical interpretation cannot justify enforcing the requirements of the practice, but some other reasons of political morality may offer at least weak reasons for doing so. If we believe there are other reasons of that sort, arguing for enforcement, then we can sensibly regard these requirements as, in the post-interpretive sense, genuine requirements of law; if we do not, then we will accept them as legal requirements only in the very different, pre-interpretive sense. (Chapter 3 of *Law's Empire* takes up this issue, and the more general issue Hart raised about the connection between legal and moral obligation, in more detail.)

1.2 Comment

RUTH GAVISON

It is very appropriate to open a discussion of H. L. A. Hart's legal philosophy by looking into the nature and status of theories about law, since Hart was one of the first scholars to make a contribution to this question. Questions such as what we expect from a theory about a phenomenon, and how we should assess the adequacy of a given theory have been asked for some time now in the context of the philosophy of science, both natural and social. In the context of law they have not received, until recently, the systematic attention that they deserve. Partial answers to these questions could be glimpsed from the arguments brought by theorists of law against other theories. Hart's analysis of a variety of legal theories and their inadequacies is justly seen as a classic in this kind of work.[2] The time has come to conduct discussions about the nature of legal theory in a more systematic way, and Dworkin, by going beyond merely proposing a new theory of law and looking into the nature of the enterprise of theorizing about law, has taken an important step in this direction.

It is almost a truism to say that a good theory of law should give us insight into the nature of law and its working and an adequate description of this complex social institution. By now we all know that the data to be adequately illuminated are themselves complex and full of apparent contradictions: as Hart pointed out, we know how to identify law, or at least the relevant sources of law, yet there is a continuing controversy about the nature of law and its meaning, and about the content of the law in particular cases. We use the word 'law' in a variety of meanings and contexts. We may say, for example, that in 1944 a certain law was passed in the German Parliament. We may also say, in a different context, that there was no law in Germany in those years. Another standard problem of jurisprudence is an adequate account of adjudication: people go to court in order to have an authoritative decision on their dispute, and are willing to accept the verdict of the law, assuming this verdict is clear. Yet they often find that lawyers and judges

[2] See especially his discussion of Austin and the Realists in *Concept* and essays 12–16 in *Essays*.

disagree about what the law is. A good theory of law, we hope, should explain and give a coherent account of these facts and apparent contradictions.

For a long time Dworkin has been criticizing what he calls the 'ruling theory of law', which is in part Hart's version of legal positivism. The novelty of his present approach is that he seems to couch his critique of contemporary theorizing about law in more general terms. Dworkin now argues not simply that there are in the field misguided and misleading theories of law, and that he can propose a better one; he claims that there is something wrong and misguided about our percep-tion of the whole purpose of seeking a theory about law. Among the misguided theories, which he dubs 'semantic theories of law', are the positivism of both Austin and Hart, legal realism, and natural law theories. In the paper before us Dworkin argues in favour of a new perception of the enterprise: articulating theories about law should be seen as an interpretive process, law should be seen as an interpretive concept. All conceptions (theories) of law should be seen as the products of such a process, and the process is a kind of general constraint on all theories of law. By implication, semantic theories of law do not meet these initial constraints. Dworkin then proceeds to sketch his own proposed conception of law.

There is a great deal one can say about Dworkin's own conception of law, but in this comment I shall limit myself to Dworkin's claims about the nature of theorizing about the law.

It is difficult to assess Dworkin's claims on the basis of a partial elaboration, as the one before us inevitably is. None the less I shall take a risk and claim that although Dworkin's analysis contains, as usual, many valuable insights, its implications are less radical than he would like us to believe. All theories of law might indeed be the products of a process of interpretation, broadly speaking. But there are many types of possible interpretations, and Dworkin is mistaken in thinking that only one sort is applicable to concepts such as law; 'semantic theories' cannot be dismissed in such a cavalier fashion (and Dworkin knows it); the virtues of interpretation are exaggerated: the process, in itself, cannot overcome the difficulties Dworkin has pointed out. And the elegance of this broad claim has lured Dworkin into disregarding some important distinctions.

Anyone familiar with Dworkin's writing knows how difficult it is to comment on his work, since it is always full of interesting details, which may not be crucial to the argument, but call for some acknowledgement none the less. I shall try to strike a balance between picking out these details and getting at the substance of his claims.

The sense of breakthrough in Dworkin's piece is generated by his success in identifying a basic flaw in all legal theorizing to date. I believe this perception is misleading. Let me start with two relatively small points, designed to support Dworkin's claim. It is important to do so before we come to the substance of Dworkin's claims, so that we may gain a clearer picture of the state of the art of theorizing about law which is the subject of Dworkin's paper.

I THE CRITIQUE OF SEMANTIC THEORIES

Dworkin argues that all previous attempts to provide a theory of law share one common feature: they are attempts to provide and articulate criteria for the use of the word 'law', criteria which will help us in making sense of our attempts to identify the law, especially in hard cases. He calls such theories 'semantic'. Dworkin argues forcefully that semantic theories cannot account for the nature of disagreements about the law, and he thus concludes that all legal theorizing has so far been misguided.[3] I believe Dworkin is constructing a straw man here. Classical legal theories have always been attempts at understanding the phenomenon of law not at defining the word 'law'. Usually, they were not directly concerned with the resolution of particular cases, either hard or easy. Legal theory was classically seen as an attempt to identify the features which make law a unique social institution, differentiated from morality and religion. The linguistic formulations of the question concealed a belief that linguistic usages reflect social reality in some way, and that there was something to be gained from attending to them. But the search has always been the same: an attempt to understand the nature of law. Thus it is not surprising that the discarded semantic theories return as conceptions of law under Dworkin's analysis. And it is similarly not surprising that Dworkin has to continue his debate with positivism although he seemed to prove its basic inadequacy by simply showing it to be a semantic theory.

In short, I do not think positivism, realism, and natural law theories are semantic theories of law. Thus Dworkin has not shown that the enterprise has been misguided. (It is curious to note, however, that even

---

[3] This point is put somewhat differently in Dworkin's contribution to the book, but his original thrust is still reflected in his reference to 'semantic' rules of identification.

if they had been semantic theories, they would not necessarily have some of the flaws Dworkin ascribes to them: Dworkin holds against semantic theories that they advocate a unified use of 'law' across countries and periods, and are thus inadequate. The literature about translations and time-sensitive theories of meaning is wide enough to suggest that such theories might not be so 'blind' after all. I shall return later to Dworkin's claim that an adequate legal theory must be time- and community-sensitive.)

II CONCEPT AND CONCEPTION

Another general complaint of Dworkin's is that theorists seek to resolve, on the level of a concept of law, questions which should be dealt with only on the level of conceptions of law. According to Dworkin we mistakenly believed that seeking a concept of law was something illuminating, which should provide some tentative answers to some basic questions of jurisprudence (for example that of the relationship between law and morals). It now seems as if we were chasing a wild dream. Such questions can only be resolved by *conceptions* of law, and regarding them as 'conceptual' is thus a category mistake.[4]

If we accept, with Dworkin, that the concept of law is merely a non-controversial statement of a consensus, then Dworkin is tautologically right; according to this analysis there cannot be a conceptual controversy by definition. Yet if one wishes to draw the concept/conception distinction as one between a root principle and instantiations of it (the way Perelman did with justice), there might be controversy on the concept, and it might be fruitful to present some of the central controversies in the field as conceptual ones.

Whatever we may think of the right way of drawing the distinction, Dworkin has not shown that a category mistake was indeed committed. In fact, he himself lapses, at times, into the convenient way of describing these central controversies as 'conceptual'.

These two points are not crucial. Yet it is important to make them before we turn to Dworkin's suggestions as to the 'true' nature of theorizing about the law. They show that the field is not empty, after all.

To argue convincingly that our conception of the enterprise of theorizing about the law should change, Dworkin must show that the old

---

[4] This point has also suffered in the abridgement. Both concepts and conceptions of law are, according to him, products of interpretation. Yet the 'concept' reflects the agreed features of the practice of law, and the conceptions reflect different, more complete and detailed theories of law.

kind of theory does not enable us to do what we can do under his kind; and that his kind of theory helps us avoid some of the immanent difficulties of the kind of theory he wishes to replace. I am afraid Dworkin fails on both grounds. Dworkin does succeed in a less ambitious claim: his analysis of interpretation deepens our understanding of adjudication (although not of the attempt of the social theorist to articulate a concept or conceptions of law).

III LEGAL THEORIES AND ANSWERING LEGAL QUESTIONS

Usually, when people think of a theory of law, they think of an attempt to identify the features which are unique to law and distinguish it from other social phenomena. This was clearly the conception shared by Austin and Hart. At times it seems that Dworkin accepts this conception. Yet at others it becomes clear that one of his theses is that a theory of law in this sense is just a part of legal practice, and that legal theory should make a difference to the way judges decide hard cases. For Dworkin, the social scientist's attempt to understand what law is and the judge's attempt to identify the law applicable to a case are questions of the same nature. The second naturally requires a much more detailed elaboration. But, basically, both are questions of an identical process of interpretation. (It has become quite fashionable lately to discuss social phenomena in terms of interpretation, but for Dworkin there is a special point in this choice of terms: hard cases are usually described by lawyers as raising questions of interpretation.)

Dworkin's approach is based on the fact that judges in hard cases argue about what the law is, that is, identification of the law of their system is an indispensable part of their work. There is no doubt that the identification of one's law on a question is central to adjudication, and that answering it involves many theoretical considerations. However, these are not considerations of legal theory, in the limited sense described above. The essence of law is not affected by the question of whether a particular law in a particular system severs the relationship between a murderer and his inheritance. Whatever the law's position on this question, a theory of law in this limited sense can 'live' with it. It follows that the theory, in itself, cannot dictate any answer to the question of what the law says or should say on such an issue. It is a question of law within this system, not a question of the general theory of law.

A possible source of confusion in this respect is that at least some of the theoretical considerations involved in solving hard cases are questions of legislative intent. Some of these questions are conceptual, and thus are not a part of any particular legal system. The logical meaning of application of rules and some of the difficulties with the idea of identifying legislative intent are indeed general, and they have to be used in interpreting particular laws in particular cases. But they are not, in the sense just mentioned, a part of an attempt to identify the unique features of law. Such theoretical analyses will form part of the general theory of law, and will apply with equal force to all legal systems. In this they are different from the traditions in a given legal system concerning interpretation or the force of precedent. These latter doctrines are clearly a part of the law, not of the general theory of law, although they may be fruitfully analysed in terms of h .se general theoretical observations.[5]

In other words, Dworkin is weakening considerably the distinction between law and theory of law, a central point in the debate between Hart and Bodenheimer.[6] The distinction is not always easy to make, but I believe that it is worth making because the law is what is binding on us, and a theory of law is our way of understanding what is binding us. The law will be binding even if we do not understand it. The rule of literal interpretation may be binding on us by precedent even if we find that this rule is not logically coherent. It is satisfying if our doctrines always fit our logic, but there is no guarantee that they must. It is useful, therefore, to maintain the distinction between the law and the theory.

I believe this confusion is intensified by the fact that both theories of law and its interpretation are, in effect, attempts at the identification of law. But here again the difference is clear: the identification of the law on a given question within a legal system is a process different from the social scientist's attempt to differentiate between law and other social phenomena.

This confusion of the identification of law in the process of adjudication and its identification in theoretical analyses of law has a number of

[5] For a good illustration of a logical discussion of the notion of rule-following and interpretation see e.g. M. Moore, 'The Semantics of Judging', (1981) *Southern California Law Review*, vol. 4 (1981), 151. Although such discussion is not system-dependent, and it might be presupposed by all law *and* legal theory, it is not a part of what is classically called 'general jurisprudence'.

[6] Bodenheimer, 'Modern Analytical Jurisprudence and the Limits of its Usefulness', *University of Pennsylvania Law Review*, vol. 104 (1956), 1080–6; and H. L. A. Hart, 'Analytical Jurisprudence in Mid-Twentieth Century', *U. Pa. L. Rev.*, vol. 105 (1957), 953–75.

important implications, some of which are problematical. The most central, to which I shall return in the next section, is the question of whether theories of law are normative or descriptive. Law itself is clearly normative, and if a theory of law is only the general part of law, it follows that it, too, is normative. In fact, Dworkin explicitly sees this conclusion as one of the virtues of his conception of a legal theory. I shall argue that it is a major disadvantage.

A second implication is that theories of law are time- and community-dependent. The more abstract parts may be applicable more widely, but basically a theory of law is a theory of the law of a community at a certain time. This implication follows not only from Dworkin's continuity between law and theory of law, but also from his conception of the interpretive process itself: it is one of the essences of this process that it is done periodically, and its product changes with the content of the practice interpreted. Dworkin specifically says that there is no reason to expect that a theory of law, no matter how abstract, could be an adequate interpretation of systems called 'law' in all societies at all times. Again, I believe that by following Dworkin on this point we are unnecessarily relinquishing a valuable tool.

IV   LEGAL THEORY: DESCRIPTION OR JUSTIFICATION?

One important implication of Dworkin's analysis is that the process of reaching a conception of law becomes *necessarily* 'reforming', since the last, or 'post-interpretive stage' in the exercise, which is none the less a part of interpretation as a whole, is to reduce the discrepancies between the pre-interpretive data, and the interpretive stage in which the practice is analysed in terms of its point. In other words, the conceptions of law yielded by Dworkin's interpretation are necessarily evaluative. The same conclusion follows from Dworkin's suggested concept of law, seeing law as a *justification* of the use of the coercive force of the community.

There is no need here to reopen the old debate within jurisprudence on the value and possibility of non-evaluative conceptions of law. I still adhere to the view that such conceptions are both possible and useful, even indispensable if we are to provide an adequate analysis of law. I have argued that Finnis in effect accepts this,[7] and I now argue that

---

[7] See my review of Raz and Finnis 'Positivism, Natural Law and the Limits of Jurisprudence: A Modern Round', *Yale Law Journal* vol. 91 (1981), 1250.

Dworkin too has to do so. He agrees that there are contexts in which the most useful way of expressing a stand on the law is by using a non-evaluative (pre-interpretive, by him) conception. We must concede that one should not advocate a system of articulating conceptions of law which inevitably excludes such conceptions. As Dworkin himself rightly insists, we should not pre-empt important questions by delimiting the rules of the game.

V THE UNIVERSALITY OF CONCEPTIONS OF LAW

Dworkin's analysis of law as an interpretive concept, under his own model of interpretation, makes classical legal theory impossible. In other words, Dworkin is challenging here the possibility and the value of 'general jurisprudence', the attempt to analyse societies at their most general (like the attempt to analyse human nature) and identify those features common to all social organizations which might lead to the need for similar institutions and practices. Law is one such social institution found in all societies and exhibiting a core of similar features. The advantages of having a universal conception of law, if it is possible, are many. The constructs of scholars such as Austin, Hart, Kelsen, and Weber, to mention just a few, were explicitly meant to be universal in this sense. I do not think it has been shown that this undertaking is impossible. On the contrary: the intellectual history of legal philosophy is full of insights gained within this kind of enterprise. So for Dworkin to propose a concept of law that will be necessarily local seems a disadvantage. What is the sense of talking about international law, for example? Why give up such an important tool of comparative sociology? It may well be that such a universal concept will have to be very general and abstract, and will not be too useful for deciding questions of law in any given community. This will again strengthen the distinction between law and legal theory which Dworkin finds wrong and misleading. But in the spirit of conceptual pluralism favoured by Dworkin it seems wrong to exclude, at the outset, through the definition of the process of interpretation, the possibility of an 'ideal type' of law of a kind that has yielded theoretical benefits in the past.

It should be added that this debate about the utility and possibility of 'ideal types' is not special to law, and indeed has been raging in sociology and psychology for quite some time. The universality of the conception reflects much more than the historical fact that different conceptions were called by the same name, and are thus strands in the same rope, as

Dworkin would have it. One does not have to be an essentialist to argue that many valuable insights may be lost if we do not, from time to time, compare our ways of dealing with human and social problems with the ways of others. I shall risk being called a 'semantic scholar' and say that for these comparative lessons to be drawn we need some universal conceptual scheme, in terms of such basic legal functions such as dispute resolution, which may help us both to understand the similarities and highlight the differences between societies.

Even if we are not sure that such concepts are useful for *all* practical purposes, why adopt constraints on theorizing which will prevent us from using them when the need arises? Dworkin does not provide an answer to this question.

These two points show that we lose something by accepting Dworkin's invitation. What are, according to Dworkin, our main gains? First and foremost is a better understanding of adjudication, and through it, of the role law plays in society.

VI THE NATURE OF DISAGREEMENTS BETWEEN JUDGES

Anyone familiar with Dworkin's work will not be surprised to learn that one of his starting points, one of the most important pre-interpretive data he identifies and seeks to explain, is the fact that there are often disagreements between judges. Furthermore, judges present these disagreements as ones about the law. If we take them seriously, we must give an account of law under which law can be controversial. Dworkin's main complaint against semantic theories of law, primarily positivism, is precisely that it refuses to allow that there may be non-empirical controversy about the identification of law. According to positivism, law consists of the pre-existing standards identified by origin or sources. Most disagreements arise in cases where the law, thus defined, does not settle the question. The judge, therefore, must go 'beyond the law' to decide the issue before him. According to Dworkin, positivism must deny that these disagreements are genuinely about the law and it must label as simple minded or fraudulent those in the legal community who claim that this is their nature.

One of the main advantages of Dworkin's picture of conceptions of law as resulting from processes of interpretation is that conceptions of law are, according to him, controversial. Thus disagreements about these conceptions, which affect judicial decisions in hard cases, are disagreements about the law. Dworkin's theory thus does justice to the way lawyers and judges talk about disagreements without seeing them as either cheaters or simpletons.

I believe Dworkin is basically right in contending that what judges disagree about is, in one sense, the law. Judges do indeed interpret the law, and I find Dworkin's model of interpretation quite illuminating: I accept that in this context of interpretation there is an inherent and inevitable reforming stage, and that this is part of the interpretive process. That is why judges claim that they are arguing about the law, and rightly so. What they are doing is all within their legal activity, and one should not forget this. Dworkin succeeds in drawing our attention to the structure of argument about the law, in contexts where the question is the identification of the content of the law relevant to a particular issue. (Dworkin's analysis is confined to 'static' interpretations and developments of the law. We should remember that most laws, unlike new rules of courtesy, are created by legislatures, in a 'dynamic' way. This is another argument for maintaining the distinction between law and legal theory.)

However, a basic rule with theory formation is that it is wise to see first if the available theories, which have made a contribution to our understanding of a phenomenon, may be adapted to the change. I believe they can, and that this adaptation is more fruitful than the total substitution Dworkin suggests. One of the virtues of the adaptation is that it does not conceal the insights gained by the 'old' theory, discarded by Dworkin's new emphases.

Adjudication is no doubt a complex social practice. In hard cases it involves interpretation. Let us accept Dworkin's model of this process. He sees that, analytically speaking, three distinct stages are involved. The question is really what we should call 'law', in a particular context: the post-interpretive conclusion of the majority, or the pre-interpretive data shared by all judges? Once we see that we have a problem of naming, much of the intensity of the debate disappears. Surely it is important to emphasize that the move from the first stage to the third involves judicial responsibilities? Surely it is important to point out that the shared pre-interpretive sources are partly what gives the whole enterprise its legitimacy? Surely it is important to be aware that the parties may be required to know the law of the first stage, and only speculate about the law of the third stage?

It follows, then, that both pre-interpretive law (the law identified by sources, or 'positivists'' law, and post-interpretive law (Dworkin's law) are important entities. But I want to go further than argue that emphasizing 'first stage law' is legitimate. I take it to be an important insight of Hart, elaborated by Raz, that what the latter calls the 'sources thesis' is not merely a contingent feature of law.[8] A more comprehensive discussion of this point will clearly go beyond a comment, but I trust that the thrust of the argument is familiar. Thus the loss of this emphasis is not merely the loss of some feature of law. It may lead us to underrate one of the important ways in which law as we know it fulfils its social functions.

One last comment is called for: Dworkin seeks to enlist our sympathies for his views by arguing that his opponents must ascribe to judges and lawyers either simple-mindedness or fraud. I agree with Dworkin that a theory which takes what judges say as reflecting what they think, and assumes that judges know what they are doing, should be more attractive than one resting on such ascriptions. However, it is not clear which of the two approaches takes more seriously the way judges feel about what they are doing. When you compare the words of candid judges out of court to their exercises in interpretation, you see that many of them fight as scholars against the rhetorical myth they must perpetuate as judges.[9] Dworkin has not linked his position on the nature of legal theory to his famous one-right-answer thesis of adjudication (a task which may prove difficult), but Dworkin himself provided the framework within which judges may make sense of what they are doing, so that they acknowledge both that their disagreements are ones about the third-stage law, and that in deciding hard cases they must go, in a sense, beyond the first-stage law.

I have enumerated above some classical problems which have been seen as crucial indicators of the adequacy of theories of law. Does Dworkin's approach improve our ability to understand these questions and deal with them? It should be remembered that the test here is a strong one, since courtesy requires that existing theories should not be stigmatized as totally inadequate unless our ability to deal with issues under the newly proposed theory is substantially improved. A mere showing that a new way of looking at things is not less helpful will not do for this purpose. I believe that Dworkin's approach is acceptable on these grounds, in the sense that it allows us to discuss these questions,

---

[8] See Raz, *The Authority of Law*, Oxford (1979), chaps. 3, 4; and *The Concept of a Legal System*, 2nd edn., Oxford (1980), postscript, 210–16.

[9] Many judges have found the tension difficult. Cardozo's classic *The Nature of the Judicial Process*, New Haven (1923) is said to have passed without calls for his resignation only because of Cardozo's undoubted integrity and stature as a judge.

but it does not seem to be superior to existing accounts. Moreover, there is a price to be paid in terms of our ability to deal with some of the issues.

VII   GROUNDS OF LAW AND FORCE OF LAW

Clearly one of the most important questions of legal and political philosophy is where to draw the line between the identification of what the law says and the moral decision of whether the law should be obeyed. One of Dworkin's initial points of criticism was that existing legal theories present many questions of law as if they were questions of fidelity to law. Yet, although Dworkin's account of the obligation to obey the law and of the division of labour between lawyers and political scientists on this matter is very illuminating, it does not differ substantially from that suggested by other scholars, no matter what their position on the nature of legal theory and on what is the best legal theory. Thus, Dworkin's specific legal theory does not offer us a better discussion of this question than is available to us under existing accounts.

VIII   WICKED LEGAL SYSTEMS

Another issue which has tested legal theories in recent history is the treatment of legal systems so wicked that they do not meet minimal standards of morality. Hart's defence of positivism was, in part, its better ability to deal with such problems: unlike some versions of natural law theories, it granted such systems the name of 'law' but denied that there was a duty of fidelity to that law, on moral grounds.[10] Fuller, on the other hand, thought a lot could be gained from a legal theory that would deny such systems the name of 'law', and would thus aid in severing the link between the system and our inclinations and sense of duty to obey.[11]

Dworkin's approach suggests that an important distinction should be made between a conception of one's own legal system and one's conception of another legal system. I believe the distinction is indeed imporatnt, and is similar to the difference, pointed out by Hart himself, between the relationship of acceptance of one's system and the record-

---

[10] H. L. A. Hart, 'Positivism and the Separation of Law and Morals', *Harvard Law Review* vol. 71 1958, 593, reprinted in *Essays*, 49, 72–8.

[11] See Fuller's response to Hart in *Harvard Law Review*, vol. 71 (1958), 630 and especially his treatment of the subject in *The Morality of Law*, revised edn. New Haven (1969).

ing of rules of conduct by an anthropologist. Yet I fail to see how this distinction improves our ability to deal with the theoretical or the practical questions raised by wicked legal systems in ways not already put forward by others.

IX CRITERIA FOR ADEQUACY: JUSTIFICATION OF DECISIONS IN HARD CASES

I shall conclude with another claim made by Dworkin, which has been referred to above. Dworkin asserts that legal theories are committed theories, that their cutting edge is the guidance of judges in hard cases. It is implied that one of the criteria of adequacy of a legal theory should be its conduciveness to the making of 'good' decisions. As mentioned above, this implication is related to Dworkin's method of deriving conceptions of law and to his refusal to draw a line between law and legal theory.

Legal theory at its most abstract does not help the judge in hard cases simply because its statements are not sufficiently specific to do so. I accept that articulations of theories of precedent and legislation are, as Dworkin says, both a part of legal theory and legal system-dependent, and that such theories may guide answers to hard cases, or at least provide rationalizations to decisions in such cases. Since previous decisions in hard cases form a part of the pre-interpretive data of this particular legal system, these doctrines are affected by such decisions in hard cases. I doubt, however, that even a theory of precedent or a theory of legislation, in itself, could dictate any answer to hard cases. In all the sample cases Dworkin cites we can easily present the disagreement in ways other than as a controversy about the force of precedent. As Dworkin himself indicates, the judgement of the majority in *Riggs* v. *Palmer* does not have to be based on the rejection of a literal interpretation of the statute. The best account may well be the idea that statutes should be read against a background of principles. Here, too, I do not see where Dworkin's new conceptual apparatus or approach aids us in understanding or talking about legal phenomena, including adjudication, in ways which are not compatible with existing theories of law. More important still, Dworkin's discussion does not support his view that theories of precedent or adjudication should be conclusively evaluated by their direct contribution to good decisions in particular hard cases.

X   CONCLUSION

To sum up, then, I agree that both the articulation of a concept of law and more detailed conceptions of law and of legal doctrines may profitably be seen as exercises in interpretation, taken in a broad sense. Articulating ideal types may be seen as interpreting reality, but the considerations of this kind of interpretation are cognitive and theoretical, not practical as they must be in the context of adjudication. I believe it is extremely important to remember that there may be different kinds of interpretations. In some contexts we are interested in understanding, not in reform; even when seeking understanding, there are many different points of view which may dictate different emphases and approaches. A general methodology of articulating conceptions of law should heed these distinctions.

Generally speaking, criteria of adequacy for theories of law cannot be uniform. Adequacy is a relative idea: we must always know the tasks we want the theory to fulfil in order to judge its adequacy. For a long time legal theorists sought legal theories without being sensitive to this plurality of tasks. Many sterile and barren debates resulted. Today we may be ready to give up hope of finding a uniformly valid legal theory and proceed to the less ambitious but more promising job of articulating conceptions of law for particular purposes, and joining them when we can to a complex picture of law. 'Classical' legal theories, Hart's included, have not been successfully dismissed by Dworkin. They still offer us many of the enduring, and possibly eternal, perspectives of analysing law.

1.3   Comment

H. L. A. HART*

Dworkin's richly suggestive paper is part of a wide-ranging restatement of his philosophy of law and it may be that when the rest of this restatement is given to us the two criticisms which I make in this brief reply will turn out to be based on a misunderstanding of his full theory. If so I apologise to him and to our audience.

I

Dworkin's paper does not, as I understand it, abandon or substantially modify the salient features of the distinctive, holistic account of the nature of law which is to be gathered from his seminal essays collected in *Taking Rights Seriously*.[12] So he still thinks of law, or at any rate law as it is to be found in countries like the United States and Great Britain, as comprising both an explicit part consisting of clear settled legal practices, enactments, and judicial decisions and an implicit part consisting of a coherent and consistent set of principles which both explains or 'fits' the explicit law up to some threshold standard of adequacy of fit and also provides the best moral justification of the explicit law.[13] Such implicit law was termed by Dworkin 'the soundest theory of the law' because it approximates to sound political morality as closely as is compatible with the requirement of 'fit' and it plays a double part. For it both constitutes a reservoir of legal standards to be used and decided in those 'hard cases' where the explicit law provides no clear unambiguous decision either way, and it also shows why and how it is that statutes and decided cases can create legal rights and duties which for Dworkin always have at least prima-facie moral force.

A main concern of Dworkin's present paper is to make clear what conflicting legal theories attempting to answer the question 'What is law', really are, once various misleading or confused accounts given by themselves of themselves, have been laid aside. For this purpose he

---

* © H. L. A. Hart 1987.

[12] References here are to the corrected impression, London (1978).

[13] Ibid., 104, 105, 107.

draws upon the distinction between a *concept* and conflicting controversial *conceptions* of a concept to which he attributed great importance at several places in his earlier work,[14] though his latest reference to it before his present paper was accompanied by the warning that he 'did not pretend to have yet given an adequate or clear account of the activity of defending a particular conception of a concept'.[15] However, a legal theory is now said by Dworkin just to be a controversial conception of the concept of law and the concept of law itself is identified by him as the abstract and at least relatively uncontroversial concept of 'those standards and procedures which must be in principle respected and followed when the coercive political power of the community is used against citizens or members or groups of these.' As a conception of that concept a legal theory is essentially normative and justificatory, not descriptive: it is concerned to provide controversial arguments to show how a community's legal principles, rules, and procedures contribute to the justification of the use of collective force. Hence Dworkin tells us that jurisprudence (not here distinguished from legal theory) is only 'the general part of adjudication' and 'no firm line divides it from adjudication or any other aspect of legal practice'. So legal theory is what judges must, in the last resort, invoke if pressed to the limit to justify their judgements directing the use of coercion.

II

This latest version of Dworkin's ideas invites criticism on two different grounds. First, since legal theory is now characterized not only as a normative justificatory enterprise but as the general part of adjudication, its perspective is that of a judge confronted in a particular system with the task of deciding whether coercion may properly be used. In my view such a characterization of legal theory unfortunately conceals the fact that there is a standing need for a form of legal theory or jurisprudence that is descriptive and general in scope, the perspective of which is not that of a judge deciding 'what the law is', that is, what the law requires in particular cases (such as those examined by Dworkin in the first section of his paper) but is that of an external observer of a form of social institution with a normative aspect, which in its recurrence in different societies and periods exhibits many common features of form, structure, and content. Among other things which such a descriptive theory should

---

[14] E.g., ibid., 134–6; 226; 291–2.
[15] Ibid., 351.

provide is an analytical account and explanation of those very legal practices which govern a community's use of force against its citizens of which legal theory, as characterized by Dworkin, offers a controversial justification. Even if it were true that legal positivism harboured the illusion about the existence of shared but unknown rules and various semantic aberrations which Dworkin in his paper imputes to it, none the less the positivist's insistence that there is a task and need for a descriptive analytical jurisprudence is salutary even if it is regarded only as a preliminary to the articulation of a justificatory theory of a community's legal practices and not, as it in fact is, a contribution to the study of human society and culture.

Of course Dworkin says *something* about the material which he terms 'pre-interpretive data' upon which a justificatory conception of the concept of law is to work. Thus he conceives the legal theorist as having no difficulty in identifying the practices that count as legal practices in his own culture: the theorist knows that there are legislatures, law courts, police, and administrative agencies and the constitution. He starts also with the knowledge that there are legal 'paradigms', that is, there are at any given time countless indubitable examples of law such as the Road Code even though he thinks these may lose their status as paradigms and be regarded as 'mistakes' as a result of the impact of some new theory which successfully catches on and offers a new vision and so a revision of what is to count as law. But it seems to me that such rough characterizations of legal practices and paradigms are not enough to answer important questions to which the existence of law has always given rise, and which are not questions of moral or political justification but concern the structure or constitution and interrelationship of legal phenomena. Answers to such questions are vital for the understanding of law.

If I may refer here to my own work, I too, in *The Concept of Law*, began my account of my form of legal theory by referring to what Dworkin calls 'pre-interpretive' material of which, as he says, there is at any given time tolerably widespread common knowledge. So I began my book with the assumption that at the point where the legal theorist raises and attempts to answer the question 'What is law?' any educated man would be able to cite as an answer to that question what Dworkin calls 'paradigms' of law (my example included rules forbidding murder and rules requiring payment of taxes) and would be able to specify the salient features of a municipal legal system. He would know that it comprises legislatures to make new rules and abolish old ones, courts to determine what the rules are and when they have been broken, and to order punishment and compensation. I then asked, in *The Concept of Law*, if so much is common knowledge what more do men want to know when they press further the question 'What is law?' So the rest of my book was taken up not with questions of justification but with describing and attempting to resolve the perplexities and need for explanation which men feel when they reflect on their common knowledge of law. Such reflection prompts the questions: What are rules? How do rules differ from mere habits or regularities of behaviour? Are there radically different types of legal rules? How may rules be related? What is it for rules to form a system? How are legal rules and the authority they have related on the one hand to coercive threats and the power to implement such threats, and on the other to moral requirements and moral pressure? So where Dworkin in his new work appears to see nothing between the specification of commonly known, easily identified legal practices and paradigms and the articulation of controversial claims concerning the fitness of legal practices to justify the use of legal coercion, I found and still find a need for a clarifying, descriptive enterprise which would answer such questions as I have mentioned and would have some claim to universality. No doubt my attempt to increase the understanding of these basic legal phenomena and to elucidate their structure may have misfired and produced not clarification and understanding but obfuscation and error. The account, for example, which I give of social rules and the conceptual tools which I invented to pick out their action-guiding and evaluation-guiding function such as the 'acceptance' of rules and the distinction between 'internal' and 'external' points of view and statements, or my conception of the identity of a legal system through time may be fraught, as some critics have claimed, with dire confusion but that only means that there is a need for a better descriptive effort or analysis which some of my critics may have supplied.

It may also be as many of my critics have claimed that my explanation and analysis of various features of law is vitiated by a particular pervasive blindness and error: that of not seeing that moral claims and moral beliefs are not merely contingent accompaniments but constituent features of the legal practices and institutions of which I sought to provide an analysis. Suppose I was mistaken in just that way, this would only call for a better and more sensitive description from the legal theorist, not a premature move away from description to controversial claims concerning the justice or injustice of the use of coercion in accordance with legal practices.

To put the point in terms of a simple example. Suppose that a satisfactory analytical account of what it is for a community to have an effective customary rule requiring its members to do or abstain from some action, shows not only that there must be general conformity in practice to the requirements of the rule and a general disposition to make and accept criticisms of deviations and demands for conformity. Suppose that the analysis shows also that conformity must be generally motivated by the belief that this will better secure some morally valuable end or purpose than if members of the community decide separately for themselves what to do, and that the members must believe that their criticism of deviations and demands for conformity are justified by that. The fact that such an analysis treats such moral beliefs and justificatory practices as essential constituents of the existence of such a rule plainly does not rob the analysis of its descriptive character.

I see now, however, that there are certain considerations which may foster the misleading idea that such an analysis must be normative or justificatory. The first is that it is indeed true that an analysis referring in this way to moral beliefs will only be intelligible to those who can understand what it is to be motivated by such beliefs and to regard moral considerations as justifying conduct. *In that sense* the theorist must 'put himself in the place' of those whose practice he is attempting to elucidate in order to portray their conduct as it appears to them. But he need not share or endorse their beliefs or regard his descriptive account as also claiming that their conduct is justified. Secondly, it is also true that an analysis which allots a place to moral claims and beliefs as constituents of a social phenomenon must itself be guided, in focusing on those features rather than others, by some criteria of importance of which the chief will be the explanatory power of what his analysis picks out. So his analysis will be guided by judgements, often controversial, of what is important and will therefore reflect such meta-theoretic values and not be neutral between all values. But again there is nothing to show that this analysis is not descriptive but normative or justificatory.

My excuse, if one is needed, for discussing what may appear elementary errors which may lead to the mistaken conclusion that a theory of law which treats moral claims and beliefs as essential constituents of legal phenomena must be a normative and not a descriptive theory is that I am at a loss, otherwise, to explain the view which apparently Dworkin now holds that theories of law purporting to answer the general question 'What is law', must be of that character.

I am also perplexed by another aspect of Dworkin's present account of legal theory. For I do not understand the relationship between legal theory characterized in his present paper as a controversial conception of the concept of law and 'the soundest theory of the law' which has figured so prominently in Dworkin's writing as the set of principles which courts are to use in deciding hard cases. Both are said to be controversial and both are normative and concerned to provide the best justification of a community's settled legal practices. Any doubt about their identity seems to be removed by Dworkin's statement in his present paper that a theory of law is but the general part of adjudication. I find this deeply puzzling; for the soundest theory of the law consists of principles used by courts in deciding hard cases and are themselves part (the implicit part) of a community's law and it is one of the chief errors which Dworkin finds in legal positivism that positivist theories fail to recognize such implicit law. But legal theory which is an implicit part of the law cannot provide answers to any general question about the nature of law. It cannot answer the question 'What is law?' but only questions asking what is the law of a particular community on particular issues.

III

My second criticism of Dworkin's paper concerns a very different issue. His present account of legal theory as concerned specifically with the justification of the use against individuals of legal coercion has caused me to consider again an objection which I made[16] to his earlier account of the soundest theory of the law as the set of principles fitting the explicit settled law of the community and providing the best justification for it. My objection was to what I took to be Dworkin's reasons for holding that legal rights and duties contrary to positivist accounts of these concepts have an essential moral component so that they constituted at least a prima-facie moral reason for action. I argued that this could not be so on Dworkin's account of the way in which legal rights and duties were identified as the requirements of principles forming part of the soundest theory of the law which must both fit the settled law and provide the best justification of it. Dworkin himself has conceded that where the settled law is morally iniquitous principles forming part of the 'best' justification of it might be morally so bad that the judge's moral duty might be to lie rather than enforce the legal right or duty

[16] In my *Essays on Bentham*, Oxford (1982), 147ff.

identified by such principles.[17] My point was that where this was so the 'best' justification of the law in such cases could only be the least odious of morally odious principles fitting morally odious settled law, and this could not constitute any form of moral justification or yield even a prima-facie moral reason for acting on rights or duties identified in this way. I also argued that these considerations cast doubt not only on Dworkin's account of the use of the soundest theory of the law in hard cases to fill in gaps left open by the settled law but also on the explanation given in *Taking Rights Seriously*[18] of how it was, even in clear cases, that legal rules and statutes created legal rights and duties with their essential moral force or component. In a reply to this criticism,[19] Dworkin insisted that I had confused 'principles that figure in the process that identifies legal rights' with 'principles that provide the moral argument for respecting those rights' and so had confused his 'account of how legal rights are identified' with his 'reasons for thinking that legal rights once identified had some claim to be enforced in court'. But this reply seems to me without substance because 'the soundest theory of the law' has, according to Dworkin, a double role, for it is both used to identify legal rights in hard cases and also figures essentially in an explanation of how it is that legal rules and statutes create legal rights and duties with their moral components and not merely legal rights and duties which the positivist would claim have, as such, no necessary moral force. So I could not see how it was possible to put forward 'the soundest theory of the law' as merely identifying a legal right and not also as providing at least a prima-facie moral reason for respecting it. Moreover, if the identification of a legal right through the soundest theory of the law constitutes no reason or prima-facie moral argument for its enforcement, this leaves unexplained why a judge should in cases where the principle identifying the right is morally unacceptable, have to lie, as Dworkin envisages he might, rather than enforce the right.

However, even if I am mistaken in my criticisms of Dworkin's argument as it stood before his present paper, his new formulation of legal theory as providing not merely the best justification of the law but of the law's use of coercion cannot accommodate the distinction between its use simply to identify legal rights and its use to provide a moral argument for respecting and enforcing those rights.

The upshot of these considerations seems to me to be the following:

[17] Dworkin, *Taking Rights Seriously*, 326–7; 341–3.
[18] Ibid., 104, 105, 107.
[19] In *Ronald Dworkin and Contemporary Jurisprudence*, New Jersey (1983), 257–8.

'the soundest theory of the law' cannot provide an explanation of how it is that legal rules and statutes create legal rights and duties constituting prima-facie moral reasons for action, and it cannot determine the existence of such legal rights and duties where the settled law is indeterminate. The soundest theory of the law could only do these things if its principles were in themselves *sound* according to independent morality which Dworkin calls background morality, and not merely the *soundest* of those theories that could fit the settled law. But no positivist who, like myself, denies that legal rights and duties are species of moral rights and duties, would ever wish to deny that legal rights and duties arising from morally sound legal principles could provide at least prima-facie moral reasons for action and enforcement. What the positivist does claim is that there are no persuasive arguments for restricting the concepts of legal right and legal duty to such cases, and that there are persuasive arguments for employing, in a descriptive jurisprudence, concepts not so restricted.

2.1 Positivism and the Foundations of Legal Authority*

ROLF SARTORIUS

In the first part of this paper I shall defend and elaborate upon, while only slightly modifying, what I understand to be the core of the account of the existence of constitutional rules to be found in H. L. A. Hart's *The Concept of Law*.[1] Stemming from a morally neutral explanation of what Hart calls the 'internal aspect' of the existence of social norms, my account of legal authority will imply neither that those in authority have a moral right to rule nor that those over whom authority is exercised have a moral obligation to obey the law. Indeed, contrary to what has been recently suggested by both Neil MacCormick[2] and Gerald Postema,[3] I shall even deny that officials in authority need have, or need believe that they have, moral obligations to one another to act in accordance with the constitutional rules which they can be said to accept. My analysis of legal authority is thus a thoroughly positivistic one. In the second part of the paper I shall turn to the question of under what conditions, if any, those with legal authority may claim a moral right to rule.

I

1 My discussion throughout shall be guided by, and I believe will lend support to, certain methodological theses which I take it are for the most part shared by Hart and myself.

In his inaugural address to the Aristotelian Society in 1953, Hart wrote:

I am not sure that in the case of concepts so complex as that of a legal system we can pick out any characteristics, save the most obvious and uninteresting ones, and say they are necessary. . . I think that all that can be found are a set of criteria

---

* © Rolf Sartorius 1987.
[1] Oxford (1961).
[2] Neil MacCormick, *H. L. A. Hart*, London (1981).
[3] Gerald Postema, 'Coordination and Convention at the Foundations of Law', *The Journal of Legal Studies*, vol. 11, no. 1 (Jan. 1982).

of which a few are obviously necessary . . . but the rest form a sub-set of criteria of which everything called a legal system satisfies some but only *standard or normal* cases satisfy all.[4]

Following this clear recognition that the concept of a legal system is what Hilary Putnam some years later described as a 'cluster concept',[5] Hart concluded that 'in the case of a concept so complex . . . we can do no more than identify the conditions present in the standard or paradigm case and consider under what circumstances the removal of any one of these conditions would render the whole pointless or absurd'.[6] The great richness of illumination offered by *The Concept of Law* is due in large part, I believe, to Hart's rejection of philosophical essentialism and his rigorous pursuit of the suggested alternative: a description of the important differences made in our lives as social beings by the presence or absence of certain central features of social order and social ordering, both legal and non-legal. An especially important instantiation of this approach is to be found in Hart's conception of *natural necessity*—the contention that there are certain salient although contingent features of human beings and their natural and social environment which provides the best of reasons why, given survival as an aim, both law and morals ought to have a certain minimal content reflected in normative requirements backed by social or legal sanctions.[7] (I shall argue in Section II that an account of the moral authority of law, while depending upon some such notion of natural necessity, must consider aims other than survival.)

Closely related to an anti-essentialist analytic posture is the view that extreme caution should be exercised in focusing upon the importance of some central features of law to the exclusion of others. What is important will depend upon what questions one is interested in, and it would be folly to claim that some single concept or small set of concepts could provide 'the key to the science of jurisprudence'. Despite occasional lapses in *The Concept of Law*,[8] I would like to believe that Hart and I are really of one mind on this score as well. For although Hart seems to have said *of* the rule of recognition that it is more important than the

[4] H. L. A. Hart, 'Theory and Definition in Jurisprudence', *Proceedings of The Aristotelian Society*, Supplementary vol. 29 (1955), 251–2.

[5] Hilary Putnam, 'The Analytic and the Synthetic', in H. Feigl and G. Maxwell (eds.), *Minnesota Studies in the Philosophy of Science*, vol. III Minneapolis (1962).

[6] Hart, 'Theory and Definition in Jurisprudence', 253.

[7] Hart, *Concept*, Ch. 9, Sect. 2.

[8] See Rolf Sartorius, 'The Concept of Law', *Archives for Philosophy of Law and Social Philosophy*, vol. LII, no. 2 (1966), Sect. 6.

other fundamental constitutional rules which he discusses, what he says *about* the different secondary rules upon which his account of the foundations of legal order relies makes it quite clear that they are equally important in their own ways.

2 Hart's discussion of the significance of the addition of secondary rules to a set of pre-existing primary rules, which marks for him the transition from the pre-legal to the legal world, overlaps with Locke's discussion of how the institution of government as 'umpire of the law of nature' may be expected to remedy the considerable 'inconveniences' of a state of nature in which individuals may protect their rights only through a resort to self-help.[9] Yet even though they seem to overlap an apparent gap emerges. The rules of recognition and change define the legislative function of government and the rules of adjudication define the judicial function. But what of the executive function without which law would be but a formal (although perhaps important) ritual? Although he introduces no label for them, Hart fills the gap when he speaks of 'further secondary rules, specifying or at least limiting the penalties for violation . . . [which confer] upon judges . . . the exclusive power to direct the application of penalties by other officials'.[10] These might have been called 'rules of enforcement'. Clearly they are as important in their own way as the other secondary rules which Hart discusses at such great length. And for one ultimately interested (as I am) in considering by what moral right some people may exercise coercive authority over others, such rules concerning the application of sanctions are in a sense the most important of all. For if anything deserves to be described as *the* distinguishing feature of the modern nation state it is that it claims and exercises an exclusive monopoly over the use of coercive force within the territory which it identifies as its own.

I am thus following Hart in identifying the foundations of positive legal authority with the complex of structures (primarily official roles with their related rights and obligations) defined by the secondary rules of recognition, change, adjudication, and (what I have called) enforcement. I shall now turn directly to the central question of the first part of this essay. What are the truth conditions for their existence? Let me first note, however, that my understanding of such constitutional norms is a broad one, embracing both constitutional law in the strict sense—that of

[9] John Locke, *The Second Treatise of Government*, New York (1952). Sects. 4–21. (Originally published 1690.)
[10] Hart, *Concept*, 95.

which courts will explicitly take notice—and constitutional conventions of which courts will not take notice but the breach of which would be viewed as an abuse of authority by officials and/or citizens.[11]

3 Just what is being claimed when it is said that a particular social norm exists in, or is accepted by the members of, a community? This question, one which must be answered if we are to understand the claims of social scientists and ethical theorists who make use of the concept of positive morality, is one which Hart treats as prior to the question of the existence of legal norms in general and constitutional norms in particular. His general approach thus follows that taken by those of his predecessors in the jurisprudential tradition whom he criticizes for their failure to provide an adequate analysis of what Hart calls the 'internal aspect' of the existence of social norms.[12] The crude behaviourism of the American Legal Realists may be said to have overlooked the internal aspect of the existence of rules entirely.[13] John Austin,[14] Hans Kelsen,[15] and Alf Ross[16] may be said to have recognized it but failed in their attempts to capture it.

It seems to have been assumed by all that, with the exception of those rules whose existence may consist in nothing more than their formal validity, a necessary condition for the existence of a social rule is that there be a sufficient degree of conformity to it to constitute a 'regularity' in the behaviour of the members of the community in which it is taken to exist.[17] This is what is called the 'external aspect' of a rule's existence by Hart and may be described by *external statements* of the sort that might be made by an uninvolved observer; for example, 'People in C customarily (regularly) do X in situations of kind K'. Hart describes the internal aspect of the existence of social rules as being manifested by certain 'reflective critical attitude[s] . . . display[ed]' by mutual demands for conformity to the rules when deviation occurs or appears imminent, by

[11] A. V. Dicey, *The Law of the Constitution*. Indianapolis, Indiana (eighth edn., 1982) 277. (Originally published 1915.)

[12] I use the term 'norms' rather than 'rules' in order to suggest that much of what is true of rules in the strict sense may also apply to other sorts of standards of conduct, e.g., principles.

[13] See Hart, *Concept*, esp. 132–44.

[14] See ibid., esp. Chap. 5, Sect. 2.

[15] See ibid., esp. 97–107.

[16] See Hart, 'Scandinavian Realism', *Cambridge Law Journal*, (1959).

[17] So MacCormick, *H. L. A. Hart*, 33, writes: '[W]hat are the attitudes to patterns of social acting which, together with some regularity in action . . . must exist or be held by human beings for it to be true that . . . a rule exists?'

criticism of deviations, and by the acceptance of such criticism as justified.[18] The internal aspect of the existence of social rules is also importantly demonstrated in *internal statements* made in the course of their application; for example, 'you're out'.

It is clear that Hart does not intend to associate the internal aspect of the existence of norms with those who accept them feeling bound to follow them; indeed, it is just here that he takes pains to distinguish his account from the otherwise quite similar one offered by Alf Ross.[19] What is not so clear is whether the reflective critical *attitudes* in terms of which the internal aspect is seemingly defined amount to anything more than the complex *behaviour* in which they are said to be displayed.

Neil MacCormick has recently argued that the internal aspect of the existence of a norm *must* involve a volitional element which is 'to be understood by reference to those who have and act upon a wish or preference for conduct in accordance with a given pattern, both in their own conduct and in relation to those others to whom they deem it applicable'.[20] He also claims that it is essential that those who prefer to follow a norm assume that others have similar preferences.[21] Yet another dimension is added when MacCormick claims that '[t]he internal point of view ... logically entails also adverse reactions to conduct departing from the pattern. Hence it is a logical truth that one who breaks such a rule incurs the disapproval of those who accept the rule. From their point of view, the disapproval is justified disapproval.'[22]

Given this understanding of the internal point of view in terms of such a complex structure of preferences, beliefs, and attitudes, MacCormick is prepared to admit that ordinary citizens need not adopt it toward the law. On the other hand, he claims that it must be involved in official acceptance of fundamental constitutional rules.

[A] legal system ... 'exists' ... only if it is effectively in force ... Almost the whole population could be in [a] state of passive and coerced obedience.

The officials themselves, however, must have a somewhat different view. For ... the 'legal system' requires by definition a rule of recognition, a rule prescribing official duties to apply certain rules as 'law'. But for that rule itself to exist, it is necessary that the officials at least observe it as a binding social rule. They must accept and observe it 'from the internal point of view' ....[23]

---

[18]   Hart, *Concept*, 56.
[19]   Ibid., 243.
[20]   MacCormick, *H. L. A. Hart*, 34.
[21]   Ibid., 35.
[22]   Ibid., 134.
[23]   Ibid., p. 22.

The complex structure of actions, preferences and beliefs involved in MacCormick's analysis provides a basis for suggesting that constitutional rules in general, and the rule of recognition in particular, provide a conventional solution to co-ordination problems which exist both between officials and citizens and among officials themselves. Such is the approach taken by Gerald Postema in another recent essay where, building upon David Lewis's notion of convention, it is argued that Hart's rule of recognition provides the basis for bridging the gap between social fact and normative value.[24] If the conditional preferences for compliance obtain, Postema argues, so too must normative (and not just purely prudential) reasons for action which provide the basis for claiming that officials have a moral obligation (although perhaps only a weak one) to apply 'the law' as it is identified by the criteria contained in the rule of recognition.

Postema's penetrating argument is so *very* carefully qualified that I am not sure if I really disagree with it. MacCormick's account of the internal aspect of the existence of rules—in particular, constitutional rules—is highly perceptive of crucial features which it might be admitted are present in the 'standard or normal case', but it must be rejected if the essentialiastic terms in which it is couched are insisted upon. Whether or not one has in mind the acceptance of social rules in general, or the acceptance of constitutional rules by officials in particular, the existence of social rules is simply too complex an affair to permit of any interesting claims about what in the nature of their existence generates moral obligations on the part of either those who apply them or those to whom they apply.

Some years prior to the publication of *The Concept of Law*, Hart noted that

. . . both general obedience and the further use of and attitudes to the law may be motivated by fear, inertia, admiration of tradition, or long sighted calculation of selfish interests as well as by recognition of moral obligation. As long as the general complex practice is there, this is enough to answer affirmatively the enquiry whether a legal system exists. The question of what motivates the practice, though important, is an independent inquiry.[25]

What this passage suggests is that the relevant preferences concerning compliance, others' preferences and beliefs, need not be present in the

---

[24] Postema, 'Coordination and Convention at the Foundations of Law', 166.
[25] 'Legal and Moral Obligation', in A. I. Melden (ed.), *Essays in Moral Philosophy*, Seattle (1958), 92–3.

case of official constitutional rule acceptance any more than they need be in the case of the ordinary citizen's rule compliance. A closer look at what is involved in the internal aspect of the existence of social rules will bear this out, revealing that the concept of an accepted social rule is a cluster concept and thus not amenable to an essentialistic analysis by way of the specification of a set of conditions which are individually necessary and jointly sufficient for its correct application.

4 Consider the following set of conditions satisfied in the normal (standard, paradigm, completely unproblematic) case of the existence of a social norm N within a group or community C.

1 Most members of C conform to N on most occasions when N applies to them, and the occasions on which N is applicable are relatively frequent. Where N is a customary norm, such a regularity in the behaviour of members of C has existed for a sufficiently long time.

2 Most members of C display the critical behaviour described by Hart toward most actual or threatened deviations from N of which they are aware (when doing so would not be redundant).

3 On appropriate occasions, most members of C make internal statements which represent applications of N.

4 Most members of C prefer that they themselves conform to N.

5 Most members of C prefer that others conform to N.

6 Most members of C feel bound to follow N: (*a*) They believe that they ought to do what N requires, and (*b*) anticipate feelings of guilt, on contemplating violation of N. Thus (*c*) they experience some anxiety on contemplating violating N, and (*d*) actually feel guilty on violating N.

7 Most members of C believe that the types of behaviours described in conditions 1–3 are justified.

Conditions 8 to 11, which complete the relevant set of first-order preferences, are generated by placing the expression 'Most members of C prefer that' before conditions 2, 3, 6 and 7.

Conditions 12 to 17, which represent a highly significant set of second-order preferences to which MacCormick has explicitly attended, are generated by placing the expression 'Most members of C prefer that' before conditions 4, 5, and 8 to 11.

Each individual's actions and preferences as well as each individual's feelings about such acts and preferences may depend to a significant degree upon what each believes about the actions, preferences, and feelings of others. This is especially true where social rules have the status of conventions. Thus the need for conditions 18 to 34, which are generated by placing the expression 'Most members of C believe that' before conditions 1 to 17.

Just as second-order preferences are important, so are second-order beliefs, for how each individual acts, prefers and feels may depend to a significant degree upon what each believes about the relevant beliefs of others. Thus conditions 35 to 51, which are generated by placing the expression 'Most members of C believe that' before conditions 18 to 34.

The conditions enumerated above represent the sort of actions, feelings, desires, and beliefs that explain in many instances why people develop firm expectations about how others with whom they share certain social norms will behave. As David Shwayder has put it:

A community rule exists if the members of a community regulate their affairs according to what other members of the community would legitimately expect them to do. The rule is at once the expectations one conforms to and what legitimizes or warrants those expectations.[26]

Where such a situation obtains, each individual will adjust his or her own behaviour with an eye to how others are expected to behave, and hence may develop *new preferences* (reliance interests) about the behaviour of others with respect to their following the norms in question. The emergence of such reliance interests may not only strengthen the preferences, feelings, and behavioural propensities described in the conditions enumerated so far. The dynamic nature of the process may also lead to the development (at least implicitly) of new preferences that the conditions underlying the system of emerging mutual expectations continue to be satisfied. This requires the addition of conditions 52 to 68, which are generated by placing the expression 'Most members of C prefer that' before conditions 35 to 51.

Second-order preferences are surely no more out of place in our list of conditions at this stage of the analysis than they were at the beginning. So we might just as well add conditions 69 to 85, which are generated by placing the expression 'Most members of C prefer that' before conditions 52 to 68.

The reason for adding the original first-order belief conditions to the original first- and second-order preference conditions calls for adding first-order belief conditions with respect to the first- and second-order preferences with which we are now dealing. Thus conditions 86 to 119, which are generated by placing the expression 'Most members of C believe that' before conditions 52 to 85.

---

[26] David Shwayder, *The Stratification of Behaviour*, London (1965), 253.

Finally, the reason for adding the original second-order belief conditions calls for adding them here as well. Conditions 120 to 153 are thus to be generated by adding the expression 'Most members of C believe that' to conditions 86 to 119.

5 I take it to be obvious that few of the conditions listed above can be claimed to be logically necessary to the existence of a social rule and that those (if any) which are such are not jointly sufficient. In particular, contrary to what seems to be a virtually universal assumption among philosophers, it makes perfect sense to speak of a social rule as existing in a community even though the external aspect of its existence—condition 1—is absent. If the relevant attitudes, beliefs, and preferences are there—the remaining 152 conditions—this is more than enough to support the claim that the rule exists. For instance, I take it that contemporary American sexual morality contains a prohibition on adultery. I also think that it might be true that the majority of married individuals commit adultery at least once in their lifetimes. The point is that it could be true without changing the fact of the matter concerning the existence of a moral prohibition on such behaviour.

Constitutional rules are importantly different on this score. They are juristic constructs, the correct description of which must fit the facts with respect to the relevant behaviour of officials and norm subjects. Like Kelsen's basic norm,[27] Hart's rule of recognition must be constructed so that its efficacy is assured. The other side of this coin, however, seems to me to be this: if officials simply enforce those rules validated by the rule of recognition, and if citizens for the most part obey them, this is sufficient grounds for claiming that the rule of recognition is accepted and that (other things being equal) a legal system exists. Perhaps Hart is correct in suggesting that the reflective critical attitudes among officials of which he makes so much must at least be present. But in a simple system containing few officials, actual or threatened deviations from the constitutional rules might be virtually non-existent and the attitudes in question might never be displayed.

The volitional element (conditions 4, 5, and 8 to 11) which MacCormick takes to be 'essential' to the internal aspect of the existence of constitutional rules surely is not required. Consider a legal system in which the officials satisfy the conformance condition and the belief conditions about preferences, feelings, and others' beliefs, but in which the beliefs are in fact false. Each official might in his or her heart reject

---

[27] Hans Kelsen, 'On the Basic Norm', *California Law Review*, vol. 47 (1959).

the values that the system embraces and wish for its downfall, but (mistakenly believing that the other officials are all good Nazis) continue to 'play along' by enforcing the system's rules from basically the same motive which both Hart and MacCormick admit could explain why citizens obey the very same rules—fear. Hart himself recognizes the basic point and I have merely tried to elaborate on its implications concerning what is required (and what is *not* required) for an internal point of view.

[A] necessary condition of the existence of coercive power is that some at least must voluntarily co-operate in the system and accept its rules . . . [B]ut it is not . . . true that those who do accept the system voluntarily, must conceive of themselves as morally bound to do so. . . In fact, their allegiance to the system may be based on many different considerations: calculations of long-term interest; disinterested interest in others; and unreflecting inherited or traditional attitudes; or the mere wish to do as others do. There is indeed no reason why those who accept the authority of the system should not examine their conscience and decide that, morally, they ought not to accept it, yet for a variety of reasons continue to do so.[28]

6 I have followed Hart to this point in focusing upon the question of what is involved in official acceptance of the constitutional rules of recognition, change, adjudication and enforcement which lie at the foundations of legal order. But what is to be said of the relationship of the ordinary citizen to such rules? In particular, what attitudes and understanding must citizens have with respect to such rules in order for them to constitute conventional solutions to problems of strategic coordination which exist between officials and citizens? I believe Postema is correct in claiming that constitutional rules may often play this role,[29] but I am afraid that what Hart claims about the ordinary citizen's typical relationship to such rules would imply that Postema's account could not possibly be correct.

Whereas officials must *accept* the constitution by way of manifesting the internal point of view towards it, all that is required of citizens, according to Hart, is that they obey the law.

[W]e can imagine . . . a simple society where knowledge and understanding of the sources of law are widely diffused. There . . . no fiction would be involved in

[28] Hart, *Concept*, 198–9.
[29] Postema, 'Coordination and Convention at the Foundations of Law', 186–93.

attributing knowledge and acceptance of [the constitution] to the ordinary citizen as well as to the officials and lawyers. . . To insist that this state of affairs . . . always or usually exists in a complex modern state would be to insist on a fiction. Here surely the reality of the situation is that a great proportion of ordinary citizens—perhaps a majority—have no general conception of the legal structure or of its criteria of validity. The law which he obeys is something which he knows of only as 'the law'.[30]

There is, I believe, a middle ground between the claim that citizens accept the constitution in the same sense that officials do and the claim that they merely obey 'the law' which the constitution validates. It is the claim that the ordinary citizen believes that *there exists* a set of constitutional rules, accepted by officials, which determines what 'the law' is which he is required to obey. With respect to it—perhaps known to the ordinary citizen in only quite vague and general terms with respect to its specific legal provisions—there may exist those beliefs and preferences concerning the behaviour of both officials and other citizens which must be adopted before an account like Postema's can take hold. It is not a fiction to insist that this middle ground obtains in most modern states. Mindless passive obedience is not the norm for the simple reason that most people tend to question just what is going on when they are met with the persistent threat of coercive force against them and where those who pose the threat claim that they do so as a matter of both moral and legal right.

II

When may those who use coercive force against others in the name of the exercise of authority be said to do so as a matter of moral right? Note how general this question is; it clearly embraces parental as well as governmental authority and might be taken to include paternalistic interference with individual liberty as well. The general question can be divided into two: (1) What are the material conditions which may justify the exercise of authority against S by someone or other? (2) What are the relational conditions which must obtain between some particular A and S in order for A to have the right to be *the one* that exercises that authority which is materially justified?

1 Let us turn to the second question first; for present purposes, it can be dealt with briefly. Although the following classification is clearly not

---

[30] Hart, *Concept*, 110–11.

mutually exclusive and may not even be exhaustive, it would seem that there are three primary sources of authority. First, authority may be based upon consent; I may, for example, authorize someone to restrain me forcibly from engaging in certain activities. In this case the material conditions appear to be primarily negative; for example, consent is not recognized as a defence against a charge of assault or murder. A second source of authority is rooted in a plea of necessity. The one who uses coercion against another claims that the material conditions which justify the exercise of authority are satisfied and that he/she is the *only one* in a position to exercise it. For example, A might be the only one in a position to prevent S from crossing a bridge which, unbeknownst to S, is ready to collapse.[31] Finally, a third source of authority is prescriptive norms, customary and/or conventional. This is the typical source of the authority of the state. To claim this is not to deny that those in political power often plead necessity in times of what they describe as political crisis nor is it to deny the existence of the contractarian tradition in political philosophy. It is merely to affirm that most governments which have existed for any length of time, whatever else they or their philosophical apologists might claim, base their legitimacy on the kind of constitutional rules discussed by Hart and others. Since the positivistic account of the existence of constitutional rules contained in Section I has no significant moral implications, the question then (to repeat) is, 'When may those who may correctly claim to act with legal authority be said to have a moral right to rule?'

2 Let me begin by explaining what I understand this claim to mean. The validation of legal rules by applying the rule of recognition, the change of legal rules by use of the legislative process, the reaching of decisions through procedures of adjudication—this all takes place within an institutional framework which presupposes the existence of what I have called rules of enforcement. This is at least true of the modern nation state, claiming as it does a monopoly on the control of the exercise of coercive force within the territory over which it asserts its sovereignty. This is not to claim that Hart is wrong in arguing that law is conceivable apart from sanctions.[32] It is merely to contend that questions about the moral rights of legal authorities would be quite different, and perhaps both less pressing and less interesting, if it were not the case that authoritative determinations of what the law requires normally imply the

[31] J. S. Mill, *On Liberty*. Indianopolis, Indiana (1956). (Originally published 1859.)
[32] Hart, *Concept*, 195.

threat of the imposition of coercive legal sanctions in the case of non-compliance. With respect to virtually all official actions, the prospect of the use of coercion by the state is understood. The moral claim of a right to exercise authority thus focuses on this coercive element.

First, it involes what Robert Ladenson has called a 'justification-right'.[33] The use of coercion is normally morally impermissible. When resorted to, it stands in need of a moral justification. As Ladenson notes, '[s]elf-defense . . ., defense of others, consent, necessity, justified paternalism, and parental authority',[34] are all bases for the assertion of a justification-right to the use of coercion. So too with the notion of a moral right to exercise those coercive powers which legal authorities are permitted—indeed, often required—to exercise.

Second, a moral right to exercise legal authority involves a claim-right against would-be, unauthorized usurpers of official activities. The kangaroo court has no right to conduct a trial, morally or legally; the lynch mob has no right, legally or morally, to punish. This claim-right aspect of the assertion of legal authority reflects the monopolistic aspect of the state's right to control the exercise of coercive force. It may be present in the case of some other forms of authority—for example, parental authority—but with most other forms of authority it would seem that only something weaker is associated with the justification-right: a claim-right that no third party act so as to prevent the justified coercion from being employed by someone or other. For example, I have no complaint, no claim-right that has been violated, if you leap to Jones's rescue before I do (the case might be one either of justified defence of others or one of justified paternalism). Note that as it has been explained the claim-right in question, in either its strong or its weak form, is against third parties; not against those over whom authority would be exercised.

It should be clear that an obligation to obey the law is not to be derived from the existence of authority as it has been described above. If a moral obligation to obey the law exists under any interesting social conditions, an argument independent from a mere analysis of the notion of a moral right to rule must be given to show that it does. I once again follow Ladenson, who points out that on a notion of authority such as my own

the claim that governmental authority constitutes a moral justification for coercion by itself implies nothing about either the subject's duties of allegiance

---

[33] Robert Ladenson, 'In Defense of a Hobbesian Conception of Law', *Philosophy and Public Affairs*, vol. 9 (1980), 137–40.
[34] Ibid., 138.

to the state or of compliance with the law. This is because the right to rule [as a relationship between the exerciser of authority and the subject of coercion], being a justification-right rather than a claim-right, entails no correlative duties.[35]

Neither can one infer from the existence of authority as I have described it that the institutional framework within which it is exercised is either just or efficient. 'Indeed, conceding someone the right to rule . . . is logically compatible with believing that the particular . . . institutions under which he or she acts ought not to exist at all'.[36] This claim is not so dramatic as it might at first appear to be. Plato, for instance, believed that monogamous marriage and the nuclear family ought to be replaced by institutions of a quite different sort; democratic political institutions, on his view, represented the worst form of government except for tyranny. Surely it could not be correct to claim that these views *required him* to reject the claims of moral authority made by Athenian parents and politicians.

3 Under what material conditions may a moral right to rule in the sense explained above be said to exist? Although I reject the conclusion which she draws on the question of the foundations of a moral obligation to obey those in authority, I believe the answer is in large part provided by Elizabeth Anscombe, in a paper entitled 'On the Sources of the Authority of the State'.[37]

According to Anscombe, government authority, like parental authority, 'arises from the necessity of a task whose performance requires . . . obedience on the part of those for whom the task is supposed to be done'.[38] The particular rights that those in authority have 'derive . . . from the fact that they are necessary to the performance of the task'.[39] One finds oneself subject to either parental or political authority 'willy-nilly';[40] the authority is rooted in the necessity of the task and what is required to get on with the task rather than in the approval, let alone the consent, of those in whose name it is carried out.

The mere existence of a task that needs to be done does not suffice to establish that one who undertakes it has a right to do so. Those who

---

[35] Ibid., 141.
[36] Ibid., 143.
[37] *Ratio*, vol. 20 (1978).
[38] Ibid., 6.
[39] Ibid., 18.
[40] Ibid., 6.

kidnap babies and rear them with love and kindness do not thereby acquire parental rights; those who usurp political authority and exercise it benevolently do not thereby acquire legitimacy. What more is called for?

Someone's [rightful] task is work which it is necessary that *he* should do or work which it is necessary that someone should do and which it is his right to do. Therefore the mere fact that someone is performing a task does not suffice to prove that he has a right to what is needed for the performance of the task. It must either be necessary that he should perform the task or be his right to do it, before he can derive a right to certain things from the fact that they are necessary for the performance of the task.[41]

With the core of Anscombe's account, as represented in the preceding paragraphs, I fully agree. In the remainder of this essay I shall amplify upon it in a manner which will link it directly to certain central aspects of Hart's work and indicate some further important points where Anscombe and I are either in accord or disagree.

(*a*) In order to preclude a possible misunderstanding of my own views at the outset, let me begin with a significant point of disagreement. I contended in the previous section that the *analysis* of the nature of authority contained therein did not imply a moral obligation of obedience on the part of the subjects of legitimate authority. I do not believe that any such obligation of obedience follows from a correct account of the *foundations* of authority in terms of necessary tasks either. On Anscombe's view, on the other hand, 'obedience/disobedience are the [logically] primary correlates of authority',[42] and it is clear that by 'obedience' she understands the existence of an obligation to obey rather than mere general compliance. 'Authority. . .,' she writes, 'is: the right to be obeyed'.[43] Anscombe's argument seems to be:

> Authorities have a right to what is necessary for the successful performance of their rightful tasks.
> Obedience on the part of those over whom authority is exercised is required for such successful performance.
> ∴ Authorities have a right to obedience on the part of those over whom authority is exercised.

The argument is obviously valid, but the problem with it is that the leading premiss is too strong. It simply begs the question on the issue of

[41] Ibid., 17–18.
[42] Ibid., 6.
[43] Ibid., 3.

a moral obligation to obey the law. What authorities have a right to on the analysis that Ladenson and I offer is limited to justification-rights in so far as norm subjects are concerned. In so far as claim-rights, which correlate with positive obligations, are involved, they hold only against third parties. So, Anscombe has her notion of authority and I have mine. How to choose between them? All I can say here is this. Neither Anscombe's understanding nor my own can be defended by an appeal to what is required by the meaning of the word 'authority'; matters here simply are not on a par with the claim that bachelors must be understood as unmarried in virtue of the meaning of the word 'bachelor'. Even if I were wrong on this score, I would be prepared to stipulate the meaning of a 'new' concept, give it whatever name you like, and defend the position that it isolated an important legal-moral-political phenomenon of considerable interest. At any rate, it is what *I* am interested in. Finally, most of us probably believe that independent argument is required to establish a moral obligation to obey the law, and the philosophical tradition beginning with Plato's *Crito* is replete with arguments of more or less complexity. If construed as an argument, Anscombe's 'argument' is simply too quick.

(*b*) Let me next turn to a point of significant agreement. I believe that there are substantive moral rights that exist outside government which both in large part set the task for, and constrain the legitimate range of, political authority. But contrary to state-of-nature theorists like Locke and Nozick,[44] I do not believe that the only rights that government may exercise are ones which in principle could have been transferred to it by individuals seeking to transform a state of nature into a civil society. Although primitive forms of a right to punish and exact reparation surely could exist simply as forms of a right to self-protection outside government, the complex procedures associated with modern forms of legislation, adjudication, and law enforcement clearly could not. As Anscombe puts it, the institution of government in large part 'creates the character of an act as one of *doing justice* on the wrongs of others . . . (C)ivil society is the bearer of rights of coercion not possibly existent among men without government'.[45] This thesis, which I have argued at length elsewhere,[46] vindicates Hart's contention that the addition of constitu-

---

[44] Locke, *The Second Treatise of Government*; Robert Nozick, *Anarchy, State and Utopia*, New York (1974).

[45] Anscombe, 'On the Source of Authority of the State', 21, 19.

[46] Rolf Sartorius, 'The Limits of Libertarianism', in Robert Cunningham (ed.), *Liberty and the Rule of Law*, Texas (1979).

tional rules of recognition, change, and adjudication, to a set of pre-existing primary rules of obligation marks a difference in the nature of social ordering so significant in kind as to warrant its being described as representing the transition from the pre-legal to the legal world.

(*c*) On the account of authority which Anscombe and I share, authority is associated with the legitimate exercise of coercive force because compliance with the norms which are enforced by those in authority is taken to be required for the successful completion of a necessary task. This suggests that there are tasks which need to be performed for the benefit of those who cannot help themselves where the beneficiaries' co-operation (in the form of obedience) is not required and that with respect to such tasks the exercise of the heavy hand of coercive authority would not be legitimate. The distinction between tasks which require various forms of co-operation on the part of beneficiaries of others' good efforts and those which do not especially inform our thinking about parental rights and responsibilities in both easy and hard cases. An easy case: affluent parents can easily assure the material well-being of a twelve-year-old child. They have no right to force the child to help support itself by getting a job delivering newspapers in the early morning hours in the harsh winter climate of Minnesota. A hard case (for many): does a parent have a right to be informed of, or even to exercise a veto over, its minor female child's decision to practise contraception? The easy case may be converted to a hard case if we suppose that the parents, rather than being affluent, are living just above the poverty line. The hard case may be converted to an easy one (for most, but unfortunately not for all) if we suppose that the child's decision involves receiving medical treatments which both she and her parents understand are necessary to save her life.

The moral of the short story of the above paragraph is simply this: the question of what means may be necessary to carry out some required tasks may be quite controversial, and the controversy may have different sources. Moral argument, not logical analysis, will be called for in such cases.

A somewhat different difficulty with the notion of what is necessary for the performance of a task requiring obedience on the part of those in whose name it would be performed is this: no particular thing might be necessary, each of a number of available means for performing it being equally sufficient (although perhaps quite different in other important respects, such as the degree to which coercion is involved or the degree to which the privacy of the beneficiary of the task is invaded). At least where the rights of those over whom authority is to be exercised are arguably involved (as they usually will be), perhaps something like the so-called 'strict scrutiny' standard of judicial review as employed in US Constitutional law ought to be the operative notion. For example, the burden of proof ought to be upon those in authority to demonstrate that they have adopted the 'least intrusive' of available means for achieving a necessary end. This will often require a weighting of the significance of different moral rights which might be differentially infringed depending upon the means adopted; for example, privacy versus freedom from coercive restraint in the case, say, of a mental patient considered dangerous to him- or herself. Once again, moral argument will be called for.

(*d*) The above difficulties centred around controversies concerning what are necessary means for the achievement of ends themselves understood to represent *necessary tasks*. But, especially where the legitimate range of governmental authority is at issue, considerable controversy may arise as to what is to be understood by 'necessary' in this context and, even with some fixed notion of necessity in mind, equal controversy may surround the question of what *is* necessary. To make matters worse, there is also room for much controversy concerning the question, Necessary *for what*? Finally, there is this question, Necessary *for whom*? (The average contemporary American? An ideally rational and moral agent? Those whose psyches have been purified in some appropriate way?) To answer all these questions would be to probe the deepest questions of political philosophy. The account of authority I have provided thus must be understood as a schema that will obviously be filled in in different ways by defenders of different political theories. The anarchist and the Marxist who seriously envisions the withering away of the state will answer these questions in ways that will militate against the possibility of the moral authority of government. The libertarian will answer them in ways which will provide for the possible legitimacy of a minimal state. The welfare statist will provide yet a different set of answers. In what follows I shall only remark briefly on the ways in which I would be inclined to answer these questions.

It is too quick a route to philosophical anarchism to deny the state legitimacy because people could *conceivably* accomplish for themselves through voluntary associations what the state can accomplish for them. The *notion* of necessary tasks may be best understood in terms of Hart's concept of *natural necessity* (see above, part I, 1). There are certain contingent but virtually universal features of human beings and their natural environment which provided *the best of reasons* why legal authorities *ought* to undertake certain tasks. A theory of morality and/or rational self-interest will be required here; not logical analysis.

What tasks are there the best of reasons for governments to undertake? On my own view, the protection of individual moral rights (not including welfare rights) and the provision of those public goods which provide the necessary background conditions for the effective exercise of individual rights (for example, national defence).

Tasks required for the achievement of what ends? Hart's notion of natural necessity is presented in terms of what there are good reasons for *given survival as an aim*. But surely room must be made for loftier human pursuits than mere survival (of either the individual or the species). I suspect that some attempt at realizing those social and environmental conditions which provide an opportunity for individuals to lead meaningful human lives will have to be made here.

Tasks which must be performed for us, with all our frailties, or for those ideally rational and moral agents which we might take (mistake?) to be our better selves? I would here suggest an approach in accord with many familiar discussions of parental authority and justified paternalism. Where the need for the exercise of political authority represents rectifiable human frailties, those in authority have the responsibility to foster their rectification. As with other forms of authority, the exercise of the awesome coercive powers of modern government ought to take place with a view toward eventually eliminating the need for it as far as possible.

2.2 Comment

JOHN FINNIS*

Sartorius's paper has two main theses with which I can concur. But I think that Sartorius fails to pursue consistently the implications of his own, and Hart's, methodology.

The first thesis guides part I of Sartorius's paper. Explanations of law, social rules, and the like had better proceed, he says, not 'by way of the specification of a set of conditions which are individually necessary and jointly sufficient for [the] correct application' of the relevant term or concept, but rather by identification of 'central features' of legal or other forms of social order and social ordering, and by consideration of the 'important differences made in our lives . . . by the presence or absence of [those] central features . . '.

The second theme runs through part II of his paper. The question which 'ultimately interest[s]' Sartorius — 'By what moral right may some people exercise coercion over others?' — is to be answered not by 'logical analysis' but by identifying, first, the 'ends' which give 'reasons' for undertaking tasks or 'responsibilities', and then by identifying 'what is required to get on with the task' in view of 'certain contingent but virtually universal features of human beings and their natural environment'.

As Sartorius rightly says, those two methodological theses were a principal source of 'the great richness of illumination offered by *The Concept of Law*'. I would go further. Those theses, subtly explored in the context of a comprehensive and precise understanding of mature legal systems, enabled Hart to restore his discipline ('jurisprudence') to the *philosophy of human affairs*[47] with all the *descriptive richness and critical openness to practical questions of good, less good, and evil* of Aristotle's original enterprise. That enterprise has long needed, of course, to be reworked, to overcome the serious limitations in Aristotle's empirical knowledge of human culture, and in his understanding of human nature (of free choice for example). Attempts to undertake this reworking have

---

* © John Finnis 1987.

[47] Cf. Aristotle, *Nicomachean Ethics*, x. 9: 1181b15: *he peri ta anthropina philosophia.*

foundered on diversions such as Hegel's or Comte's *gnosis* about the meaning of history, Bentham's hedonist determinism, Weber's value-demonism . . . and many others. Hart has distanced himself from such diversions and shown how one can get on with the job of overcoming both the complacent eclecticism of the legal practitioner and academic, and the arbitrary scepticisms of empiricists like Bentham and, at a remove, Austin, of neo-Kantians like Kelsen, and of behaviourists like the Scandinavian and American Realists.

One sign of Hart's openness to reality has gone unnoticed by Sartorius. In *The Concept of Law*, the end or 'aim' which is the basis for the 'natural' or, better, 'rational necessity' of the central features of law is said to be 'survival'. Sartorius rightly suggests that 'surely room must be made for loftier human pursuits than mere survival . . .' But Hart got there before him; in his 1967 essay 'Problems of the Philosophy of Law', Hart proposes as the final point of law not mere survival, but rather that 'whatever other purposes laws may serve, they must, to be acceptable to any rational person, enable men to live and organize their lives *for the more efficient pursuit of their aims* . . . certain rules [are] necessary *if fundamental human needs are to be satisfied.* . . .'[48] No doubt the faithful and cautious interpreter of Hart's works might see in this shift no more than a new stratagem in the unaltered grand strategy of declining to participate (or at least to involve jurisprudence) in the great 'dispute'[49] about the point of human existence, the basic forms of human flourishing and the basic requirements of practical reasonableness; the new stratagem is that so amply developed in Rawls's 'thin theory of the good' — of saying (no more than): *if anything* is wanted, these [primary goods] will be needed. But one who speaks at all of human needs and human rationality cannot prevent his hearers reflecting that human intelligence can also understand some 'ultimate' wants as really no more than worthless means to self-gratification while other objects of desire are really desirable or worthwhile. Human rationality can also reflect that the arbitrariness involved in unrestricted self-preference is itself a deviation from 'rationality' and something one *needs to avoid* whatever else one's wants . . . As Sartorius's whole paper hints, Hart's method points out a land which is left to his readers and hearers to hazard to enter.

[48] Hart, *Essays*, 113 (emphases added).
[49] Cf. Hart, *Concept*, 187–8.

I

That the analysis of legal authority yielded by part I of Sartorius's paper would be 'positivistic' was pre-determined by the restricted nature of his question in that part, 'just what is being claimed when it is said that a particular social norm exists in, *or is accepted by* the members of, a community?[50] If one's interest in the 'existence' of social (for instance, legal) norms is restricted to the question, 'When are they accepted?', one will be a positivist simply by narrowness of theoretical concern.

Every competent 'natural law theorist' (Plato, Aristotle, Aquinas) can produce a 'positivist' analysis of what is involved in people accepting a rule, that is, of what is involved in the pragmatic 'existence' of such a rule (for example, of the 'existing law' of a corrupt and tyrannical democracy such as executed or judicially/legally murdered Socrates). What would strike these theorists as odd, and in need of explanation, is that some 'social scientists and ethical theorists' apparently consider such an 'analysis' somehow an interesting and complete topic in its own right. After all, law's existence in this pragmatic sense will be evident enough to anyone who strolls into the marketplace and attends to the goings-on of courts, hangmen, secret and not-so-secret police, barrackroom lawyers in the legislature . . . Such an observer might, I suppose, get interested in what is involved in *acceptance*, as part of (say) a Thucydidean enquiry into the likelihood of breakdown, revolution, and civil war or counter-revolutionary suppression; or as part of a Weberian enquiry into the fate of bureaucratic mass democracy. But he will hardly turn to a philosopher's 'analysis' to help him.

Sartorius ignores the claim made by Joseph Raz and other students of Hart that, in the world of social life and common speech which lies open to our 'analysis', we find statements about the existence of norms — that is, statements of the form 'N [a law or other social norm] still exists as part of English law', 'N is a valid law', 'There is in England a law, N', 'By virtue of N, X has power to . . .', — statements which may be understood in three ways, one of which is *basic* or *primary*, the other two being secondary and derivative or even parasitic;[51] and that the basic or primary form of such statements is that in which the statement asserts

[50] Emphasis added. The next sentence begins 'This question . . .', thus establishing that the 'or' in the sentence quoted signifies synonymity, not alternatives. That the question is indeed restricted to 'acceptance' is made clear by the phrasing in other places.

[51] Joseph Raz, *Practical Reason and Norms*, London (1975), 172. See Finnis, *Natural Law and Natural Rights*, Oxford (1980), 234–6. Likewise Neil MacCormick, *H. L. A. Hart*, London (1981), 39–40.

that N gives *good reason* for acting in a certain way. I am not going to explore this claim here; for Sartorius does not confront it. I shall simply observe that legal theorists who are not determined a priori to restrict their theoretical enquiries after the manner of Sartorius's 'positivistic' part I, can undertake an enquiry which I suggest is more enticing: What sort of good *reasons* are there for thinking that laws or other social norms can and sometimes do *give good reasons for acting?*

What is the attraction of such an enquiry? Well, it permits *all* the hard-headed, undeluded, undistracted attention to social facts which a 'positivist' (or an Aristotle!) could desire; for social facts both affect one's choice or approval of means in one's practical reasoning, and serve as a stock of reminders of reasons which other people have considered to be good reasons and which may thus be plausible. And at the same time it opens up a line of thought to which a philosopher could hope to contribute much, namely the analysis of reasons *as reasons*.

The attractive power of such more-than-positivist enquiry is indicated, perhaps, by the way in which Sartorius strays across his own self-imposed boundaries. Consider the following:

Whether or not one has in mind the acceptance of social rules in general, or the acceptance of constitutional rules by officials in particular, the existence of social rules is simply *too complex an affair to permit* of any interesting claims about what in the nature of their existence generates moral obligations on the part of either those who apply them or those to whom they apply. (emphasis added)

This seems to suggest that if the facts involved in acceptance were less 'complex', one might be able to say that something about 'the nature of their existence' (scilicet about that acceptance) 'generates moral obligations'. But how do facts, simple or complex, 'generate' moral obligations? How does the question of generating moral obligations arise in the course of a 'positivistic' discussion of what counts as acceptance of social rules? Sartorius seems, similarly, to have confused MacCormick's claim — that rules cannot be said to be accepted unless people have a certain set of preferences and beliefs including a belief that the rule is [morally] binding — with the quite distinct claim that where the rule is thus accepted it does indeed 'generate' moral obligations. We shall see, in our discussion of part II of his paper, that Sartorius really does speak as if an 'analysis' of terms or 'phenomena' might, in principle, yield a moral conclusion. I must say that the main stream of natural law theorizing never falls into this sort of confusion, which is by no means peculiar to Sartorius.

Following Aristotle, Aquinas, and Hart, I agree with Sartorius that any useful theoretical concept of *legal system*, or of *acceptance*, had better be a 'cluster concept'. So I may be excused from dwelling on Sartorius's interesting discussion of the 153 conditions which might, he thinks, have to be acknowledged by someone who misguidedly sought a set of necessary and sufficient conditions for the existence/acceptance of a legal system;[52] or on his argument that none of the 153 is in fact a strictly necessary condition.[53]

Nor do I wish to dwell on the fact that Sartorius himself seems to engage in a bit of 'essentialism' when he opines that 'constitutional rules ... are juristic constructs, the correct description of which *must* fit the facts with respect to the relevant behaviour of officials and norm subjects.' The truth is that the concepts of *juristic construct* and *correct description of juristic constructs* are each concepts which had better be treated as cluster concepts. One may readily see this, in precisely the context of constitutional rules, if one reflects on the rival 'correct juristic descriptions' which can intelligibly and reasonably be given of the constitutional situation in a civil war, or during an enemy occupation and 'government in exile', or in circumstances such as prevailed in and in relation to Rhodesia in the years after its Unilateral Declaration of Independence from the United Kingdom in 1965. In such circumstances, one can of course *adopt* a particular viewpoint from which one and only one description of the constitutional rules will be 'correct'. But to assert that only one such particular viewpoint can be correct is to distort both common opinion and practice, and the legal and moral complexities of the situation.

The most substantial point I want to make about part I is that Sartorius has not followed through the implications of his recognition that the analysis had better be by way of cluster concepts. For, as he

[52] I am not to be taken to agree that the generation of most of the 153 conditions is sound; one wonders whether it takes sufficient account of the point made by the classical natural law theorists: doing justice (in whatever capacity) is a matter not of having the right attitudes but of right *practice* regardless of attitude: e.g. Aquinas, *Summa Theologiae* II–II, q. 57, a.1c. Why should people bother to have all, or even any, of these preferences (or even of these beliefs) about other people's preferences or beliefs, so long as the others are *complying?*

[53] I think his argument about adultery in contemporary American sexual mores is weak; the fact that most people commit adultery at least once would not nearly show that the rule had no 'external aspect'; the proper question (relative to this so-called external aspect) is whether most people *usually* abstain from adultery when occasion offers. (Perhaps they do not, but Sartorius does not tell us about that). But I do not want to question his point that condition 1 may not be necessary.

acknowledges from time to time, a cluster concept is not a shapeless sprawl of features. It is a set of criteria or features all of which are satisfied in 'standard or normal' cases, and some of which, with due (extreme) caution, can be recognized to be 'central' or 'crucial'. But what makes a feature 'crucial' or (better) 'central'? And what makes an instantiation of the concept 'standard or normal'? As to the latter question, it is perhaps significant that Sartorius spends time on 'insist-[ing]', against Hart, that 'mindless passive obedience is not *the norm*' (emphasis added). Why should Sartorius want to insist on this purely empirical question of what 'obtains in most modern states'? I fear it may be because he lacks any clear conception of what should count as the central case or cases (instantiations) of a theoretical concept such as *legal system* or *internal attitude*, and equally of what should count as the central or crucial features of that concept.

Weber was right, I believe, to insist that social science advances understanding by identifying not the universal, or the common, or the average (or, one might say, the Sartorian 'norm'), but rather the characteristic, the culturally significant, the intelligible and meaning-ful.[54] And certainly, when it is a question of developing a theoretical concept encapsulating a clarified and improved understanding of a range of social phenomena (such as the concept of law developed by Hart in the book of that name), one should share Hart's assumption that 'the extension of the general terms of any serious discipline is never without its principle or rationale'.[55] The project of identifying such a principle or rationale should be particularly easily distinguishable from the question of either universality or even frequency of instantiation, when the relevant term and concept signify a range of social phenomena constituted principally by *reasons*, good and/or purportedly good, for action. For the coherence and mutual supportiveness of reasons is certainly distinct from the question of how frequently those reasons, or any sub-set of them, are actually adopted and acted upon. Thus, for example, Hart's critique of Kelsenian reductionism ('distortion as the price of uniformity')[56] does not depend on demonstrating that the law-abiding man's attitude to law is more *common* than the 'bad man's' perspective. Nor does his critique of 'realism'[57] depend on showing that

[54] Max Weber, *The Methodology of the Social Sciences* (ed. E. A. Shils and H. A. Finch), New York (1949) 43, 90; Susan J. Hekman, *Max Weber and Contemporary Social Theory*, Indiana and Oxford (1983), 22, 25, 48.
[55] Hart, *Concept*, 15, 210; also 234; also Hart, *Essays*, 22, 30 n, 43 ff.
[56] Hart, *Concept*, 38–41.
[57] Ibid., 81–2; 'Scandinavian Realism', in *Essays*, 165.

judges never or rarely fail to use the law as a reason for their judgements; rather, it suffices that the whole idea of having rules which courts are to apply to the litigants who were subject to those rules — an idea central to any plausible project of distinguishing law from other forms of coercive social ordering[58]—would be unintelligible if rules were not reasons for judgement but mere predictions.

I quite agree with Sartorius that it is possible to envisage a legal system in which every official in his heart rejected the system's values and wished for its downfall and continued to play along largely or 'basically' out of fear. Equally, I agree with Hart that 'allegiance to the system may be based on many different considerations', such as 'calculations of long-term interest . . . an unreflecting inherited or traditional attitude; or the mere wish to do as others do'.[59] But I would like to suggest again what I have argued elsewhere. 'All these considerations and attitudes . . . are manifestly deviant, diluted or watered-down instances of the practical viewpoint that brings law into being as a significantly differentiated type of social order and maintains it as such. Indeed, they are parasitic upon that viewpoint.'[60] For, unreflecting traditionalism or sheer conformism, while capable (up to a point) of maintaining a legal system in being if it already exists, are blind or practically indifferent to the need to remedy the defects of a pre-legal (or post-legal!) social order; that is, they do not share the concern which Hart himself treats as the explanatory source of legal order. Likewise, the man motivated dominantly by calculations of long-term self-interest will dilute his allegiance to law and his adherence to legal processes with doses of that very self-interest which, on everybody's view, it is an elementary function of law to subordinate to social needs.

I will not here repeat the whole argument in favour of identifying, as the central case of allegiance to law (the 'internal viewpoint'), the attitudes of one who considers that morality, and a rationally imperative impartiality of concern for others, require him to co-operate in establishing and/or maintaining legal order as distinct not only from anarchy but also from discretionary or statically conventional forms of social ordering. I have argued elsewhere that this is the set of attitudes that should be taken as the standard of reference by the theorist seeking to describe the features of legal order. A principal attraction of this

---

[58] See Raz, *Practical Reason and Norms*, 136, 137, 139.
[59] Hart, *Concept*, 198; also 111, 226.
[60] Finnis, *Natural Law and Natural Rights*, 13–15.

method, for me as for Plato[61] and Aristotle and Aquinas, is this: the mature person of practical reasonableness (whose relevant attitudes I have just sketched) can understand and appreciate the concerns and the reasons for action of the merely self-interested, the mere conformist, the mere careerist, *but the converse does not hold*. So, adoption of this person's practical concerns as the criterion for discerning what features really do 'cluster together' as a coherent, meaningful, and important social institution will make possible not only the most intelligible account of legal reasons for action (including reasons for having law and the rule of law at all) but also the best *empirical* account of this aspect of human affairs.

But since Sartorius's paper does not advert to this type of objection to Hart's refusal to identify a central case of the internal point of view, I shall not labour the matter further here.

II

Why should someone who is 'ultimately interested . . . in considering by what moral right some people may exercise coercive authority over others' *want* a 'positivistic' account of the existence of a legal system? Why should he want an account which treats some rather indeterminate (we may not talk of 'necessary and sufficient conditions') cluster of facts about practices and attitudes as amounting to the acceptance (by a community) of a legal system?

I suspect that the reason is a fear that the moral enquiry will somehow be *prejudiced* unless the object of that enquiry has been first identified in morally neutral terms.

As a reason for sponsoring a 'positivistic' general theory of law or legal system, this would be, I suggest, a muddle. For, as Hart reminded us many years ago,[62] we begin our enquiry—*any* theoretical enquiry— about law with a wide knowledge of the facts about law and legal systems. We already know, before we start either 'positivistic' description or moral argument, that in our own society as well as in others, there are existing institutions of courts, legislature, police and bailiffs, lawyers, enactments, valid and invalid instruments, and so forth. This knowledge is not going to be lost during the development of a descriptive general theory, and is perfectly sufficient to permit us to raise,

---

[61] *Republic* IX, 582a–e; III, 408d–409e.
[62] *Concept*, 4–5.

without any prejudgement, the question whether these institutions have any moral justification and make any morally obligatory claims upon us.

What, then, is the point of a descriptive general theory? It is, as Hart also taught us, by word and example, to *explain* the *function*, the practical point, of the various aspects and components of law and legal systems, so as to show *why* there is *good practical reason* for these aspects and components to cluster together as a distinct social enterprise.[63]

And that is why a fruitful, descriptive general theory of law cannot proceed at all without adopting and seeking, as Hart would say, to 'reproduce' a particular practical viewpoint.[64] Hart identified that viewpoint as 'the internal attitude'. He characterized that viewpoint more closely than Sartorius, for he treated merely fearful compliance as not 'internal'.[65] In this, his view is to be preferred to Sartorius's. It matters not that one can imagine a society in which every single person complies only out of fear. For such a society, as Sartorius himself points out, would have to be founded on a vast series of factually mistaken beliefs (about the attitudes of everyone else). And no illumination *about law* is to be gained by reflecting on this grossly pathological social condition.[66]

I have argued, above, that the practical viewpoint from which to explain the point of a legal ordering would be better characterized even more closely than Hart does, by treating as insufficiently illuminating those explanations which would satisfy the mere conformist or careerist or traditionalist, and by looking further, for explanations which would satisfy someone with a sound morality, that is, a fully reasonable person.

You will say that descriptive jurisprudence cannot, on this view, be safely done until one has completed a moral enquiry into the foundations of the moral authority of law. I reply that the moral enquiry cannot be safely done until one has an exact knowledge of the functions of legal ordering and of the institutions and devices which have been devised to serve those functions. The truth is, then, that *explanatory descriptive general theory* of law and *the moral justification and critique of law for the guidance of one's own conscience* are radically inter-dependent intellectual enterprises.[67]

---

[63] Finnis, *Natural Law and Natural Rights*, 6–7.
[64] See Hart, *Concept*, 88; see also *Natural Law and Natural Rights*, 12.
[65] Hart, *Concept*, 88.
[66] By which I do not *mean* 'rare' (though I think it is).
[67] Finnis, *Natural Law and Natural Rights*, 16–19.

III

The question addressed in part II of Sartorius's paper is: 'When may those who correctly claim to act with legal authority be said to have a moral right to rule?'

Sartorius's first move is to explain 'what [he understands] this claim to mean'. I want to raise two sorts of doubts about the explanation he offers: the first, about the content of his analysis of the claim to a moral right to rule; the second, about what he thinks, or seems to think, *might* be established by any such analysis.

Sartorius's analysis of the claim to a moral right to rule identifies it as a compound of two elements: (*a*) a claim to a 'justification-right', that is a claim that A (the bearer of legal authority) is morally justified, by virtue of his authority, in using coercion against S (his legal subject); (*b*) a claim to a claim-right against usurpers, who thus are said to have a correlative obligation not to usurp the processes of, for example, trial and punishment by kangaroo courts or lynchings.[68]

The point that Sartorius seems to want to make is that this claim does not include a claim that S has a moral obligation to obey the law.[69]

The effort to keep S out of the picture of A's moral right to rule leads to some oddities. It is odd to think of the obligation not to usurp being owed (as Sartorius insists) not to S (the victim of the usurping kangaroo court or lynch mob) but to A. I would be prepared to grant that A does have some rather secondary and not very interesting Sartorian claim-right not to be usurped; but, in relation to usurpation, I should say that his primary right is his justification-right (and responsibility) to take coercive steps to deter, resist, and punish usurpers. And I can see no ground, either in common opinion or sound political philosophy, to doubt that it is S who has the primary and interesting claim-rights (*a*) against usurpers, that authority over him shall not be usurped, and (*b*) against A, that A shall resist usurpers.[70]

Much more odd is the following implication of Sartorius's analysis: to

[68] In one place, Sartorius loosely expresses this obligation or duty to abstain from usurpation as a mere 'no right'. In another he correctly identifies the correlative of the claim-right as a '[positive] obligation'.

[69] It is hard to be sure about Sartorius's point here, because neither he nor the quoted passages from Ladenson distinguish between deriving the *existence of an obligation* from an (*existing*) (*moral*) *right to rule*, and deriving *the existence of an obligation* from a (*mere*) *claim to have a* (*moral*) *right to rule*.

[70] I do not say that Sartorius denies these rights of S; but neither does he mention them; secondary takes the place of primary, and primary is not mentioned, in his analysis.

claim that A has a moral right to rule is to claim that A is morally justified in coercing S, by trial and punishment, for an action *that S had and has no moral obligation to abstain from*. For this is the implication of Sartorius's assertion that A's justification-right has no correlative obligation. I do not say that this defies 'logic'. On the contrary, there has been for centuries an important and influential strand of Western political philosophizing which contends that many laws are 'purely penal', that is, that the enactment of the laws is morally justified, but that the laws themselves impose no moral obligation to comply with their legal-obligation-imposing content, but only a moral obligation to submit to the legal penalty for non-compliance, or alternatively and more popularly, a disjunctive moral obligation to either comply or submit to penalty.[71] Those who have defended this interpretation have occasionally visualized the logical possibility that S has no moral obligation even to submit to the penalty. But this logical possibility seems to have almost no moral plausibility. For if the structure of the situation is such that A really is morally entitled not only to enact the law but also to impose really coercive penalties on S, what could be the features of that structure that would relieve S of the moral obligation to co-operate with A, if not by complying with his law at least by submitting to the penalty?

It would have been helpful if Sartorius had indicated where he stands in these debates about 'purely penal laws'. I cannot discern from his paper whether or not he thinks that S, whom he envisages as having no moral obligation to *comply*, has any moral obligation to submit to the penalties which A, on Sartorius's own analysis, has the moral justification-right to impose on him.

And I confess that I am simply defeated by his discussion of the legitimate exercise of coercive force. I cannot be sure how it is supposed to stand in relation to the principal thesis that a moral right to rule does not entail a moral obligation to comply. For at one point the picture is that 'authority is associated with' [oddly weak phrase] 'the legitimate [scilicet justified] exercise of coercive force *because* compliance with the norms which are enforced by those in authority is taken to be *required* for the successful completion of a necessary task', and then the next sentence 'suggests' that where 'co-operation (*in the form of obedience*)' [no 'purely penal law' here!] 'is *not required*' then 'the exercise of the heavy hand of coercive authority would not be legitimate' (emphases added).

But the important thing to establish is not whether Sartorius is wholly

[71]   For an account of these theories, and of the reason for the label 'purely penal law', see Finnis, *Natural Law and Natural Rights*, 325–7, 346–7.

consistent, but how he can suppose (as he seems to) that *what is being claimed* by those who claim a moral right to rule is that the imposition of coercive measures (by those with that right) is morally justified even though those on whom the morally justified penalty/punishment is imposed had no moral obligation to abstain from the conduct for which they are being penalized/punished (and [?] have no moral obligation to submit to, that is, not obstruct the imposition of, that penalty/punishment). In the hazy area of 'regulation', where language, institutional practice, and common attitudes neglect or smudge the distinction between tax and fine, and where 'penalty' does not necessarily connote punishable desert or culpability, there is both logical space for and some arguable moral/political ground for this supposition. But as a general analysis of authority to impose the *serious* penalties/punishments involved in any serious exercise of governmental authority in the modern state, it has, I think, no claim to represent common opinion, and no intrinsic moral plausibility.

Now for my second doubt about Sartorius's procedures in part II. A theme of part II is that, to justify a claim that S has a moral obligation to obey A, one must supply more than a 'mere analysis of the notion of [A's] moral right to rule'. I quite agree; it is fundamental to clear thinking that the mere analysis of *what a [moral] claim comes to* can never suffice to establish that the claim *is* morally justified, whether generically or in a particular case. What is so surprising is that Sartorius seems to think, at least some of the time, that the need for a *moral argument* (to show that S has a moral obligation to obey), an argument supplementing the analysis of the moral claim, arises only because the *claim* in question does not, on analysis, *include* or *[analytically] entail* the claim that S has such an obligation. The truth, I suggest, is that even if the analysis of the claim to a moral right to rule did disclose or include or entail a claim that S has a correlative duty to obey, *nothing would follow, morally*, about whether anyone really has a moral right to rule or a moral duty to obey.

What is the function of an analysis of the sort supplied by Sartorius? Perhaps it is intended to be an exploration of the meaning (or one meaning) of the term 'authority'. But it is also called an 'analysis of the nature of authority', and Sartorius declares himself more or less indifferent to the question of whether his use of the term (and presumably also of correlative phrases such as 'right to rule') amounts to stipulating for it a new sense which it does not ordinarily possess. Then he says that his analysis 'isolated an important legal-moral-political phenomenon of considerable interest'. But what is the 'phenomenon'? If

Sartorius is not here making an assertion about common speech, is he asserting that, in some actual communities known to us, people (A) *are considered* to have a moral right to rule coercively while their subjects (S) are considered not to have a moral duty to obey but only a moral duty not to usurp? No reason is given for supposing that this assertion is true. And even if it were true, Sartorius would still have to show why that sort of social order is 'important' and 'interesting' and more worthy of our attention than the alternative social order envisaged by Anscombe (and, I venture to think, much more familiar in thought and in social life to all of us), in which the needs and facts which are considered to form a basis for a moral right to rule are equally considered to be the basis for a moral duty/obligation to comply with the rules of the rulers.

The one thing certain is that no moral argumentation was supplied as the analysis unfolded. And there was no argumentation there, to show the importance and interest of the perhaps rather novel conjunction: moral-right-to-rule-with-no-duty-to-obey-but-duty-not-to-usurp.

But is some moral argumentation supplied by Sartorius later, to justify his claim that it is important to acknowledge that this strange (to me) conjunction has some kind of priority in a discussion of the moral relationship between A and S? There is only the passage which dismisses as 'too quick' Anscombe's premiss that authorities have a right to what is necessary for the successful performance of their tasks; 'too quick', he says, because 'independent argument is required to establish a moral obligation to obey the law'. But 'independent' of what? Certainly, any conclusion like Anscombe's needs argument which is 'independent' of the fact that A has *legal* authority; that such independent argument is needed is a central claim of the whole natural law tradition, at least. But Sartorius is asserting that 'independent' argument is required over and above (*a*) the *fact* (Anscombe's unchallenged second premiss) that authority's tasks cannot be successfully performed without obedience, and (*b*) the *evaluative [moral] assessment* that authority's tasks are simply 'required' that is, necessary for the necessary end(s) of protecting moral rights and conferring fundamental benefits. He does not even hint what such an independent argument might be.

For my part, I do not see how any argument that is independent in this last sense is either possible or needed. Nor do I see that Anscombe's argument for a moral obligation to obey is any 'quicker' than Sartorius's own argument for a moral right to rule and impose coercion and resist and punish usurpation.

Is it not the case, *pace* Sartorius, that the human needs to which he refers bring in the whole set of rights and obligations, or bring in none of them? If they bring in the fearsome right to rule coercively, they bring in, equally, the obligation to obey.

This assertion of mine does not rely on any 'analysis' of authority, nor on any 'logical' inference about the 'correlatives' or 'entailments' of a right to rule. It relies (like Anscombe's) on a moral assessment of what is humanly appropriate in face of the needs for co-operation in its many forms. *After* one has made that moral assessment, and has drawn the moral conclusion in the way I have just (very summarily) drawn it, one is equipped with a (morally justified) concept of authority, and within the conceptual framework thereby established it will be possible to say that right to rule entails obligation to obey. If, as I believe is the case, this morally justified concept coheres quite nicely with standard English usage and common political thought, that is a bonus. But all the work for the moral conclusion must be done by one's assessment of human good and what, in the human situation, is needed to attain it.

I have just said that in the morally justified, political-philosophical concept of authority, right to rule entails obligation to obey. But this must not be misunderstood as the relationship of claim-right to duty, in which S's duty would be an obligation owed *to* A, the holder of the claim-right. On the contrary, I think that in *that* (quasi-Hohfeldian) sense of 'right', rulers have no right to be obeyed.[72] Rather, rulers have the right (Hohfeldian power-right) to make laws which, once made, impose on their subjects an obligation (presumptively or defeasibly a moral as well as a legal obligation) to do or abstain from certain acts. If one had to locate a party to whom the obligation is owed, would it not be one's fellow-subjects, particularly the law-abiding, rather than the rulers (legislators, judges, administrators, police)?[73] Some of the recent crop of arguments against the existence of a generic prima-facie moral obligation to obey the law are shipwrecked because their authors suppose that such an obligation would have to be (and/or is commonly supposed to be) *to officials*.[74] This supposition, I suggest, falsifies both common opinion and critical moral plausibility.

[72] Finnis, *Natural Law and Natural Rights*, 359; see also 332–7. See also Max Weber, *Economy and Society* (ed. Roth and Wittich,) Berkeley (1968), 218.

[73] See Hart, 'Are there any Natural Rights?' *Philosophical Review*, vol. 64 no. 175 (1955) at 185, quoted by Sartorius, 'Political Authority and Political Obligation', *Virginia Law Review*, vol. 67 (1981), 3 at 14.

[74] See, e.g., Gerald Postema, 'Coordination and Convention at the Foundations of Law', *Journal of Legal Studies*, vol. 11, no. 1 (Jan. 1982), 165 at 196.

2.3 Comment

HANINA BEN-MENACHEM*

In the first part of his paper Sartorius provides us with an elaborate analysis of the concept of a social rule. His main question is 'just what is being claimed when it is said that a particular social norm exists in a community?' In answering this question Sartorius lists no less than 153 conditions which 'are satisfied in the normal standard paradigm, completely unproblematic case'. It is a major thesis of the paper that, similar to many other legal concepts, the concept of an accepted social norm is a cluster concept, meaning that few of the 153 conditions which exist in the normal case, are necessary. Sartorius illustrates the clustered nature of the concept of a social rule by the conformance condition. We are told that it makes perfect sense to speak of a social rule as existing even though the external aspect—condition 1—is absent. As a case in point Sartorius cites the example of American sexual morality which contains a prohibition on adultery even though the majority of married individuals commit adultery at least once in their lifetimes.

Let me first observe that the notion of a cluster concept as presented in Sartorius's paper, and in greater detail in his book, *Individual Conduct and Social Norms*,[75] does not demand that all components of the concept are dispensable. Rather, it means that not all are necessary. So Sartorius could hold his notion of a cluster concept and maintain at the same time that condition 1 is necessary. His assertion that condition 1 is not necessary is therefore not logically derived from his conception of a cluster concept. So he must have another motivation for that assertion which calls for justification, or at least for clarification. For as we shall see this position has methodological shortcomings; furthermore, Sartorius himself does not remain faithful to his position throughout.

Sartorius's example of American sexual morality is, contrary to what we are told, in full accord with condition 1. Let me remind you what condition 1 is: 'Most members of C conform to N on most occasions when N applies to them'. In order to show that condition 1 is not satisfied, it must be the case that most married individuals commit

---

* © Hanina Ben-Menachem 1987.
[75] Eacino, California, 1975.

adultery on most occasions. Now, I do not think Sartorius wants to make this claim. Nor should we regard Sartorius's illustration merely as a poor example. This flaw is instructive. It originates, it seems to me, from the realization that it is indeed very difficult to assume that we can omit condition 1 and keep all the other 152 conditions intact. If indeed condition 1 is absent and the majority of married individuals commit adultery on most occasions, then it is hard for me, and perhaps for Sartorius too, to see how they would still sincerely hold this sophisticated web of beliefs and preferences concerning the prohibition on adultery.

I would even go a step further and argue that on Sartorius's own terms it is at least conceptually problematic to maintain that condition 1 is absent yet the remaining 152 conditions exist. Let us look at condition 1 itself. Either conformance is a cluster concept or it is a concept which we can define precisely. Since Sartorius holds that 'the key concepts of social union and the rule of law are cluster concepts', I too shall begin by assuming that it is. Indeed, would Sartorius not say that conformance to a norm is too complex an affair to permit any determination of precise and necessary conditions that must obtain? If so, we can apply Sartorius's own analysis. Let us ask as before, 'Just what is being claimed when it is said that most members of C conform to N?' In other words, when will an external observer conclude, on the basis of visual and auditory impressions, that most members of C conform to N? Consider the following partial list of conditions

1 Most members of C act upon N.
2 Most members of C display critical behaviour towards most actual deviations from N.
3 Most members of C, on appropriate occasions, make internal statements which represent applications of N.
4 Most members of C say that they prefer that they themselves act upon N.
5 Most members of C say that they prefer that others act upon N.
6 Most members of C say that they feel bound to follow N.

(In conditions 4 to 6 I have added the requirement that most members say that '.....' so that what they say can be picked up by an external observer. I have added this only for the sake of clarity, and it does not add anything substantial to the original conditions 4 to 6: the fact that members say it is implied in conditions 4 to 6 (otherwise, how would we know?))

It is obvious that an external observer could conclude that most members of C conform to N without conditions 2 to 6 being satisfied. But can he conclude that there is no conformance if only some of the conditions are satisfied? I think that, on Sartorius's analysis, for condition 1 to be absent, it must be the case that most of conditions 1 to 6 do not hold; which in turn means that the parallel conditions on Sartorius's list do not hold either. The omission of condition 1 entails the omission of further conditions and I wonder whether, this being the case, Sartorius would still be willing to talk about the existence of a social rule.

Reformulating condition 1 so that it has 'most members act or do' will not be of great help, since acting, doing, or whatever, when applied to a complex social situation, should be viewed, on Sartorius's account, as cluster concepts. The only ways out, as far as I can see, are either to argue that conformance is not a cluster concept or, that it is but that condition 1 is necessary. But then some justification is required for treating the concept of conformance differently from the concept of a social rule.

In order to evaluate Sartorius's claim that condition 1 is not necessary let us assume that it is possible to conceive of a community which does not conform to a certain norm yet holds the relevant set of beliefs and preferences concerning the behaviour prescribed by the norm. Let me first say what I take this claim to be: If the 152 conditions exist, the question whether condition 1 exists as well is immaterial for the assertion that a rule exists. In other words, condition 1 will not change the fact of the matter concerning the existence of a social rule. Consider two communities A and B in which the same social rules exist, the only difference being that in community A, with respect to one social rule, condition 1 is not satisfied. How would we express the difference between these two communities in terms of their social rules? Could we say, for example, that in community A there is a social rule that is not practised? Though Sartorius speaks about 'accepted social rule' as if one could speak about 'unaccepted social rule', I think this would undermine the Hartian notion of a social rule as a social fact. Or should we, perhaps, say that in both communities there is one and the same rule? This would be very misleading. Suppose I want to join one of the two communities and my choice is to be made on the basis of their respective social rules. Suppose I feel very strongly about not being able to practise the behaviour in question. In this context I believe it would be a distortion to say that both communities are identical and it does not matter which one I join. It is one thing not to be able, socially speaking, to act in a certain way. It is quite another to share a critical attitude to a commonly practised behaviour, that is to be a hypocrite.

If the formulation of social rules that exist in a given community is meant, among other things, to help us make practical decisions, Sartorius's analysis seems to fail on this score. But the formulation of social rules is also meant to help us form an evaluative assessment of a given community and here again the analysis does not provide us with the necessary tools. Here it might be useful to ask why condition 1 is absent. At least two answers seem possible: firstly, condition 1 is not satisfied because most members of C cannot resist the temptation to violate the norm. Secondly, condition 1 is not satisfied because there is an objective obstacle; for example, there is a social rule that people ought to bring an offering on certain occasions but the site to which the offering is to be brought is in ruins. (I am ignoring here a third possibility, namely, that condition 1 is not satisfied because the occasion for acting does not occur, because this is ruled out by Sartorius.) A crucial difference between these two cases relates to the possibility of ascribing to the community the relevant set of attitudes and preferences concerning the behaviour that is not practised.

Consider the first possibility. What we have here is a Victorian community, one in which there is hypocrisy concerning say, sexual morality. In this case there is a gap between what is said and what is done. Compare it with a pious, honest, one-standard society. One of the adequacy requirements on an analysis of the type here considered, is that differences which we can intuitively grasp and describe in ordinary discourse should find their expression in the analytic discourse. If Sartorius's analysis lacks the means to distinguish between the two communities, it fails to comply with this adequacy requirement. If, however, one were to argue that two different social rules exist in the two communities, it would mean that, contrary to Sartorius's claim, actual conformance does make a difference. The same would apply to the second possibility. The analytic discourse should allow for a distinction between aspirations on the one hand and norms that govern daily life on the other.

I said earlier that Sartorius does not remain faithful to his own assertion that condition 1 is not necessary. Having argued that condition 1 is not necessary, Sartorius qualifies what he has just concluded: 'Constitutional rules are importantly different on this score. They are juristic constructs, the correct description of which must fit the facts with respect to the relevant behaviour of officials and norm subjects. Hart's rule of recognition must be constructed so that its efficacy is assured.' What disturbs me most here is not the tension *per se* that exists between his assertion that condition 1 is not necessary and his claim that it is different in the case of constitutional rules, but rather his account of constitutional rules themselves. How does Sartorius analyse the concept of constitutional rules? Hart's analysis of social rules is primarily intended, as Sartorius himself observes, to accommodate the rule of recognition in the broader social context. The importance of the theory of social rules and its being the key for the concept of law lies precisely in that it enables us to view the rule of recognition as a social rule, without assuming any special and distinctive features of the rule of recognition.

Hart's methodology would suggest, it seems to me, either that we abandon the idea that condition 1 is not necessary and instead consider it an indispensable element of the cluster concept of a social rule, constitutional rules included; or extend the assertion that condition 1 is dispensable to constitutional rules as well. This latter possibility would, admittedly, widen the scope of the phenomena discussed and described by the science of law.

Let me add one final remark that might explain what you might call my obsessive treatment of condition 1. It is precisely here, if we entertain the idea of applying Sartorius's claim to constitutional rules, that his analysis, in spite of its shortcomings, appears attractive to me. As a student of Jewish law I have long been puzzled by the question of how one can approach the phenomenon called Jewish law in Hartian terms. I do not mean that Jewish law presents difficulties to the legal historian. It is rather a jurisprudential account of Jewish law at present that seems problematic. When it is said in ordinary discourse that Jewish law is a legal system that is no longer practised, what is meant is that its constitutional rules, viewed from the perspective of social rules, do not satisfy condition 1. However, there is an identifiable community which displays the relevant attitudes and preferences concerning these constitutional rules. In that sense Jewish law, unlike other ancient legal systems such as Roman law, is an existing social phenomenon.

If an indispensable condition for the existence of constitutional rules and thus for the existence of a legal system is that they be founded on existing practice, a Jewish legal system cannot be said to exist. This conclusion, however, is counter-intuitive, at least from the point of view of members of the community who share and display these attitudes and preferences. A modified version of Sartorius's analysis might thus suggest a way to approach this phenomenon in Hartian terms. Here, however, much is yet to be done.

3.1 The Normativity of Law*

GERALD J. POSTEMA

A central task of philosophical jurisprudence is to explain and reconcile two (sometimes apparently conflicting) sets of widely shared beliefs about our legal practices. On the one hand, we recognize that the notion of law is essentially practical. 'Law' lives in the familiar environment of 'rights', 'obligations', 'reasonableness', and their cognates, all of which derive their distinctive character from the roles they play in the practical deliberation and guidance of rational agents. We acknowledge that the concept is appropriately used for purposes of social description, explanation, and prediction, but its suitability for such purposes is determined and limited by the shape imposed on it by this primary practical environment.

On the other hand, we believe that law is essentially a social phenomenon—a complex of social institutions which can be studied by external observers and participants viewing their practices as external observers. We know that different societies and cultures can have strikingly different legal practices; that, although the law makes claims upon our allegiance, its claims nevertheless can be extravagant and unwarranted; and that we have no guarantee that the law automatically satisfies standards of justice.

The problem of accounting for the normativity of law is the task of explaining, illuminating, and where necessary reconciling these beliefs. Over the years Hart has done much to clarify this problem for us, and to define the terminology needed to address it profitably. He has taken us a long way towards its solution. His classic discussion of the problem in *The Concept of Law*[1] has been refined and extended in his recent *Essays on Bentham*[2] and I shall take the latter for my text and primary focus.

I OBSERVERS, PARTICIPANTS, AND DETACHED JUDGEMENTS

Hart's formulation of the problem is shaped by his critical appreciation

---

* © Gerald J. Postema 1987.
[1] H. L. A. Hart, *The Concept of Law*, Oxford (1961) hereafter *Concept*.
[2] H. L. A. Hart, *Essays on Bentham*, Oxford (1982), hereafter *Bentham*. See especially Introduction, and Chaps. VI, X.

of the classical positivist tradition. The 'permanently valuable feature' of Bentham's jurisprudence, he says, lies in its insistence on the *conceptual separation* of law and morality.³ Especially valuable was Bentham's attempt to define a concept of law and legal obligation in descriptive and morally neutral terms and so make it clear that, although laws require certain behaviour of a subject, nothing follows about the moral reasons the subject has for obeying the laws. Following Bentham's lead, Hart seeks a general theory of law which simultaneously 'reproduces the way in which law in modern societies appears to many of its subjects' *and* 'is applicable to legal systems whatever their moral quality'.⁴ In particular, Hart wishes to preserve the positivist idea that the expression 'Jones has an obligation to A' has a quite different meaning depending on whether it is used in a legal or moral context.⁵

Bentham's theory failed not in the conception, but in the execution of this noble project, Hart argues, because it tried to reduce all apparently normative legal statements—statements of the law or the legal position of persons under the law—to ordinary historical and empirical statements *about* the law, or about the actions of officials or subjects of the legal system. Thus, it failed to capture the normativity of such statements.⁶ For legal statements are characteristically used to assess behaviour or to guide it;⁷ they set out what is required, prohibited, permissible, or normatively possible according to the law. In fact, Hart insists, the 'standard normal form of descriptions of the content of law' is that of statements in the normative vocabulary of 'obligation', 'rights', 'powers', and the like. The problem of explaining the normativity of law, he suggests, is (at least in part) that of explaining the possibility of this characteristic use of normative language, while remaining faithful to the separation thesis.⁸

The Concept of Law sought the solution in the fact that in any legal system in force in a community most law-applying officials and many law-subjects take an 'internal attitude' towards the law. They characteristically use normative language to express their acceptance of the law (or its fundamental constitutional rules) and use the rules as guides for their own actions and standards for the evaluation of the actions of

---

³ Hart, *Bentham*, 19.
⁴ Ibid.
⁵ Hart, *Bentham*, 147.
⁶ Hart, ibid., 144–5.
⁷ Hart, ibid., 144.
⁸ Hart, ibid., 144–7.

others. Furthermore, Hart insisted that it is a necessary condition of the existence of a legal system that at least law-applying officials take such an internal attitude. Thus, Hart distinguished between 'internal' (or 'committed') normative statements which express a participant's acceptance of the rules, and 'moderate external' statements which report *the fact that* participants take this attitude.

But this proposal is not entirely satisfactory, for it restricts the use of straightforwardly normative language to those who are actually committed to the validity of the law whose content their legal statements describe. Following Joseph Raz (and Hans Kelsen),[9] Hart now acknowledges a third category of legal statements distinct from both 'committed' statements and 'reports'. These 'detached' judgements are statements of law or legal obligation *from the point of view* of one who accepts or regards as valid the laws in question, but without committing the speaker to that point of view. Detached obligation statements, like reports, imply no commitment on the part of the speaker to the truth or validity of the claims made by committed speakers. They differ from reports, however, in that they are not *about* the beliefs or attitudes of committed participants, but rather (in Hart's view) genuinely assess actions, albeit from the point of view of one who is committed to the validity of the normative standards in question.

Details of Hart's definition of the category of detached judgements aside, it is clear that it picks up a familiar feature of our ordinary practical landscape.[10] However, the addition of this category of judgements to our theoretical repertory cannot take us very far towards a solution of the problem of normativity of law.

It is true that the distinction can be used to block the inference from, for example,

(*a*) 'Jones has a legal obligation to A' to (*b*) 'Jones morally ought to A' or even to (*c*) 'Jones has reason to A'. For, if (*a*) expresses a detached judgement, then nothing follows about the (non-relativized) reasons Jones has to A, let alone his moral reasons to do so. But that,

---

[9] J. Raz, *The Authority of Law*, Oxford (1979), Chaps. 7, 8.

[10] 'You must follow suit', could well be said, with full intelligibility, by one who believed that bridge is a frivolous activity not worthy of a serious person's time. In fact, detached legal judgements are a species of a genus of implicitly relativized rationality or ought judgements, i.e., of judgements of what a person ought to do or what is rational to do *relative to* certain norms or desires or other assumptions, on the validity or rationality of which norms or desires the speaker takes no position. See generally, S. Darwall, *Impartial Reason*, Ithaca (1983), 14–16, 44–50. Aquinas seems to make a similar point about judgements of 'good'; see *Summa Theologiae*, I–II, question 92 art. 1.

of course, is merely to say that detached judgements do not logically entail committed judgements. Nothing follows from this about the inference from 'Jones has a legal obligation to A' to judgements about Jones's moral (or non-moral) reasons *holding the perspectives of the judgements constant*.

More specifically, this distinction does not support the idea (which Hart thinks is important) that the notion of obligation has a *different meaning* in legal and moral contexts. For we can also block the inference from 'Jones has a *moral* obligation to A' to judgements about what Jones *morally* ought to do or has reason to do in the same way we blocked the inference to them from the judgement of *legal* obligation. But it would be a mistake, surely, to say that this shows that there are different notions of *moral* obligation. Moreover, we can distinguish legal from moral obligation on the basis of this distinction between kinds of normative judgements only if we could reasonably say that 'legal obligation' could only be used in *detached* judgements. But that would deprive committed participants of the terminology they need to express their committed judgements, and at the same time empty the detached judgements of any content. (Since detached judgements are simply judgements made from the point of view of one who makes committed judgements.) Clearly, if Hart is to insist that 'legal obligation' and 'moral obligation' have different meanings, he needs more than this distinction.

It might be thought, however, that this distinction between kinds of normative judgements is useful in another way. For it seems to suggest a way of resolving the long-standing dispute between positivist and naturalist theories of law. Observe that the distinction marks a difference between perspectives from which the law of a given community may be viewed. *Self-identified participants*, we might say, tend to make committed judgements, whereas *observers* make reports or detached judgements. As participants, we may be concerned with how we ought to behave, what our rights and duties are, when we may fall back on the framework of law to defend our rights or justify our actions, or the extent to which the law legitimately claims our allegiance. As observers, we might be concerned with the relationship between legal practices and other central social institutions, or with the history of the legal system of a society, or even with the problem of arranging our activities to avoid obstacles the law puts in our way (the aim of the 'bad man').

We might, further, distinguish jurisprudential *theories* in terms of whether they attempt to give systematic accounts of participant judgements or of observer judgements. An *observer theory* would, *inter alia*, attempt to set out the truth conditions of detached judgements or the conditions that must be met if a legal system is to be in force in a community. A *participant theory* would attempt to set out in a systematic way the truth conditions of committed legal judgements. We might even say that the aim of observer theory is to define and defend an observer conception of law, and the aim of participant theory to do the same for a participant conception of law.

Now it is tempting to try to settle the differences between naturalism and positivism by assigning them exclusively to one or the other of these types of theory of law.[11] But this, I think, is a mistake, because it ignores the resources within each of these traditions for addressing issues arising in observer theory and issues of participant theory (although we may be forced to recast the disputes between the naturalist and positivist in light of the distinction). For example, Hobbes's theory of law, and I believe Bentham's as well, offers powerful arguments *from substantive political theory* for a conception of law which permits identification and application of law and legal obligation entirely apart from questions of their moral merits. Ronald Dworkin appears at certain points in his writing to offer important morally substantive arguments against this positivist participant theory of law. By the same token, the naturalist offers an account of the general features of the point of view of a self-identified participant in a legal practice which makes an important contribution to the debate within observer theory. And Hart puts forward a positivist account of the normativity of law in his *Essays on Bentham* which takes as its main rival this (observer) version of naturalism. I shall not at present discuss further the naturalist–positivist dispute within participant theory. Rather I will devote the rest of this essay to a discussion of the dispute within *observer theory*.[12] In this context Hart makes some of his most intriguing and provocative claims.

[11] See, for example, J. Finnis, *Natural Law and Natural Rights*, Oxford (1980), 21.
[12] It is not clear to me at this point whether the distinction between observer and participant theories, and the perspectives they seek to express, can be made with the sharpness and clarity I would like. The issues raised by this distinction, I now see, are very complex, and the distinction may even collapse in some very important cases. But I cannot explore these issues or defend this distinction further in this essay. I shall rely on the distinction in the remainder of this essay despite some worries because I believe the distinction, or something very like it, is implicit throughout Hart's writings on the question of the normativity of law.

II NORMATIVITY IN *THE ESSAYS ON BENTHAM*

In his recent *Essays on Bentham*, Hart replaces the troublesome notion of rules, which was at the centre of his theory in *The Concept of Law*, with the technical notion of an 'authoritative legal reason', which both is more abstract and admits of more precise analysis. The key to explaining the distinctive normativity of law, while preserving the conceptual separation of law and morality, Hart now insists, lies in recognizing a special kind of normative attitude characteristic of self-identified participants in legal practices, namely, the standing recognition of, or willingness to regard, certain events or states of affairs as constituting 'peremptory' and 'content-independent' reasons for action.[13] Where such an attitude is widely adopted, the occurrence of the events will have not only natural, but also *normative* consequences—certain actions will be made right or obligatory, others wrong or offences, by those events.[14]

'Authoritative legal reasons' are a sub-class of such reasons. They are *content independent* in the sense that neither the nature nor the strength of the reasons is influenced by the character of the actions for which they are reasons.[15] Thus, the recognition of such reasons in no way depends on an assessment of the desirability or moral merits of the actions in question. The reasons are *peremptory* in the sense that they are both (*a*) positive reasons for action, and (*b*) reasons against acting on the agent's own deliberation or assessment of the merits of the actions.[16]

The notion of authoritative legal reasons is arrived at by placing the above notion in the distinctive institutional context of law. The account here is familiar and I can be brief. Legal systems are distinguished from other normative systems by the fact that the validity of legal norms is determined by recognition of the norms by certain primary institutions charged with interpretation and application of the norms of the system (namely, the courts). Validity is a function of a rule's being properly related to some already recognized *source* of such rules (for example, legislative enactment, administrative promulgation, custom, precedent). For every legal system there is an ultimate source, a rule of recognition which is the basis of all legal norms either directly or indirectly. The rule of recognition defines the ultimate criteria of validity for laws of the system and thereby isolates from the universe of practical considerations

[13] Hart, *Bentham*, 256, 18.
[14] Hart, *Bentham*, 259.
[15] Hart, *Bentham*, 254.
[16] Hart, *Bentham*, 253.

the range of relevant and legally binding grounds for judicial decision within that system. The rule of recognition, being ultimate, rests not on some further standard of validity, but simply on the social facts of the court's practice of identifying the norms of the system. But these are social facts with a normative dimension, for self-identified participants in the practice adopt a distinctive normative attitude: the standing willingness to regard the fact that a norm satisfies the criteria of the rule of recognition as a peremptory and content independent reason for identifying, applying, or in other appropriate ways following the norm.

Against this background we can summarize Hart's preferred account of the normativity of law in four propositions.

A.   Detached statements of law are possible because it is a necessary condition of a legal system's being in force in a community that court officials make committed statements of law; detached statements are made from the point of view of those who make committed legal statements.

B.   Justice Smith, uttering 'Jones has a legal obligation to A', expresses a committed legal judgement if and only if (1) Smith accepts in common with other judges of the legal system the rule of recognition, R, which defines criteria for identifying norms of the system which they as judges have a duty to apply and enforce; (2) there is a rule, L^*, identified by R; and (3) L^* warrants the conclusion 'Jones has a legal obligation to A'.

C.   If conditions B1–3 are met, then the fact that L^* satisfies the criteria of validity of the system constitutes *for Smith*, an authoritative legal reason for his complying with L^*—that is, a reason for treating L^* as a standard for evaluation of the conduct of all agents falling within its scope and determining what demands may properly be made upon those agents.

D.   Thus, 'Jones has a legal obligation to A'—when it expresses a committed judgement—means that A may properly be demanded of, or if necessary extracted from, Jones according to the rules regulating such demands.[17]

This account of the normativity of law severs the alleged connection between law and morality with three *separate* blows. First, on this view, committed judgements of legal obligation do not entail corresponding committed moral judgements. Indeed, from Justice Smith's utterance of

---

[17] Hart, *Bentham*, 160.

the committed judgement 'Jones has a legal obligation to A', *nothing* follows regarding Smith's view of the reasons Jones has to A. All that follows is that Smith regards *himself* as having reason to hold Jones to the standard and to evaluate and even punish Jones's behaviour by appeal to this standard. (Smith may also believe Jones to be morally bound to A, or to have moral reason to A, but this is not entailed by the legal judgement Smith makes.)

Second, Justice Smith's reason for following the law is, on Hart's view, peremptory and content independent. It is constituted solely by the fact that L^* meets the criteria defined by the rule of recognition and depends in no way on the moral (or other) merits of the action required, or of the rule itself.

Third, the fact that L^* satisfies the rule of recognition provides Justice Smith with a reason to follow L^* *simply because* Smith, in common with other judges in the legal system, has a standing disposition to regard rules which satisfy the rule of recognition as authoritative legal reasons. According to Hart, it is entirely irrelevant what reasons moved Smith (or reasons Smith had) to adopt this attitude. In particular, Hart denies that self-identified participants in the legal practice (must) adopt the criteria in the belief that they are (or compliance with them is) morally legitimate.

Now this account of normativity of law is, in my opinion, open to challenge at each of the three points just mentioned, but in what follows I will ignore the second and concentrate only on the first and third of Hart's devices.

III REASONS AND OBLIGATIONS

Let us begin with the first of Hart's devices for severing law from morality. We can agree that there is no contradiction or paradox in a judge's making a committed statement of legal obligation while recognizing that the subject of the obligation, or even the judge himself, could utter the corresponding *detached* legal judgement (and that from the latter judgement nothing would follow regarding the subject's reasons to obey). But Hart's claim is different and stronger. As I understand him, Hart maintains that officials, in uttering committed legal judgements, are committed (*a*) to the view that *because* the law meets accepted criteria of validity *they* have reason to follow it, and (*b*) to the view that nothing follows from this about the reasons persons who are subject to the law have to comply with it.[18] But this is counter-intuitive. What inclines Hart to this view?

Two different sources of this doctrine are evident in Hart's *Essays on Bentham*. The first is his assumption of a rather strong internalist thesis about the nature of reasons.[19] On this view, R is a reason for J to A if and only if R is capable of motivating J to A, and that is so, on this view, if and only if R is (or, perhaps, upon reflection would be) an object of J's desire, aims, purposes, or commitments.[20] Thus, from Justice Smith's saying 'Jones has a legal obligation to A' it follows that Smith has reason to obey the rule because it expresses *Smith's acceptance* of the criteria of validity. But nothing follows about Jones's acceptance, and so Smith must admit that nothing can be inferred about Jones's reasons for action. We might say that, on this view, law, whatever its pretensions to the contrary, is simply a system of hypothetical imperatives.

This version of internalism is, of course, controversial, but we need not address the question of its adequacy to realize that it cannot support Hart's analysis of legal obligation. The problem is that the internalist thesis is a *general* claim about reasons; it is not restricted to reasons arising from law. It may force us to regard *both* law and morality as categorical only in their surface logic, but this provides no basis for blocking the inference from legal to moral obligation. Smith may be barred from inferring from the committed judgement 'Jones has a legal obligation to A' that Jones has any (non-relative) reasons to A, but it alone does not bar the inference to 'Jones morally ought to A'.

A second possible source of Hart's analysis of legal obligation lies in more directly jurisprudential concerns. Hart wants to allow for the possibility of judges coming to realize that the legal system in which they work is so bad (at least as it affects certain portions of the society) that some of its subjects simply have no reason whatsoever to comply

---

[18] In *Bentham*, 266, Hart says that when judges make such legal judgements they 'speak in a technically confined way. They speak as judges, from within a legal institution which they are committed as judges to maintain, in order to draw attention to what by the way of action is "owed" by the subject, that is, may legally be demanded or exacted from him.' Either this is equivalent to what I have said in the text, or Hart is saying that these judgements must be regarded as detached obligation judgements. But the latter is a mistake, for detached judgements are possible only if there is a point of view from which the committed judgements are made. The theoretical issue focuses on what exactly is expressed, or entailed, by these committed judgements. The fact that detached judgements can also be made is not relevant at this point.

[19] Hart, *Bentham*, 151–60, 266–7.

[20] For an extended discussion of this form of internalism see Darwall, *Impartial Reason*, especially Chaps. 1–7.

voluntarily with its demands,[21] but also that they, nevertheless, are bound to apply and enforce those rules. Hart's analysis of committed legal obligation statements allows for this possibility, for such judgements simply set out what the law demands, with the implication that the judge has reason to apply it, but imply nothing about the reasons the subjects may have to obey.

However, several questions arise about this approach to the problem of 'the wicked legal system'. First, this is a more puzzling conundrum than is often realized. It is not at all obvious, as many have supposed, that we naturally say of victims of politically organized and firmly institutionalized repression and violence that they have legal obligations but no moral obligations to comply with the law (unless, by 'legal obligation' we mean nothing more than the minimal claim that subjects are liable to suffer for non-compliance). The linguistic evidence here is conflicting and entirely inconclusive, and this suggests that, as a matter of substantive belief, we can be genuinely ambivalent about specific cases.

There are good reasons for this ambivalence, for our usually univocal common sense observations pull, in these cases, in quite different directions. Normally, the views of officials and ordinary citizen-participants in the legal system largely coincide. But the case of the wicked legal system drives them apart. Hart assumes that observer theory must take up the point of view of the official and law elite (and perhaps, the beneficiaries) and leave the victims to make only detached judgements.[22] But why must we do that? The victim has an intelligible *participant* view of the situation as well. The committed judgement, that demands imposed on victims by the organized powers in a territory generate no obligations whatsoever and therefore cannot be regarded as valid or binding, is a perfectly legitimate, intelligible judgement. If there cannot be found even minimally persuasive reasons for victims voluntarily to comply with the dictates of those in power, then those dictates cannot be regarded as binding. The judgement expressed in the previous sentence is a committed, participant judgement, not a detached one. But Hart's approach does not permit us to express this committed judgement, and thus ignores an important part of participant views of existing legal practices. In fact, Hart's observer theory seems to pre-judge a question which is clearly a participant question: whether or not the judge *must* indeed follow the law and hold the victim-subject to it even when the latter has no reason voluntarily to comply with it.

---

[21] Hart, *Concept,* 195–8; *Bentham,* 150–1.
[22] Hart, *Bentham,* 257.

Moreover, I am not convinced that the most natural, and least misleading, way to express the view of sensitive officials who are aware of both the position of the victims and their own position, is to say that the victim has a legal obligation but nevertheless no reason to comply. It seems more natural, and less obscure, for the judges to say that they regard themselves bound to apply the formally validated law to the victim, but that the victim has *no obligation* (legal or moral) to comply with them.[23] Of course, the pragmatic circumstances of their public position may bar judges from saying this. But those same pragmatic circumstances, it would seem, would probably bar their admission that the victim has no reason (save the prudential one of avoiding punishment) to comply with the law.

Secondly, Hart accounts for the sensitive official's view of such cases by insisting that one can *never* legitimately infer that a person subject to a valid law has any moral obligation or reason to comply. But this is not the only way to explain the case. For it is plausible to say that, under normal circumstances, such an inference is legitimate, but that the reasons generated by the fact that one is subject to a formally valid rule of law are *simply extinguished* (the obligations normally generated are void *ab initio*) under certain specified circumstances. Of course, an argument would have to be marshalled to support the claim that formally valid laws, in virtue of their existence alone and not in virtue of their content, generate such presumptive reasons. But the possibility of a case in which victims have no reason (even prima-facie reason) to comply does not show that no such argument is possible. Formally valid laws which, however, fail to meet certain conditions of justice, can be regarded as void *ab initio*, just as immoral promises are.

Thirdly, situations may arise in which officials correctly regard themselves as bound to follow rules which, they must admit, make no rational claim upon their subjects. But, I shall now argue, this cannot be a permanent or pervasive feature of a legal system.[24] The argument for this claim rests on three important premises. (1) Law is a distinctive way of directing human social behaviour. It seeks to guide the behaviour

---

[23] The phenomenon of the wicked legal system forces us to break the links between a) the existence of a formally validated rule of law, b) the existence of an obligation to comply with it, and c) the existence of reasons to do so. Hart's account makes the break between the existence of the obligation and the existence of reasons. This seems counter-intuitive. The more natural place to introduce the break is between the existence of the formally valid rule of law and the existence of an obligation to comply.

[24] This is not, I think, a moral or empirical claim, but rather a conceptual truth, or as close to a conceptual truth as it is possible to get in jurisprudential theory.

of rational beings through rational means, that is, through addressing to them public general rules to which they are expected to conform in their behaviour. (2) If law is to succeed even minimally in this distinctive task there must be a shared context of interpretation of the rules in which law-makers, law-appliers, *and* law-followers participate. That is, rational direction of action through public rules requires communication, and communication entails interdependence among law-makers, law-appliers, and law-subjects.[25] The interpretation which law-subjects put on public rules depends on their expectations of how officials will understand and apply them; but likewise, officials will interpret them on the basis of their expectations of the understanding given them by law-subjects. The shape the laws must take depends importantly on how they will be understood and applied by those subjects to them. Thus, for law-making and law-applying officials to achieve whatever substantive purposes they have through the distinctive mechanism of law, it is necessary for them to look at the rules and directives from the point of view of law-subjects, to understand the role the rules can be expected to play in the practical reasoning of law-subjects. (3) The property that distinguishes law from other exercises of social power is that the law—or rather its officials—claim authority to issue directives, as well as to back them up with threats of force. We are forced to deny even *de facto* authority to imperatives backed by threats if those who issue them cannot themselves claim legitimacy without contradiction or self-deception.

Now, on the basis of these three premises we can argue that, if it is a permanent and pervasive fact in a society that a substantial part of its population has no reason voluntarily to comply with the dictates of those in power, then we have good reason to say that there is no legal system in that society (or if that is too strong, then that there is no law for those systematically excluded), despite the fact that a certain coercive order is maintained in the territory. This is so because in such a situation functionaries (and beneficiaries) of the system voluntarily accept the rules, but they cannot regard them, or their exercise of power over the victims, as legitimate without self-deception. For if they purport to direct the social action of the victims in the way distinctive of law, they must look at their exercise of power through the eyes of the victims. But they will be forced to see that such victims have no reason voluntarily to

---

[25] I argue this point in greater detail in 'Coordination and Convention at the Foundations of Law', *Journal of Legal Studies*, vol. 11 (1982), 187–93.

comply with their dictates. In the face of this, it will be impossible to maintain the belief in the legitimacy of their exercise of power and of their laws without self-deception. And if they cannot claim legitimacy for themselves, we have no basis on which to accord them even *de facto* legitimacy. But then there is a straightforward sense in which the institutionalized coercive force cannot be regarded as law.

Thus, there may be cases in which judges are bound to apply valid rules which those subject to them have no reason to obey, but these cases are likely to be much rarer than Hart seems to think. And this is precisely because in many of the cases to which the description might at first seem to apply, we have good reason to challenge the judge's claim that he or she is bound to apply the rule (on other than purely personal or prudential grounds). Consequently, neither Hart's internalist account of reasons, nor his worries about explaining the possibility of a wicked legal system force us to accept his account of legal obligation, and so, we have no reason yet to think that 'obligation' has a different meaning in legal and moral contexts, as Hart insists.

IV NATURALISM VERSUS CONVENTIONALISM

Consider now the third of Hart's devices severing law from morality. Observer theories of law attempt to give an account of the structure of the point of view of self-identified participants in a legal practice. According to Hart, such participants *accept* the fundamental law (or rules of recognition). But a dispute between naturalist and positivist observer theories takes shape at this point regarding the nature and grounds of this acceptance. At the core of Hart's version of observer theory is a two-part thesis: (*a*) that distinctive of the point of view of self-identified participants is the standing acceptance of the rule of recognition as providing peremptory and content-independent reasons for (judicial) action; and (*b*) that it is no part of the legal point of view that this acceptance rests on a conviction of the moral legitimacy of general compliance with the rule of recognition. In fact, Hart insists that this normative attitude may be adopted for *any* sort of reason: moral, prudential, purely personal, or even for no special reason at all.[26] In contrast, naturalist observer theory seems to hold that acceptance of the fundamental law of a system must rest on a conviction of the moral legitimacy of that law or of compliance with it.

[26] Hart, *Bentham*, 256.

In this respect, Hart argues, naturalist observer theory simply conveys 'an unrealistic picture of the way in which the judges envisage their task of identifying and applying the law'.[27] For, upon taking up the office in an established legal system, judges find a settled practice already firmly in place, according to which they must apply laws identified by special criteria.

This settled practice is acknowledged as determining the central duties of the office of a judge and not to follow the practice would be regarded as a breach of duty . . . [moreover] demands for compliance would be regarded as proper [and to be expected].[28]

Furthermore, judges follow this practice out of a 'settled disposition' without considering the merits of doing so in each case. Indeed, judges 'would regard it not open to them to act on their view of the merits'. From this Hart concludes that, although

the judge is in this sense committed to following the rules, his view of the moral merits of doing so . . . is irrelevant. His view of the merits may be favourable or unfavourable, or simply absent, or, without dereliction of his duty as a judge, he may have formed no view of the moral merits.[29]

In these recent essays Hart has added a new wrinkle to the familiar argument of his *Concept of Law*.[30] He stresses not only the facts of the established practice, but also the special nature of the settled disposition involved. But his appeal to this special disposition does not substantially strengthen the original argument. Let me briefly say why.

First, Hart seems to call into service his notion of authoritative legal reasons and thus the peremptory and content-independent character of the reasons which, in the judges' view, are provided by the fact that the laws in question satisfy the criteria of validity. However, this cannot advance his argument, because it runs together (*a*) excluding consideration of the moral merits of *particular laws* validated by the rule of recognition with (*b*) excluding consideration of the moral merits of *complying with the rule of recognition itself*. And it is the latter which is now at issue. Exclusionary reasons of the sort Hart thinks operate in the legal context are not self-validating. The issue here is what sorts of reasons

[27] Hart, *Bentham*, 158.
[28] Hart, *Bentham*, 158–9.
[29] Ibid.
[30] Hart, *Concept*, 103–7, 245.

are characteristically given by self-identified participants in the practice (or what sorts of reasons are they committed to giving) for regarding satisfaction of the criteria of validity as peremptory and content-independent reasons. Even if officials take the distinctive normative attitude described by Hart, it does not follow that they do so without regard for the moral merits of adopting the attitude. Hart's notion of authoritative legal reasons simply can be of no help at this point in his argument.

Secondly, Hart appeals to the acknowledged fact that officials adopt the rule of recognition *as a rule*. But this also fails to advance the argument. For it implies only that judges do not and need not raise *in each case* the question of the moral merits of applying the criteria of validity defined by the practice. It does not follow from this that officials do not believe that sufficient moral reasons are, and must be available for their accepting and applying these criteria. Nothing in this argument forces us to the conclusion that, *from the participant's point of view*, the moral merits of accepting the criteria defined by the practice are irrelevant to the practical authority of those criteria.

I conclude from this that the full weight of Hart's objections to naturalist observer theory on the present issue must rest solely on considerations made familiar in *The Concept of Law*.[31] There Hart maintained that the question of the authority of the rule of recognition simply does not arise in the normal course of adjudication, and when judges are forced to reflect on the criteria themselves, and their own continued use of them, they simply recognize that the criteria are established in the judicial practice. The authority of these criteria, on this account, rests entirely on the social fact that the practice manifests their general use and acceptance.

But there is a problem with the way Hart sets up the question of the authority of the criteria of validity. He considers the views of a judge who *stands outside* the practice as an observer. This, I believe, invites confusion of the observer perspective with the participant perspective on the question. We can all agree that *an observer* is indifferent to the reasons for which the participants accept the criteria, but it does not follow that *self-identified participants* are indifferent. And it is the point of view of this participant which Hart's observer theory seeks to capture.

Against this Hart suggests in *The Concept of Law* that to take up the question of the authority of the criteria of validity is to take up a question

---

[31] Hart, *Concept*, 103–7, 245.

that can *only* be raised from the perspective of the observer (the 'external point of view'). It is not a question self-identified participants can put to themselves,[32] for this is to shift from questions of proper use of the criteria constituted by judicial practice to questions regarding the facts of the practice itself. But I see no reason to accept this argument. There is nothing in general to bar a participant in a normative system or practice from having, *as a participant*, a view of the practical significance of the fundamental rules of the system. Indeed, these views may well be partially constitutive of the kind of enterprise or normative system involved. (It is partly definitive of recognizing a practice as a game, for example, that one recognizes that its requirements are largely autonomous from other practical considerations.) Nor is there anything preventing the participant from regarding the social fact of others participating, accepting the constitutive norms, as crucial to the normative significance of constitutive norms of the system.

In order to avoid the confusion of observer and participant perspectives, then, Hart's claim must be restated. But this can be done in two different ways. (1) We might say that, although it is a social fact about judges in any given legal system that they all accept the basic criteria of validity, there nevertheless is no uniformity, no distinctive pattern, in the reasons they give for accepting them. Some accept for moral reasons, others for prudential reasons, others for quite idiosyncratic reasons, and some for no reason other than the fact that it is done. Thus, self-identified participants in this kind of normative system have in common only their acceptance of the criteria of validity, and to specify the legal point of view any further would do violence to these facts. I shall call this the *simple convergence thesis*. (2) But we might say, rather, that self-identified participants themselves recognize the fact that there is a wide range of reasons for acceptance of the criteria of validity, but those reasons (they believe) are irrelevant to the question of the authority of the criteria. For that authority (they hold) all that is necessary is that the criteria be accepted and practised widely. I shall call this the *strict conventionalist thesis*.

It is difficult to say which of these two theses Hart accepts, but I will not try to settle that issue here. Rather, I will consider each thesis in its own right and as rivals to the naturalist thesis. It would be instructive, then, to contrast these two different observer theories of law with the naturalist observer theory.

---

[32] Hart, *Concept*, 107.

The naturalist and simple convergence theories agree in two important respects: (*a*) that from the point of view of the self-identified participant the fact that others accept the criteria of validity is neither necessary nor sufficient for their authority, but also (*b*) that in order for there to be an effective legal system there must be *in fact* a broad convergence on the criteria accepted. Thus, one might say that naturalism embraces an *enriched* convergence thesis. Naturalism departs from the simple convergence thesis in holding that, from the point of view of the participant, it is not true that *just any* kind of reasons for acceptance will do. The participant recognizes wide disagreement about the reasons offered for the authority of the criteria of validity, but insists that they be regarded as reasons of moral-political theory, reasons that purport to show that the criteria are, at least in some limited sense, morally legitimate.

The *strict conventionalist* agrees with the naturalist that an accurate account of the view taken by participants must restrict the range of reasons participants have for accepting the authority of the criteria. But on this thesis, participant judges regard the criteria of validity as the basis, the defining ground rules, of the enterprise. They are regarded as, in Dworkin's phrase, 'true by convention'. Other reasons may be given for them, but such practical support is not necessary. Their authority stands or falls entirely on whether or not the criteria are widely accepted.

Hart rejects the naturalist thesis in favour of either the simple convergence thesis or the strict conventionalist thesis. I believe none of these three theses is correct, but we can gain insight into a more adequate account of the phenomena here if we pay careful attention to the dialectic that develops among these three theses.

Consider first the simple convergence thesis. The latitudinarian posture of this thesis, it seems to me, is unacceptable if we take seriously the general aims of observer theories to give an account of the point of view of the *self-identified* participant in the legal system. No doubt it is possible for judges to identify and apply laws in the standard way, to follow the rule of recognition, without regarding themselves as genuine participants. A radical critic of the existing legal structure, for example, may believe that the most effective way to bring the present system to its knees is for its judges to expose its absurdity through strict adherence to its foundational principles. Another might see participation in the practice as nothing more than a necessary means of self-advancement. Each has reasons for following the practice, but the reasons are only accidentally and extrinsically related to the nature and mission of the law.[33] Both judges may find it necessary to make a pretence of regarding the law in the manner of a self-identified participant, but that just shows that the latter attitude is theoretically primary, the former parasitic.[34]

We can state the objection in a slightly different way. First, we must distinguish two ways in which norms or rules can figure in the practical reasoning of a person who falls within the scope of the norms or rules. (*a*) They can function as standards guiding decision and action, or (*b*) they can function as constraints structuring the situation within which the practical deliberation takes place. Now self-identified participants, who accept the legal norms, regard them in the first way. However, simple convergence theory cannot make this crucial distinction and so cannot distinguish central from peripheral cases of 'acceptance' of the criteria of validity of a legal system.

These are not the only problems facing the simple convergence thesis. Both the naturalist and the conventionalist offer persuasive objections against this thesis. The naturalist, for his part, maintains that self-identified participants do not regard the law or the rule of recognition on which it rests as simply supplying personal reasons to act in a certain way, but rather as defining a framework of public justification for their actions, and, in the case of judges, defining judicial duties. For example, consider the activities of *lawyers*, not merely advising clients, but actively manipulating legal machinery to achieve results for their clients, or the activities of *citizens* using the law to advance personal objectives (perhaps at the expense of others or the community at large), or the activities of *judges* applying and enforcing the law. These situations share certain common features: the parties are actively involved and personally implicated in the acts and their consequences, the activities call for some sort of special justification (the interests and rights of others and the community are at stake in some way), and appeals to the law play an important role in the justification these active parties offer for their actions. It is not enough for them to be able to show how the 'justification' might go within some system of norms. They must regard (or at least pretend to regard) that justification as applicable to their activities, as vindicating their actions.

---

[33] Compare here Joseph Raz's argument against sanction theories of normativity of law in his *Practical Reason and Norms*, London (1975), 161–2.

[34] It is not inconceivable that each official in a legal system makes a pretence of participation, but it is impossible that each official does so *and* that this is a matter of common knowledge. For then we would no longer have adjudication or law-applying, but only a sinister charade. It would be a charade because no official claims, or believes any other official claims, authority for the 'law' they 'identify and apply'.

Take judicial decisions, for example. The naturalist argues that they are (and typically are regarded as) inescapably moral or political decisions—not in the sense that it is impossible to protect them from moral or political bias, but in the sense that they deal with and directly affect, and are *intended* to deal with and affect, matters of immediate moral and political significance. Not only do they directly and publicly address matters that touch morally important concerns of individuals and the community alike, but they also direct the exercise of the coercive power of the state.[35] Such decisions are not self-justifying. Thus, if it is believed that sufficient justification for such activities can come from appeals to the law, and the fundamental principles on which it rests, then it must be because these principles are themselves regarded as morally legitimate. No self-identified participant in the judicial practice can be satisfied with frivolous, purely personal reasons for following that practice, since the practice must provide moral justification for his or her actions, and such reasons will not be sufficient for such justification.

The strict conventionalist also rejects the simple convergence thesis but for different reasons. Again we can begin from the observation that self-identified participants regard the rule of recognition as defining obligations imposed on them and others. They do not obey merely for their own part only. Hart puts the argument well:

But this merely personal concern with the rules, which is all the ordinary citizen may have in obeying them, cannot characterize the attitude of the courts to the rules with which they operate as courts. This is most patently the case with the ultimate rule of recognition in terms of which the validity of other rules is assessed. This, if it is to exist at all, must be regarded from the internal point of view as a public, common standard of correct judicial decision, and not as something which each judge merely obeys for his own part only.[36]

That is, participants in the judicial practice not only accept the criteria of validity, they *accept* them as *common public standards* of judicial decision. This is not an accidental fact about the attitudes of participants, Hart insists, rather, 'the characteristic unity and continuity of a legal system ... depends on the acceptance, at this crucial point, of common standards of legal validity'.[37] And, we might add, since self-identified participants would not be indifferent to the conditions necessary for achieving and maintaining 'the characteristic unity and

---

[35] This is a familiar argument of Ronald Dworkin's.
[36] Hart, *Concept*, 112.
[37] Hart, *Concept*, 113.

continuity' of their legal practice, they would regard the fact that the criteria are widely accepted and practised as an essential part of their argument for the authority of those criteria.

There seems, then, to be sound reasons for abandoning the simple convergence thesis. But, if you find the above arguments at all persuasive, as I do, we face a paradox—or at least a puzzle. For, if the naturalist's argument against simple convergence theory is sound, it is equally sound against strict conventionalism; and similarly, the conventionalist's argument applies equally against any convergence thesis, including naturalism. I believe this puzzle can be solved, but the way to do so can best be seen by returning to the naturalist and conventionalist arguments once again, this time addressing them to each other, rather than to a common foe.

To begin, consider the naturalist's objection against strict conventionalism. Naturalists sometimes argue,[38] that the judicial convention on which the law rests consists of nothing more than the settled uniform responses to a certain range of standard situations, that is, to the settled law already explicitly accepted. The convention, we might say, is, on this view reified in the behavioural uniformities of the participants. But, the naturalist objects, self-identified participants in legal practices do not view the fundamental criteria of validity in this way. Rather they see them as dynamic and changing, as subjects of potentially conflicting views. Thus, the criteria cannot be regarded as conventional.

There may be something in this criticism, but it rests on a very implausible conception of social conventions which the strict conventionalist need not accept. There is a great deal more freedom, openness, and creativity possible within social conventions than this argument allows. The argument assumes that learning or adopting the rules of a practice amount to nothing more than acquiring a limited repertory of stock responses to standardized situations, which (one knows) other participants have acquired as well. But this mistakenly equates social practices with stylized rituals and petrified customs. Learning how to participate with a living social practice, in contrast, necessarily involves acquiring the capacities to *create or discover* for oneself, and to recognize in the actions of others, *novel* applications of its rules.[39] The practice

---

[38] Most notably Dworkin in 'Model of Rules II', in *Taking Rights Seriously*, Cambridge, Mass. (1978), especially 80.

[39] Compare here the learning of language. See, e.g., J. F. Rosenberg, *Linguistic Representations*, Dordrecht (1975), 3, and generally R. Brandon, 'Freedom and Constraint by Norms', *American Philosophical Quarterly*, vol. 16 (1979), 193–5.

provides a framework within which one can move from existing patterns to new situations in a regular, orderly, and yet creative way. Furthermore, these capacities are *social* capacities, because they are essentially capacities to recognize what *would be* regarded or accepted by the community as proper actions within the practice. It is the shared experiences and shared constraint of the existing patterns of behaviour that give shape and content to the exercise of these capacities.

The naturalist, however, can concede this richer account of convention and still press two important objections against the strict conventionalist. First, if appeals to existing law are to justify judicial decisions and exercises of coercive power, they must rest on something morally more substantial than the mere fact that others follow the rules. Law is different from most games and etiquette in this respect. With regard to the latter, it is usually enough to say (and normally all that can be said is) that there is a general acceptance of the rules one proposes to follow and they constitute the rules of the game, or simply that 'it's done'. But this is not enough in the case of appeals to law, because, both as a matter of fact, and a matter of design, law much more directly touches matters of public moral significance. Arguments adequate for games or etiquette are unsuited to this task.

Secondly, it seems just false to maintain, as the strict conventionalist does, that the criteria of validity are regarded by self-identified participants as constitutive rules of the enterprise which cannot be questioned (without abandoning the perspective of a participant). On the contrary, these criteria can be, and often are challenged. (The issue of the binding force of precedent in British law in the nineteenth century and again in the recent past is, perhaps, an example of such a dispute.) Changes and developments in the practices at the foundations of law can take place not only as a result of the novel application of rules described above, but also through direct challenge to the prevailing or orthodox understanding of the constitutive rules. For the strict conventionalist to reply that such challenges come from *outside* the practice, and so must be regarded as proposals for replacing the accepted rules with new rules, simply begs the question. It assumes that there is a sharp difference between arguments within the rules and arguments about them, and that the latter cannot be taken up by self-identified participants. But earlier in this part we have considered reasons for rejecting this claim.

However, even if these arguments are sound, only half of the naturalist's position has been established. It has not been shown that conventionalist considerations are *irrelevant* to the participant's view of the authority of criteria of validity, but only that they are not sufficient. And the conventionalist offers a strong case against embracing the naturalist thesis without qualification. The naturalist, after all, must regard convergence of conviction regarding the proper criteria of validity in a system of law to be a necessary condition of the existence of law while at the same time insisting that this convergence is, *from the point of view of participants*, nothing more than a happy accident. There is nothing logically contradictory in this, but it is implausible. The conventionalist will point out that participants will not be indifferent to conditions necessary for the existence and continuity of their practice if they are aware of them. And this is not a condition difficult to grasp, so it is unlikely that they will be unaware of it. Thus, participants will not regard the convergence as merely a happy but unintended accident.

But we might consider a more sophisticated observer theory naturalism suggested by some of Dworkin's work. Convergence is not a mere accident, one might argue, because judges in any established legal systems are set the task of constructing a general public theory of their common practice, and all start from the same data, namely, the settled rules and uniform patterns of behaviour in the practice. This is still a naturalist observer theory because it requires that these judicial theories of the legal practice attempt to *justify* the bulk of the practice on the basis of recognizably moral-political principles. And the fact that a given theory is widely accepted is still not, on this account of the participant point of view, relevant to the truth or authority of the theory.

But this modified naturalism cannot consistently grant the importance of settled law as a starting point for the construction of judicial theories of the practice without granting that agreement or consensus (either actual or potential) on the theory of the institution is *essential* to its claim to truth or authority. First, officials, on this view, might simply regard the settled decisions and patterns of the practice as so much behaviouristic data. But this would be to deny them the status of public rules, and it is essential to their claim to be regarded as starting points of any theory of the institution so that they be accorded this status. If, however, officials who are engaged in construction of such a theory were to recognize the settled cases as public rules, they must also appreciate that the content of the rules is dependent upon what other officials and citizens in general take them to mean.[40] General acceptance of the

---

[40] See my discussion in part III above regarding the essential interdependence of legal practice.

settled rules is relevant not only to the fact that they are *settled*, but also, and importantly, to the fact that they are *public rules of law*. But then no theory of the institution can ignore or treat as irrelevant the question of whether a proposed theory of the fundamental criteria of validity is (or upon reflection and public argument could come to be) accepted as the theory of the institution.

The conventionalist's argument could also be put in another way. According to the naturalist, participant officials are charged with constructing a general public theory of the practice. But their task is different from that of theoretically inclined observers of natural phenomena. For the practice is, in part, *constituted by* the understanding participants put upon their activities in the practice, and so by the general interpretations of the practice by officials that are constructed for practical (intra-practice) purposes. Participant theories do not have the distance from the phenomena for which they try to account or that observer theories sometimes enjoy. Thus, while different and mutually incompatible observer theories may be possible without the coherence and orderliness of the phenomena being compromised, this is not true for participant theories of social practices. The regularity, order, and significance of legal practices are partly a function of the mutual coherence of different interpretations implicit in the actions and decisions of participants (especially officials). Because of the dominant position of officials in the complexly interdependent relations between officials and citizens, officials are required to act on the basis of not only a coherent general theory of the institution, but of a theory of that practice which renders that practice coherent (or as coherent as is practically possible to make it). Bentham, in his (otherwise unfair) criticism of the Common Law, correctly perceived the absurdity of a theory of law which allows that

from a set of data . . . law is to be extracted by everyman who can fancy that he is able: by each man, perhaps a different law: and these then are the *monades* which constitute the rules which taken together constitute [the law].[41]

The problem with such a theory is that it transforms a matter of *public* rules into a matter of essentially and unavoidably private conjecture. Rousseau neatly sums up the difficulty facing naturalism of the sort we are considering here:

[41] J. Bentham, *Of Laws in General*, ed. H. L. A. Hart, London (1970), 192.

Whatever is good and in conformity with order is such by the nature of things independently of human conventions. All justice comes from God; he alone is its source. But if we knew how to receive it from so exalted a source, *we would have no need for government or laws*. Undoubtedly there is a universal justice emanating from reason alone; but this justice, to be admitted among us, ought to be reciprocal . . . There must therefore be conventions and laws to unite rights and duties and to refer justice back to its object.[42]

If these arguments are persuasive, then we cannot accept either naturalist or strict conventionalist observer theories as adequate accounts of the point of view of the self-identified participants in legal practices, and so of the normativity of law. But the arguments suggest the possibility of a marriage of the surviving portions of each account. I shall call the product of this union 'constructive conventionalism'. On this view, officials recognize, and are committed by their actions and arguments to recognize, that their joint acceptance of the criteria of validity must be linked to more general moral-political concerns. Only in this way can their appeal to those criteria, and the practice on which they rest, provide the right sort of justification for their exercise of power in particular cases. But they also realize that *an essential part* of the case to be made for the criteria rests on the fact that they jointly accept the criteria, or *could come to accept* them after reflection and participation in a forum in which reasoned and principled arguments are exchanged amongst equals. That is, officials recognize that the law they identify and administer is a collective product, and the process of determining its main outlines is essentially a collective and public process. Thus, the participant theoretical interpretations of the foundational rules of the system are subject, on this view, to two constraints: the constraint of conviction of the moral legitimacy of the criteria (or of compliance with them) and the constraint of seeking general consensus for one's account of the criteria and the basis of their authority.

It is impossible at this point to assess the adequacy of the constructive conventionalist thesis and the account of the normativity of law it suggests, without a detailed articulation and defence. But its Hartian pedigree is not in doubt. Of course, the sire may choose to disinherit his offending offspring.

---

[42] J.-J. Rousseau, *On the Social Contract*, vol. II, vi, transl. and ed. Donald A. Cress, Indianapolis (1983), (emphasis added).

3.2 Comment

NEIL MacCORMICK*

To comment on a paper so rich in interesting themes as Gerald Postema's is a difficult task; all the more difficult when the paper itself is a comment on equally rich and intricate recent work of Hart's. In a broad way I am in agreement with Postema, at least in this: we neither of us accept Hart's latest statements of his positivist position, and especially not his claim that 'obligation' is a term with a different meaning in the phrases 'legal obligation' and 'moral obligation'.[43] The assiduous student (I use the singular advisedly) of my book *H. L. A. Hart*[44] would note that the Hartian doctrines in *The Concept of Law* which seemed to me soundest in themselves and yet to require redevelopment in certain ways are the very doctrines Hart himself has either abandoned or restated quite differently in his latest writings. Like Postema, I have to accord to the sire—or grandsire—the right to disinherit his offending issue, to say nothing of pronouncing upon them a declarator of bastardy.

Or should we be so quick about supposing that a right of disinheritance is so uncontroversial? Under Scots law, after all, children, even illegitimate ones nowadays, have against their parents legal rights of succession which prevail no matter what the deceased parent's will may say. English law is different in this, even though the rigours of outright disinheritance are now mitigated by statute law under which judges may make discretionary provision for a deceased person's family out of his/her estate where he/she has wholly failed to make any reasonable *inter vivos* or testamentary provision for them. No doubt robuster customs prevail wherever the old English common law remains in full vigour without abatement at the hands of paternalistic legislators. Perhaps it is so in North Carolina.

Let this ramble, or meander, into comparative law not be thought wholly irrelevant to the present theme of the normativity of law. For what does it show? It shows that as to the very same topic, different systems of positive law may accord different rights. Scottish testators

* © Neil MacCormick 1987.
[43] See H. L. A. Hart, *Bentham*, 147.
[44] London (1982).

have neither right nor power to disinherit their children at law, and the executors of their estate are duty-bound to secure the legal rights of the children against the estate. English and *a fortiori* North Carolinan testators have such right and power and their executors are subject to no such duty.

If there are such different laws, different rights, different powers and different duties in our three jurisdictions, all on the same topic, is it possible that somebody somewhere has made a mistake about law, legal rights, legal powers, or legal duties? Of course not. Everyone, even the most perfervid jusnaturalist, acknowledges the possibility of variance in positive laws. The validity of positive law is jurisdiction-relative and accordingly the existence and import of legal rights and legal duties is jurisdiction-relative, to some extent at least. That the law makes different provision on the same topic in three jurisdictions is simply a mark of that relativity and is wholly unsurprising. In this sense and to some extent at least the 'validity'—*legal* validity—of legal provisions is surely *content independent*. And of course the judicial duty of applying valid laws is a peremptory one.[45] A judge in Scotland and a judge in England might each think that the balance of reasons actually favours the provision of the other's law. But neither could justifiably re-interpret the scheme of legal rights as a discretionary family provision scheme, nor vice versa.

The moral rights and wrongs of the matter are another thing altogether, and no doubt a controversial one. Some think *any* succession to property rights iniquitous, some think any impediment to the utmost freedom of testation iniquitous, some back the idea of partial testamentary freedom, some back the idea of discretionary powers and so on. Certainly circumstances alter cases, as much in morals as in law. But the *mere* circumstance of domicile in Scotland, England, or North Carolina can hardly be thought decisive of the *moral* question of what is the morally proper way to regulate family provision in the law of succession. Where people disagree about that, they disagree. It is of the nature of an opinion on a moral question that it is universalizable and thus contradicts any different opinion on that question. That each of us must judge for ourself in such matters does not mean that each is a jurisdiction to him- or herself. Someone who judges morally that all children have a right to be provided for out of the assets of their deceased parents necessarily concludes that parents have no moral right

---

[45] Cf. Hart, *Bentham*, 256.

to disinherit their children; and therefore necessarily concludes that those who judge that parents have the right to disinherit have reached a wrong judgement, though not necessarily an arbitrary or irrational one.

It follows that not all positive laws on such matters can be of equal moral soundness. Of course, moral reasons can be given for and against the differing solutions, and reasonable persons can differ both as to the moral rights which are at stake and as to the moral rightness of different solutions, all things considered. But although reasonable persons can differ as to which law on family provision is the morally best or morally right one, this does not of itself authorize us to say that all the rival solutions are equally good or right; if one is right, or is better, the others are necessarily wrong, or worse. But this will not affect their legal validity. Whatever is in your view or mine or anyone's the morally right disposition of these things, the rule of family rights is valid in Scotland, that of testator's right of total testamentary freedom is valid in North Carolina and that of testamentary freedom subject to judicial discretion is valid in England.

What I take out of this, then, is that legal validity is a jurisdictionally relative concept; and, accordingly, legal rights and legal duties or obligations are also jurisdictionally relative. If I am the child of a person domiciled in Scotland, I have legal rights which the child of a person domiciled in England or North Carolina who is otherwise identical with me does not have—so much so, indeed, that my parent can divest me of the right simply by acquiring a domicile of choice in England. That my parent shifts from Gretna Green to Carlisle with the intention of making a permanent home there automatically changes my legal rights of succession to his or her estate. One could not conceive of any rational conception of morality under which such a change of residence would *of itself* change moral entitlements as between parent and child. That this is inconceivable indicates that moral entitlements are not jurisdictionally relative.[46]

This in itself is amply sufficient to establish the conceptual distinctness of legal and moral rights, duties, and obligations. If legal rights and

[46] Although a change of residence does not change moral rights of succession as between parent and child, it does not follow that the change of residence would be wholly irrelevant from a moral point of view. Among our prima-facie moral rights is the right as against public officials that they secure to us upon demand whatever we have a legal right to. The moral right to get what one has a legal right to get is a content-independent one; but only a prime-facie right, and not a right (all things considered) to things which it is morally wrong that one should have, e.g. slaves, even when the law treats us as having a right to them.

obligations can vary or be varied without corresponding variance in moral rights or obligations; if I can only know what your legal rights or duties are relative to some jurisdiction (and, let it be added, some time), but can discuss your moral rights and duties regardless of jurisdiction and time; then it follows that systematically different grounds exist for legal and for moral rights and obligations.

What does not follow is that the term 'right' or 'obligation' has a different meaning when qualified as on the one hand 'legal' or on the other 'moral'. Railway tickets are not steamer tickets, but this does not make them 'tickets' in different senses of the term 'tickets'. Legal obligations are not moral obligations, but this does not make them 'obligations' in different senses of the term 'obligation'. (Contrast the two senses of 'interest' which occur in 'mortgage interest' and 'life interest'.) Thus if Hart suggests that legal obligations or duties are to do with what is legally due from or owed by us, and thus with what can be properly demanded of us, these demands being enforceable by due process, it will follow that moral duties or obligations are to do with what is morally due from or owed by us, and thus with what can be properly demanded from us—moral demands being in their nature above and beyond enforcement by institutional and coercive processes.[47] Whatever differentiates legal obligations from moral obligations, it is not (as Postema rightly observes) some kind of pun on the term 'obligation'. But in my suggestion, which is at least compatible with, if not derivable from Postema's view about 'conventionalism', the differentiation arises from the difference of justifying grounds of ascription of legal and of moral right and duty, the former being jurisdictionally relative while the latter are not.

The same distinction is of help if we now turn to consideration of the topic of 'committed' versus 'detached' normative statements, dealt with by Postema in the first section of his paper. Here I agree with him that 'J has a moral obligation to A' no more entails the committed conclusion that 'J morally ought to O' than does 'J has a legal obligation to A', if both obligation statements are taken to be detached ones. But I think that the concept of detachment needs more consideration here. It seems to me that 'detachment' does not apply in identically the same way to statements of law and statements of morality. Since, as we have seen, the

---

[47] At the symposium in Jerusalem, Hart indicated that he agreed as to the analogical applicability of his elucidation of legal rights to the case of moral rights, and had not intended his remarks about a difference of meaning between the two cases to convey the opposite impression.

correct answer to any question of legal right or duty can only be an answer relative to some jurisdiction and time, it follows that different answers may be correct for different jurisdictions and times. If the legal obligations of executors are different in Scotland and in England, it does not follow that anyone has made a mistake about what is legally obligatory or about what it is for someone to have a legal obligation.

Moral differences are different. A Nazi regards racial discrimination as obligatory, a liberal regards racial non-discrimination as obligatory. This is not a divergence between two moral systems supposed to have different jurisdictions; it is a contrariety of opinion upon one and the same issue—our moral obligations to our fellow humans. There are not two moral jurisdictions, Nazism and liberalism, each with its own valid moral norms which can without contradiction or error diverge from those of the other. There are two rival moral creeds, Nazism and liberalism. They are rival creeds because they are beliefs about one and the same thing.

This has an important bearing on the possibility of detachment in statements of law as against statements of morality. A statement of law has to be a statement of law in respect of some time and jurisdiction, and one can make it without any logical or pragmatic implication as to one's approval or endorsement or disapproval or non-endorsement of that body of law wholly or in part. In making a statement of morality, however, I necessarily make a statement either of my view of what is morally right or obligatory or of somebody else's view of what is right or obligatory. When I detachedly remark that racial discrimination is obligatory—from a Nazi's moral point of view, that is to say—my statement can count as detached only if it is clear that I convey *no* opinion as to the correctness of the view, and that my view may differ. I cannot be saying that the answer which is correct from their point of view is *therefore* correct wherever that point of view is valid, but there may be a different point of view for me. For either the point of view is valid universally and the view from that viewpoint correct or not. To be detached in moral matters is to refrain pro tem from having *any* view of one's own in order to appreciate others' views; but this requires abstention from any supposition that theirs is a correct view—any ascription of correctness is a matter of commitment. To be detached in legal matters is precisely to discover what the correct view of the law somewhere is. To acknowledge a statement of law as correct is to make a cognitive commitment, not a practical one. But one cannot acknowledge a statement of morality as correct without thereby making a practical commitment.

Accordingly, detached moral statements are statements of somebody's view of morality, not statements of what is moral; whereas detached statements of law are not statements of somebody's view of legality, but statements of what is legal—in some jurisdiction at some time. Although neither sort of detached statement implies or entails commitment to a moral ought, the reason for the absence of such implication or entailment is different. What Postema and I agree on here is the non-entailment; whether we agree on what lies behind it, I am less sure.

Anyway, as is often the case in discussions of the 'conceptual independence' question, it turns out that assumptions about morality are at least as important as assumptions about law. In the above I have assumed that morality is intrinsically universalistic as well as practical, and only under that conception of morality is what I say true. But it is only on that conception of morality that there is even an interesting question about the conceptual independence of the legal and the moral. If we interpret '*morality*' as *mores*, such that each group's mores are its morality; that is, if we take morality as being 'positive morality'; then of course positive law is one special case of positive morality—it is *a* morality among moralities; that it is not every or any morality is just trivially true; that there can be moralities which are not laws and that laws are not the same as those moralities is too obvious to be worth saying. If there is *a* positivism versus natural law question (which I rather doubt) it is only capable of being an interesting question given universalistic assumptions about morality. So I have made these assumptions here.

Be that as it may, any discussion of detachment properly leads us to asking, 'detachment from *what*?'. What is the nature of the commitment I do not make when I make legal statements non-committally? Since we all agree that there would not merely be nothing to detach oneself from, but indeed nothing about which to make statements at all if no one were committed in any way to legal systems as practical normative orders, it matters greatly what a practical commitment to law amounts to, for that is what makes it normative.

Like Postema, I find myself at variance with Hart's latest statement on this. Whereas the Hart of *The Concept of Law* wanted to differ from the Kelsenian thesis that all legal norms are primarily norms for official conduct, Hart's latest thesis about judicial statements of legal obligation seems to coincide with, if not to adopt, the Kelsenian view.[48] For Hart's thesis now is that the judicial statement of the citizen's legal obligation as a committed statement is only a statement of the reasons the judge has for holding the citizen to a certain line of conduct, not a statement of reasons the judge supposes there to be for the citizen to do something.[49]

This seems to me to confuse two things: what the law says to the citizen, and why the law which says that is one which the judge should implement. As to the former, laws regarding crimes and civil wrongs of all sorts (this includes but is not exhausted by breaches of obligations) at least purport to set *categorical* requirements, minimal requirements for conduct to be acceptable within this jurisdiction. Only on the supposition that the legal system intelligibly sets such a standard as a requirement can we make intelligible the *secondary (per Concept of Law)* responsibility of the judge to implement the law as a law of this character.[50] The judicial commitment has to be *inter alia* a commitment to treating as wrong what valid law characterizes as wrong conduct, *even if* in the absence of such a law there would seem nothing wrong in what is prohibited, and *even if* in a concrete case the soundest moral judgement might be that, all things considered, there was nothing wrong either in doing the deed the law characterizes as wrong, or in breaking the law by doing that deed. *This* commitment to the 'peremptoriness' of law is indeed a commitment which only judges need make, and only in their judicial capacity—and surely we have moral reasons for wishing it not to be an absolute commitment even for judges in their judicial capacity.

The issue raised by Hart and debated by Postema, however, is not whether the judicial commitment is absolute but whether it is moral. It seems that we have to ask what are the reasons for the commitment—if the reasons are moral reasons, the commitment is a moral commitment and if they are not or need not be, then the commitment need not be a moral commitment. And in that case the conceptual independence of law from morals is established.

Yet the case is not as easy as that after all. What kind of reasons are we talking about here? Exciting reasons (motivating reasons) or justifying

---

[48] See Hart, *Concept*, 35–40, criticizing H. Kelsen, *General Theory of Law and the State*, trans. A. Wedberg, Cambridge, Mass. (1945), 58–63 and 143–4. For a similar view of the 'sudden Kelsenian twist to Hart's view of legal duties' as stated at p.160 and pp.266–7 of *Bentham*, see J. Raz, 'Hart on Moral Rights and Legal Duties', *Oxford Journal of Legal Studies*, vol. 4 (1984), 123–31 at p. 131.

[49] Hart, *Bentham*, 160, 266–7.

[50] See Hart, *Concept*, 40 on 'the inversion of ancillary and principal' involved in Kelsen's 'extreme view', and chap. 5 on the 'secondary' quality of rules of adjudication.

reasons?[51] Why a judge does make such a commitment (money, power, greed, stupidity, acceptance of tradition, moral uprightness, patriotism, commitment to democracy) and why a judge should make such a commitment are different questions, the difference being much obscured by the odd current view that statements about what ought to be done are made more lucid by being translated into statements about reasons for doing things. Surely there could not be justifying reasons for a judicial commitment to the peremptoriness of valid law in a given jurisdiction unless these reasons were moral ones and were not all content-independent reasons. But there could be motivating reasons having nothing to do with morality. The motivating reasons need not be the same ones for every judge and need not be a standard set. But the judicial pretension to justification in administering the law as distinct from mere justification by the fact that it is law one is administering amounts to a pretension to having some justifying reason for one's judicial commitment, even though one's actually motivating reason were immoral or amoral or a mere unthinking acceptance of a traditional practice. Such a pretension to justification in administering the law does seem to me to be implicit in the activity of implementing as categorical requirements what the law treats as categorically required.[52]

It is possible that judges are either mistaken or insincere as to the justification of what they do. It is possible that their motivating reasons conflict with any legitimate justifying reasons there might be for what they do as judges. But surely what they do as judges essentially includes reference to a conventional, not a merely convergent, set of criteria of the validity of laws.

Conventionalism is all that we should need in order to account for the possibility of true detached statements of law for a given jurisdiction at a given time. That those conventions are the conventions of those who effectively administer 'justice' is sufficient to identify what their law is and what it requires or permits. But so long as law is viewed detachedly it

---

[51] Francis Hutcheson, in *An Essay on the Nature and Conduct of the Passions and Affections. With Illustrations on the Moral Sense*, 3rd ed. (1742), quoted in D. D. Raphael, *British Moralists*, Oxford (1969), vol. 1, 308, draws our attention to this distinction between exciting and justifying reason, '. . . what is this *conformity of actions to reason*? When we ask the reason of an action, we sometimes mean, 'What truth shows a quality in the action, exciting the agent to do it?' . . . Sometimes for a reason of actions we show the truth expressing a quality, engaging our approbation . . . The former sort of reasons we will call *exciting*, and the latter *justifying*.' The distinction remains an important one, if not much noticed in the current literature.

[52] For elucidation of the sense of 'categorical requirement' meant here, see MacCormick, *H. L. A. Hart*, London (1981), 61–5.

is only hypothetically normative—the view is of what you must do supposing you have any reason or wish to conform to the law of that jurisdiction.

It is only in discussing law as categorically normative that we are committed to presupposing some justifying reason for endorsement of the system, some underpinning reason for acceptance of a rule of recognition. This, I think, does lead to the conclusion that Postema's 'constructive conventionalism' may be necessary for committed participation in a legal system. To say this would be to acknowledge that the concept of law is the concept of a mode of social regulation which committed participants deem in some way morally justified. No explanation of law is then possible without some account of the nature of moral justification. But law thus explained will not be explained as something which is in its nature morally justified. This is to repeat the point that detached legal statements are statements of what law correctly is in some jurisdiction and at some time; not statements of what it is correct (justifiable) for law to be.

3.3 Comment

DAVID LYONS*

Gerald Postema seeks to reconcile contemporary representatives of traditionally opposed legal theories. His complex and subtle paper focuses on the meaning of statements made within and about the law, but he begins by referring to a wider issue: 'A central task of philosophical jurisprudence is to explain and reconcile two (sometimes apparently conflicting) sets of widely shared beliefs about our legal practices. On the one hand, we recognize that the notion of law is essentially practical ... [O]n the other hand, we believe that law is essentially a social phenomenon ....' I would like to explore that suggestion. For I suspect that we cannot make much progress towards solving the theory-motivated problems probed by Postema until we have a better grasp of the background he has sketched, the tension in our ordinary beliefs about the law and the idea that Postema makes the theme of his paper, 'the normativity of law'.

With Postema's concurrence, I shall use this opportunity to consider problems that are largely presupposed by his discussion. As I proceed, however, I shall also offer some related observations on aspects of Postema's paper.

I

Postema refers to a clash between the 'practical' and 'social' aspects of law. These characterizations are too loose to suggest contradiction. Cookery-books and instruction manuals, for example, can be considered both practical and social, but that seems no cause for philosophical concern. What then is the problem? As I pursue this, I shall pay special attention to the idea of law's 'normativity'.

Postema says that law 'seeks to guide the behaviour of rational beings through rational means, that is, through addressing to them public general rules to which they are expected to conform in their behaviour'. This suggests a blending of the practical and social, but it still offers no

* © David Lyons 1987.

appearance of inconsistency. Postema goes further: 'The property that distinguished law from other exercises of social power is that the law—or rather its officials—claim authority to issue directives, as well as to back them up with threats of force.' What seems important here is not enforcement but rather the claim of authority. This needs interpretation; but first a general comment.

I do not believe that this property is peculiar to the law or legal officials. Others, ranging from bishops to revolutionaries, can and do claim authority, in the names of their respective groups or institutions, to use social power in such ways. But all of that seems irrelevant. The question is why our ordinary beliefs about the law are threatened by contradictions. The difficulty need not be limited to law. I think, in fact, that the problems here are *not* peculiar to the law, but affect any institution with properties like those sketched below.

What kind of authority is claimed by officials in the name of the law? It is not, presumably, the authority that goes with expertise. Officials need not be specialists in social engineering to claim authority to engage with it.

For present purposes, it would not be helpful to identify the relevant authority as 'legal'. In order to explain this I must suggest what I take the relevant sort of authority and normativity to be.

As a first approximation, let me suggest that the relevant claims of authority involve the idea that legal standards *justify doing things to people which require justification*, such as depriving people of life, liberty, or other valued goods.

Here is why it will not help to identify the relevant sort of authority, normativity, or justification as 'legal'. Suppose the law requires that a particular person be burdened in a certain way. I can fully appreciate this fact and still sensibly ask *how* such an action or decision *could be justified*. That the law *requires* the decision and the corresponding actions may be taken as implying that they are 'legally justified'. But that fact was not at issue in my question.

We can characterize what is at stake here by saying that *the law has moral pretensions*. It claims to provide some measure of justification (in a sense that is not narrowly 'legal') for doing what it does to people. Of course, to *claim* authority is one thing, to *possess* it quite another. Legal positivism, roughly speaking, seems committed to denying that law always automatically lives up to its pretensions, while natural law seems to claim the oppposite.

The way I have put this may already make clear that 'moral' here

cannot refer to arbitrary or indefensible standards that may be laid down
or accepted by some person or social group. The pretension is that of
providing *sound* justifications, so the morality in question must be
capable of providing it.

Is there any such morality, consisting of sound principles, capable of
truly justifying things and discriminating right from wrong? We do not
need to answer that question here. We need merely observe that the
context presupposes it. The nature of the authority claimed by law or its
officials presupposes that moral judgements are not inherently arbitrary
and indefensible. More generally, the issues here arise precisely
because it is assumed—with good reason, I believe—that some of what
law does to people *requires* justification, in a sense that is not narrowly
legal. This assumes that there are sound objections to doing such things
to people (such as depriving them of life, liberty, or other valued
goods)—objections that the law's moral pretensions simply can be
overcome. And all of this assumes, in turn, that there are sound
standards for evaluating such things. *Those* are the standards to which
we refer, in this context, under the heading of 'morality'.

If we did not assume that there were such standards, then none of
these issues would arise. Not only the possibility, but the very need for
such justification presupposes that there are sound standards for
evaluating what we do to one another, standards that apply to what is
done in the name of the law. (All of this applies, of course, to other
familiar ideas, such as the idea that one is under an obligation to obey the
law.)

But this first attempt at explaining the normativity of law will not do,
for two reasons. For one thing, there is, as we shall see, another kind of
'normativity' that can be attributed to law; that will come up in the next
section. Secondly, what has been said so far does not account for a
credible threat of inconsistency in our beliefs about the law. That is
because we have no difficulty recognizing that the law might simply fail
to live up to its extravagant moral pretensions.

This has to do with what Postema refers to as the 'social' aspect of law.
What I mean, at any rate, is this. Law is the product of human action and
decision. These are fallible in relevant ways. We cannot assume that
individual laws or entire legal systems are wise, just, or morally
defensible. Indeed, we have excellent reason to judge some laws and
systems as unwise, unjust, and morally indefensible. But the moral
pretensions of law are *not* limited accordingly; they extend to laws and
legal systems that are unwise, unjust, and morally indefensible.

Now, it may be true, as it is often assumed, that those who make and enforce the law characteristically claim and even, by and large, sincerely believe that law always merits some measure of respect, that it always provides some measure of justification for doing the things that it does to people. But we have quite good reason to suppose that they are at least sometimes mistaken. Since it is plausible to suppose, therefore, that law can fail to live up to its moral pretensions, our account does not yet seem to generate any inconsistency in our beliefs about the law.

Such a threat emerges when we develop a point made in passing by Postema. The law does not simply set standards to be followed and claim authority to enforce them: it is understood specifically to generate *rights and obligations*. This is relevant because rights and obligations are understood to demand some measure of respect and can therefore be seen as providing at least some of the justifying power that we have been considering. This can be suggested as follows. If I fail to live up to an obligation or fail to respect another's right, and I lack sufficient reason for my failure, that is understood to count against both me and my performance. Such conduct is *wrong*. Thus rights and obligations are understood to provide reasons for action and relevant justifications. They would seem, at least, to justify some negative appraisals of behaviour.[53]

In other words, rights and obligations seem to have what may be called 'moral force'. This provides some desperately needed support for the moral pretensions of law, but it also helps to generate the spectre of inconsistency that Postema perceives in our beliefs about the law. Inconsistency threatens because the rights and obligations that depend on law can sometimes seem deeply suspect and problematic—so much so, that we can reasonably question whether those rights and obligations always *do* merit the respect that we associate with rights and obligations.

It is important to observe that no inconsistency is threatened if we merely suppose that all the rights and obligations that are generated by law possess the limited moral force that we attribute generally to rights and obligations, and that this moral force is sometimes overridden by conflicting moral factors. Within the framework we are now using, inconsistency is threatened if, but *only* if, our beliefs about the law appear to commit us to both of the following propositions: that rights and obligations *always have* some moral force, however slight it may be in

[53] Some would go further and say that rights and obligations justify their own enforcement. I discuss Hart's suggestion of this in *Rights*, California (1984), 3–4.

some cases; but that *some* rights and obligations that are generated by law possess *no* moral force at all.

To suggest how rights and obligations that are generated by law might merit absolutely no measure of respect, we can refer to conditions that, unfortunately, have not been uncommon in the history of law. The relations between a slave-owner and his slaves, for example, may be established in terms of 'rights' and 'obligations'. But these rights and obligations can be morally indefensible, and can be held to merit not the slightest measure of respect. I do not mean that someone who owns slaves has no rights that merit respect, but only that this may be true (for example) of his rights as slave-owner. And similarly for a slave: the indefensibility of his status does not nullify all moral constraints on (for example) the way he may treat the person who is regarded in law as his owner. But a person whose condition as slave could not be justified would *not* seem subject to *sound* criticism for failing to live up to at least some of the obligations that the laws concerning slavery may be understood to impose on him. His slave status may provide *absolutely no sound moral reason against* his refusing to obey his legal owner's lawful orders or his seeking by unlawful means to secure his own freedom.

But to suggest that some rights and obligations lack moral force entirely is to suggest that they lack some of the attributes and obligations. Hence the threat of inconsistency to our ordinary beliefs about the law.

II

There are at least two ways of trying to dissolve the apparent inconsistency. Each focuses on a different aspect of our assumptions about the rights and obligations that are generated by law. One distinguishes 'legal' from 'moral' rights and obligations, while the other introduces a similar distinction within the law itself.

The first strategy, suggested by Hart, takes for granted that legal requirements and prohibitions generally give rise to rights and obligations, but it distinguishes the rights and obligations that law is *always* capable of generating from those that *by their nature* merit some measure of respect. It does so by treating law and morality as analogous systems of evaluation. Just as 'moral' rights and obligations can be understood to possess 'moral force', so 'legal' rights and obligations can be credited with 'legal force', in terms that are internal to the law. My failure to live up to a legal obligation or to respect another person's legal right counts against my performance, in the eyes of the law. Such conduct is legally wrong, or unlawful.

In other words, law's 'normativity' can be seen as having two aspects. Legal relations have important legal implications, and law furthermore has moral pretensions.

The analogy between legal and moral evaluations should be clarified in one respect. We can acknowledge 'moral systems' that are fully analogous to legal systems in that they may be claimed to have, but may nevertheless lack, the justifying power that we discussed earlier. That is, we can recognize moral systems that merely happen to be accepted. Within such systems, whose principles may turn out to be arbitrary and indefensible, 'moral force' cannot be assumed to have more than internal significance, just as legal force cannot be assumed to have more than legal significance within a given system. But when, as in the present context, the only moral standards in which we are interested are those that are sound, then law and morality are importantly disanalogous. For then the reasons and justifications that are provided by morality are not merely internal to a system that may be arbitrary and indefensible; they are assumed to be sound. That is the context in which one worries about the problematic relations between law and morality.

This sort of distinction between the legal and the moral does not deny that law can have moral significance. It would of course allow law to have moral significance when it satisfies some minimal moral conditions. One can go further. The distinction should not, I think, be taken as excluding the possibility of some significant, non-contingent links between law and morality. In these respects, it might turn out that legal evaluations always possess some kind of 'moral force'. But the distinction tells us that *this cannot be assumed.*

When we limit our attention to the possible connections between law and *sound* morality, the point of the distinction is suggested by our previous observations about the moral fallibility of law. Our moral experience and our exercise of reasonable moral judgement would seem to warrant a further presumption against there being significant, non-contingent links between law and sound morality. But the distinction alone tells us only that we cannot assume that legal rights and obligations have the specific kind of 'normativity' that amounts to sound moral force. It therefore explains how the rights and obligations that are generated by law can lack the attributes of rights and obligations when the latter are assumed to possess such force. It dissipates the threat of inconsistency to our beliefs about the law by implying, in effect, that the rights and obligations that are generated by law can fail to live up to their moral pretensions.

Postema appears unhappy with this way of drawing such a distinction between law and morals, at least when Hart employs it, because it does not guarantee the fully-fledged positivistic 'separation of law and morals'. That is, the distinction, so drawn, does not insist that law, on its own, lacks sound moral force. The distinction leaves this issue open.

I think that Postema asks too much of such a distinction. The distinction I have sketched acknowledges two identifiable realms of evaluation, warns us neither to confuse them nor to assume significant non-contingent connections between them, but leaves open the possibility of such links. This makes the mere distinction appropriately less ambitious and less controversial than the fully-fledged positivistic 'separation of law and morals'. That is as it should be. For the full separation of law and morals is rooted not in theoretical distinctions but rather in our pre-analytic exercise of moral judgement.

At any rate, Postema seems to prefer a different way of dissolving the apparent inconsistency in our beliefs about the law. The second strategy is suggested by some of Postema's remarks about the ascription of legal obligation.[54] Here one does *not* assume that leagl restrictions can generally be understood to generate rights and obligations. Only some of them do; that is, when the resulting rights and obligations can be held (on independent grounds) to possess sound moral force and to merit some measure of respect.

It would seem that on this second approach we should find ourselves recognizing fewer legal rights and obligations than we should recognize on the first approach. That is because the second approach imposes a moral condition on genuine rights and obligations: they must possess sound moral force. But in another respect the two approaches are identical. For neither lays down any moral restrictions on what counts as *law*. The second approach does not deny that law exists when the system in question merits no respect at all.

So the two approaches differ with regard to what they take to be the proper application in terms like 'right' and 'obligation'. This is understandable. As Postema observes, the proper use of such terms is in relevant respects unclear. Neither approach seems required or prohibited by the mere concept of a right or obligation.

If that is right, then we seem to have ways of avoiding inconsistency.

[54] Cf. *Ronald Dworkin and Contemporary Jurisprudence*, Marshall Cohen (ed.), New Jersey (1984) 256–60.

Our recognition of the fact that law can be so morally defective as to merit not the slightest measure of respect enables us to perceive the need for distinctions that our ordinary ways of talking may obscure. No matter how we draw these distinctions, however, they turn upon the moral fallibility of law.

III

Some might complain that I have not shown how to dissipate the apparent inconsistency in our beliefs about the law because I have not yet identified the source of that perceived tension. The very fact that we use terms like 'right' and 'obligation' to characterize both legal and moral relations and feel the need to deal with the threat of inconsistency may be taken as prima-facie evidence that there are significant non-contingent links between morality and law.

This may be explained as follows. Law is not simply a collection of standards that some people, who *claim* authority to do so, have laid down and are prepared to enforce. Legal standards are created, identified, and applied by those who *have* authority to do so. This very fact suggests a link between morality and law. While it may be granted that specific legal standards are not always justifiable on their merits and that legal systems may fall short of satisfying minimal moral standards, they may be held to merit respect, none the less, because they result from the exercise of legitimate authority.

This idea is connected with some contemporary positivistic theorizing about the law. It is widely believed, for example, that the existence, and therefore the authority, of law essentially involves the 'acceptance' by those who occupy official positions within a certain type of institution of the most fundamental rules of that institution. They characteristically take an 'internal attitude' towards those rules. When officials apply ordinary rules of law, they express this internal attitude by making 'committed judgements' about what the law requires or allows, or about legal rights and obligations.

Such committed judgements have something like moral force. Someone who makes a committed judgement expresses the conviction that either he or others have reason to comply voluntarily with the rules. I say 'either he or others' to cover the two versions of Hart's interpretation of committed judgements that are discussed by Postema. On one version, a committed judgement ascribing a legal obligation to someone implies that the person with the legal obligation (the subject) has a reason to comply; on the other version, a committed judgement implies only that the person making it (the official) has reason to respect and apply the rules.

Hart deliberately declines to assume that the implied reasons for action should be classified as 'moral'. But he does appear to mean that one who makes a committed judgement expresses the conviction that the reasons are sound. That is why I have said that these judgements are understood to have 'something like' moral force.

Hart distinguishes committed judgements from 'detached judgements' of law. They can be expressed by using the same words and are exactly alike except that detached judgements lack the semblance of moral force just mentioned. One who makes a detached judgement of, say, legal obligation does not thereby express the conviction that the rules provide sound reasons for action.

Detached judgements are important because they represent the fact that one can make legal judgements without assuming that law possesses moral force. Postema seems concerned that Hart's distinction between committed and detached judgements does not secure the positivistic separation of law and morals. From the distinction it does not follow that law in fact lacks moral force. As I suggested when the analogous point came up earlier, this seems the proper way to understand such a distinction. It enables us to accommodate the separation of law and morals but the distinction, as drawn, would seem appropriately less controversial than the thoroughly positivistic doctrine.

The problem that we need to face can be set out in the following way. According to this type of positivistic theory, there cannot be law unless officials are prepared to make committed judgements. For there to be law, those judgements must themselves be true. But this seems to imply that there cannot be law unless the rules *succeed* in providing sound reasons for action (if not for those subject to them, then at least for those who administer them). Thus, the role of committed judgements in this sort of theory would seem to *contradict* the positivistic separation of law and morals!

This problem arises, however, only if we understand committed judgements in a problematical way. The difference between committed and detached judgements is that one expresses and the other fails to express a conviction that law provides sound reasons for action. The foregoing argument assumes that this corresponds to a difference in their *meaning*, and that all such elements of committed judgements must be *true* for there to be law. If the conviction that law provides sound reasons for action is part of the meaning of a committed judgement and must be true for there to be law, then there cannot be law unless there are at least some sound reasons for respecting its directives.

Now, I confess I am not persuaded that there cannot be law unless officials by and large sincerely believe that the law provides some sound reasons for action and, moreover, express that conviction in their legal judgements. But no matter; let us suppose *this* to be true. It does not follow that there cannot be law unless *their conviction* is true. For it is plausible to suppose that the alleged conviction can be distinguished from the specific content of the legal judgement and its grounds. It is one thing to believe that law requires or allows someone to behave in a certain way, for example, quite another to believe that someone has sound reason to respect the law. Similarly, it is one thing to *assert* the former belief, about the content of the law, another to *express* the latter belief, about the existence of someone's sound reason to respect the law.

We can suppose that what is common to committed and detached judgements is their identical meaning and that what distinguishes them is not part of the meaning of either. We can suppose that one who makes a committed judgement makes the same *assertion* as one who makes the corresponding detached judgement but additionally *expresses* (without asserting) the conviction that someone has a sound reason to respect the law. Not all things that are expressed by making an assertion are part of its meaning. We have so far been given no reason to suppose the contrary, that the conviction in question must be construed as part of the meaning of a committed judgement, and a part that must be true for there to be law. It would seem gratuitous to assume this, and we have some reason to doubt it. For, as we have been told, corresponding detached and committed judgements can be expressed in exactly the same terms, on the same substantive grounds. This gives a good reason to suppose that the added conviction distinguishing committed from detached judgements is *not* part of the former's meaning but is instead a belief that can be attributed to officials under certain circumstances and that can be expressed when they make their legal assertions.

There is added reason for construing committed judgements in this alternative way, if they are in fact essential to the existence of law. For we have reason to deny that the *truth* of such a conviction is essential to the existence of law. That is, we have reason to suppose that law sometimes fails to provide sound reasons for action. This reason is suggested by the moral judgements that lay behind the positivistic separation of law and morals. In sum, the existence of law might require that officials by and large believe that law provides some reason for action, but this *belief* might none the less be false.

We shoud not be misled by the moral pretensions of legal authority. Its claims are extraordinary. I have the capacity to create obligations for myself, but I cannot so easily impose obligations on others. And, when I can, conditions can diverge significantly from what one finds within the law.

It is generally assumed, for example, that parents have the moral capacity to impose obligations on their children. But there are limits to parental authority. The moral capacity of those who are charged with the care of children to impose obligations on those children is somewhat contingent on the caregivers' success and their benevolent intentions. Neither of these conditions are automatically or always satisfied. So, while one may doubt the aptness of a paternalistic model for legal authority, it makes no difference for present purposes. We cannot assume either the benevolence or the beneficence of those who make, interpret, and enforce the law.

People can acquire the authority to impose obligations on others within voluntary associations, as a consequence of the acceptance of such authority by those who freely participate in the associations. But this too does not seem an appropriate model for legal authority, as law does not confine its claims to those who freely participate or otherwise voluntarily acquiesce in such rule. And it is arguable that there are limits to the moral capacity of authority even when one voluntarily accepts it.

The idea that legal authority has automatic moral force is inherently problematic. It is implausible to suppose that legal authority merits some measure of respect when it fails to satisfy some significant moral conditions.

Postema would seem to agree. This may be obscured by his suggestion that one can 'legitimately infer that a person subject to a valid law has [a] moral obligation or reason to comply'. But his point is that such an inference can *sometimes* be made, 'under normal circumstances'. The problem is that Postema appears gratuitously to asume that the requisite moral conditions are 'normally' satisfied under legal systems. When one considers the conditions of most people under most legal systems that have existed, one finds, I believe, reason to doubt this assumption.

IV

Postema suggests, finally, that we should consider marrying the salvageable elements of what he calls 'naturalism' and 'conventionalism' to explain 'the point of view of the self-identified participants in legal practices' and 'the normativity of law'. I shall conclude with some comments on this proposal. It will be useful to quote a good part of one passage in which Postema sketches the resulting theory:

> On this view officials recognize, and are committed by their actions and arguments to recognize, that their joint acceptance of the criteria of validity must be linked to more general moral-political concerns. Only in this way can their appeal to those criteria, and the practice on which they rest provide the right sort of justification for their exercise of power in particular cases. But they also realize that *an essential part* of the case to be made for the criteria rests on the fact that ... the law they identify and administer is a collective product, and the process of determining its main outlines is essentially a collective and public process.

I have three difficulties with this suggestion. First, it is clear that these conditions are supposed to ensure that law has some relevant sort of 'normativity', but the latter itself is not entirely clear. The context suggests that Postema has in mind the sort of normativity that he associates with committed judgements, that is, the belief (which Postema might assume is true) that someone (either the official or the person subject to the law) has sound reason to respect the law.

The conditions sketched by Postema seem to require that officials make a conscientious effort to exercise power in a justifiable manner. If so, that might be ground for all to respect their efforts and intentions, but that does not seem adequate ground to respect their product. They could make a conscientious effort and still fail badly. Then there may be 'victims' (as Postema refers to them) of the system who would seem to have no good reason voluntarily to comply with its requirements. So, if the conditions provide reasons for anyone at all, it must be for the conscientious officials themselves. The question, then, is whether a conscientious effort automatically gives one sound reason to respect the result. I do not yet see that it does, so I am doubtful that Postema's conditions secure the relevant sort of 'normativity' for law.

Second, it is not clear to me that the law can merit respect only when officials are as conscientious and public-spirited as Postema's conditions suggest. I do not mean to underestimate the importance of such attitudes and concerns on the part of officials. But it seems possible that law could be, say, fair and useful even when those who make the law have quite different preoccupations. So I do not think that Postema has given us conditions that are generally necessary for law to merit respect, though they may be necessary if officials are themselves to believe sincerely that they have sound reason to respect it.

Finally, I am struck by the severely limited applicability of Postema's characterization of officials' attitudes and circumstances. Take, for example, the idea that the official determination of law (or at least 'its main outlines') 'is esentially a collective and public process'. This is put even more strongly when Postema refers to 'the constraint of seeking general consensus for one's account of the criteria and the basis of their authority'. In the first place, it does not seem generally true that in legal systems officials deliberately seek a 'general consensus', if that means anything like a fully informed and free agreement on the part of the community at large. In the second place, the class of those who exercise power can be extremely limited, relative to the community at large. So the 'consensus' that must be referred to here either can be so narrow as to provide no basis for the claim to legitimacy (in anything but the narrowest legalistic sense), or else the account is simply inapplicable to most legal systems.

4.1 The Obligation to Obey the Law[1]*

PHILIP SOPER

I PRELIMINARY ISSUES

Questions about the obligation to obey the law may be structural or substantive. Structural questions enquire into the characteristics of political obligation without assuming that there is any such thing. Substantive questions ask, within the constraints thus established, whether or not there is an obligation to obey.

In this paper, my concern is primarily with the substantive issues: I shall defend the view that there is a prima-facie obligation to obey the law. That such a view needs defending might surprise many people, for most Western thought seems to assume that the obligation to obey is one of the paradigms by reference to which one determines the parameters for other kinds of obligation. Hart, for example, in an influential article published thirty years ago,[2] compared political to promissory obligation and placed both in the special class of cases where the language of obligation is appropriate. Somewhat earlier, Socrates in the *Crito* even argued, according to some interpretations, that the obligation to obey is absolute—not subject to being outweighed by other considerations.[3] Few defend such a strong view today. But almost all discussions, until recently, have been consistent with the view that law imposes at least a prima-facie obligation to obey.[4]

A philosophical assumption, of course, does not become true through adverse possession—just because it has been around for a long time without being contested. Still, a tradition so long accepted ought to make one cautious about concluding, as one commentator does, that the

[1] This paper is adapted from a chapter in *A Theory of Law*, Harvard (1984).
[2] See H. L. A. Hart, 'Are There any Natural Rights', *Phil. Rev.* vol. 64 (1955), 175–91, reprinted in *Political Obligation*, A. Quinton (ed.) Oxford (1967), 53–66.
[3] See W. Powers, 'Structural Aspects of the Impact of Law on Moral Duty Within Utilitarianism and Social Contract Theory', *UCLA Law Review*, vol. 26, 1263–64 n.2 (noting inconsistencies in Socrates' views as expressed in the *Apology* and the *Crito*); A. Woozley, *Law and Obedience*, Chapel Hill, N.C. (1979).
[4] See, e.g., R. A. Wasserstrom, 'The Obligation to Obey the Law', *UCLA Law Review*, vol. 10 (1963), 780.

view that law does not obligate is now 'becoming more popular'.[5] A two-thousand year tradition ensures that such a claim cannot fail to be true so long as the qualifier 'more' is included; but even with that qualifier, 'popular' suggests a greater consensus or trend than the evidence or passage of time will yet support. Philosophical traditions, although they may not place the burden of proof on those who challenge them, do introduce the additional puzzle of explaining why the tradition came to be: why might we have assumed for so long that laws impose at least prima-facie obligation, and what might explain the sudden enlightenment?

A neglected structural question

Before turning to the substantive issues, I want to suggest a possible answer to this last question. I shall describe a structural enquiry that has been little explored in the literature and that may harbour an answer to the question of what has caused the recent divergence of views on the substantive question. I shall do no more at this point than describe the enquiry, leaving fuller exploration and resolution for another occasion. But I shall return briefly at the end of this paper to consider how the enquiry might affect the thesis developed here.

Structural questions are of two sorts. The more familiar kind are internal questions. These ask, for example, what one means by 'obligation' or by 'prima-facie' or by an obligation 'to obey the law'. An example of an internal structural constraint is the widely accepted idea that the obligation at issue is an obligation to obey law *in general*—just because it is the law—not because of some independent argument for compliance applicable only to particular laws or in a particular context.

Structural questions may also be comparative. These ask how the obligation to obey the law, if any, would compare to other obligations, or how the enquiry into political obligation relates to other moral enquiries. An example of a comparative structural argument is John Finnis's response to the claim that the obligation to obey, even if it did exist, would be trivial. Finnis notes that the argument for triviality, advanced by M. B. E. Smith, would apply with equal force to the obligation to keep a promise.[6] If Finnis is correct, as I believe he is, the obligation to obey is

---

[5] J. Raz, 'Authority and Consent', *Virginia Law Review*, vol. 67 (1981), 103 (citing: Raz, *The Authority of Law*, Oxford (1979), 233; A. J. Simmons, *Moral Principles and Political Obligations*, Princeton (1979); Woozley, *Law and Obedience*; M. T. B. Smith, 'Is There a Prime Facie Obligation to Obey the Law?', *Yale Law Journal*, vol. 82 (1973), 950; R. P. Wolff, *In Defense of Anarchism*, New York (1970)).

[6] See J. Finnis, *Natural Law and Natural Rights*, Oxford (1980), 345.

thus restored, as against this particular argument, to the same level of comparative importance as the obligation to keep a promise which for many people still seems a relatively safe paradigm. Another example of a comparative, structural enquiry is the question, explored in a recent symposium: what is the connection between conclusions about the obligation to obey the law and conclusions about the legitimacy of state authority?[7]

The enquiry that I have in mind resembles this last example in asking about the relationship between political obligation and another field of enquiry, rather than another type of obligation: what is the connection between conclusions about the obligation to obey the law and conclusions about the nature of law? Does the problem of explaining law's normativity, for example, have any bearing on the substantive question of political obligation?

That this enquiry has been neglected is easy to establish. Almost all discussions of the obligation to obey proceed on the apparent assumption that one does not need to turn first to legal theory to decide what 'law' is before considering whether it obligates. No one has done more than Hart to alert theorists to the connection between the *idea* of law and the *idea* of obligation. But this is still connection at the level of legal theory, not moral theory. Whether law connotes obligation and in what sense is a different question, most assume, from whether there is obligation in fact.

I said that proving that this enquiry has been neglected would not be difficult. The difficult part, some might think, is proving that the neglect is undeserved. What reason is there to think that the disputes about the nature of law or about the proper description of the normative attitude entailed by statements of legal obligation have any bearing on the issue of whether there is a moral obligation to obey? But this question invites an obvious retort; how can one decide whether law obligates if one *does not* know what 'law' is? In the parallel case of promising, arguments about whether and why promises obligate presumably begin with a shared understanding of what one means by 'promise', distinguishing promises, for example, from mere statements of future intent. What is the analogous understanding of 'law' with which moral philosophers begin when asking whether it obligates? And is it really possible that no matter what position one takes on the disputes within legal theory, the conclusion about the obligation to obey the law will remain unaffected?

[7] See Sartorius, 'Political Authority and Political Obligation', *Virginia Law Review*, vol. 67 (1981), 3; Raz, 'Authority and Consent', 103.

That this last question requires a negative answer should be clear. There is at least one view about the nature of law that would necessarily affect conclusions about the obligation to obey. That is the classical natural law view (in some versions, at least) that 'law' refers only to directives that already pass minimum moral muster. From this perspective, the conclusion that there is an obligation to obey follows from the definition of law.[8] Thus, critics who deny that there is such an obligation must be assuming that this natural law view is incorrect. One may think that this assumption is justified and easy to defend; the point remains that it is an implicit assumption about 'law' that establishes at least one connection between the substantive moral enquiry and a traditional strand of legal theory.[9]

What other implicit connections between political and legal theory might there be? An assumption about what law is *not*, after all, does not yet tell us anything about what philosophers assume law *is* when they deny that it obligates. It is this enquiry, into the positive characteristics of law implicitly assumed in discussions of political obligation, that may yield explanations for the recent change in view. For if current and traditional views about political obligation rest on different implicit ideas about what 'law' is, divergent conclusions are obviously possible.

To illustrate, consider M. B. E. Smith's recent attack on the existence of an obligation to obey. Smith begins by recalling H. A. Prichard's remark that 'the mere receipt of an order backed by force seems, if anything, to give rise to the duty of resisting, rather than obeying'.[10] If this casual reference is taken as a clue to the pre-analytic phenomenon whose capacity to obligate is in question, then the conclusion that there is no obligation seems to depend on the assumption that 'law' is not relevantly distinguishable from the coercive confrontation with any gunman. But the excuse for not pausing to defend this implicit assumption is not nearly as obvious as the excuse for implicitly rejecting the natural law view. If the pure idea of force—an order backed by a

[8] See Raz, *The Authority of Law*, 137.

[9] Wasserstrom is one of the few participants in the contemporary discussion to consider explicitly (and reject) the possible definitional connection between the concept of law and the obligation to obey, although he seems to leave open the possibility that there may be such a connection between law and prima-facie obligation. See Wasserstrom, 'The Obligation to Obey the Law', 786–90. The best discussion of the entire problem, at least within legal theory, may be found in J. Raz, *Practical Reason and Norms*, London (1975), 163–70.

[10] Smith, 'Is There a Prima Facie Obligation to Obey the Law?', 950 (quoting H. A. Prichard, 'Green's Principles of Political Obligation', in *Moral Obligation*, Oxford (1949), 54).

threat—is an inadequate model of law because it fails to convey even the idea of obligation, as Hart has shown, then it should hardly be surprising that such a concept does not entail obligation as a matter of moral philosophy either.

I said that I do not want to explore this issue in detail at this time. But if I am right that this structural question about the relationship between political and legal theory is unavoidably implicated in any discussion of the substantive question, then I too must indicate what I take 'law' to be in some acceptable pre-analytic sense before defending the view that law obligates. How does one do that without plunging into a full-scale examination of legal theory as a preface to examining political theory? In the end, I think that there is no good answer to this question. The positivist's claim that law and morals are separate need not entail the conclusion that legal and political theory are also separate; indeed, I argue elsewhere that the contrary is the case.[11] For the purposes of this paper, however, I propose to shortcut the problem in two ways. First, instead of asking whether law obligates, I shall ask what 'law' would have to be if it were to obligate. This hypothetical approach allows one to establish the conditions that must be met if political obligation is ever to exist; it leaves open the question whether 'legal system' or 'law' designates just those regimes or directives that satisfy those conditions. Second, even the hypothetical question—what must law be if it is to obligate?—assumes some pre-analytic phenomenon to which 'law' refers. I shall at the outset take that phenomenon to be what is implicit in Prichard's remark about orders and threats. I shall start, that is, with the concept of the purely coercive social organization with which almost all legal theorists begin in describing the basic features of legal systems. One would no doubt want to add that such coercive systems are supreme and comprehensive in ways that differentiate them from lesser organizations like social clubs. The important point is that it is not necessary at this stage to distinguish this pre-analytic idea from what Hart has called the 'gunman situation writ large'. Rather than ask, as Hart does, what alterations one must make in this coercive model in order to yield a correct legal theory, I shall ask what alterations one must make in order to yield political obligation.

Terminology

I shall begin by setting out the structural constraints that will guide the

---

[11] See P. Soper, *A Theory of Law*.

rest of the discussion. My claim is that there is a prima-facie obligation to obey the law. By 'prima-facie' I intend the generally accepted distinction between an obligation that can be outweighed in appropriate circumstances by other obligations, as opposed to one that is absolute. By 'obligation' I mean only some moral reason to do what the law requires. Thus, disputes about whether 'obligation' is a stronger concept than the morally correct, or discussions about the relationship between 'obligation' and 'duty', I shall take to be irrelevant to the present enquiry. Finally, by obligation 'to obey the law', I mean to accept the generally recognized constraint already referred to—the constraint of generality—according to which the moral duty or reason to obey must arise just because something is required by law, not for independent moral reasons.[12]

Three comments are in order about this list of structural assumptions. First, I do not believe that anything substantive hinges on the choice of terminology. The sense of the question is equally well conveyed by any of the standard formulations of meta-ethics. Thus, one could just as easily ask what law must be to entail a moral reason, however weak, or a prima-facie obligation or duty, however weak, to obey. What is essential is the idea that one is seeking a basis for even the most minimal attitude of moral respect for the law.

Second, it is worth noting that the question I have put is at the other extreme from the question posed by some versions of natural law theory. Instead of defining law to ensure that it always obligates, I seek an account that explains why it has any tendency to obligate at all. In this way, one preserves an independent concept of law, distinct from that of morality, while at the same time leaving room for the intuition that law has some moral authority.

Finally, I shall anticipate the objection that the virtue just described is also a vice in that it seeks too modest an account of the moral authority of law. Political obligation, the objection would continue, is a much stronger bond than minimal respect, and thus an account that justifies the latter may yet fail to establish the former. To this, two replies suffice.

---

[12] Recognition of this constraint on any successful solution to the problem of political obligation is widespread. See Smith, 'Is there a Prima Facie Obligation to Obey the Law?', 951–2; Raz, *The Authority of Law*, 233–4; A. J. Simmons, *Moral Principles and Political Obligations*, 30–5.

In addition to the constraint of generality, it is sometimes suggested that there is also a constraint of specificity: a requirement that a unique obligation be established between a citizen and his country. Thus, Simmons claims that an obligation to support 'just' governments would violate this constraint by leading to an obligation toward all such

First, to provide even a minimal basis for the moral authority of law is an accomplishment that some critics now claim to be impossible.[13] Secondly, once it is conceded that the political bond is not absolute, the only problem that remains concerns how much weight to accord to the obligation—a nuance that, like the choice of terminology itself, may be allowed to escape us as it undoubtedly escapes the ordinary citizen or, for that matter, as it escapes the attention of most theorists. Moral philosophy, after all, is notorious for its inability to assign weights to, as opposed to characterizing the form and ground of, the normative requirements of life.

II THE FAILURE OF THE STANDARD ARGUMENTS

To show that there is a prima-facie obligation to obey requires one either to rescue one of the standard arguments from the assault of recent theorists, or to develop a new argument. The arguments under assault are of two main sorts. The first is a straightforward utilitarian defence of obligation; the second analogizes political obligation to, or tries to subsume it under, one or more standard paradigms such as promise, estoppel, or fair play. Hart's views, set forth briefly in the article mentioned earlier, are of the latter sort; they provide the starting point for recent analyses of what is now called the argument from fair play.[14]

A Utilitarianism

Before considering Hart's suggestion and the possibilities for its defence, it is worth noting why the other standard arguments are thought to fail. Utilitarian arguments typically begin by positing that legal systems, however imperfect, are better than no law at all. This

governments in existence at a given time. See ibid., 31–2. Simmons's example, however, violates the constraint of generality (the obligation arises because the government is just, not because the directive is law). Moreover, to make specificity into an independent constraint seems at best unnecessary and at worst misleading. The problem of political obligation begins with a confrontation with force. It may turn out that this *de facto* authority is legitimate only in certain cases, for example between a country and its citizens (although the common intuition probably is that there is an obligation to obey the laws of the country one visits). But there is no need to pre-judge this issue in advance of the attempt to distinguish those situations of effective force that are legitimate from those that are not.

[13] See, e.g., Raz, *The Authority of Law*, 235, arguing that 'obligation' to obey means more than merely having a good faith reason to obey, but that even in this 'modest' sense there is no such obligation.

[14] A. J. Simmons suggests that the principle was first given this name by John Rawls, see Simmons, *Moral Principles and Political Obligations*, 213 n.1; Rawls, 'Legal Obligation and the Duty of Fair Play', in Sidney Hook (ed.) *Law and Philosophy*, New York (1964), 9–10.

assumption is then coupled to a second assumption, namely, that any act of disobedience threatens or endangers the system. These two premisses, it is claimed, yield the conclusion that there is an obligation to obey the law. The invalidity of the argument is due to the implausibility of the second premiss: laws can be and are regularly disobeyed without endangering the legal system. Indeed, sometimes disobedience has beneficial effects on the system. Thus the argument establishes at best only an obligation to obey whenever it would maximize utility to do so, not just because something is law; it fails to satisfy the constraint of generality.

I shall not try to rescue this argument by considering, for example, whether one could shore up the implausible second premiss through some form of rule utilitarianism. First, I doubt that any such attempt would succeed.[15] Secondly, the inevitable digression into arguments about how best to characterize and evaluate various forms of utilitarianism seems at best a sidetrack not peculiar to political obligation, and can be bypassed if there is another route to one's goal. Finally, there is an important objection to the utilitarian account which Hart raises and which has implications few commentators have noted. Even if one could establish the connection between any act of disobedience and the required undesirable effect on the legal system, that feature by itself would not explain political obligation because:

the obligation to obey . . . is something distinct from whatever other moral reasons there may be for obedience in terms of good consequences (e.g., the prevention of suffering); the obligation is due to the co-operating members of the society as such and not because they are human beings on whom it would be wrong to inflict suffering.[16]

In context, of course, this objection depends on restricting the language of obligation in a way that I have declined to do in this paper. Hart's point seems to be that the utilitarian argument explains at most what one 'ought' to do, not what one has an 'obligation' to do. To explain obligation requires one to focus *on the relationship* with the person to whom the obligation is owed, rather than on the effects of disobedience on that person's welfare or, even, on the system as a whole. This objection is thus unavailing if one does not distinguish between moral reasons in general and the special case of obligation. But Hart's

[15] See Smith, 'Is There a Prima Facie Obligation to Obey the Law?', 965.
[16] Hart, 'Are there any Natural Rights?' 62.

observation has significance beyond the linguistic or meta-ethical point and will become important later in comparing the argument from fair play to the argument of this paper.

B *Promise, estoppel, fair play*

I shall not review in detail here the reasons for the failure of promise and estoppel as paradigms for political obligation. Both encounter a similar objection. Based as they are either on voluntary or negligent action, they cannot apply to those who do not consent and are not negligent. Since the class of citizens who fit this dual description is not empty—or at the very least must be determined empirically—these paradigms necessarily fail to satisfy the constraint of generality. Whether one has an obligation because one has consented or because one has induced others to rely on an attitude of apparent moral respect for law will depend on contingent features, not true of all citizens wherever there is law.

The appeal of the fair play argument lies precisely in its contrast in this respect with these paradigms. The fair play argument purports to establish obligation simply through the benefits enjoyed within a legal system, rather than through conduct that could have been avoided. Hart states the argument 'in its bare schematic outline' as follows: 'When a number of persons conduct any joint enterprise according to rules and thus restrict their liberty, those who have submitted to these restrictions when required have a right to a similar submission from those who have benefited by their submission.'[17]

The major question that has been raised about this argument concerns the extent of the participation that is necessary before one who benefits from an enterprise can be said to be obligated to reciprocate. The problem can be seen by comparing the legal analogy of unjust enrichment. A claim for unjust enrichment, as developed in the common law, arises when benefits are received under circumstances that cannot be taken to imply a promise to pay, even though the benefits were not intended as a gift. If I overpay my account at the grocer's, I will have a legal claim for the excess even though the grocer made no promise to return the amount and was not responsible for my mistake. But though the receipt of benefits may be a necessary condition for the legal claim, it is clearly not a sufficient one. If, uninvited, I paint my neighbour's house while she is away, my neighbour has no obligation to pay for the benefits even though she may be delighted and enriched by

[17] Ibid.

the result and even though I may not have intended to confer a gift. The law in such cases brands me an 'officious intermeddler',[18] partly because my neighbour cannot easily return the benefits thrust on her, but also because I have deliberately avoided the obvious means of first ensuring through contract that—and how much—the exchange was desired. In contrast, for example, the doctor who renders aid to an unconscious victim, expecting to be paid, may recover for his services on the assumption that it was reasonable to think that the victim would have agreed to pay, though under the circumstances could not do so.[19]

A more appealing case than the officious intermeddler's is that of the person who cannot avoid giving me the free ride for which he later tries to bill me. But here, too, the law generally is sceptical of unjust enrichment claims. I am not liable to pay for the increased value of my house or to contribute my share when my neighbours embark on a clean-up campaign that results in benefits for all. Presumably, if one is not making an estoppel argument, my neighbours had self-interested reasons for their venture that do not depend on my willingness to contribute, even though I indirectly benefit. To be obligated to play fair, one must first be a player.

Both Robert Nozick and A. J. Simmons rely on examples such as these of free riders and officious intermeddlers (though without reference to the legal analogy) to conclude that the argument from fair play requires more than passive receipt and enjoyment of benefits.[20] For Nozick, the something more that is required is nothing short of consent so that the fair play argument collapses into promise. Only people who have 'agreed' to the enterprise or the rules will find that they are the kind of players who have obligations to do their share. Simmons agrees with Nozick that some kind of active acceptance of benefits is a prerequisite for obligation, but argues that such acceptance does not necessarily collapse into consent. Simmons's example, however, is unfortunate. He imagines a person first voting against a community project to dig a well, then, after the well is dug, taking the water while still declaring he does not consent to pay.[21] But one does not need theories of unjust enrichment to explain why actual consent is irrelevant to the obligation to pay when one snatches goods that *are* excludable and that have been

[18] See George Palmer, *Law of Restitution*, Boston (1978), vol. II, 359.
[19] Ibid., 374–83.
[20] See Robert Nozick, *Anarchy, State, and Utopia*, New York (1974), 93–5; Simmons, *Moral Principles and Political Obligations*, chap. V.
[21] Simmons, *Moral Principles and Political Obligations*, 126–7.

made available only on the condition that a price be paid. Theories of theft (conversion) or imputed promise will suffice here, and such theories fail to explain political obligation for oft-rehearsed reasons: the excludable benefits of society are few; they are not ordinarily offered with an accompanying price tag of obligation; and even if they were, most people would find it easy to avoid being in the position of having grabbed such benefits from those whose efforts went into making them.

What must be imagined if one is to distinguish unjust enrichment from promise or theft is a case in which one seizes benefits that are not the excludable property of others, but are nevertheless made possible only because of the efforts of others. Assume, for example, that Jones and Kafka are left property under identical provisions of a disputed will. Jones, but not Kafka, pursues the disputed point in litigation and succeeds in defending an interpretation that ensures that Kafka will now take his share without the need for further litigation. Is Kafka, in accepting these benefits that are clearly his, obligated to share the expenses of the litigation with Jones? Can Jones's attorney collect an additional fee from Kafka, who, after all, is not his client and never agreed to litigate the matter?

These questions, unfortunately, are just as vexing in law as in morals. Lawyers, for example, increasingly do recover from strangers for benefits produced through proceedings never requested by the latter.[22] Whether such special treatment represents a defensible exception to the general rule or marks instead the beginning of the rule's demise is a matter of academic speculation.[23]

One could, of course, dismiss this area of doubt as irrelevant in any event: the case just described involves unsolicited benefits that are happily seized, whereas the benefits of the rule of law, as noted, are not the sort that one has any chance to decline short of leaving the country. Indeed, this involuntary, passive stance of most of those who benefit from a legal system has led John Rawls (as well as Simmons) to conclude that the argument from fair play established obligation only for officials and others who affirmatively assume valuable positions or roles, not for the populace as a whole.[24]

I do not believe, however, that one can dismiss the fair play or unjust

[22] See generally, Palmer, *Law of Restitution*, vol. II, 431–5.
[23] See John Dawson, 'Lawyers and Involuntary Clients: Attorney Fees from Funds', *Harvard Law Review*, vol. 87 (1974), 1597; id, 'Lawyers and Involuntary Clients in Public Interest Litigation', *Harvard Law Review*, vol. 88 (1975), 849.
[24] See Rawls, *A Theory of Justice*, Harvard (1971), 113–14.

enrichment idea just because benefits were unsolicited and unreturnable. If, in order to develop his land, Jones drains water from his swamp thereby inevitably draining Kafka's swamp as well, the question whether Kafka, who can now develop his own land more profitably, should share the expenses of the drainage does not seem all that different from the question posed in the case of the will. The fact that Kafka cannot refuse to 'accept' the drained land may make us cautious in concluding how much or whether he actually values the improvement. And indeed the general legal result, perhaps for this reason, still gives Kafka in this case his 'free ride'.[25] But there are exceptions to the general rule that I have not explored. To explore the exceptions with the aim of trying to show how they do or do not apply in the political context is to place too much strain on the method, which already bears the burden of a difficult analogy between the general benefits of society and the more particular benefits that give rise to unjust enrichment claims in the law. It is enough to note that the exceptions underscore the possibility that here at least the moral issue may not coincide with the legal result. We are dealing, after all, with cases in which the producer of benefits had self-interested reasons for his actions, even without forced contribution from incidental beneficiaries. That may be reason enough for the law not to intervene, however valid the moral claim for contribution. Both the strength and the weakness of the moral claim are aptly summarized by John Dawson:

> The underlying assumption, which at times seems almost to rise to the level of a moral judgment, is that self-serving enterprise, which claims the privilege of defining its own incentives, should make its own way and is not entitled to subsidies. Discussion could end at this point if it were not for the source of the subsidy sought. If awarded, it would be drawn from those who themselves have gained without effort or contribution of their own and who can offer no more persuasive reason for refusal to contribute than: 'We never asked for it.' So there is always present that underground spring of resentment that was so successfully tapped by Henry George with the polemic phrase 'unearned increment', and even more successfully, long before, by the Book of Matthew, which described as a 'hard man' one who reaps where he did not sow.[26]

I shall not then reject out of hand the possible application of the unjust enrichment or fair play idea to the case of political obligation even though, I shall assume, one is dealing largely with unsolicited and

[25] See *Ulmer* v. *Farnsworth*, 80 Me. 500, 15 A. 65 (1888); Palmer, *Law of Restitution*, vol. II, 418–19.

[26] John Dawson, 'The Self-Serving Intermeddler', *Harvard Law Review*, vol. 87 (1974), 1409, 1457.

unreturnable benefits. For there is another objection to benefit-based theories of obligation that is even more problematic than those based on the application of the paradigm. This objection concerns the content of the obligation that the paradigm is supposed to yield. I have been rather loosely assuming that the obligation generated by benefits received from a legal system is the obligation to obey the law. In fact, however, the paradigm suggests only that the obligation is to return a proportionate share of the benefits received. Since not all submissions to law are beneficial, one does not necessarily find oneself faced with a general obligation to obey the law even if the paradigm applies. Instead, as Smith argues, one is faced only with the narrower obligation of obeying whenever it is beneficial to others to do so.[27] The paradigm again fails to satisfy the constraint of generality.

This objection brings us back to Hart's claim about the peculiar nature of obligation. If obligation arises because of the actual benefits or harms that result from disobedience, then Smith's objection seems unassailable. If, however, obligations arise, not because of the effect of action on another's welfare (objectively measured), but because of the special, subjective interest of the right-holder, then the objection is misplaced. I shall show later in this paper how this idea can be used to generate the specific content of an obligation to obey the law.

Although the applicability of the fair play idea thus remains in doubt, one can at least draw a few conclusions from this discussion to guide the attempt to develop an alternative theory. The strength of the argument from unjust enrichment depends on the motives and actions of both the benefactor and the recipient. The argument is weakest, indeed fails convincingly, when the benefactor acts 'officiously' to confer benefits precisely in the hope of charging for them without first securing consent. The argument is strongest when the benefactor has made a mistake, not easily chargeable to his own negligence. In between are the problem cases involving benefactors who are independently motivated by reasons of self-interest. On the recipient's side, the argument is weakest when the benefits cannot be rejected and are not even desired in the first place (in which case it is probably a mistake even to call them 'benefits'). The argument is strongest when the recipient indicates through word or deed that he values the benefits, is happy to have received them, and indeed would probably have taken steps to secure them himself even

[27] Smith, 'Is There a Prima Facie Obligation to Obey the Law?', 956–7.

though we cannot put that conclusion to the test where the benefits are literally unreturnable or unrefusable.

This last observation may explain the appeal of the fair play argument. The appeal may stem from the fact that most people concede that there are more benefits than burdens in the rule of law. This claim about the value of law in general also constitutes, we have seen, the first and more plausible of the two premises in the utilitarian argument, considered earlier. The problem is to develop an argument for political obligation that preserves this appeal of the fair play argument, while avoiding the objections that theory encounters in application.

III A FRESH START; AUTONOMY AND AUTHORITY

A *Wilful assent and the paradigms of complicity*

There are other routes to establishing obligation than those that begin with standard paradigms. Some discussions, for example, appeal directly to an intuitive understanding of the ideas of autonomy and authority in an effort to determine whether these ideas are ever compatible. Recasting the problem of political obligation into the problem of reconciling autonomy and authority helps explain, in fact, the failure of two of the standard paradigms. Promise and estoppel both generate obligations structured in some sense around actions within the control of the individual. This structure confronts the individual with his responsibility for the situation in which he finds himself, thus reducing to some degree the clash between authority and autonomy. The theories fail in the political context because the confrontation of the individual with the legal order is not the product of wilful or negligent action at all.

B *Rational assent and the paradigms of respect*

Because complicity-based paradigms of obligation do not apply to all citizens, the only course left is to construct an argument that appeals directly to the beliefs and attitudes of rational individuals in situations analogous to the situation one confronts in the case of law. I shall do so by considering two other paradigms, also frequently discussed in the literature. Both share a critical feature with the political situation and the fair play argument in that both describe confrontations with *de facto* assertions of authority in circumstances not chargeable in any normal sense to the complicity of the individual.

The first paradigm, that of the family, has a long history as a possible analogy for political obligation. Thus Socrates in the *Crito* personifies the laws and has them speak in a tone which, if the matter were not so serious, would sound like an original stereotype of the guilt-inducing parent, confronting the thankless 'child':

Are you not grateful to those of us laws which were instituted for this end, for requiring your father to give you a cultural and physical education? . . . We have brought you into the world and reared you and educated you, and given you and all your fellow citizens a share in all the good things at our disposal.[28]

Modern commentators have both defended and attacked the paradigm of filial duty as an analogy for political obligation.[29] But defenders and attackers alike centre their discussions once again on benefits conferred. This preoccupation with duties arising from benefits makes it difficult to distinguish the alleged debt of gratitude from the obligations based on unjust enrichment that have already been considered. Indeed, one recent summary of the necessary conditions for a debt of gratitude coincides remarkably with the conditions necessary for legal recovery on a theory of unjust enrichment in such cases as those of the doctor rendering aid to the unconscious victim.[30]

This focus on benefits still leaves unsolved the problem of deriving the specific content of an obligation to obey the law. (It is one thing to berate a child for ingratitude and conclude that he ought therefore to pick up the phone and call; it is quite another to suggest that gratitude requires that he drink up the hemlock and die.) More fundamentally, the focus on benefits overlooks the most significant aspects of the confrontation of child with parent. What is it that lessens the impact of the parental directive on the child's increasing sense of autonomy? What is it that distinguishes a parent's or guardian's directive from that of a playground peer or an adult stranger who just happens to be momentarily in a position to enforce a command?

It should not be difficult to see plausible answers to these questions that do not depend on being able to show *specific* rewards reaped during one's life in the family. The confrontation of two personalities, one demanding compliance, the other resisting, is too basic a clash to be mediated by the plea to 'consider all I've done for you'—particularly

---

[28] Plato, *Crito*, 50d–51d.
[29] Compare A. C. Ewing, *The Individual, the State, and World Government*, New York (1947), 218, with Simmons, *Moral Principles and Political Obligations*, chap. VII.
[30] Compare Simmons, *Moral Principles and Political Obligations*, 178, with *Restatement of Restitution*, St. Paul (1937), 483–4.

when what was done was usually motivated in the first place by feelings of benevolence or by the immediate rewards of parenting, rather than by expectations of future repayment. (The 'debt' never arose in the first place or has long since been repaid.) More likely, mediation occurs because there is something about the particular person the child confronts that unites child and parent at the same time that the conflict repels. Ideally, what unites is love, which need not be biologically based and which need not reflect notions of gratitude. If those I care about (for whatever reason) demand my compliance, my concern *for them* (not for what they have done for me) is one reason to comply, one reason to consider along with the other reasons produced by my independent evaluation of the action on its merits. But love is only the ideal end of the available spectrum for mediating this clash of will. At the other extreme, the appeal need be only to the child's recognition of the value of some family, some parent or guardian, compared to the alternative of none at all. That concession provides a basis for respect for the framework of the family, for the kind of values and functions it serves. From this basis of respect for the general enterprise, one need add only one additional requirement in order to lay a basis as well for respect for the particular person and particular enterprise one confronts. That is the requirement that the parent or guardian is in good faith trying to act in the interests of the child by acting in the interests of the family as a whole.

These two features of the situation may be summarized in the following hypothetical reaction to any confrontation with authority:

1.   Here is a job—directing an enterprise—that I concede someone needs to do.

2.   The person who just happens to be in charge is trying to do that job in good faith, taking my interests into account along with the interests of others who also find themselves in the same scheme.

3.   That effort deserves my respect and provides me with a moral reason to go along (although at some point this reason may be outweighed by the seriousness of the error I think is being made).

One could perhaps be more explicit about the ultimate source of this attitude of respect.[31] One could connect the above reaction, for ex-

---

[31] For a cogent analysis that resembles the argument of this paper in finding both governmental and parental authority in necessity rather than in benefits conferred, see Elizabeth Anscombe, 'On the Sources of the Authority of the State', *Ratio*, vol. 20 (1978), 1, 6. See also A. Honoré, 'Must We Obey? Necessity as a Ground of Obligation', *Virginia Law Review*, vol. 67 (1981), 39.

ample, to themes in moral philosophy and literature that stress the virtue of empathy (how would I want others to respond if I happened to be in charge), and the dangers of hubris ('I could, after all, be wrong about what ought to be done'). But at some point, 'proof' in ethics cannot go beyond putting an account in a way that rings true in light of experience and reflection.

Consider then a second example: the lifeboat. Like the family, the idea of the lifeboat also recommended itself to political theorists as a source of analogy long before the image came to be applied metaphorically to the earth as a whole. The source of its appeal is identical to that of the family. Here is another situation, less commonly experienced but easily imagined, in which one confronts demands for compliance unmediated by complicity in creating the situation. Indeed Hume uses the boat analogy to parody arguments seeking to infer tacit consent from residence. 'We may as well assert that a man, by remaining in a vessel, freely consents to the dominion of the master; though he was carried on board while asleep and must leap into the ocean, and perish, the moment he leaves her.'[32]

Assume, then, a variant of Hume's case (omitting the element of abduction). One wakens, following shipwreck let us say, to discover someone in *de facto* control issuing orders. What reason does one have to obey? We have already noted that answers can be given to this question that do not imply respect for authority *simpliciter*. Thus R. P. Wolff uses a similar example to show that one might obey the particular person in charge 'since the confusion caused by disobeying him would be generally harmful'.[33] The failure of this utilitarian argument contrasts instructively with the alternative account of the basis for respect that I am advancing here. On confronting the situation, two things become obvious. First, somebody needs to be giving orders. A single boat and a single tiller require conflicting opinions about the direction to steer to be resolved. Secondly, although I may have views of my own about the direction to sail, the forced submission to the opposing views of those in charge loses some of its sting if my views and arguments are considered and in good faith rejected. That provides a basis for respect in my acknowledgement that those in charge, after taking my interests into account, are doing no less than I could if I were in charge—namely, acting in good faith as they think best for all. Of course, if I feel strongly

---

[32] Hume, 'Of the Original Contract', in Charles Henkel (ed.) *David Hume's Political Essays*, New York (1953), 56.
[33] Wolff, *In Defense of Anarchism*, 16.

that the orders given will lead to disaster, I may decide I have no ultimate obligation to comply, but should instead try to sabotage the existing leadership. The point is that one now has a basis for prima-facie obligation that does not depend on an implausible connection between disobedience and the success of the enterprise. What is relevant is not the effect of my decision on the venture, but the effect on the person who stands in front of me trying to do his best to accomplish ends thought to advance the interests of the group as a whole, including myself.

IV   A THEORY OF POLITICAL OBLIGATION

I have said enough to make fairly transparent the features I claim are sufficient to establish political obligation. Those features are: 1) the fact that the enterprise of law in general (including the particular system that confronts an individual, defective though it may be) is better than no law at all; 2) a good faith effort by those in charge to govern in the interests of the entire community, including the dissenting individual.

I shall explore these features and strengthen the plausibility of the claim that they are sufficient conditions for obligation in three steps. First, I shall consider why it is that both features are necessary. Second, I shall consider how this theory of political obligation might be expressed in either utilitarian or deontological terms. Finally, I shall connect the theory with the discussion of the neglected structural enquiry with which this paper began and describe some issues that seem to require further investigation.

A   *The value of law and the mutuality of respect*

By insisting that obligation exists only if legal systems are in fact better than no law at all one introduces a gap into the solution of the problem of political obligation. In essence one concedes that there is no obligation if the anarchist is correct in claiming that all legal systems are undesirable or immoral. To complete the argument, one would have to show that the anarchist is wrong.

I shall not undertake this task in any systematic way for several reasons. First, the standard explanations for the value of law in promoting security and stability are almost universally accepted. One need not agree with Hobbes that security is the entire *raison d'être* of the state in order to acknowledge that it is one very good reason for preferring organized society to the state of nature. Secondly, it is important to note how tiny the gap in the proof is and how starkly the conclusion reached here contrasts with the conclusion of current theorists who deny the existence of obligation whether or not anarchism is correct. It is, after all, hard to find a real, live anarchist among contemporary political theorists. Even those most critical of state intrusions on individual liberty remain persuaded of the legitimacy of the state, however ultra-minimal.[34] Thus the practical effect of the theory on the ordinary citizen who wants to know whether he has a duty to obey is not likely to be affected by noting that the theory assumes the falsity of the anarchist's view. Finally, as I have previously noted in considering the most common utilitarian argument for obligation, the suspect premiss in that argument is the assertion of a connection between disobedience and the collapse of the legal system, not the claim that legal systems in general are valuable.

Instead of recounting familiar arguments for rejecting anarchism it is more important to understand why it matters whether the anarchist is correct. The requirement that there be positive value in the type of enterprise an individual confronts stems from the need to accommodate the concern for autonomy. That the requirement accomplishes this much, at least where the individual *himself acknowledges* the value of the enterprise, is reinforced by the earlier discussion of the nature of autonomy as well as by the conclusions reached in connection with the unjust enrichment paradigm. Let us recall that the strongest claims of unjust enrichment arise when the person benefited affirms as valuable the choices that others, for whatever reasons, have made. Thus this requirement—that the value of law be conceded—connects with the most plausible aspect of the appeal to benefit-based theories of obligation.

A more difficult question is whether the individual who honestly believes all law is bad has any obligation. Even if one assumes his belief is wrong, there is now no shared value between him and those in charge. The assault on autonomy must be assuaged by the appeal to reason alone, rather than by the fact of a shared commitment. This difficulty, however, is simply a variation on a familiar problem in moral theory. Individuals (subjectively) can only do what they think is right, even though (objectively) they may be wrong. One who thinks anarchism is correct will conclude he has no obligation. But if he is wrong about anarchism, he will also be wrong (objectively) about whether he has an obligation.

[34] See Nozick, *Anarchy, State and Utopia*, 68.

But why must one assume that the anarchist is wrong? Suppose he is right. Does the theory not suggest that one could construct an argument for obligation even in that case? I have stressed, after all, the link between obligation and the idea that people who have good faith disagreements about value judgements deserve moral respect as individuals equally concerned with the struggle to identify and defend value. Why not say, then, that the anarchist, even if he is correct in his views, has a minimal basis for respect for the law—a prima-facie obligation to obey—based on the same dual considerations of a shared commitment to the search for truth and humility about the correctness of one's own conclusions?

This question illumines the dangers of moving so quickly between the concepts of 'respect' and 'obligation'. Although I shall continue to defend the decision to use these concepts interchangeably, one must be careful to recall that it is respect *for the law* that is in question. Although the theory developed here ultimately rests on an appeal to the respect that other moral beings deserve (as, indeed, any moral theory must if it is to steer clear of mysticism), it nevertheless remains a theory that links respect to the will of others as expressed in law. Respect for the wishes of others as expressed apart from law may obligate the anarchist to listen to, and seriously consider, opposed views; but if the anarchist is correct about the lack of value of law in general his obligation cannot extend even prima-facie to require compliance except by undermining autonomy. However much he may remain connected to others in some respects—for example, in the commitment to the search for truth—as respects the dispute over the value of law the anarchist is not connected to those he confronts either objectively through reason, nor subjectively through shared values.

It may now seem that I have defended the claim that obligation depends on the falsity of anarchism with an explanation that would apply as well in less extreme cases. One may, for example, admit to the value of law in general and yet deny the value of a particular legal system or of a particular law. After all, what is at issue when it comes to the demand for compliance is *this* system, *this* law, not legal systems in general. If autonomy is strong enough to prevent obligation attaching in case there is no value to law in general, then why does a particular, worthless, legal system not require only that one listen, not that one obey?

In some cases this conclusion is appropriate. A particular legal system that has so deteriorated as to deny even the minimal security that makes the general enterprise valuable will not yield obligation. But the same conclusion does not hold just because a particular law is immoral or a particular system unjust—socialist instead of capitalist, or vice versa.

This claim, that there is a morally relevant difference between the value of the enterprise and the value of a particular law or legal system, rests on the plausibility of distinguishing disagreements about the *kind* of legal system that is best from disagreements about whether any legal system is defensible at all. The former disputes raise central issues in moral and political philosophy whose intractibility is reflected in stubbornly opposed theories of distributive justice and in conflicting solutions to the problem of proportioning state power to individual prerogative. Arguments about these issues, like arguments about the merits of particular laws, are part of the process by which disagreement is resolved. Arguments about the legitimacy of the state, in contrast, are seldom heard outside an academic context. In one sense, the choice between anarchy and law is both more fundamental and at the same time less open to individuals than the choice of types of law or type of legal system. For these reasons, if the anarchist is correct, the only option open consistent with his autonomy is moral escape from the obligation to obey the law. But for those who accept the value of law, the story is different. Disagreements now are measured in degree, not kind. Coupled with the second requirement—good-faith concern for the community as a whole—the possibility of persuasion appears both mutual and real in proportion to the merits of the case and the openness of the society.[35]

Any other conclusion, of course, makes autonomy so strong a concept that by definition the problem of political obligation cannot be solved. There is just as much reason to suspect definitions that make the problem unsolvable as there is to suspect definitions that solve the problem by fiat (as in the case of some natural law theories). If the persistent efforts of political theorists are accepted as evidence that one is dealing with a real phenomenon, then there is much to be said for a

---

[35] The point can also be made conceptually. Imagine attempting to argue along the lines of this paper that the only 'enterprise' that is necessary is one that involves a limited exercise of force. Any state that exceeds these limits, by regulating, for example, private affairs as well as open clashes, is not the kind of enterprise that triggers the obligation of respect. Such an argument could succeed only if the concept of a state itself entailed inherent limits of the sort described. But if the idea of a state includes all régimes with a monopoly on force, then arguments about whether a particular state is exceeding its proper bounds are normative arguments about how the monopoly on force should be used, not arguments which show that the regime in question is no longer an instance of the basic enterprise. The question, in short, is whether one is deriving alleged limits on the obligation to obey from the concept of a state, or from the concept of a good state.

theory of obligation that depends on the falsity of anarchism but does not further depend on the correctness of the underlying political or moral principles of a particular society.

This discussion also helps explain the importance of the second condition for obligation. Acknowledgement of the value of law arises out of a rational appraisal of one's self-interest in the maintenance of a coercive social order. To confront, then, a particular system that ignores one's self-interest undercuts the basis for the bond between ruler and ruled. Respect, if it is owed, is also owing and for essentially similar reasons: my acknowledgement that you are trying to do a job that must be done and that you think requires my compliance is mirrored by and dependent on your acknowledgement in turn of my own autonomy. And in each case the specific content of the resulting obligation is determined by the nature of the interests of the person confronted. Respect for those in charge is a reason for doing what these persons believe I should do: comply with the law. Conversely, respect for my autonomy in evaluating for myself the extent to which law reflects my interests requires that rulers at least consider those interests in exercising their authority.

B   Standard theories compared

The last observation indicates how the problem of translating theoretical arguments for obligation into the specific obligation to obey the law is met by a theory that focuses on the personal encounter with authority. We saw that a general utilitarian argument that focuses on the effects of disobedience on the enterprise would at best establish only an obligation to perform optimific acts, not to obey all laws. In contrast, focus on the person seeking my compliance gives a reason to do what is desired quite apart from its overall effects on the enterprise. Similarly, by dispensing with specific benefits received as the basis for the obligation, one avoids the objection that the only obligation is to obey whenever it is actually beneficial to do so. In legal terms, 'benefits' here are to be measured subjectively, by the wishes of the person whose efforts generate the obligation, not by some objective or market measure of 'value'.[36]

The reason why the content of my obligation is determined in part by what others desire stems from the fact that the theory sketched here combines both objective and subjective elements. Other citizens[37] have

[36] See generally, D. Dobbs, *Handbook on the Law of Remedies*, St. Paul (1973), 261–2.

[37] I have cast the theory of this paper in terms of respect for officials or 'those in charge' only because, in Hart's terms, that is the limiting case of law. Only 'officials' need accept the basic rules in order to have a legal system. In most cases, however, as Hart recognizes,

a 'right' to my compliance with their desires, as expressed in the laws they accept, partly because of the objective value of legal systems, but partly also because of their subjective good faith in holding out the system as just. The content of my obligation thus also has both objective and subjective components. Objectively, one sometimes shows respect by doing the right thing, rather than what is desired. But this possibility should not obscure the fact that respect for good faith *effort* is shown by complying with (rewarding) subjective desire. This tension between rewarding honest (but unsuccessful) effort on the one hand, and, on the other, rewarding only successful effort is a familiar one in daily life (consider children and students). The tension does not appear just because in a particular case the pull toward doing what is objectively correct proves stronger than the pull toward rewarding good faith attempts to discover what is correct. That is why, after all, the obligation is only prima facie. (Going along, even when others are wrong, 'only encourages them' to keep getting it wrong; on the other hand, refusing to go along where others tried hard to get it right, discourages the effort of pursuing justice, and encourages reliance on force alone.)

This way of putting the matter may lead one to try to recast the argument in 'simpler' utilitarian terms in the following manner. If satisfaction of desires is a good thing, then the fact that by obeying I will please the person who demands my compliance provides a reason to obey. Thus there is always a reason to obey the law simply in the fact that some good will result: that is, some people will be pleased. This positive consequence of obedience is then to be weighed against negative consequences in deciding what my ultimate obligation is.

This argument makes the gunman and the taxman once again indistinguishable. Pleasing the gunman would also have to count as a reason to obey. Though I have tried to skirt the problem of explaining just what a prima facie obligation or reason is, this example should caution against an interpretation that yields a prima-facie obligation to perform any act, however obviously outrageous, just because some good effects would be realized along with the bad. As Smith puts it, we should hardly say that one has a prima-facie obligation to kill the next person one meets just because that act will have some beneficial effect on the over-population problem.[38]

---

the system will enjoy the support and acceptance of many citizens as well as officials. In these cases, those who deserve respect under the theory will include all who accept and support the system and urge compliance with its laws—citizens as well as officials.

[38] Smith, 'Is There a Prima Facie Obligation to Obey the Law?', 965.

To see what has gone wrong and how one might cast the argument in acceptable utilitarian terms, compare the gunman with the beggar. In the latter case, it is not nearly so implausible to suggest that the satisfaction the beggar receives from my alms is a good reason to heed his request, although at some point it will be outweighed by the disutility to me of parting with the money. Indeed some utilitarians argue forcefully that utilitarianism requires giving relief to the severely distressed until one is left with just enough for one's own subsistence. But suppose now that the beggar displays the gun he has been concealing all along beneath his coat and thus makes clear that if his appeal to conscience fails, he will resort to force to get his way. On the assumption that the relative utilities of parting with and receiving the money remain unchanged, one might think that the gun should be irrelevant and that the utilitarian should still conclude that one should hand over the money.

This conclusion, I take it, is completely counter-intuitive. The beggar who displays the gun thereby destroys whatever sympathy I may have had for his appeal to me as a fellow human being in distress. It is as if, once again, the insult to my autonomy represented by the gun cancels out whatever moral, rational basis underlay the initial appeal for help. The utilitarian has familiar devices for accommodating this intuition in his theory. He will shift his focus from the relative utilities of these two persons immediately before and after the transient encounter, and consider instead 'the long run' and the effects on 'overall' utility if gunmen's demands were so easily accorded moral sanction. In so doing he can now suggest quite reasonably that more harm than good will result from following a rule (of thumb or of steel) that money should be given to gunmen on the same basis as to beggars. If one did not recognize the illegitimacy of the resort to force, one could expect an increase in muggings and a distortion of the calculation of relative utilities in ways that make one confident that overall utility would probably decline rather than increase.

If this is what prima-facie obligation means for the utilitarian, one can construct a similar argument for the theory of political obligation developed here. One begins with the same initial premiss of the argument considered earlier: legal systems are better than the alternative of no law at all (the plausible premiss). The second premiss connects disobedience, not to the disintegration of the legal system (the implausible premiss), but to the subjective satisfactions to be gained by those who desire my compliance. This way of putting the argument brings to the fore the essential shift in the account I have given, focusing on the persons one confronts and their response to my disobedience rather than on the effects of disobedience on the enterprise itself. Disobedience cannot easily be linked to societal disintegration. But it can be linked in an ascending scale to sadness, disappointment, concern, anxiety, and fear on the part of those who think the laws are important and my obedience desirable.

Recasting the utilitarian argument also reveals the role of the initial premiss in the argument and the basis for its appeal. Recognition of the value of legal systems is necessary, not to show that an admittedly valuable thing is endangered by disobedience, but to counteract the insult from the threat of force that would otherwise cancel out the respect owing to those who care about my obedience. The premiss thus serves to distinguish legal systems from gunmen and restores credibility to the utilitarian argument that failed in the case of the mugger: the force that backs the legal demand for compliance is now seen, not as an unwanted and ultimately counter-productive feature of the encounter, but as an aspect of a coercive social order which, by hypothesis, is admitted to represent an overall gain in utility.

The above sketch of how a utilitarian might recast the argument for political obligation is intended to aid in understanding the features of the theory rather than as a claim that the theory is essentially utilitarian.[39] Indeed, it should be clear that one could just as easily cast the argument in non-utilitarian terms. In fact the terminology I have used sits much more comfortably with the tradition that traces the source of all moral obligation to the respect that is due to other, equally autonomous, rational beings, equally concerned for each other.

One final observation is in order. My concern has been to show that

[39] Although I have tried to give a utilitarian cast to the theory, mainly in order to highlight the change that has been made in the usual argument, I confess that the utilitarian model fits uncomfortably. Thus, one might suggest that a theory based on the reactions of others to one's disobedience only counsels keeping disobedience secret, giving rise to obligation only where disobedience is likely to be discovered. In that case, there would be no 'generic' solution to the problem of political obligation. One may perhaps counter that the possibility of discovery (unlike the possibility that trivial acts of disobedience will adversely affect the system) can never safely be ruled out (one might confess, if nothing else), and that this standing possibility is all one needs for a prima-facie case of obligation (a rule of thumb?). It seems more persuasive to suggest that it is the *hypothetical* discovery that one must consider, and thus act like any other rational person in society—a Kantian explanation that forces one to evaluate action from the viewpoint of the rational other, rather than the contingent, actual other. In the end, I suspect difficulties with the utilitarian account stem from the incoherence of the idea of prima-facie obligation itself within a utilitarian theory.

there is a prima-facie obligation to obey the law, not to indicate how strong the obligation is or in what circumstances it must yield to conflicting obligations. But the theory has relevance for the latter problem by indicating what to look for in assessing the weight of the obligation. One critic, for example, suggests that even if there were an obligation to obey the law, it would be of trivial weight. This, we are told, is because:

a prima facie obligation is a serious one if, and only if, an act which violates that obligation and fulfills no other is seriously wrong; and second, a prima facie obligation is a serious one if, and only if, violation of it will make considerably worse an act which on other grounds is already wrong.[40]

Thus murder which is already wrong is not made significantly more so because it is also against the law. And morally trivial acts, like driving through a stop sign at two a.m. when no one is around, are not made serious because such acts violate the law.

I suggested above that Finnis is correct in observing that the same tests for seriousness will likewise trivialize the prima-facie obligation to keep a promise.[41] Murder is not made more reprehensible because one promised not to kill. And a trivial act—running the stop sign—is not made seriously wrong because one promised never to run stop signs. An argument that so casually dismisses a tradition that takes promise as the paradigm of prima-facie obligation deserves to be met with some scepticism. But whatever one thinks about the strength of these two prima-facie obligations, to admit that the obligation to obey the law is on a par with (no less serious than) the obligation to keep promises is to solve the problem of political theory. Every theorist has assumed that consent-based theories provide a basis for obligation in the necessary sense if only they could be made to fit the facts of the political context. There would be little reason to explore the defects of such consent theories if, even with consent, disobedience is a 'mere pecadillo'.

The theory advanced here provides a key to the weight of the obligation to obey the law that does not trivialize the obligation and that probably reflects common sense conclusions. The seriousness of the obligation is directly proportional to the seriousness (as indicated no doubt by the severity of the attached sanctions) with which those who demand my compliance will view disobedience. If I do not believe that abortion is wrong, the intensity with which others hold the opposite

[40] Smith, 'Is There a Prima Facie Obligation to Obey the Law?', 970.
[41] See discussion at note 6, above.

moral view makes the obligation to obey a law against abortion strong, subject to being outweighed only by an equally strong moral view of my own (concerning the right to privacy, for example)—not by reasons of mere self-interest or convenience. Conversely, if no one cares much about running stop signs at two a.m., the breach of the law will be easier to justify. Ultimately some such explanation probably accounts for the doctrine of desuetude: a law on the books that the court concludes nobody cares about any more simply does not obligate—legally or otherwise. But any case that falls short of desuetude, any case in which I am potentially subject to legal sanction, by implication means that someone cares, however slightly. What matters is how much it matters to others.

V THE UNFINISHED AGENDA

Two conditions, I have argued, are sufficient to provide a moral reason to obey a coercive political directive. First, the directive must be part of a supremely effective coercive system, thus providing the security that makes legal systems preferable to no law at all. Secondly, the directives must be defended by those who accept and enforce them as 'just': in the interests of all, including the citizen whose obedience is in question. Several questions obviously remain to be explored.

The first involves the structural problem mentioned at the outset of this paper. Does 'law' or 'legal system' in fact refer only to regimes in which officials defend the justice of the accepted rules? If not, the theory fails to satisfy the constraint of generality. I shall not explore this question in detail here, but only note that the claim that 'law' does imply a good faith official belief in the justice of the system is supported in part by investigations of contemporary legal theorists.[42] I also note that counter-examples to the linguistic claim—regimes that one would clearly call 'legal' but in which there is no official belief in the justice of the system—are more difficult to find than counter-examples to the parallel natural law claim. That is because *belief* in the justice of a system is obviously both possible and frequently encountered, however unjust the system may be in fact.

Second, much obviously needs to be done in explaining what is meant by 'good faith' belief in the justice of a coercive system.

Finally, one might think that the modern state is a far cry from the

[42] See J. Raz, *The Authority of Law*, chaps. 4, 8; id., *Practical Reason and Norms*, 123–9, 146–8, 162–77.

paradigms of lifeboat and family which I used to construct a theory of obligation. Indeed, one may wonder whether the face-to-face confrontation that leads to respect in those paradigms can be said to have a counterpart at all when the confrontation in society is largely with institutions as impersonal as court and legislature or administrative agency. But behind courts and legislatures and agencies are people, and it is this sense, that there are people who are about the laws they enact, that warrants extrapolating from the simple case of personal, to the general case of political, obligation. One may concede that this sense of personal confrontation is impaired in proportion to the degree that structure, rather than people, control. The bureaucratization of the courts,[43] the unthinking invocation of standard ideologies, the conversion of response and dialogue into ritual and rote—all erode the sense that one confronts people who care and with it the case for obligation. But these are still largely tendencies, realized in varying degrees, rather than fully established aspects of most societies. As long as there are 'officials', in Hart's sense, whose acceptance of the basic rules makes law possible, there will be people who can, by accepting and defending those rules on moral grounds, fulfil the conditions specified here for obligation.[44] In this respect, the amendment one must make to Hart's

[43] See J. Vining, 'Justice, Bureaucracy, and Legal Method', *Mich. Law Review*, vol. 80 (1981), 248; id., *Legal Identity*, New Haven (1978).

[44] The claim that the State is too impersonal to justify the analogy with more intimate relationships can be understood in two ways. First, one might be claiming that there simply are no persons 'out there' who could be the object of respect under this theory. Similar claims have been made, for example, about the existence of an Austinian sovereign. But the 'officials' and citizens who deserve respect under this theory are simply those that Hart, for example, identifies as persons who 'accept' the basic rules of the system. Objections to the possibility of finding an identifiable sovereign apply no more here than in Hart's case.

The second, and more serious, objection is that even if one locates the relevant officials and citizens who accept the system, these persons do not 'care' in the relevant sense about disobedience. In evaluating this claim, several points need to be kept in mind:

1) The theory does not require personal, psychological 'affront' in reaction to disobedience, as some of the simpler examples used in the text might suggest. All that is required is belief by others that the laws are important, justified, and should be obeyed.

2) If the claim is that no one 'cares' even in this non-psychological sense, one must find some way to deal with the anomaly of people punishing others for doing acts which, by hypothesis, no one cares about. That those who enact, enforce, or support laws implicitly care about the acts prohibited or regulated lends force to the view that law is perceived by those who accept it as presenting 'exclusionary reasons' for acting. See generally, J. Raz, *Practical Reason and Norms*, chaps. 1, 5.

3) Finally one must take care to determine that behaviour actually is desired. (Contract law may require one only to perform or pay, whereas the availability of punitive damages in torts suggests no such option is available for a wilfully committed assault.) Further, in the case of private law, doctrines requiring some link between the plaintiff and the violation

own legal theory in order to ensure that 'law' entails political obligation is slight. The potential amendment one thus makes to the assumption that legal and political theory are separate may be much greater.

sued for, such as that of standing, may limit the relevant persons whose 'concern' can invoke the legal obligation (if the owner does not 'care' enough about minor trespasses to bring suit, he may thus release me from both my moral and legal obligation not to trespass. But the law typically gives at least nominal damages to the owner who does care to bring suit even for the minor trespass.)

4.2 Comment

KENT GREENAWALT[45]*

I INTRODUCTION

Philip Soper's rich and subtle paper accepts the view that people have a prima-facie obligation to obey the law. Although he finds the paradigms that now dominate discussion—consent and fair play—inadequate bases for this obligation, he suggests that a novel approach, which we may roughly label respect for those with authority, does establish a prima-facie obligation. In this essay, I argue that his novel approach does not solve the problems cast up by other, more traditional perspectives, and that it suffers the liability of drawing attention away from the most significant reasons to obey the law. I also explore the implications of the duty of fair play, which constitutes H. L. A. Hart's major suggestion about why people have a moral duty to obey the law. I conclude that the scope and importance of that duty differ importantly from what is sommonly assumed.

Professor Soper's whole discussion is informed by his concentration on two major issues, and my response reflects my attention to subjects that vary from these. Following a centuries-long tradition, Soper explicitly sets out to deal with the problem of a general obligation to obey the law, whereas I am much more interested in trying to ascertain which sources of obligation apply on which occasions. While I believe that Soper's *search* for a general source of obligation leads him to strain his argument about respect for authority beyond the breaking point, I mention my own interest here mainly because it is the primary force behind my discussion of fair play.

The narrow problem on which Soper focuses is whether one has a prima-facie obligation to obey *unjust laws*. He does not state that this is the only or primary problem about the obligation to obey, and his discussion of the obligation to obey is not so narrowed. Yet his broader

---

* © Kent Greenawalt 1987.

[45] Editor's note: Professor Greenawalt's paper was distributed at the conference in Jerusalem but because of his absence, owing to illness, it was not delivered. The duty of fair play is discussed at greater length in *Conflicts of Law and Morality* to be published by Oxford University Press in 1986.

concern with defining law in relation to the obligation to obey, his development of the argument for respect for authority, and a few occasional remarks strongly suggest that unjust laws are at the centre of his mind. A powerful illustration is what he says about 'classical natural law', which takes the view that 'law refers only to directives that already pass minimum moral muster'. According to Soper, '[f]rom this perspective, the conclusion that there is an obligation to obey *follows from* the definition of law. Thus, critics who deny that there is such an obligation must be assuming that this natural law view is incorrect.'[46]

This comment is wrong and revealing. Many violations of perfectly just laws have no foreseeable harmful consequences. Someone may believe that the law of trespass is as just as it could be, and still suppose that no moral duty bars him from walking across someone's land when he will not be seen and will not damage the land. To say that a law is moral does not *settle* whether one has a prima-facie obligation to obey it in all situations; and building a criterion of justice into one's definition of law would not itself resolve whether one has such a prima-facie obligation to obey all laws. No doubt an affinity exists between a natural law approach to definition and the assumption that legality determines one's moral obligation to obey; but Soper is wrong in suggesting that the relation is a simple one of logical entailment. Soper's comment is revealing because it displays his overriding concern with the unjust law and his comparative inattention to the problem of 'trivial' violations of ordinary laws. Although Soper recognizes that a persuasive account of a general obligation to obey must deal with that problem, I shall try to show that his own theory does not adequately do so.

II RESPECT FOR THOSE WHO GOVERN

A *The basic account*

Soper's theory of obligation can be summarized as follows. Coercive government is necessary for human beings, so those who try to govern in the interests of their subjects are not committing a moral wrong against them. Subjects should respect the good faith efforts of those with authority and a crucial way to show this respect is by obeying their directions. Subjects have a prima-facie obligation to obey the law because those with authority care about whether the law is obeyed and they deserve respect.

[46] Emphasis added.

The analogy to the family that Soper draws help to clarify the approach. A sensitive daughter in a good family recognizes the need for parental authority, and understands that her parents are trying to exercise their authority in her interest. Since her refusal to comply with their directions will cause them disappointment or unhappiness, the love, or at least respect, that she feels for her parents provides an important moral reason to do what they direct. The daughter's obligation is similar to the duty of fair play in arising from the efforts of others, but it does not rest on any parental expectation of reciprocal benefits,[47] nor is it limited to the daughter's contributions to a co-operative enterprise. Not depending upon mutuality of restriction, the obligation reaches the many situations in which the only way the disobedience of children adversely affects a parent's self-interest is by causing psychological pain.[48]

In anchoring an obligation to obey government officials on the claim that political authority, like parental authority, is valuable, Soper relies on a premiss that strongly underlies traditional utilitarian and natural law accounts of obedience to law, as well as the recent argument by Tony Honoré that necessity is the ground of obligation.[49] Soper recognizes that the difference between legitimate political authority and a robber is that the former's interference with autonomous choice is morally acceptable and the latter's is not. Avoiding the fallacy that the very notion of legitimate authority implies an obligation to obey, Soper uses the propriety of the efforts of officials as the reason why they warrant respect and co-operation.

Soper shows that respect for officials is often a good moral reason for obeying the law. His argument is flawed, however, by insufficient analysis of the conditions that bring that reason into play, and it fails to establish that respect for officials is a reason for obeying the law that is uniquely powerful or uniquely broad.

---

[47] Of course loving parents are positively affected by responsive love, but usually they are not counting on specific reciprocal benefits from children. Even if they entertain a hope that mature children will care for them should the need arise, that hope is not a primary motivation for their own efforts when the children are younger.

[48] Even to talk in this way falsifies the strong sense of identification that many parents feel in relation to their children. Reduced to the practical level, the point is that Soper's theory includes a parental directive to do homework as well as a directive to set the table.

[49] A. Honoré, 'Must We Obey? Necessity as a Ground of Obligation', *Virginia Law Review*, vol. 67 (1981), 39. Although Honoré's argument is interestingly similar to Soper's in many respects, the notion of respect for those who govern is not critical to it.

B Injustice, autonomy and the conditions for a duty of respect

Soper acknowledges that if 'real' anarchists[50] are right, the obligation to obey does not exist. Although obedience might still be a way of showing respect for officials as persons, we cannot have a prima-facie obligation to obey those who undermine our autonomy and commit a moral wrong against us. So, Soper's obligation depends on a rejection of anarchism. Soper believes that a person does not have an obligation to obey if officials do not have a good faith belief in the justice of the system, or if the person's interests are not taken into account along with those of other subjects.[51] Other species of injustice, Soper claims, do not undermine the obligation to obey.[52] The analysis supporting this claim is sketchy and raises difficulties concerning appraisals of whole systems and the significance of individual acts of injustice.

Soper calls differences over the proper sort of government ones of degree, rather than kind, and claims that arguments over these matters are part of the process by which disagreements are resolved. In so far as his point is that acceptance of an obligation to obey should survive moderate differences over ideal forms of government and society, it may be conceded. But some people regard issues about whether a social order should be capitalist or socialist as absolutely fundamental, believing that the form they reject involves blatant denial of moral rights or frustrates all opportunities for persons to become truly human. According to Soper, '[a]cknowledgement of the value of law arises out of a rational appraisal of one's own self-interest in the maintenance of a coercive social order'. But if someone regards a government as extremely bad, much worse than possible alternatives for his genuine interests and those of his fellows, why should his view that even such a government is better than anarchy control the question of obligation?

[50] I use the term 'real' anarchist to distinguish persons like Robert Wolff, *In Defense of Anarchism*, New York (1970), who say nothing inconsistent with the propositions that government is necessary and that those who govern are acting in a morally acceptable way.

[51] I have drawn this principle by implication from what Soper says in generalizing from his family analogy. In the draft of his paper prepared for the conference, Soper spoke of interests being taken 'equally into account', thereby implying that if one's interests were given less than equal consideration one might not have an obligation to obey. He now speaks only of interests being taken 'into account', apparently not wishing to impose the more stringent condition. Presumably, however, if one's interests are taken into account only in a grossly unequal way (say, as Western societies may now take the interests of domestic animals into account), the obligation to obey would not arise.

[52] Despite a caveat about the openness of a society, Soper apparently does not suppose that the obligation to obey arises only in open societies.

This question is particularly pointed if one thinks that anarchy is not, in fact, a realistic long-term option for human beings, so that a comparison of very bad government with it hardly seems relevant.

One suggestion Soper makes is that the political process is a battleground where people can fight in a reasonable way over the proper forms of government, but that is only partly true. Even in the United States, an open society, the advocate of divine right monarchy or of a rigid dictatorship of the working class gets no more serious attention than the outright anarchist. Altogether, Soper presents no clear reason why a person who believes that the society he is living in is highly unjust should regard himself as obligated.

Of more practical importance for those living in societies they regard as reasonably just is the import of Soper's approach for persons faced with particular unjust laws. The essential drift is that authorities do not forfeit their right to respect because of occasional mistakes, especially given the difficulty of deciding which acts are mistaken. No doubt, reasonable disagreements about the justice of particular laws should not undercut an obligation to obey; but views about injustice are hardly that simple, even in a just society. Many regard certain laws as obvious responses to improper power and influence, or as wholly outside the domain of legitimate authority.

Suppose someone had the following attitude about laws regulating consenting sexual behaviour among adults:

I concede that government is necessary and that officials generally act in good faith. But I deny that government is necessary to regulate consenting sexual acts and I deny that such matters are the government's business. Further as to these laws, I do not believe most officials are really acting in good faith. Either they are wilfully enforcing their own blind prejudices or they are pandering to the prejudices of a narrow-minded minority of voters.

Why should the person with such an attitude have to take the government and its laws whole? That those in authority are generally performing a necessary function in a good faith way is apparently enough for Soper. At least as plausible is the conflicting view that if the particular function of the government is wholly unnecessary, and a crucial component of the basic justification for the obligation to obey is therefore absent, both the legitimacy of interference with autonomy and the ground for obedience disappear.

C The uniqueness of respect for authority

Despite Soper's contention that respect for those in authority is the key to political obligation, such respect is not typically the most important basis for obeying when it is relevant, nor does it enjoy unique breadth as a source of obligation.

Understanding why respect for authority is not usually the most important reason for obeying the law helps us to put that ground of obligation in perspective. Of course, independent moral reasons for refraining from acts are more important than any reasons that derive from their legal prohibition; but even among grounds that derive from the existence of the legal directive, respect for authority will not usually predominate. Soper's lifeboat example provides an apt, though extreme, illustration.

Soper assumes that a passenger wakens to find someone in *de facto* control, someone (unlike a ship's officer) who has neither a special claim to, or special qualification for, the position. Responding to Robert Wolff's proposal that one might go along because of the confusion disobedience might cause,[53] Soper stresses 'the effect on the person who stands in front of me trying to do his best to accomplish ends thought to advance the interests of the group as a whole, including myself'. A moment's reflection suggests how little the feelings of the *de facto* authority count here in comparison with the *success* of the endeavour in which he is engaged. The reason why Soper does not emphasize the latter is his recognition that much disobedience does not threaten the success of the broad purposes of law; none the less when accomplishment of the proper purposes of government is seriously implicated, it provides a much stronger reason to obey than the feelings of officials.

More broadly, Soper's focus on relations with officials settles on a source of obligation that is less significant than relations with fellow citizens. This conclusion is easier to assert than demonstrate, but let us imagine two societies with the same reasonably just structures of government and reasonably just laws. In the first most citizens are fair and conscientious, but most officials are self-interestedly trying to increase their power and wealth and are kept in check only by other selfish officials who try to win approval of the general populace by exposing their wayward fellows. In the second society the officials evince a disinterested concern for subjects but most of the population is corrupt and rapacious, paying attention to the law only out of fear and

[53] Wolff, *In Defense of Anarchism*, 16.

greed. My sense is that the citizens of the first society, whose fellow members self-consciously contribute to maintenance of the legal order, generally have more powerful reasons to obey than do the citizens of the second society. This unreal contrast may help to show that in actual modern societies, where officials and citizens alike act from mixed and complicated motives, the relationship with fellow citizens is the more central.[54]

Nothing I have said thus far about the *power* of respect for officials contradicts any claims made by Soper. Although *my* interest includes the comparative strength of sources of obligation, Soper's concern is their generality. What he does claim is special about respect for officials is that it alone is a ground of obligation that reaches all laws. I shall now turn to difficulties with that claim.

Soper argues that respect for those exercising political authority in good faith is a moral reason for obeying the law in every instance. I first suggest that respect may sometimes call for a different response and then discuss more troubling questions about the nature of the claimed obligation.

I agree with Soper that if one cares for and respects a person exercising authority, an important way to show one's concern is to comply with his good faith directions. But in personal relations, at least, directives are occasionally so misguided they reflect either a lapse from what is rationally defensible or a deep-seated failure of comprehension about what human relations should be. The person subjected to such a directive may regard it as an unacceptable infringement of his autonomy, but even if he decides to concentrate exclusively on showing respect for the person who issued it, easy compliance may not be the answer. Respect for that person's rational and moral capacities may

---

[54] In footnote 37 Soper comments that he has concentrated on officials because their acceptance of the rules is a minimal condition of law for Hart. Neither the relevance nor the importance of this observation is obvious to me. Hart accepts as a legal system a social order in which officials do not care about the interests of all subjects and do not believe in the justice of the system, but display the internal attitude because doing so promotes their self-interest. See H. L. A. Hart, *The Concept of Law*, Oxford (1961), 198–9. So Soper has already added significantly to Hart's minimal conditions of law in discussing grounds of obligation. Why the additions concern attitudes and behaviour of officials rather than citizens is not explained. In any event, we can probably assume that in virtually any society (at least any society that is not ruled by invaders) where officials concern themselves with the interests of all and believe in the justice of the system, *many* citizens will also believe in the justice of the system and will act to promote the values of the legal order. If that is correct, it is distinctly possible that in virtually every modern society satisfying Soper's conditions for obligation, responsibility to fellow citizens will be a more important reason for obedience than respect for officials.

require bringing sharply to his attention the unacceptability of what he has directed, and sometimes open disobedience may be the only forceful way to do that. For this reason, we cannot lightly assume that compliance with directives is *always* a better way than disobedience to show respect for the person in authority who generally acts in good faith.[55]

Much more pervasive problems with Soper's approach are raised by official ignorance and indifference. Since Soper wants to present his position without taking sides on certain controversial issues about the nature of moral obligation, exactly what amounts to a failure of respect is not entirely clear. But much of the paper, including the analogies employed, gives the impression that what is at stake in law compliance is not disappointing and rebuffing officials who are doing their best on our behalf.[56] Were the obligation so understood, it would not reach the many circumstances when law violation is unlikely to have that effect.

An initial problem here is figuring out just what laws matter. Soper says that a law unenforced for so long that it loses validity under the doctrine of desuetude no longer creates any prima-facie obligation to be obeyed. Less sweeping failures of enforcement do not vitiate the obligation, though they may well reduce its force. Soper is thus committed to the view that an obligation to obey laws survives their sporadic enforcement. To illustrate, many American cities forbid jaywalking, that is, pedestrians crossing streets against lights or in the middle of blocks. So long as anyone is ever prosecuted, or perhaps even waved at by a police officer to cross 'properly', everybody else retains the obligation to obey; although in some cities tens or hundreds of millions of violations occur for each instance of enforcement. A further difficulty here is the unreality of Soper's fleeting reference to desuetude. One study indicates that desuetude is not typically recognized in American criminal law.[57] When the doctrine does apply, non-enforcement must be the pattern for many years before a law loses validity. Thus, if desuetude is really the key, citizens have an obligation to obey some laws that have received no enforcement in recent years.

[55] Soper apparently concedes the force of this point, but wishes to cast it differently. His view is that even if one focused on respect for an official, the respect showed by obedience could be outweighed by the respect showed by doing 'the right thing'. This formulation allows the respect shown by obedience to count as a reason for obeying, even when it properly gives way to a competing kind of respect for the same person.

[56] In footnote 44, however, Soper indicates that he is not talking only about a psychological affront.

[57] L. Rodgers and W. Rodgers, 'Desuetude As A Defense', *Iowa Law Review*, vol. 52 (1966), 1. Prosecution under an old criminal statute not enforced for many years might raise constitutional problems of due process and equal protection.

The status of civil duties is faced by Soper only in his concluding footnote. Do we have a prima-facie obligation to do everything that amounts to a legal duty under the civil law? Some contract law theorists talk about economic breaches, and how the law of damages encourages those. Do parties have a prima-facie obligation to keep the terms of every contract or for some contracts is the prima-facie obligation only to keep the contracts or pay appropriate damages?[58] What apparently counts for Soper in answering questions about this and other civil duties is whether officials (or perhaps citizens) genuinely desire the duty to be performed.

If we limit analysis to criminal laws that are presently enforced with some regularity (the sort of laws Soper mainly has in mind), we still face difficulties. Officials never learn about a great many violations, and often those committing them are aware that the likelihood of officials finding out is exceedingly slight. A theory of obligation based on the hurt and disappointment that diligent officials will feel does not easily cover a violation one knows will never be discovered.

Even with respect to known breaches of law, Soper's account has a certain air of unrealism. Facing the argument that officials in a large bureaucratic state do not personally care whether particular individuals violate the law, he responds that officials do care in some degree that laws are observed. This response may be satisfactory if one focuses on serious criminal acts, but it is highly strained if one considers the vast numbers of violations of highly technical provisions, about which no official cares in a personal sense. But, could it be said that the legislators, at least, must care or they would not have created the duty?[59] Much legislation contains provisions that are so complex no legislator really understands many of the activities that will be affected. And, with some frequency legislation is designedly made substantially broader than the evil at which it is aimed, the idea being that the wide net will simplify enforcement efforts. To say that legislators care about all the behaviour that they do not understand is affected or that falls outside their real aim is implausible.

We can, in fact, even think of situations in which officials welcome disobedience. This may be the case in small communities where the

---

[58] A rare modern attempt to resolve this issue is found in J. Finnis, *Natural Law and Natural Rights*, Oxford (1980), 325–37. After delving into an extensive literature of the sixteenth and seventeenth century, he concludes that people have an obligation to adhere to the terms of contracts.

[59] Perhaps (living) past as well as present legislators may count as relevant officials.

enforcement of reasonable laws against speeding provides a substantial source of revenue; the benefits of the penalty are thought by officials to outweigh the risks to the community in the violations, and overall, they view the violations as allowing them to perform their jobs more effectively.

The strain of extending respect for officials as a reason to obey the law in these sorts of situations highlights deep conceptual uncertainties about Soper's whole approach: what exactly are the conditions that allow one to speak of a prima-facie obligation and what are the grounds for this particular obligation?

Let us initially grant the (implausible) assumption that in every case of disobedience of law an official will or might suffer disappointment. We would now have *a reason* for obeying the law in every instance. Although Soper makes clear that his usage does not restrict 'obligations' to claims voluntarily undertaken, he recognizes that having *a reason* to obey is not always enough to create a prima-facie obligation. Although every murder may help alleviate the overpopulation problem, we do not have a prima-facie obligation to commit murder, nor do we have such an obligation to give robbers money though our submission will please them. To generalize, we do not have a prima-facie obligation to do things that are independently wrong or are wrongly demanded of us. Do we have a prima-facie duty to do something which there is always *a moral reason* for doing and which would not be an independent wrong or represent a submission to a wrongful demand? Do I have a prima-facie obligation to vote Republican in every election, if there is always at least one good moral reason for doing so? Perhaps the account could be narrowed by saying that we have a prima-facie obligation to do things asked of us by people performing useful or important social functions. But the Republican candidate may be such a person. So also may be those who solicit charitable contributions by mail. Yet, despite the fact that we know those doing the soliciting will be more pleased by contributions than by disregard, most of us do not suppose that each request casts upon us a prima-facie obligation to contribute.

Soper's notion of prima-facie obligation appears to be broad enough to include these choices. Someone might argue that obedience to law is special because *widespread* disobedience would be destructive of social order, but Soper does not want to rest his argument for obedience either on the danger that individual instances of disobedience will have destructive effects or on a principle of generalization that would rule out individual acts of disobedience because of the hypothetical effects of widespread disobedience. Nor does he rely on any claim that the disappointment and resentment caused by disobedience of law will be greater than its positive effects, although an implicit judgement of this kind may well underlie his comfortable assumption about the presence of a prima-facie obligation.

The plausibility of Soper's approach may rest on a very weak notion of prima-facie obligation that effectively denies uniqueness to respect for officials. If the obligation of respect is understood in a utilitarian sense, other utilitarian reasons seem as general. Soper claims that respect for officials has greater breadth than the danger of disintegration of the law; but that danger is hardly the only other utilitarian reason for obeying the law. Because we are influenced by our own prior actions and the examples of others, each violation of law somewhat increases the likelihood of future undesirable violations of law. That danger seems at least as plausible as a *general* utilitarian reason for obeying law as the possible disappointment of officials. Thus, among the whole range of utility reasons, official disappointment does not enjoy special breadth. Nor does it have any special power. Cast in utilitarian form, respect for officials is simply one factor among many to go into an overall weighing of consequences, not ever requiring a decision that contravenes that overall balance.

In sum, if respect for officials is conceived as a reason for obedience based directly on likely harmful consequences, the reason seems not to come into play when official ignorance or indifference is predictable. When the reason does come into play, it is one consequential reason among many with no special status, and can be called a 'prima-facie obligation' only if that term is understood in a very broad way.[60]

These difficulties might be largely met if the obligation of respect is conceived as some sort of deonotological duty.[61] So understood, it might very well have power to require obedience to law even when the

---

[60] Unembellished act-utilitarians are often said to *reject* a prima-facie obligation to obey the law because they do not accept any reason for obedience that weighs against consequences. David Lyons develops such a position in 'Utility and Rights', in J. R. Pennock and J. W. Chapman (eds.), 'Ethics, Economics, and the Law', Nomos XXIV (1982), 107. A rule-utilitarian who adopted a particular level of generalization or an act-utilitarian who adopted a two-level theory might accept a prima-facie obligation to obey in a stronger sense. But Soper indicates no reliance on such a theory. For such an approach see R. M. Hare, 'Utility and Rights', comment on David Lyon's Essay, 148.

[61] Soper recognizes in note 39 that despite the utilitarian cast of much of his discussion, it is doubtful if his account can provide a general basis of obligation if it is understood in a utilitarian way.

balance of predictable consequences would fall moderately on the side of disobedience. More important for Soper's purposes, it might then be capable of possessing the generality that he claims.[62] In answer to the worry about official ignorance, one could speak about how officials would hypothetically react if they learned about disobedience. Whether the deontological version of Soper's account can also handle the problem of official indifference is less clear, but perhaps one can say that some officials would care somewhat if they knew about violations and that that would be enough to generate a slight obligation to obey.

The major stumbling block to accepting Soper's account as supporting a deontological duty is that he presents no convincing suggestion as to why an argument concentrating on the feelings of those in authority should be conceived as deontological. In this regard, the political context seems far removed from the family analogy. When people have a close personal relationship, failures to obey may lead to covering lies or to restrained communication. The duty to obey may best be conceived as one that does not rest on predictable consequences in particular instances. But most undiscovered violations of law do not subtly damage any personal relationships between the actor and officials. As the charitable solicitation example indicates, we do not have a deontological duty of respect to respond favourably to all reasonable requests for action by those who are performing useful social functions and care about our interests, and I am unable to discover in Soper's essay the grounds for according a special status to the directives of officials.

Although Soper's focus on the necessity of government, the value of official roles, and the importance of respect for officials is fruitful, his attempt to build a general theory of obligation is not successful. In shifting attention from the mutual restraints of citizens to what citizens owe officials, the theory is actually retrogressive. Even if one wishes to focus on respect for those who want compliance and will suffer disappointment at instances of disobedience, it would be mistaken to attend exclusively to officials. Many citizens also care about whether laws are observed and by their own compliance perform a function, admittedly one less specialized than that of officials, that is necessary for social life. If Soper's theory were developed in this direction, it would more closely approach the duty of fair play, to which I next turn.

Even were Soper's own account wholly persuasive, it would not eliminate the need to investigate other grounds of obligation, since the

---

[62] See note 39.

person choosing to obey or not should be interested in all the moral grounds that support obedience. But further investigation of the duty of fair play is specially warranted if, as I claim, Soper's theory does not provide an answer to the deepest questions about political obligation.

III   FAIR PLAY TO FELLOW CITIZENS

In 1955, H. L. A. Hart suggested that political obligation was intelligible only in terms of mutuality of restrictions.[63] He explained: 'When a number of persons conduct any joint enterprise according to rules and thus restrict their liberty, those who have submitted to these restrictions when required have a right to a similar submission from those who have benefited by their submission.'[64]

Almost a decade later, John Rawls put forward a similar account in much greater detail and coined the term 'duty of fair play'.[65] Largely because of his highly influential treatment, the main force of the duty has been perceived as concerning just and voluntary arrangements and as explaining why one has an obligation to obey even when disobedience would produce a balance of desirable consequences. In this effort to explore the scope of the duty, I shall suggest that it applies to many schemes that are not voluntary or just and that much of its importance lies in its capacity to make into duties certain actions that are conducive to utility.

1   The duty in its clearest form

It will help to begin with an illustration of the duty's undisputed application.

Having been left a hard tennis court by the builder, all residents of a new housing development agree that upkeep will be provided by residents who use the court, paying $.50 for each hour of use. The Monroes then move in with no previous awareness of the existence of the court or the scheme for its upkeep. When they learn of the court, they decide they would like to use it when no one else is doing so. Their use would not

---

[63] Hart, *Philosophical Review*, vol. 64 (April 1955), 175.
[64] Ibid., 185.
[65] Rawls, 'Legal Obligation and the Duty of Fair Play', in S. Hook (ed.), (1964) *Law and Philosophy* 3.

add at all to the costs of upkeep. They announce that they do not consent to the scheme because use is not worth $.50 an hour to them.[66]

Putting aside longer-term ramifications, utility would be served by the Monroes using the court and paying nothing or a lesser amount than $.50. Yet, if the other residents do not agree to scale down the price for them, and that refusal is not unfair, the Monroes must, morally, choose between paying $.50 for each hour they play or not playing. If they voluntarily accept the benefits of this scheme of mutual co-operation, benefits conferred by the willing payments of others, then they must adhere to the rules of the scheme.[67]

2 Problems of application to political communities and the law

Both the acceptance of benefits and subjection to the rules of the tennis court scheme are voluntary; the Monroes by refusing the benefit of using the court can avoid any obligation with respect to it. Participation in political communities is voluntary in neither sense. Many important legal duties do not depend on the voluntary acceptance of benefits and many benefits cannot be refused. In his discussion of the duty of fair play, Rawls presupposed a constitutional democracy[68] and spoke of 'a

[66] In most hypotheticals in which the duty of fair play seems most clear, a plausible argument that a person is bound by express or implied consent can also be made. If the Monroes were aware of the tennis court scheme and then chose to purchase a house and move into the development, it might be argued that they had implied their consent to abide by practices within the development, including the scheme for the court's upkeep. The caveat about no previous awareness is meant to meet this possibility; though it might still be argued that the Monroes had implied their consent to all prevailing practices about which they could have learned. Such an extension of implied consent seems dubious to me; but we might imagine instead that the Monroes consistently said prior to their purchase that agreement to buy the property did not carry consent to the scheme. They and the seller, and any development officials involved in approving the purchase, might have agreed simply to leave this issue unresolved when the property passed.

In any event, the point of this hypothetical example for my purposes is to establish a clear case for the duty of fair play from which variations can be considered, not to establish that the clear case involves no overlap between it and obligations of consent. My purpose would not be undermined even if such an overlap existed. As subsequent discussion shows, I believe the outer reaches of the duty of fair play include many situations for which no plausible consent argument could be mounted.

[67] Soper urges with respect to a similar hypothetical case employed by John Simmons that '[t]heories of theft (conversion) or imputed promise will suffice'. The question, however, is why society is willing to react in these ways to a taking of benefits that involves no deprivation of value for those from whom the benefits are taken. Something like the duty of fair play informs the moral judgements that a promise to pay should be imputed upon such a taking and that an uncompensated taking should be treated as theft.

[68] Rawls, 'Legal Obligation', 5.

mutually beneficial and just scheme of social cooperation'.[69] John Simmons, in his probing and careful treatment of the subject, cautioned that '[o]nly political communities which at least appear to be reasonably democratic will be candidates for a "fair play account" to begin with'.[70] Although the flavour of these passages is that only in relatively voluntarist political societies will a duty of fair play arise and the apparent assumption is that only liberal democracies qualify, we shall see that the very strategies that make the duty convincing for that political context suggest its broader application.

Some benefits provided by the state are accepted voluntarily, in the manner of the community tennis court. One may or may not use a state park or museum for which a fee is charged. Some benefits, such as military and general police protection are open, available to everyone whether they want them or not and regardless of their actions. Some benefits, such as basic education, involve action by recipients but that action is compelled. Other benefits may be refused, but the state's control over options leaves little real choice; no one need call the fire department when his house is burning but the state's monopoly over fire-fighting forecloses other possibilities for relief. Since acceptance of the comparatively few benefits about which one has a really free choice is an inadequate basis for an obligation to obey all or most laws, the main problem for the duty of fair play in the political context is how receipt of benefits that is not genuinely voluntary can give rise to the duty.

One possibility for rescuing the duty in the political context is that receipt of valuable benefits triggers the duty whether one wants the benefits or not. On this view, a pacifist would have a duty to contribute his share for a (genuinely valuable) military defence that he abhors. As Robert Nozick has illustrated with a number of ingenious examples,[71] forcing 'benefits' upon us that we do not want cannot place us under a duty of fair play to do our 'share', and this conclusion holds even if the benefits are 'really' good for us, and even if our being forced to accept them is not wrongful.

A more promising possibility is that acceptance of benefits with a certain attitude may be sufficient to invoke the duty of fair play. As John Simmons suggests, if I am delighted to receive 'open' benefits, if I understand the co-operative scheme by which they are supplied to me,

---

[69] Ibid., 10.
[70] A. Simmons, *Moral Principles and Political Obligations*, Princeton (1979), 136–7.
[71] R. Nozick, *Anarchy, State and Utopia*, New York, 93–5.

and if I further believe that the share required of me is perfectly fair, then I may be in the same position as someone who has genuinely chosen to receive a benefit he could freely refuse.[72]

Simmons's supposition that understanding of all these matters is crucial for the duty to come into play raises the question of when that understanding must be achieved, and whether it is even necessary. Ordinarily, the duty relates to a continuing enterprise in which one's present and future acts are based on assessment of how one's fellow participants have acted in the past and on expectations of how they will act in the future. But the duty may also appear on what one should do about receipt of past benefits; indeed, Soper's discussion in terms of unjust enrichment is particularly apt for this setting.

The Monroes have used the community tennis court for a month believing use is free and that the builder is paying for upkeep. Their ignorance is the product of a neighbour's dog taking from their doorstep a notice setting out the terms of the upkeep system. At the end of the month someone comes around to collect. The Monroes acknowledge that they think the scheme is fair, that they would have agreed to it if asked, that their use of the court was well worth the money to them, and that their misunderstanding did not affect their frequency of use or other expenditures.

Under these conditions, the Monroes should recognize that they have a duty of fair play to pay their share for past benefits.

If the acquisition of relevant knowledge can lead one to accept a duty of fair play that requires compensation for past benefits, how are we to describe the situation in which a person would accept the duty if acquainted with the relevant facts but, through no one else's fault, is ignorant of these facts? We might say either that the person lies under an unrecognized duty of fair play or that he is subject to a potential duty that can be brought into being by his acquaintance with the relevant facts. The terminological quandary here reflects more than the familiar problem in moral theory that '[i]ndividuals (subjectively) can only do what they think is right, even though (objectively) they may be wrong'.[73] Some duties, for example, not to inflict needless suffering, are put in a way that does not depend on personal attitude. Other duties depend on attitudes a person already has. If the duty is to help persons for whom

[72] Simmons, *Moral Principles and Political Obligations*, 132.
[73] Soper above. The context of the quotation is Soper's discussion of an anarchist.

one feels friendship, then the total absence of such feeling toward someone shows that *this* duty does not exist toward him. The difficult intermediate situations are those in which the duty may depend on having certain attitudes, but the attitudes are ones that reasonably well-informed people should have. That seems to be the apt characterization of the person who does not recognize the sacrifices of fellow citizens. It is difficult to say that a person is 'acting unfairly' if he is unaware of the sacrifices of others. Unless his failing to inform himself is unfair to others, talk of a potential duty of fair play may be more apt for his circumstance than talk of an already existing duty.[74]

3 The force and scope of the duty for political communities

I shall say more about the conditions under which the duty of fair play arises, but I pause here to draw two significant distinctions between the duty's application in the original tennis court example and its application in the political context. Since one is neither free to refuse most benefits of government nor to escape most legal duties, the 'scheme' does not have the take-it-or-leave-it character of the tennis court. For precisely this reason, a participant may not be in the position of having to accept the community's judgement of how much his fair share is or of how he should contribute that share. To take the latter point first, consider the person who thinks he is highly fortunate to be a citizen and does not believe *too great* a share is demanded of him. Yet he thinks the government's policy on nuclear weapons is suicidal, and he interferes with tests of a nuclear submarine, believing that the result will be a jail sentence for him. His perception is that he is sacrificing himself for the benefit of his fellows; how can he be violating a duty of fair play, particularly if he accepts the idea that others willing to make similar sacrifices for different causes are morally free to do so?

As to amount, a person may believe that the demanded share is too great. In that situation, his willing acceptance of open benefits goes only so far as what he thinks his fair share for the benefits is and the duty of fair play compels him to contribute only that much. How exactly one would decide a fair share would be highly complex. One perspective might be whether total benefits outweighed the cost of one's share. Unless a person is an anarchist or believes that his society is extremely repressive toward him, he will be likely to conclude on due considera-

---

[74] It may matter precisely how the duty is put. We might more easily say that ignorant A's failure to do his share violates a duty of fairness than to say that it violates a duty to act fairly.

tion that the total benefits he gets from government and law are greater than the total costs. But that enquiry does not end the matter. He may think that the benefit-cost ratio would be much better under a different sort of government or that beyond a core of virtually invaluable services what his government does is wasteful or counter-productive; in either event he might suppose that a good government could provide equal benefits at half the cost. Or he might object to his share of costs as it compares with those of other subjects. He might think that his prescribed share is unfair in comparison with other prescribed shares or that the failure of others to perform up to their prescribed shares makes his prescribed share unfair. If someone reaches the judgement that overall his mandated share is excessive, then his duty of fair play may extend only to what he thinks would constitute a fair share.

If the duty of fair play is so limited, it still retains a double importance. Although it may not demand compliance when one's judgement is that breaking a rule will actually contribute to the welfare of one's fellow citizens, it does require 'doing one's share' even when a failure to do so would have desirable consequences because of effects on oneself or persons outside the community. In such situations the duty remains a source of an obligation to obey that would not be present under a simple act-utilitarian account. More often, the duty indicates the same actions as utilitarian perspectives. Here its significance differs. Many, including myself, believe that the utilitarian premiss that one's duty is always to promote the general welfare is unpersuasive, at least if the premiss specifies a standard that people are expected to meet and can be blamed for failing to meet, rather than a perfectionist aspiration. When the duty of fair play applies, it transports the welfare-promoting action into the realm of duty or obligation, providing a powerful moral reason why people should not disregard overall welfare in pursuit of self interest.

It might be argued that I have too quickly circumscribed the scope of the duty, that within liberal democracies citizens should recognize that all have a fair and equal share of basic liberties and participatory rights, and that these are the shares that matter most. Thus, citizens who have an opportunity to debate and vote on political issues should regard their overall shares as essentially fair even if they think their shares of economic burdens and benefits are unfair. Although this view warrants more careful attention than I shall give it, it rests on an unrealistic assumption about the overall fairness of political processes in liberal democracies and on a mistaken judgement about the comparative importance for most people of political rights and economic status.

Decent processes of government do greatly affect how someone should view the fairness of his share, but they do not give the duty of fair play the same scope it has for truly voluntary schemes.

4   Injustice

A co-operative scheme can be unjust to non-participants or to some or all of the participants themselves. A system of slavery may involve mutual sacrifices and an equitable distribution of burdens and benefits among slave-owners, but it does a terrible wrong to its victims. I agree with John Simmons, who criticizes Rawls's assumption that a duty of fair play can arise only from a just scheme;[75] in the slavery example, the slave-owner does, as Simmons indicates, have a duty of fair play toward other slave-owners, although that duty is far outweighed by his moral duties to the slaves.

The other basic kind of injustice is to the participants themselves. Often the problem is that some participants deprive others of a fair voice in decisions or impose on them an unfair share of burdens. As I have just mentioned, one participant's fair share *vis-à-vis* others could well depend partly on the extent of his say in decisions. Possibly if a political order is very unjust, those who lack a fair say may not have any duty of fair play to the participants who have set up the unjust procedures, even if those without a voice do not object to the substantive benefits and burdens assigned to them.

In many political communities, however, the situation is rather different. The vast majority of participants have no responsibility for the processes of decision, because a small minority has seized control or an outside regime has imposed its will. What then of the duty of fair play?

A militaristic neighbour conquers a small democratic country, Pastoria, to render its own borders more secure. Wishing to keep the Pastorian population as sympathetic as possible, the invaders keep all basic laws in place. Revenues are spent much as before, and the invader finances its military forces and governing apparatus from its own treasury.

The Pastorians owe no moral duty to the new government as such, but what of their duty to their fellow citizens concerning laws that establish mutual restraints and impose financial burdens for public programmes? The duty to one's fellow citizens should not shift radically when, through no fault of theirs, the government has suddenly become

---

[75] Simmons, *Moral Principles and Political Obligations*, 109–11.

illegitimate. In fact, after invasions or internal takeovers by autocratic regimes, the basic rules of criminal and civil law of previously democratic societies often do not change very much. It would be surprising if the moral duties of citizens with respect to those laws lapsed suddenly with the change in political power. In respect to these kinds of laws, a reflective citizen who had lived *all his life* under a morally illegitimate government might still recognize the fairness of his share of burdens borne.

Having thus far suggested the relevance of the duty of fair play to political orders that do serious injustice to most participants, I now want to go a step further and ask whether the duty may apply even to situations in which the total scheme produces nothing approximating a fair balance of burdens and benefits.

Tim, the tyrant, has become very angry with a local village and insists that each healthy resident of the village perform the back-breaking, unproductive work of smashing one large rock into pieces every day. If an inadequate number of rocks is smashed at the end of any day, one villager at random will be jailed for six months. Ray alone realizes that Tim's minions have miscounted the number of healthy villagers and that at the end of each day they are finding what they believe is a surplus of five smashed rocks but which in fact represent exactly the number of healthy villagers. Ray understands that most other villagers are doing their share not only to protect themselves but also to protect their fellows.[76]

No harm will come if Ray stops smashing rocks, but does he have a duty of fair play to his fellow villagers either to continue smashing rocks or to distribute the benefits of relief from smashing more widely? Although the scheme overall is not beneficial for the participants, Ray is receiving a kind of benefit from his fellows; their efforts, co-operative in a sense, are reducing the risk that Ray will be jailed, a possible outcome if the scheme fails. Ray's obligation to his fellow villagers is substantial enough so that he should spread the relief from smashing rocks if that is feasible.

What if telling others about the surplus is too dangerous (Tim may find out) and Ray's failure to smash rocks will not be noticed? If no one else even knows this benefit is available, the duty of fair play would not

---

[76] As put, this example partakes of fantasy, but invaders do often demand assistance for their own enterprises, with no reciprocal benefits going to those whose help is demanded.

seem to require Ray to exert himself doing something that is totally useless and that the participants have not chosen to undertake. Perhaps Ray can view himself, by dint of his fortuitous and exclusive knowledge, as being in a unique position, different from that of the other villagers. This conclusion suggests how closely ordinary notions of fair play depend on there being either shared knowledge of free-riding opportunities or the possibility of spreading benefits.

5 Motivations

In each example I have discussed so far, I have talked about other participants restraining themselves in part for the benefit of their fellows. Simmons says the duty of fair play can arise 'even if the individuals' reasons for making the sacrifice [are] purely self-interested . . .'[77] Without doubt, the duty of fair play can arise after people have entered a co-operative scheme for selfish reasons; the tennis court example shows that. What is a much more troublesome question is whether the duty exists if the reasons why others perform their requirements under the scheme are purely selfish.

Soper, drawing from the law of unjust enrichment, and considering situations in which the beneficiary is not actually involved in a co-operative scheme with the person creating the benefit, asks if the indirect conferment of benefits may trigger a moral duty to pay. Although traditionally the indirect receipt of benefits produced by the self-interested actions of others has not been a source of a duty to pay, Soper points to contrary authority involving lawyers' fees. Soper recognizes that the legal analogy is significantly different from the moral issue, and suggests that one's moral duty may be broader than one's legal duty. No doubt one reason for the law's hesitancy to allow recovery is uncertainty about the value of benefits someone has taken no positive steps to acquire (though this problem is minimal if benefits and costs are purely monetary). The difficulty of outsiders calculating benefits has little bearing on the moral duty of a person who does regard the benefit as well worth the share he might pay. On the other hand, there are rather different reasons that may suggest that a moral duty might be less extensive than one's legal duty.[78] Recovery for lawyers' fees might be mainly a utilitarian technique for encouraging suits when many people

---

[77] Simmons, *Moral Principles and Political Obligations*, 172.

[78] I here exclude from consideration a moral duty that *arises* because the legal duty is created. In this context, the use of the legal analogy is meant to help reveal what is an independent moral duty.

suffer small similar losses and problems of co-ordination and prospective free riding discourage litigation unless those who do pay for it are assured of contributions from others who benefit. If this were the basis for the legal rule, it would have little bearing on the moral duty of the incidental beneficiacy who has not intentionally manipulated the situation to his advantage.

The problem of the selfish conferment of benefits can arise within a scheme that may loosely be called co-operative.

Each of two strangers, both under imminent attack from a vicious gang of criminals, realizes that, whatever the other does, he will have a better chance to live if he runs away, so long as co-ordination is not possible. Each also realizes that if both stay and fight, they will both have a better chance to live than if both run away. The diagram indicates the possibilities.

		A	
		Runs	Stays and fights
B	Runs	A − 25% B − 25%	A − 10% B − 90%
	Stays and fights	A − 90% B − 10%	A − 60% B − 60%

The strangers distrust each other so completely that neither is willing to count on any agreement to stay and fight; but they do agree that they will simultaneously chain each other to posts, and they do so. Neither is counting on the other's sense of obligation and each knows that the other is not counting on him. B has managed to chain A effectively, but A has botched the job. B realizes in the midst of the attack that he can manage to run away.

I am inclined to think that B has no duty of fair play to stay, since neither stranger has asked for or counted on the other's self restraint.[79]

[79] A has at least shown B the minimal respect of not pulling his gun on B and chaining B while he, A, remained unchained. But this degree of restraint from doing a wrong to B, which has already been reciprocated by B, would not seem to be enough basis for B to have a duty to stay and protect A.

Generalization from this example may be treacherous, but perhaps if all initial agreement does is to produce an effective engine of sanctions, and if compliance flows *solely* from fear of sanctions, participants do not have a duty of fair play to each other. (Or, if they have any such duty, it is much weaker than one arising when other participants act from a sense of obligation.) The duty of fair play arises when the self-restraint of most participants flows from a sense of what is owed to others, and when the actor realizes that his fellow participants are exercising self-restraint. The necessary attitudes need not involve precise understanding of people's places in a co-operative scheme. It is enough that fellow participants act out of feelings of duty, and that the actor has a vague understanding that others are making sacrifices toward common ends.

6   Fair play and a prima-facie obligation to obey

The duty of fair play, outlined here, does not establish a prima-facie duty on the part of all citizens to obey all laws. Unless one injects an assumption that citizens act unfairly even to determine independently of the law what will serve their fellows, the duty does not even establish a prima-facie obligation on the part of some citizens to obey all laws. Yet the duty provides a very powerful reason why many citizens should obey many laws. Its application to the political context, where, as Soper puts it, 'the confrontation of the individual with the legal order is not the product of wilful or negligent action', suggests a breadth to the duty that has not commonly been recognized, one that extends well beyond liberal democracies.

CONCLUSION

I accept Professor Soper's basic claim that social contract, estoppel, and fair play do not establish a prima-facie obligation to comply with all legal requirements; and I reject his claim that respect for authority can do so. I am sceptical that citizens have any prima-facie obligation that applies to all laws and serves as a counter to an overall appraisal of consequences, but if one is to be found, the search for it needs to be along the lines of traditional natural law or some other notion of natural duty, or in terms of a rule or two-level utilitarianism. In my view, much more promising than the search for an elusive general obligation is close attention to the scope and power of those sources of obligation that have been identified. Here, there is ample room for exploration of quite different sources and Soper's claim that respect for officials matters is compatible with claims that fair play matters. None the less, my own judgement is that respect for officials has much less overall significance for why modern citizens should obey the law than does the duty of fair play, the understanding of which is built on the foundation laid down by Hart.

4.3 Comment

CHAIM GANS*

Philip Soper begins his paper by pointing out a historical fact from which he attempts to establish a presumption against the recently growing consensus among philosophers concerning the question of the duty to obey the law. The consensus is that there is no such duty.[80] The historical foundation underlying this presumption is the fact that the view of the last fifteen years has developed a position entirely opposed to the tradition of more than two millennia. Soper ends his paper with a philosophical confirmation of this historical presumption, thereby disputing the current consensus. He provides us with a new argument for the duty to obey the law.

I agree with Soper that reversals of philosophical consensus such as that regading the duty to obey the law require re-examination or at least explanation. However, I disagree with his particular treatment and the results of this re-examination. Under the conceptual clarifications made by recent writers with regard to the thesis that there is a duty to obey the law, especially the universality of that duty and the way it is understood, any argument purporting to support that duty seems to me doomed to fail. Soper fully subscribes to these conceptual clarifications. His original argument for the duty to obey the law is yet another victim of them. This I shall immediately try to show. I shall attempt to arrive at the same conclusion as Soper's, namely, that there is a duty to obey the law, by using an entirely different strategy. I shall not occupy myself with original substantive arguments purporting to support the duty to obey the law, but I will deal more with what we mean when we claim that we have such a duty. I think it is logically and practically possible, as well as

* © Chaim Gans 1987.
[80] See M. B. E. Smith, 'Is there a Prima Facie Obligation to Obey the Law?' *Yale Law Journal*, vol. 82 (1973), 950; R. A. Wasserstrom, 'The Obligation to Obey the Law', in R. S. Summers (ed.), *Essays in Legal Philosophy*, Oxford (1979), 233; Raz, 'The Obligation to Obey the Law' in *The Authority of Law*, Oxford (1979), 233; Simmons, *Moral Principles and Political Obligations* and also most of the participants in the Symposium in Honour of A. D. Woozley: Law and Obedience, published in the *Virginia Law Review*, vol. 67, no. 1 (1981).

desirable, to understand such a duty in a way less stringent than recent writers have done. If this is so, then some versions of old arguments can be used to support it.[81]

But first I shall attempt to explain my impression that Soper's argument does not succeed in showing what it claims to show, namely, that there is a duty to obey the law understood as a universal duty.

As noted above, Soper constructs his argument by making analogies between the situation under the law on the one hand, and the life-boat and child–parent situations on the other. He has tried to get something new out of these long-standing analogies by emphasizing aspects of them which have been neglected by other writers who have exploited them. The traditional utilitarian analogy to the life-boat example was based on the assumption that every single act of disobedience will bring about disorder and, therefore, will put both the disobedient passenger and the group as a whole in a worse position than had they obeyed. But the assumption that every single act of disobedience will bring about disorder is patently false (as an early work of David Lyons showed with great detail and rigour).[82] Soper moves therefore to a different aspect of the situation. He says: 'What is relevant is not the effect of my decision on the venture, but the effect on the *person* who stands in front of me trying to do his best to accomplish ends thought to advance the interests of the group as a whole, including myself.'[83] The traditional analogy between the citizen–law situation and the child–parent one has concentrated on the debt of gratitude a child owes his parents because of benefits bestowed upon him by them. Here again, Soper shifts the focus in a similar manner. He says: '. . . My concern *for them (not for what they have done for me)* is one reason to comply . . .'[84]

My doubts about this argument have to do with its two premises. I doubt whether the aspect of the relations between child and parent or between passenger and de-facto commander, which Soper emphasizes,

---

[81] I myself have tried elsewhere to show how a version of a consequentialist argument from co-ordination can explain the rational normativity and non-optionality of the law. In the context of legal systems which are on the whole moral ones, I believe this argument can establish a moral duty to perform acts ordered by the law. Presupposing the morality of the system as a whole does not trivialize the claim that there is a moral duty to obey the laws belonging to it. On the contrary, laws belonging to legal systems which are on the whole moral, may be themselves immoral, and the thesis that there may be a moral prima-facie duty to obey immoral laws, is not trivial at all. *See* 'The Normativity of Law and its Co-ordinative Function' *Israel Law Review*, vol. 16, no. 3 (1981), 333.

[82] Lyons, *Forms and Limits of Utilitarianism*, Oxford (1965).

[83] Emphasis added.

[84] Second emphasis added.

produces a duty of universal obedience of the former to the latter. Secondly, I doubt whether the legal situation is similar in relevant aspects to these examples. Hence, if the duty derived from these situations is dubious, it is *a fortiori* dubious in the case of law.

The focus on respect for the persons to whom the duty of obedience is said to be owed does not secure such a duty, at least not a universal duty. One reason for this is that as a matter of fact not every act of disobedience need necessarily be taken by those persons as disrespectful or offensive. Another reason is that as a matter of morals it is not at all clear that a person in authority should desire full compliance with his orders and feel dishonoured or be offended should they not be complied with completely. At least it is not clear whether persons who do feel offended whenever disobeyed should, as a matter of institutional morality, be in authority. To this it may be answered that we do not choose or nominate parents and men in charge of emergencies of the sort to which the lifeboat case belongs, and therefore, facts about their character and views should determine how they ought to be treated and not vice versa. This may be partly the case, but I am not certain that it should be the whole case. Should, however, facts about their character give rise to their subordinates' duty of obedience, then what is it that guarantees their character to be such that they take offence at any single act of disobedience?

The main point is that the case of the legal system is importantly different from the cases to which it is being compared. In the case of the legal system, we do have control over choosing or nominating the persons who are in authority. We can and we should nominate those whose temper is such that it can fit within the desirable range of the duty of obedience, rather than dictate the range of this duty. Moreover, in the context of the law the assumption that there are persons in authority to be offended because of disobedience is somehow implausible. Of course, legal systems are administered by individuals, but the complexity of this administration, the anonymity of most of the officials and the indirect connection between them and the subjects of the system, make the whole enterprise highly impersonal. Therefore, the point about the cases to which the analogy is made, namely, that the persons in charge may not in fact be offended, and morally should not be offended (at least in cases where they know the disobedience not to be harmful, and committed by agents who know their disobedience not to be harmful) are much stronger here, in the case of legal systems.

It seems to me that Soper's argument does not succeed in showing that there is a duty to obey the law, a duty to perform acts specified in laws just because they are thus specified. But as I said at the outset, I share Soper's feeling that the opposition between the recent consensus on the duty to obey the law and the tradition of more than two millennia preceding it, requires an explanation, perhaps a softening. The first thing to notice about that opposition is that its implications are not very revolutionary.

It seems that a major practical motivation which led philosophers to argue for the duty to obey the law was the preferability of a situation with law to one without it. The writers of the new consensus do not deny this thesis. Hence the practical significance of the change of mind is not great. Until the beginning of the seventies philosophers had told us that it was all right to experience moral compunction after crossing the road against a red light at 3.00 a.m., even when nobody sees such an act. Now they tell us that this compunction is superfluous. But philosophers do not tell us now, and never have told us, that we may violate the law for political purposes, that we are justified in committing civil disobedience without an adequate defence.[85] The significance of the contrast between the two opposing views seems therefore to lie more in the field of theoretical precision than in practice.

Let me move now to the area of theoretical precision and examine the validity of, and the considerations which led to, the conclusion that since neither of the arguments for the duty to obey the law shows this duty to be universal, we had better give up the thesis that there is such a duty. I want to put forward three arguments against this conclusion. The first relates to the price we have to pay for it in terms of how we express our duties in general. The second and third concern the possible logical and practical grounds for continuing to speak about the duty to obey the law despite an important sense in which it is not universal.

A long time ago philosophers gave up the idea that the universality of general duty claims implies the necessity of performing all act-tokens falling under the duty-act-types mentioned in general duty claims.[86] When philosophers nowadays talk about the universality of general duty claims they seem to mean that every single act-token, falling under a duty-act-type, is actually *required* by the reasons justifying the duty. (That they are actually required by these reasons does not automatically mean that they must be performed, since they might be outweighed by

---

[85] E.g., Raz, 'A Right to Dissent? I. Civil Disobedience' in *The Authority of Law*, 262.

[86] W. D. Ross was the first to make this move, when suggesting and elaborating on the notion of prima-facie duty in Chapter 2 of his *The Right and the Good*.

other reasons. It means only that the reasons requiring them exclude or trump or necessarily outweigh some other reason, and ought to be weighed against reasons which they do not exclude or necessarily outweigh.[87] This understanding of the universality of duties—which is not the universality of *performance* but the *universality of being required by* a sort of peremptory but not absolute *practical force*—seems to follow logically from another conceptual constraint which applies to general duty claims and which I shall call the constraint of non-contingency. If there is a duty to obey the law or keep promises, then actions falling under these duties are dutiful by virtue of having the characteristic 'ordered by a law' or 'having been promised', and not because of any other characteristic they happen to have. In order to show that there is a moral duty to obey the law, we cannot rely on the fact that many acts ordered by the law, such as not murdering, not stealing, keeping promises, are morally dutiful, regardless of the fact that the law orders them.[88] We must show how the fact that these acts are specified in the law adds to their obligatoriness. In order to show that there is a moral duty to obey the law we must then show that the characteristic of being ordered by a law is one which renders them dutiful. And if this is so, how can it be that there are some act-tokens having this characteristic which are not dutiful, which are not required? Hence, the conceptual thesis of universality as explained above, follows logically from the undeniable conceptual thesis of non-contingency. (Soper gives the impression that the universality and non-contingency are one and the same thing. If so, this is a mistake. Although they seem to imply each other, they do not mean the same thing, and if the second argument below is plausible, then it is certainly worth while to insist on distinguishing between them.) Since none of the arguments for proving the duty to obey the law, including Soper's, succeeds in showing that every single act-token falling under the act-type of 'obeying the law' is required by peremptory practical force, there is no duty to obey the law.[89]

[87] The concept of duty was accounted for by various writers in terms of its special peremptory practical force. This practical force seemed to be most problematic because it could not be explained in terms of reasons *simpliciter*, important reasons or conclusive reasons. Joseph Raz explained them, therefore, as exclusionary reasons. (*Practical Reason and Norms*, London (1975).) Ronald Dworkin would probably have explained them as he explained the notion of rights, namely, as trumps. I have tried to suggest that duties represent practical priorities which are absolute with respect to *sorts* of reasons for action. (Gans, 'The Concept of Duty', D. Phil. Thesis, Oxford, 1981.)

[88] See Smith, 'Is There a Prima Facie Obligation to Obey the Law?', 951 and Raz, 'The Obligation to Obey the Law', 234.

[89] This is Smith's and Raz's strategy in showing that there is no duty to obey the law.

The first thing to notice about this argument is that it works well not only with regard to the duty to obey the law but also with regard to duties such as keeping promises and not killing humans. These duties were taken by philosophers to stand in need of further justifications, and *were* given further justifications.[90] It can easily be shown that these justifications do not apply to every single act-token falling under these duty-act-types, and, therefore, that there is no duty to keep promises, no duty *not* to kill humans. In reference to this second duty philosophers have claimed, convincingly I believe, that this duty is based on two main grounds: firstly, in the value of the life of creatures capable of enjoyment and happiness, and secondly, on the special value of life in creatures capable of self-consciousness, rationality, or autonomy. But surely there are human beings who are capable of neither happiness, nor autonomy. One valid conclusion to be drawn from this is that, in regard to certain human beings, no peremptory practical force against killing is exerted.

The cases for euthanasia and for abortion are at least partly based on this conclusion and the line of thought leading to it. It follows that the duty not to kill humans is not universal in the sense explained. The same can be shown with regard to the duty to keep promises.

But do we want to move from this conclusion, namely, that the duties of keeping promises and not killing humans are not universal, to the conclusion that there is no duty to keep promises, and no duty *not* to kill humans? This price seems high. In fact, it is higher than it seems. We have to give up almost all our beliefs in duties of a manageable degree of specificity.[91] But since logic requires it, is there a way of not paying this price?

I think there is, and it is to be found in a more liberal understanding of the constraint of non-contingency, an understanding which will not entail the universality thesis as explained above, but will explain universality of duty claims in a different way.

Philosophers are undoubtedly right when claiming that when we say that there is a duty to obey the law or that there is a duty not to kill humans, then a non-contingent link must be shown between the fact that act-tokens belong to these categories and their becoming obliga-

---

[90] See e.g., MacCormick, 'Voluntary Obligations and Normative Powers', *Proceedings of the Aristotelian Society*, Supp. vol. 46 (1972), 59; Narveson, 'Promising, Expecting and Utility', *Canadian Journal of Philosophy*, vol. 1 (1971), 207; P. Singer, *Practical Ethics*, Cambridge (1979); J. Glover, *Causing Death and Saving Lives*, Penguin (1977).

[91] It seems that the only duties we are left with are those formulated in the most basic and abstract first principles of the ethical theory we hold (e.g., the principle of utility and the categorical imperative).

tory. But we must be cautious about what we mean exactly by this non-contingency. One thing we may mean is that belonging to this act-type, and not any other characteristic of the act-token in question, is the characteristic which renders it obligatory. But we may satisfy the requirement of non-contingency by meaning less than that. We may mean not that belonging to *this act-type simpliciter* is the characteristic which renders the act-token obligatory, but rather that the characteristic or characteristics which make this act-type obligatory *typically* belong to act-tokens in this category.

For example, the act-type of killing humans typically involves extinguishing creatures capable of joy, rationality, or desires; the act-type of breaking a promise typically contributes to weakening a system of interpersonal reliance in society; the act-type of breaking a law typically undermines stability, security, order, and co-ordination within a society. These values typically exert peremptory practical force on act-tokens belonging to the act-types mentioned, and these values are linked to these act-types not just by accident.[92] Hence, the non-contingency of the link between the fact that an act-token belongs to the duty-act-type and its being obligatory is ensured, but it does not automatically mean that every single act-token belonging to that act-type is, in fact, being required by practical force.

In other words, in order to meet the requirement of non-contingency of the link between belonging to a certain act-type and becoming obligatory, it is enough to answer positively questions such as, Is there something typical about the law which renders many or some acts specified in laws dutiful? Is there something typical about killing humans by virtue of which some acts of that sort are forbidden? It is not necessary to answer positively the more ambitious questions: Is there something intrinsic in the law which renders *all* acts specified in laws dutiful? Is there something about humans by virtue of which all their killings are forbidden?

So far I have tried to show that it is possible to understand the conceptual thesis of non-contingency in a way that will not entail the kind of universality explained above—the universality of being required by peremptory practical force—of general duty claims. I hope also to have shown that if this step is not taken, then the price we are committed to pay for this entailment is much higher than merely giving up the thesis that there is a duty to obey the law. I want to add now a third

---

[92] I have discussed the particular nature of the link between one of the values obligating act-tokens of obeying the law and the law elsewhere. See note 81 above.

consideration for remaining committed to general duty claims, including the one that is the subject of this discussion, namely, that there is a sense in which they are universal.

This consideration concerns the functions of general duties in our practical and moral reasoning. They have an important role in this reasoning even in cases of duty-act-tokens where the justifying reasons of the general duty were found not to apply (that is, not to exert any practical force in favour of performing these particular acts). Sticking to general duty claims such as that there is a duty to obey the law, that there is a duty to keep promises, that there is a duty not to kill humans, accommodates this important fact. General duty claims such as the ones just mentioned indicate not only act-types relative to whose act-tokens there are certain typical reasons which might establish a *conclusive case* for their performance, but also the reasons which must at least be *considered* in favour of those acts (and which necessarily outweigh or exclude *some* other reasons and desires which might weigh against those acts).[93] General duty claims indicate that such reasons are either extremely important or highly probable or at least of enough combined probability and importance that we must always confirm whether these reasons obtain.

In other words, that an act-type is thought of as a duty means firstly that there is a factual presumption that typically a certain reason exerts peremptory practical force on act-tokens falling under that act-type. This factual presumption and the process of rebutting it or confirming it is the first stage of our reasoning about duties. At this stage, duties such as the one to obey the law, not to kill humans, and to keep promises are universal. The fact that an act is specified in a law, that it is an act of breaking a promise, or an act of killing humans, requires that we ask whether a reason typically exerting peremptory practical force on acts of these kinds does exist and is applicable in the case of the act in question. Hence, at this stage of reasoning about duties, the stage of factual enquiry, duties are universal. It is only at the second stage, the stage of weighing them against other reasons, that they cease to be universal. Naturally, we do not consider reasons in situations where we find them not to apply. The obligating reasons become even less universal at the third stage, the stage of requiring decisive action. So perhaps we ought to distinguish three stages where universality might be intended to apply

---

[93] See note 87 above. Apart from exerting special peremptory force, the reasons which justify duties exert ordinary practical force. Like all reasons requiring actions, they ought to be weighed against all other reasons arising from the situation in question.

to duties: the universality of becoming conclusive (or the universality of performance), the universality of exerting peremptory practical force and of having to be considered, and the universality of factual enquiry into whether the justifying reasons of the duty arise. All are stages in our reasoning about duties. The thesis that duties are universal in the first sense, namely, that they always provide conclusive reasons for act-tokens falling under the duty-act-type, was given up by philosophers a long time ago.[94] Duties are understood as prima-facie, or as providing *trumps* or exclusionary reasons or only relatively absolute reasons. It is time for us to give up this universality as well. If we want to preserve our linguistic practice of talking about general duties, we had better understand their universality as relating to the stage of factual search for the reasons typically obligating the act-tokens falling under the act-types they specify. We had better understand general duty claims as claims that in each and every case of act-token falling under the duty-act-type it is necessary to see whether a certain reason typically linked with the duty-act-type and obligating act-tokens falling under it, does, in fact, apply to the act-token in question.

These are good reasons for continuing to talk about duties such as not killing, or keeping promises. For it seems justified and important to have distinct expressions to indicate the kinds of actions which are often required by reasons which, relative to these actions, outweigh important or widespread desires.

This is perhaps a proper place to say something more about how to evaluate the importance of duties in general, and the duty to obey the law in particular. Soper has already quoted M. B. E. Smith on that matter and has joined John Finnis in criticizing Smith's test of importance. From Smith's test it follows not only that the duty to obey the law is trivial, but also that the duty to keep promises is trivial, and a test 'that so casually dismisses a tradition that takes promise as the paradigm of prima-facie obligation deserves to be met with some scepticism'. But perhaps Smith's test is correct and the duty to keep promises is unimportant? There is surely some truth in Smith's test, truth which derives from the fact that some instances of the moral duty to obey the law, if it exists, are instances of trivial duties: disregarding them will do some, but not much, harm. The same, I think, is true with regard to promissory obligations. Some are instances of trivial obligations. However, it is wrong to conclude from the triviality of some legal and

---

[94] See note 86 above.

promissory obligations that the general duties of obeying the law and keeping promises are trivial. That some legal and promissory obligations are trivial is because the dangers to the values that the duties of obeying the law and keeping promises protect depend on factual probabilities, and therefore vary from one case of disregarding these duties to another. The value of preserving a system of interpersonal reliance within a society can be damaged differently in different cases of breaking promises. But from this it does not follow that the general duty of keeping promises is unimportant. The same holds for the duty to obey the law. Both duties protect values which are of great importance and are therefore important duties.

Furthermore, the importance of general duties is a function not only of the importance of the general value they protect but also of the frequency with which these duties might apply, and the frequency with which the reasons necessarily outweighed by these duties might arise in our lives. Minor wants of ours are tautologically trivial, unimportant. But minor wants are omnipresent in our lives. If a certain general duty (necessarily) outweighs only them, then, given that the occasions for performing duty-act-tokens falling under this general duty are significantly frequent, the fact that we subscribe to such a general duty is a significant fact of our practical life, although the duty does not protect an important value. If we hold such a duty, this means that we do not allow ourselves, in cases where it applies, to act for the reasons which often do determine our actions.

The duties to keep promises and obey the law are important, however, on all three scores mentioned above. The occasions for their performance are frequent; the reasons they necessarily outweigh, even if we are minimalists and think these are only minor wants, arise frequently in our lives, and finally they protect important, though not the most imporatnt, values: interpersonal reliance, stability, security.

I want to conclude with a final comment. There is one thing I have not done in this paper: I have not attempted to provide an argument which will establish the duty to obey the law. I believe, however, that some versions of at least one traditional argument, of what has been termed 'the utilitarian argument', can establish this general duty, if we expect it to be established only on the basis of non-contingency and universality as defined here.

I have tried elsewhere[95] to use this utilitarian argument in order to

---

[95] See note 81 above.

explain the normativity of law. Some modifications are required in that argument so that it establishes a moral duty to obey the law. The space here will not suffice for that purpose.

PART II
LEGAL RESPONSIBILITY

5.1 The Middle Way in the Philosophy of Punishment*

IGOR PRIMORATZ

I INTRODUCTION

Through most of its history, the philosophy of punishment has been marked by a division into two opposed and—on the face of it, at least—irreconcilable approaches. If one proposed to justify legal punishment, one had to choose between the claims of justice and desert, and those of the common good; one had to present punishment either as retribution, or as an indispensable means for attaining socially desirable objectives. No synthetic theory seemed possible, for each side in the debate totally repudiated the basic contentions of the other. Utilitarians tended to depict the retributive view as irrational, vindictive, reactionary, and to deny it any intellectual or moral respectability, echoing the crushing verdict passed by Plato at the very beginning of the debate:

In punishing wrongdoers, no one concentrates on the fact that a man has done wrong in the past, or punishes him on that account, unless taking blind vengeance like a beast. No, punishment is not inflicted by a rational man for the sake of the crime that has been committed—after all one cannot undo what is past—but for the sake of the future, to prevent either the same man or, by the spectacle of his punishment, someone else, from doing wrong again.[1]

Retributivists, on the other hand, pointed out the obliviousness of utilitarianism to the claims of justice as an autonomous principle, and the consequent tendency of its proponents to accept, and even call for, various types of obviously unjust punishment, whenever they turn out to be socially useful. Some of these unjust but expedient types of punishment are so appalling to anyone but the out-and-out utilitarian, that Westermarck wrote that 'those who would venture to carry out all the consequences to which [the utilitarian theories of punishment] might lead would be regarded even as more criminal than those they punished,

---

* © Igor Primoratz 1987.
[1] Plato, *Protagoras*, 324ab, trans. W. K. C. Guthrie, in E. Hamilton and H. Cairns (eds.), *The Collected Dialogues of Plato*, Princeton (1973), 321.

not only by the opponents, but probably by the very supporters of the theories in question'.[2]

Still, there have been philosophers who believed that both theories of punishment, over and above their undeniable difficulties, have an important contribution to make—that each has grasped a part of the truth about the moral basis of punishment. They held that the way leading to a satisfactory theory of punishment is the middle way, that the theory of punishment must be a synthetic theory. One should try for a synthesis, which would avoid the one-sidedness, exaggerations, and outright mistakes of both utilitarianism and retributivism, while incorporating the important insights contained in both; a theory which would bridge the gap between, and reconcile the claims of, justice and the common good, the past and the future.

These attempts at a middle-of-the-road, synthetic view of punishment have one thing in common: the methodological point of departure. When philosophers set out to bridge a gap, to synthesize theories which seem to be mutually opposed and even irreconcilable, usually the first thing they do is introduce a distinction. This has been the case in all important attempts at a middle-of-the-road philosophy of punishment. All these attempts have proceeded from a distinction which was overlooked, or at least whose import was not appreciated, in the preceding debate: either the distinction between the question of the meaning of the word 'punishment' and that of moral justification of what the word stands for; or between the ultimate end of punishment and the means indispensable for achieving it; or between the rationale of the institution of punishment and the principle, or principles, governing its application to particular cases. The synthesis was to be accomplished by working out a division of labour between the two theories, on the basis of the distinction seen as crucial.

In this paper I propose to analyse these attempts at a middle way in the philosophy of punishment, and to try to show that none of them has been entirely satisfactory.

II   THE WORD AND THE THING: A. M. QUINTON

In a short, but very influential article 'On Punishment', published in *Analysis* in 1954, Anthony M. Quinton attempted to solve what he called

---

[2] E. Westermarck, *The Origin and Development of the Moral Ideas*, 2nd edn. London (1912), vol. 1, 81–2.

'a prevailing antimony' in the philosophy of punishment. The two traditional theories of punishment seem to be irreconcilably opposed to each other. If we believe that punishment is justified, we have to choose between the two. But the choice is difficult, for each has been shown by its opponents to be thoroughly unattractive. Retributivism is characterized by 'vindictive barbarousness' which calls for the infliction of suffering for suffering's sake, while the utilitarian theory is plagued by 'vicious opportunism', which culminates in the willingness to justify punishment of the innocent, whenever that would be expedient. No third option is available, for if punishment is justified, it is justified either intrinsically, as the retributivists submit, or extrinsically, as the utilitarians claim.

This antimony can be solved if we attend to the distinction between two levels of discourse, the logical and the ethical; that will enable us to understand the real nature of the two theories, and to bridge the gap between them. For the confrontation between them, which has been going on for centuries, is basically misconceived; it is but a result of a confusion of the two levels or, to be more precise, of 'a confusion of modalities, of logical and moral necessity and possibility, of 'must' and 'can' with 'ought' and 'may'. In brief, the two theories answer different questions: retributivism the question 'when (logically) *can* we punish?', utilitarianism the question 'when (morally) *may* WE or *ought* we to punish?'' [3]

The retributive theory, in its most complete form, contains four tenets. There is the doctrine of punishment as 'annulment' of the crime, and the thesis that it is a right of the criminal himself. There is also the demand for proportion between crime and punishment. In Quinton's view, these three theses are clearly untenable. The main thesis of the theory, however, is a different matter. This thesis, which he formulates as the claim that 'punishment is only justified by guilt' or, alternatively, that 'it is necessary that a man be guilty if he is to be punished', strikes us as quite compelling.

There is a very good reason for this difference in force. For the necessity of not punishing the innocent is not moral but logical. It is not, as some retributivists think, that we *may* not punish the innocent and *ought* only to punish the guilty, but that we *cannot* punish the innocent and *must* only punish the guilty. Of course, the suffering or harm in which punishment consists can be and is inflicted on innocent people but this is not punishment, it is judicial error or

---

[3] A. M. Quinton, 'On Punishment', in H. B. Acton (ed.), *The Philosophy of Punishment*, London (1969), 55–6.

terrorism or . . . 'social surgery'. The infliction of suffering on a person is only properly described as punishment if that person is guilty. The retributivist thesis, therefore, is not a moral doctrine, but an account of the meaning of the word 'punishment'.[4]

This not only cuts retributivism down to size, but also takes care of the main objection to the utilitarian theory—the one on punishment of the innocent. Such a thing simply cannot happen; it is impossible in the strongest sense, that is, logically.

The general result is that:

the retributivist case against the utilitarians falls to the ground as soon as what is true and essential in retributivism is extracted from the rest. This may be unwelcome to the retributivists since it leaves the moral field in the possession of the utilitarians. But there is a compensation in the fact that what is essential in retributivism can at least be definitely established.[5]

It is established, and also contained in the utilitarian theory of punishment by virtue of the fact that the latter is a theory of *punishment*.

Now Quinton is right as to the meaning of the word 'punishment', and therefore also as to the logical impossibility of punishing the innocent. Still, his interpretation of the main thesis of the retributive theory as an analytic statement, and the synthesis of the two theories based on it, is misconceived. He neither manages to trivialize the main retributivist tenet, nor to save the utilitarian theory from the punishment-of-the-innocent objection.

Quinton phrases the main retributivist thesis in two alternative ways—'Punishment is only justified by guilt' and 'It is necessary that a man be guilty if he is to be punished'—believing that these two formulations come down to the same thing. They do not; only the first is an accurate expression of what the retributivists are saying. And it is certainly not an analytic statement. If this is not obvious consider the following: (*a*) 'Punishment is not justified only by guilt', and (*b*) 'Is punishment justified only by guilt?' If the thesis were analytic, (*a*) would have to be a contradiction, and (*b*) a self-answering question; clearly, neither is the case. When putting forward the thesis that 'punishment is only justified by guilt', retributivists are not stating the logical truth that, in order that the word could be correctly applied, the person at the receiving end must be guilty; they are making a genuine ethical claim that the fact of his guilt is the sole justification of the suffering inflicted

---

[4] Ibid., 58–9.
[5] Ibid., 62.

on him, the sole ground of the state's right to do that to him. They are not talking about a word, they are using it to say something about the morality of what it stands for.

On the other hand (and Quinton could see this as a compensation for the failure of his interpretation), if it were true that the main thesis of retributivism—that punishment is only justified by guilt—is an analytic truth, that would make the main thesis of the opposing, utilitarian theory, which he wishes to uphold—the thesis that punishment is justified by its good consequences—analytically false. The aim of trivializing the main thesis of the retributive theory in order to add it as an innocuous, logical appendix to the utilitarian theory of the moral basis of punishment, would have been achieved at the price of doing away with the latter in the process.[6]

With the second line of Quinton's argument—the attempt to rebut the crucial objection to the utilitarian view by reminding us of the meaning of the word 'punishment' and the implication that punishment of the innocent is not really punishment—I can deal quite briefly. This manœuvre—which Hart has termed the 'definitional stop'—will not help.[7] Punishment of the innocent is logically impossible, but something very similar to it is not: 'punishment' of the innocent. And that is precisely what the utilitarian would be committed to in the situation described in the argument: to say that we ought to inflict upon the innocent man the suffering which, if he were guilty, would be punishment; which, since he is not guilty, cannot be properly termed punishment, but must be called something else (victimization, social surgery); and which must be falsely presented to the public at large as punishment, that is, as suffering inflicted on the culprit for his crime, because only thus can the good results of the whole proceeding, which provide its moral justification, be achieved.

III THE END AND THE MEANS: A. C. EWING

The late A. C. Ewing's original and unjustly neglected attempt at a reconciliation of the two theories[8] is also offered as a solution of an antinomy. Both theories have grasped an important truth, but these

---

[6] For a detailed analysis of Quinton's argument see my 'Is Retributivism Analytic?', *Philosophy*, vol. 56 (1981).
[7] H. L. A. Hart, *Punishment and Responsibility*, Oxford (1968), 5.
[8] 'Punishment as a Moral Agency: An Attempt to Reconcile the Retributive and the Utilitarian View', *Mind*, vol. 36 (1927); *The Morality of Punishment*, London (1929).

truths seem to be mutually opposed. Retributivism has one great merit: it enables us to make sense of the reference to the past in punishment, to talk of it in terms of guilt, desert, justice. But it absolutizes this perspective, and denies any moral relevance to the good consequences of punishment. These are put forward as its justification by the utilitarian theory, but only at the cost of dissociating it completely from considerations of justice and desert and the retrospective reference implied in it. A satisfactory account of the moral basis of punishment will have to allow for the reference to the past implied in every punishment, its connection with the offence committed, and thus with desert and justice, while stopping short of the retributivist claim that just punishment is good in itself in any great measure; at the same time, it will have to justify punishment in terms of the good it produces, but not at the price of ignoring justice and desert in the pursuit of the good, which the traditional utilitarian doctrines of punishment were all too ready to pay.

These conditions, Ewing believed, can be met if we view punishment as a special kind of language. The pain of punishment is not pain pure and simple; it has certain significance, a certain message to convey. Its distinctively moral function is to express the emphatic moral condemnation of the crime by society. This has a twofold purpose: to bring home to the offender the high degree of wrongness of his misdeed, and to teach all potential offenders in the public at large the same lesson. This is not to be confused with the deterrent effects of punishment. The message is not about the dangers of breaking the law, but about the gross immorality of doing so; the aim is not to get both the actual offender and the public to accept the prudential rule that crime does not pay, but to strengthen in them those distinctively moral motives which will ensure that they do not commit crimes even when it pays to do so. Of course, it is not claimed that people need criminal law and punishment to teach them that such things as murder, rape, or theft are wrong; but the fact that some of them do commit such acts shows that they do not realize strongly and vividly enough just how very wrong they are. This is the lesson taught by punishment; it contributes to the reformation of the offender, and the moral education of the public. In this way punishment helps prevent crime. Given crime prevention as the ultimate goal of punishment, it is obviously much more important that the message be conveyed to, and the lesson impressed on, the public at large, than that the same effect be attained with regard to the actual offender. This function of punishment as a means of moral education of the public— which Ewing terms 'educative', to distinguish it from the reformation of the offender—is its distinctively moral function, and its basic moral justification.

Now if it is to serve this purpose, punishment must satisfy certain conditions. As an expression of society's moral condemnation, punishment makes sense only if it is addressed to the offender and his offence. If it is inflicted upon an innocent man, it can have no desirable effects, either on him or on the public at large; it can only confuse and corrupt both the man 'punished' and everyone else. This is where the reference to the past and the considerations of justice and desert come into the picture. They also come in when the severity of punishment has to be decided upon. There must be certain proportion between the crime committed and the punishment meted out for it: more serious crimes ought to be punished by harsher punishments, and vice versa. For 'in a given society a certain amount of pain is a suitable way of expressing a certain degree of disapproval, just as one tone of voice may be a more suitable way of expressing it than another'.[9] If this proportion is not ensured, punishments will confound moral judgements about comparative wrongness of offences, and thus fail to achieve their purpose.

Thus a division of tasks is made, and a reconciliation of the utilitarian and retributive views of punishment effected, on the basis of the distinction between the end of punishment and the means indispensable for attaining that end. This is made possible by positing as its end the moral education of the public—something that had been almost entirely disregarded by the traditional utilitarian theories of punishment. This novel, 'educative' theory solves what Ewing calls 'the fundamental antinomy in the theory of punishment':

It seems an essential part of punishment that it should be inflicted for a past offence and not merely as a means to a better future like a surgical operation . . . Yet if it is inflicted for the past and not the future, what is the good of it? It cannot change the past and make the evil act undone. Hence the fundamental antinomy in the theory of punishment. One side says—punishment must be for a past act, otherwise it would be unjust; the other side says—punishment can only be justified by the good it does, but the good it does is not in the past, it can only be in the future. My solution would be that punishment is only justified by the good it does, but it can only do that good if it is for a past offence. If punishment serves as a kind of moral education for the community, it is far from purposeless, yet it can only serve this purpose if it is substantially just. . . . Because punishment is directed towards the past it does not follow that this is its ultimate end; on the

---

[9] Ewing, *The Morality of Punishment*, 105.

contrary we have only justified the reference to the past by showing that without it the future effects desired by us cannot be obtained. It should be inflicted because of a past offence, but we must add also 'as a means to a future good'.[10]

However, this reconciliation is problematic; in certain circumstances it would prove to be merely apparent. That is so because of the status accorded to the considerations of justice and desert: these are first and foremost means to an end. Ewing concedes that justice in punishment may be valuable in itself, but emphasizes that its intrinsic value is very small indeed when compared to its value as a means. It is of great importance as a means because only punishment seen as deserved and just will get across the message in which he sees the main moral purpose of punishment and its real justification. To be sure, a punishment will be normally seen as just if it *is* just—but then it ought to *be* just, essentially, so as to be *seen* as such. And if it can be seen as just without being so, that will also do quite well, for the intrinsic importance of justice in punishment is not great. This shows that Ewing would be committed to 'punishing' the innocent no less than a traditional, Benthamite utilitarian. For the latter, the same as Ewing, could not accomplish his aim except by presenting the innocent man 'punished' to the public at large as the culprit; this kind of merely apparent justice is presupposed in the argument. So long as the public is deceived into believing that the innocent man is guilty, his 'punishment' will deter potential offenders; so long as it is so deceived, the 'punishment' will carry the moral message to those of the public that are in need of it. Ewing's 'fresh purpose to justify [punishment]' can legitimize unjust punishment no less than the aim of deterrence which the traditional utilitarian theory saw as its main justification.

IV   THE INSTITUTION AND THE PARTICULAR CASE

1   Rule-Utilitarianism[11]

Still another attempt at a synthetic theory of punishment, far more influential than those I have considered so far, has been made in the context of developing rule-utilitarianism. The main motives behind this reconstruction of utilitarianism have been the need to account for the role moral rules play in our moral thinking, and to avoid various

---

[10] Ewing, 'Punishment as a Moral Agency', 300.
[11] In this section I draw on material in section IV of my 'Utilitarianism and Punishment of the Innocent', *Rivista Internazionale di Filosofia del Diritto*, vol. 57 (1980).

compromising implications of the old 'act' variety of the theory. Both are clearly at work here, the implications to be avoided being that various kinds of unjust punishment, with 'punishment' of the innocent understandably topping the list, might be justified. In addition, the rule-utilitarian theory of punishment is meant to transcend the confrontation between utilitarianism and retributivism by providing a synthesis which is basically utilitarian, but makes room for considerations of justice and desert as well. The distinction which ought to make this possible is the one between the institution of punishment and the particular case falling under it.

The classic and still unsurpassed formulation of this theory is presented in 'Two Concepts of Rules' by John Rawls:

> One must distinguish between justifying a practice as a system of rules to be applied and enforced, and justifying a particular action which falls under these rules; utilitarian arguments are appropriate with regard to questions about practices, while retributive arguments fit the application of particular rules to particular cases.[12]

An analogous distinction must be made between the roles pertaining to these two levels: the role of the legislator, who sets up the institution of punishment, guided by considerations of the common good, and that of the judge, who applies the rules of the institution to particular cases, giving offenders punishments prescribed by law for their offences, and acquitting those proven innocent.

> The judge and the legislator stand in different positions and look in different directions: one to the past, the other to the future. The justification of what the judge does, *qua* judge, sounds like the retributive view; the justification of what the (ideal) legislator does, *qua* legislator, sounds like the utilitarian view. Thus both views have a point . . . and one's initial confusion disappears once one sees that these views apply to persons holding different offices with different duties, and situated differently with respect to the system of rules that make up the criminal law. . . . One reconciles the two views by the time-honoured device of making them apply to different situations.[13]

The law is primary in relation to particular cases that fall under it; the role of the legislator is primary in relation to that of the judge.

---

[12] J. Rawls, 'Two Concepts of Rules', in M. D. Bayles (ed.), *Contemporary Utilitarianism*, Garden City (1968), 62.
[13] Ibid., 63–5.

Accordingly, this synthesis is basically utilitarian, with retributive considerations being assigned a secondary, subordinate role.

Is this, then, a successful synthesis of utilitarianism and retributivism, and a plausible view of punishment? The answer to this question will depend mainly on the capacity of this theory consistently to rule out 'punishment' of the innocent and other kinds of unjust punishment. To keep to the issue of 'punishing' the innocent, what reason would this theory give for holding to the rule that only the guilty are to be punished even in a case when the utilitarian aim of the institution of punishment, the prevention of crime, would be best served by making an exception?

Here a rule-utilitarian might try several lines of argument.

(*a*) He might refer to indirect, long-term effects of making an exception. No matter how great a contribution to the aim of the institution might be secured at the time of 'punishing' an innocent man, when the truth about his innocence eventually becomes known to the public this will undermine the rule broken and the whole institution to such an extent, that the harm caused will by far outweigh the benefit originally achieved. Therefore, when a long-term view is taken, it turns out that 'punishment' of the innocent can never really be socially useful, and therefore a utilitarian will never be committed to such a course of action.[14]

This retort can easily be met. It is enough to introduce an additional assumption into the argument: that it is possible to make sure that the truth about the innocence of the man sacrificed to the common good will never become known. In such a case no indirect adverse consequences of the breaking of the rule have to be taken into account, and the balance of consequences remains as before, in favour of making an exception and 'punishing' the innocent man.

(*b*) Another possibility would be to refer to the logical nature of the rule that only the guilty are to be punished. This is not an empirical generalization allowing for exceptions, but an institutional rule—a rule which partly defines the institution of punishment and the institutional role of the judge. It does not leave the person playing the role the discretion to make exceptions to it, but makes it incumbent upon him to apply it in all cases of punishment. The argument on 'punishment' of the innocent assumes that the judge has the authority to decide particular cases on utilitarian grounds, disregarding the rules which make up the institutional context; but such authority is logically precluded by the very notion of such rules.[15]

---

[14] Cf. W. Lyons, 'Deterrent Theory and Punishment of the Innocent', *Ethics*, vol. 84 (1973/4).   [15] Cf. Rawls, 'Two Concepts of Rules', 76–8, 87–90, 92, 94–5.

This defence, however, misses the point of the argument. There is no denying that the rule that only the guilty are to be punished, being an institutional rule, aspires to universal validity, and that the role of the judge does not give him the authority to make exceptions to it. For the import of the argument is that in a situation in which the best consequences would be secured by 'punishing' an innocent man there is no good utilitarian reason for the judge not to *ignore* the claim of the rule that only the guilty shall be punished to universal validity, not to do something which his role does *not* authorize him to do—namely, to break the rule and 'punish' the man.

(*c*) The discussion so far has been in terms of a choice between keeping to the rule that only the guilty are to be punished, and making an exception to it. Rawls holds that this is not the right approach at all; what is being discussed is *rule*-utilitarianism, so the choice ought to be presented as one between that rule and an alternative rule. Faced with the argument on 'punishment' of the innocent, the rule-utilitarian 'must describe more carefully what the *institution* is which [the argument] suggests, and then ask . . . whether or not it is likely that having this institution would be for the benefit of society in the long run'.[16] Rawls contends that a utilitarian justification of an institution for 'punishing' the innocent whenever that is in the best interest of society—he calls it 'telishment'—is 'most unlikely'. Why? For one thing, because the dangers of abuse by the officials of the institution would be great. This is not very convincing, for there are hardly any institutions which cannot be abused; we can assume, for the sake of argument, that enough reliable, honest people can be found to ensure that abuse is reduced to an acceptable minimum.

Rawls's second reason is that in a society which replaced the institution of punishment as we know it by telishment, the uncertainty as to whether people fined, put in prison, or executed were punished or telished, and the unpredictability of one's own fate, with all the psychological and social repercussions of such a state of affairs, would be just too high a price to pay. However, all this would not be a consequence of the institution of telishment as such, but of the public knowledge about it. Rawls says that, as a matter of logic, institutional rules have to be publicly known. Now this is right in the sense that an institutional rule cannot be private—known to one person only and secret with regard to everyone else. But this is not to say that they have to

[16] Ibid., 70.

be public in the widest sense possible, that is, known to the whole public at large. The rules of telishment could be internal institutional rules— they could be known to the officials of the institution, but not to the public. Then those harmful consequences on which Rawls bases his claim that telishment could not have a utilitarian justification would not be produced. The circumstances which would provide for such justification would be the same that make a particular act of 'punishing' an innocent man justified from the utilitarian point of view, only they would not be transient, but would have a degree of permanence. That would give rise to a social need of some permanence, to be met by an appropriate institutional arrangement.

Thus rule-utilitarianism does not really effect a synthesis of the utilitarian and retributive views of punishment; it does not really integrate retributive considerations in such a way as to avoid the commitment to socially expedient injustice in punishment, which vitiates the old, 'act' variety of the theory. Rules or no rules, a utilitarian will have to put aside considerations of justice and desert when that is the option with the best consequences.

2   H. L. A. Hart

In some respects, Hart's highly influential views on punishment are rather similar to the rule-utilitarian account. He sets out by claiming that a 'morally tolerable' theory must display the complexity of punishment, and 'exhibit it as a compromise between distinct and partly conflicting principles'.[17] The way to do that is by distinguishing the question of justification of the institution of punishment or, as he puts it, of its 'general justifying aim', and those questions that arise in particular cases of punishing, that is, questions of its distribution: who gets punished, and how much? As an answer to the first question, retributivism will not do; the institution of punishment has to be legitimized in terms of its general justifying aim, which is the prevention of crime by way of general deterrence (conceived in a less rationalistic and mechanistic way than in the traditional, Benthamite version of the deterrence theory). At the level of distribution, however, both utilitarian and retributive considerations are relevant. The question of liability to punishment has to be answered in purely retributivist terms: only those who have broken the law, and have done so voluntarily, may legitimately be punished. The amount of punishment is to be decided upon partly by

---

[17]   Hart, *Punishment and Responsibility*, 1.

considerations of deterrence, which are determined by the purpose and justification of the institution of punishment, and partly by criteria on which the retributivist would insist. Punishments ought to be measured out so as to serve the end of deterrence in an efficient, but also economic way. At the same time, there ought to be some proportion between crimes and punishments. And in cases of diminished responsibility, the severity of punishment ought to be mitigated.

On the face of it, this looks rather like the rule-utilitarian view discussed in the preceding section. Whether it is but another formulation of that view, open to the same objections, depends on the status of those principles of justice which, according to this theory, have an important role to play at the level of distribution of punishment. On this question Hart is not entirely unequivocal. At times he seems to lean towards a purely utilitarian understanding of those principles; he seems to imply that they are subordinate to the justifying aim of the institution. Thus he says that:

fairness between different offenders expressed in terms of different punishments is not an end in itself, but a method of pursuing other aims which has indeed a moral claim on our attention; and we should give effect to it *where it does not impede the pursuit of the main aims* of punishment. . . . The idea of proportion . . . has still a place in an account of the values which a theory of punishment should recognize. But it is a modest place . . . .[18]

He also says, more generally, that 'justice is a *method* of doing other things, *not a substantive end* . . . .'[19] However, these formulations are atypical; the dominant view is significantly different. The principles of justice or fairness which, in combination with utilitarian considerations, determine the distribution of punishment, are to be understood as *different* from, *independent* of, and partly *conflicting* with, its general justifying aim. And it is no accident that they conflict with it; for they are meant to *limit* the pursuit of the utilitarian aim, to make sure that it is not striven for in ways which are unjust, that the individual is not denied his rights and unjustly used by society, or even sacrificed to it, in ways which unqualified pursuit of deterrence would call for. In this respect punishment is like other major social institutions: 'Just because the pursuit of any single social aim has its restrictive qualifier, our main social institutions always possess a plurality of features which

---

[18] Ibid., 172–3 (emphasis added).
[19] Hart, *The Morality of the Criminal Law*, Jerusalem (1964), 54 (emphasis added).

can only be understood as a compromise between partly discrepant principles'.[20]

Thus, with regard to liability to punishment, the principle that only those who have broken the law, and have done so voluntarily, may legitimately be punished, cannot be established on utilitarian grounds. To try to show that 'punishment' of the innocent could not possibly be socially expedient in the long run is to miss the point: '. . . though such answers *can* be made they do not seem to account for the character of the normal unwillingness to 'punish' those who have not broken the law at all . . . .' For this unwillingness 'would still remain even if we were certain that in the case of the 'punishment' of one who had not broken the law the fact of his innocence would not get out or would not cause great alarm if it did'.[21] Nor can the requirement of *mens rea* be plausibly defended by the argument from 'inefficaciousness' of punishment of the insane or those who have violated the law unintentionally. Hart shows Bentham's rationale of excuses to be a 'spectacular *non sequitur*': true, such punishment would not make sense in terms of special deterrence—but that it could contribute significantly to general deterrence, which is the main purpose of punishing. Our rejection of such punishment implies our willingness to do without that contribution. Generally, the operation of 'punishing' the innocent for the sake of the common good, and programmes of abolishing the *mens rea* requirement and meting out punishments in accordance with 'objective liability' (Holmes), or of doing away with the intuition of punishment altogether and replacing it by some therapeutic system of social control (Lady Wootton), cannot be plausibly rejected from a utilitarian point of view; they have to be repudiated in the name of justice or fairness as an irreducible, independent principle of considerable weight. This principle can be supported by arguments from liberty as a paramount moral and social value. Only a system of crime control which incorporates the principle that only those who have broken the law, while having a fair opportunity not to do so, may be punished, maximizes freedom of the individual within the coercive framework of law. It lets his own decisions determine his future, and also enables him to predict it, in a way and to a degree which would not be possible were this principle to be discarded.

With regard to the severity of punishment, over and above the utilitarian concern for economical deterrence, entailed by the general

[20] Hart, *Punishment and Responsibility*, 10.
[21] Ibid., 76, 77–8.

justifying aim of the institution, there are some requirements of justice to be met. First, there ought to be a certain proportion between the punishment and the crime; disproportionately harsh punishments are unacceptable, not because they would be uneconomical (they might not be), but just because they would be disproportionate. This demand for proportion is supported both by considerations of utility and of justice:

There are many reasons why we might wish the legal gradation of the seriousness of crimes, expressed in the scale of punishments, not to conflict with common estimates of their comparative wickedness. One reason is that such a conflict is undesirable on simple utilitarian grounds: it might either confuse moral judgements or bring the law into disrepute, or both. Another reason is that principles of justice or fairness between different offenders require morally distinguishable offences to be treated differently and morally similar offences to be treated alike.[22]

Secondly, there are considerations of mitigation. It is justice, not utility, that requires that those who faced special difficulties in obeying the law they have broken should be punished less severely. If utility were all there is to it, it would have to be the other way round.[23]

These, then, are the main points of Hart's theory of punishment. It has been criticized on several counts. The notion of a 'general justifying aim' has been challenged. It is ambiguous between an aim or purpose of punishment and its justification, and these are not the same, 'except in the eyes of those who have travelled so far down the utilitarian road that they never question the means if the end is desirable'.[24] Now Hart certainly does not fit this description. The criticism misses the mark, for the notion is not used in order to advance a utilitarian rationale of the institution of punishment under the guise of a normatively innocuous formulation of the question to be dealt with; the claim that the institution has to be justified in terms of deterrence is put forward as an expressly normative one, and the alternative, retributivist answer to the same question is explicitly repudiated on the same, normative level.

It has also been pointed out that the mere fact that we can ask those particular questions distinguished by Hart:

---

[22] Hart, *Law, Liberty, and Morality*, London (1963), 36–7.
[23] Cf. J. Bentham, *An Introduction to the Principles of Morals and Legislation*, W. Harrison (ed.) Oxford (1960), 290–1.
[24] K. G. Armstrong, 'The Retributivist Hits Back', in H. B. Acton (ed.), *The Philosophy of Punishment*, 141.

is consistent with *all* the answers being solely in terms of prevention, or solely in terms of desert. There is no reason for thinking that some separate-questions procedure inevitably or logically leads one to a compromise theory. The existence of separate questions does not constitute an *argument* for the conclusion that punishment must be justified by several principles.[25]

This is not a valid objection either. The compromise view which Hart advances as the right solution of the problem of justification of punishment is not presented as following from the division of the relevant questions, nor are those out-and-out utilitarian and retributive theories dismissed as somehow logically flawed, because they do not allow for the fact that there are several distinct questions involved. On the contrary, Hart repudiates both purely retributive and purely utilitarian theories of punishment for expressly moral reasons. The separation of questions does not logically lead to a compromise, but opens up a possibility of it; it is not a sufficient, but merely a necessary condition of a synthetic, middle-of-the-road theory.

Finally, this synthesis itself has been questioned; it has been asserted that it is based on a distinction which Hart, as a utilitarian, is not entitled to make. If one opts for utilitarianism as the answer to the question of the general justifying aim of punishment, one is thereby committed to going by utilitarian considerations, and such considerations only, at the level of distribution. A 'thoroughgoing utilitarian' may not introduce restrictions upon the pursuit of the aim which justifies the institution, except such as may themselves be based on utilitarian grounds.[26] This criticism is beside the point. Hart is not a thoroughgoing, but a qualified utilitarian. He is not trying to 'append' a principle of justice onto the principle of utility, but offers a theory which allows for both, conceived as distinct and independent principles.

Other attempts at a middle way in the philosophy of punishment, discussed in preceding sections, have one thing in common: there is a willingness to find room for considerations of justice and desert, but justice is never seen as a truly independent moral principle. It is either a mere logical appendix to a utilitarian ethical theory (Quinton), or a means to a utilitarian end (Ewing), or an internal rule of an institution justified by its utility, and accordingly a rule predicated upon its own utility (rule-utilitarianism). Having been given such a low status, justice

---

[25] T. Honderich, *Punishment: The Supposed Justifications*, rev. edn. Harmondsworth (1976), 151.
[26] S. Gendin, 'A Plausible Theory of Retribution', *The Journal of Value Inquiry*, vol. 6 (1972), 10–11.

proves incapable of ensuring that unjust but expedient punishment is ruled out. With Hart things are significantly different. Justice is introduced expressly as an independent principle, irreducible to utility and based on grounds other than utility; therefore his theory does rule out injustice in punishment such as disproportionately harsh penalties, punishment of the irresponsible, or 'punishment' of the innocent. This has been accomplished by giving up the simplicity of a thoroughgoing utilitarianism, which is the source of most of its problems, but also one of the main reasons for its wide appeal, and developing a qualified utilitarian theory of punishment, which is complex, but also much more plausible. This theory has 'delineated a middle ground, whose existence had not before been so clearly perceived, between the retributivists and the utilitarians'.[27] It has been widely influential; it has been said that it 'clearly shows how in philosophy—and all the more in the philosophy of punishment, which deals with an institution affecting so closely the dignity, liberty and security of men—balance and moderation are worth more than absolute and exclusive fidelity to a single principle'.[28]

Still, Hart's theory of punishment is exposed to some objections.

(*a*) According to the theory, the severity of punishment is to be determined partly by considerations of deterrence, and partly by those of justice. The utilitarian view of punishment has been charged, *inter alia*, with committing us to draconian punishment. If we fix the punishment on the principle of deterrence, writes K. G. Amstrong, for instance, 'why stop at the minimum, why not be on the safe side and penalise [the offender] in some pretty spectacular way—wouldn't that be more likely to deter others? Let him be whipped to death, publicly of course, for a parking offence; that would certainly deter *me* from parking on the spot reserved for the Vice-Chancellor!'[29] Now this is not a good argument even against an out-and-out utilitarian view of punishment:

---

[27] R. A. Wasserstrom, 'H. L. A. Hart and the Doctrines of *Mens Rea* and Criminal Responsibility', *The University of Chicago Law Review*, vol. 35 (1967/8), 125.

[28] M. A. Cattaneo, 'La Retribuzione Penale nell Interpretazione e nella Critica di Herbert L. A. Hart', in G. Tarello (ed.), *Materiali per una Storia della Cultura Giuridica*, vol. 4, Bologna (1974), 699.

This pluralistic approach to punishment—which would be apt concerning other major social institutions as well—is very much in the spirit of the repudiation of the 'metaphysical chimera' that the realm of values must be essentially harmonious, all values ultimately compatible, all value conflicts capable of a 'final solution', in the writings of philosophers such as Sir Isaiah Berlin ('Two Concepts of Liberty', *Four Essays on Liberty*, Oxford (1969)) and Bernard Williams ('Ethical Consistency', *Problems of the Self*, Cambridge (1973); 'Conflicts of Values', *Moral Luck*, Cambridge (1981)).

[29] K. G. Armstrong, 'The Retributivist Hits Back', 152.

no utilitarian would want to prevent offences by causing more harm than would be brought about if those offences were committed. In Hart's theory, this requirement of utilitarian economy sets an *upper* limit to the severity of punishment. The upper limit is determined from the other side as well, by the demand for some sort of proportion between punishments and offences. Even when efficient in an economical way, disproportionately harsh punishments may not be meted out; for such punishments would be unjust. But this principle of proportion is merely negative, a constraint upon the pursuit of the aim of punishment. So it does not at the same time determine the *lower* limit of the severity of punishment—that is decided upon on the grounds of deterrence only. Interestingly enough, this purely negative interpretation of the principle of proportion can also be met in the writings of some self-styled retributivists.[30] Its consequence is that if, for example, six months in prison turned out to be deterrent enough with regard to rape, or if a year's term turned out to be enough to deter potential murderers, these would be punishments right and proper for such crimes, when committed. We would not be justified in going beyond them. Thus Hart's theory would not justify disproportionately severe punishment, but it would justify *disproportionately lenient penalties.*

(*b*) With regard to liability to punishment, the theory advances only considerations of justice and desert, on which the retributivist insists. Only the voluntary commitment of a crime gives the state the *right* to punish or—as Hart puts it—the moral licence to use a man for promoting the aim of deterrence. Thus 'punishment' of the innocent is effectively ruled out. But this negative significance of the fact that someone has committed a crime is all the moral significance the fact has by itself. It by no means entails the *duty* of the state to punish; that is based on the deterrent effects of punishment, and on those effects only. Hart repeatedly and emphatically repudiates retribution as a principle calling for punishment to be meted out independently of whether it will help deter crimes in the future or not. Thus the theory implies that in cases when considerations of deterrence do not apply, the guilty may not be justifiably punished. No matter how grave and morally reprehensible a crime is, if by punishing for it no deterrent results are to be attained, it ought to remain unpunished.

This argument on *non-punishment of the guilty* seems to carry greatest weight in cases of the gravest crimes of all—those committed against

---

[30] Cf. ibid., 154, 157–8.

humanity.[31] Was it, for example, justified to punish Eichmann? The answer suggested by Hart's theory is that it was, provided that punishing him served the purpose of deterring potential Eichmanns from committing genocidal acts in the future. Now this does not seem to be a very satisfactory answer. For we can assume, for the sake of argument, that there are no potential Eichmanns left in the world or, alternatively, that those that remain, and those still to come, are beyond deterrence. Not that the history of the last forty years or so has convincingly testified to the deterrent efficiency of such punishments. The death sentences meted out at Nüremberg, or the one given to Eichmann, did not deter mass murderers who came later, such as Idi Amin, Pol Pot or Enrique Macias and their henchmen. If, from the point of view of deterrence, those punishments have failed, should we conclude that Rosenberg or Eichmann ought not to have been punished? Or that we should not bother to search out and bring to justice those who have committed mass murder, nor punish those who might do the same in the future?

(c) In connection with Hart's claim that the institution of punishment is to be justified solely in terms of deterrence, R. A. Wasserstrom says the following:

There is a real sense in which Hart's position is less a justification of punishment than a justification of the threat of punishment. It is clear that if we could convince the rest of society that we were in fact punishing offenders we would accomplish all that Hart sees us as achieving through punishment. This is so because it is the *belief* that punishment will follow the commission of an offense that deters potential offenders. The actual punishment of persons is necessary only to keep the threat of punishment credible. Punishment is, therefore, in Hart's view, to be conceived as a necessary evil rather than a positive good. It follows, and this, too, is surely one of the merits of Hart's view, that punishment is something that society ought always seek to minimize if not eradicate.[32]

Rather than being a merit of the theory, I should say that this brings it dangerously close to the old Benthamite view of punishment, with its distinction between real and apparent punishment and the thesis that it is the latter only that deters, while the former is needed solely for the sake of the latter and, being in itself but an evil, ought to be minimized or avoided altogether whenever possible. 'If hanging a man *in effigy* would

[31] Cf. R. A. Wasserstrom, 'H. L. A. Hart and the Doctrines of *Mens Rea* and Criminal Responsibility', 109–10.
[32] Ibid., 111.

produce the same salutary impression of terror upon the minds of the people', Bentham wrote, 'it would be folly or cruelty ever to hang a man *in person.*'[33] This example may not be entirely felicitous here, for Hart does not believe in the deterrent effectiveness of the death penalty; but it does illustrate the kind of *deception* and *manipulation* of the public that a theory which sees the positive value of punishment exclusively in its utility as a means of crime control could justify.

V RETRIBUTION AS A POSITIVE PRINCIPLE

In contrast to other attempts at a synthesis of utilitarianism and retributivism, which do not take retributive considerations seriously enough and therefore do not effectively rule out those unjust punishments which compromise utilitarianism pure and simple, Hart's theory provides for an autonomous and significant role for considerations of justice and desert, and is therefore immune to most arguments against the utilitarian view of punishment. But it has one thing in common with other middle-of-the-road theories: like those theories, it seeks to accommodate the retributive principle as a *negative* principle only. The principle of just deserts figures merely as a constraint upon the pursuit of the aim of punishment: it provides the basis of the state's right to punish and delimits the scope of this right. So it precludes 'punishment' of the innocent, but does not call for punishing the guilty; it sets the upper limit to the severity of punishment, thus prohibiting disproportionately harsh punishments, but does not relate to the lower limit of punishment, does not call for the full measure of proportion to be secured when punishing. The duty of the state to punish and the lower limit of punishments are determined by entirely different considerations—those of deterrence.

To say that retribution not only gives the right to punish, but also imposes the duty to do so, and not only sets the upper, but also the lower limit to the severity of punishment, would for all practical purposes mean to embrace the idea as the justification of the institution of punishment. About this kind of retributivism as a distinctive theory of punishment (and not merely part of the case for legal moralism) Hart does not have much to say. He calls it 'stern', 'severe', even 'fierce',[34] and sometimes seems to imply that it is enough to display it for what it

---

[33] Bentham, *Principles of Penal Law, Works*, J. Bowring (ed.) New York (1962), vol. 1, 398.
[34] Hart, *Punishment and Responsibility*, 232, 236–7.

is—namely, a theory which would call for punishing, and giving the full measure of deserved punishment, even in cases when no utilitarian aim would be served by doing so—in order to dispose of it.[35] Apart from that, his main objection seems to be that it avoids the question of justification of punishment rather than providing an answer to it.[36] This is an old argument, but not a very strong one; for it is based on a narrow notion of justification as a procedure showing that the *justificandum* has instrumental value. There is no obvious reason why we should conceive of justification in such a narrow utilitarian manner. Still, the argument does point at something which might be seen as a disadvantage of retributivism: while the utilitarian view of punishment follows from a more general ethical theory, the retributive view seems somehow to stand on its own, to lack more general theoretical support.

It should not be an impossible task to build a general theory of justice into which the retributive view of punishment could be fitted. But I do not see why that should be a precondition for advancing this view. I see nothing methodologically unsound in putting forward the crucial tenet of retributivism, that punishment is morally justified in so far as it is just, that justice is *the* moral consideration with regard to punishment, as a fundamental moral principle—fundamental in the sense that it is not deduced from a more general ethical theory. A retributivist can put forward his basic thesis in this way, and then go on to explain what he means by it, and to support it in a non-deductive way. By way of elucidating it he will say that punishment is just when it is deserved, and it is deserved by the commission of an offence. The offence committed is the sole ground of the state's right and duty to punish, and accordingly the measure of the severity of punishment as well. 'Justice' and 'just deserts' are not meant merely negatively, as constraints, but also positively, as demands for punishment of the guilty and the full measure of proportion between the punishment and the offence. It is unjust to 'punish' the innocent; or to punish the guilty by disproportionately harsh punishments; but justice is also not being done when the guilty go unpunished, or when they are punished in a disproportionately lenient way. Justice in these matters is just to treat offenders according to their deserts, to give them what they deserve—not more, and not less. By way of arguing in favour of his theory, the retributivist can set out from the

---

[35] See ibid., 75.

[36] Ibid., 9, 235. For a thorough and sympathetic study of Hart's treatment of various kinds of retributivism and the denunciatory view of punishment see M. A. Cattaneo, 'La Retribuzione Penale nell Interpretazione e nella Critica di Herbert L. A. Hart'.

assumption that the institution of punishment is not unjustifiable in principle, that at least some punishments are legitimate and called for, and then display the particular implications of the competing justifications of punishment. With regard to the utilitarian theory, he will point out those unjust punishments which could be expedient, and thus also justifiable in utilitarian terms. As to Hart's 'middle way' in the philosophy of punishment, he will note that it would justify disproportionately lenient punishment, non-punishment of the guilty, including those guilty of extremely heinous crimes, and making a show of punishment instead of actually inflicting it. And then he will submit that his theory, and his theory only, ensures that none of this is justified.

Admittedly, this will work only with those who hold that the unjust punishments to which a thoroughgoing utilitarian is committed, and also disproportionately lenient punishment, non-punishment of the guilty, and shows of punishment, are morally unacceptable. Those who do not will easily outwit the retributivist at this point, by saying that such courses of action *are* justified, if and when they are options with the best consequences. And there might also be those who take exception to the method of appealing to our particular moral convictions (intuitions, feelings, attitudes) in moral philosophy.[37] Hart, for one, should not be expected to object to the method, for he himself frequently appeals to moral convictions of 'most thinking people', 'moral convictions which most of us share', or 'our moral code', when criticizing unqualified utilitarianism or arguing for his own theory. And he is also alive to the weight of the argument on non-punishment of the guilty, at least:

Even the most faithful adherents of utilitarian doctrine must have felt tempted at times to acknowledge the simple claim that it is right or just that one who has intentionally inflicted suffering on others should himself be made to suffer. I doubt if anyone, reading the records of Auschwitz or Buchenwald, has failed to feel the powerful appeal of this principle; perhaps even the most reflective of those who supported the punishment of the criminals concerned were moved by this principle rather than by the thought that punishment would have beneficial future consequences.[38]

If we accept this claim with regard to the crimes committed in Auschwitz and Buchenwald, why not accept it with regard to crimes

---

[37] Taking exception to what has been the standard method of argument in moral philosophy in general and in the philosophy of punishment in particular will have to be substantiated by something more than a variety of the genetic fallacy, on which the thrust of Y. Shachar's response to my paper is based.

[38] Hart, *Law, Liberty, and Morality*, 59.

against humanity of lesser magnitude? And if we accept the claim with regard to the latter as well, why not with regard to murder of a single human being? And with regard to other crimes, less serious than murder? Or, if we are not willing to go all the way with this demand that justice be done and the criminal paid back in full, where, precisely, shall we draw the line? And why at that particular point, and not a degree or two higher, or lower, on the scale of crimes?

Admittedly, retribution as a positive principle seems to have greater force in cases of more serious crimes than in those of petty offences. In cases of the latter sort we may be more inclined to let the offender 'get away with it', if no effects of deterrence are to be achieved by having him punished. If so, we should be able to account for the difference in our moral judgement in terms of a general theory of the gravity of offences which would justify the different treatment: a theory which would allow, and even call for, the application of the principle of just retribution regarding the most heinous crimes man is capable of perpetrating, and others somewhat less abominable, and then others less abominable still, and then suspend the principle at a certain point on the scale of crimes, and replace it by considerations of entirely different nature—those of deterrence. Lacking such a theory,[39] we seem to have two options. Faced with the records of Auschwitz and Buchenwald, we can appeal to the idea of justice as a positive principle, which not only allows us to punish criminals, but also demands that we do so, independently of the effects in terms of deterrence to be reaped from the punishment, and then proceed to apply the principle to other crimes, serious and not so serious. Or we can stick to the position that retribution ought not to be exacted if no deterrent effects are to be expected from punishment, which may seem to come naturally in cases of petty offences, and then go on to dismiss, along the same lines, the idea of punishing Eichmann.

VI   DENUNCIATION

In a review of the main varieties of retributivism, Hart points out that 'in its most interesting form modern retributive theory has shifted the

---

[39] The distinction between legal offences which are also morally wrong (*mala in se*) and those which are intrinsically morally indifferent (*mala prohibita*) (see P. Devlin, *The Enforcement of Morals*, London (1965), Chap. 2, and Hart, *Punishment and Responsibility*, 235–6) will not help here, for many offences regarding which we may be willing initially to desist from punishment if it would be useless in terms of crime control, belong to the first category.

emphasis, from the alleged justice or intrinsic goodness of the return of suffering from the moral evil done, to the value of the authoritative expression, in the form of punishment, of moral condemnation for the moral wickedness involved in the offence'.[40] That punishment has something to do with expressing condemnation or denunciation of the offence by society has been recognized by many authors. Accounts that point out this dimension of punishment are sometimes termed 'expressive' or 'denunciatory' theories; but these labels are too indefinite and potentially misleading. For one can analyze punishment as a practice that has this dimension, and even present it as the essence of punishment, without taking sides in the controversy about the moral justification of punishment thus analyzed. In such a case we have a view or account or analysis of punishment, but not a theory of punishment in the sense usually assumed in the debates on punishment in moral and legal philosophy.[41]

But even if this expressive aspect of punishment is brought up in the context of discussion of its moral basis, there are two different ways in which this can be done. It may be claimed that punishment is justified as the expression of condemnation or denunciation, because that is how it serves its social purpose. This mechanism can then be described in more than one way. One could say, with J. F. Stephen, that society as a matter of fact feels hatred and vengefulness towards the offender, that this is 'a healthy natural sentiment',[42] and that it ought to be given a socially recognized and regulated form in punishment rather than be left unchannelled and likely to break out in various disruptive ways. In this sense it could be said—to quote a famous formulation of Stephen's—that 'the criminal law stands to the passion of revenge in much the same relation as marriage to the sexual appetite'.[43] Or one could see this expression of condemnation of the offence in the light of its contribution to the moral education of society, as in A. C. Ewing's 'educative' theory of punishment. It could be claimed, with Durkheim, that the expression of moral condemnation through punishment serves to reinforce the 'collective consciousness' of society. An offence is, first and foremost, a violation of this consciousness; the latter 'would necessarily lose its

---

[40] Hart, *Punishment and Responsibility*, 235.

[41] Cf. e.g. J. Feinberg, 'The Expressive Function of Punishment', *Doing and Deserving*, Princeton (1970).

[42] J. F. Stephen, *A History of the Criminal Law of England*, London (1883), vol. 2, 82.

[43] Stephen, *A General View of the Criminal Law of England*, 2nd edn., London (1890), 99.

energy, if an emotional reaction of the community [i.e. punishment] did not come to compensate its loss and [this] would result in a breakdown of social solidarity'.[44] Still another possibility would be to suggest some combination of these various uses of the expressive possibilities of punishment, as in *The Ethics of Punishment* by W. Moberly,[45] or in the view suggested by N. MacCormick in his recent monograph on Hart as one that would tie in nicely with Hart's analysis of 'rules of obligation' and bring out the contribution of punishment to general prevention in a more sophisticated way than the deterrent account pure and simple does.[46]

However, one could also put aside all such forward-looking, utilitarian considerations, and maintain that the expression of condemnation of the offence in the form of punishment is *intrinsically* right and called for. When discussing this view in the context of his critique of legal moralism, Hart objected that it 'represents as a value to be pursued at the cost of human suffering the *bare* expression of moral condemnation, and treats the infliction of suffering as a uniquely appropriate or "emphatic" mode of expression. But . . . is the *mere* expression of moral condemnation a thing of value in itself to be pursued at this cost?'[47] To this one could reply that to dissociate punishment as the expression of condemnation from those prospective considerations utilitarians would see as crucial is not to make it into a *bare* or *mere* expression. By expressing condemnation of the misdeed committed, punishment *vindicates* the law broken, *reaffirms* the right infringed, and *demonstrates* that the deed *was* an offence.

Rules which express standards of behaviour and command categorically automatically imply that their breaches are wrong, and that such breaches are to be condemned, denounced, repudiated. Expressions of such condemnation and repudiation are the index of the validity of the rules and of the acceptance of the notion that their violations are wrong in society. If actions of a certain kind do not revoke such a response from society, that goes to show that no rule prohibiting such actions is accepted as a valid standard of behaviour. Moral standards, expressed by moral rules, evolve in society in a diffuse, non-institutional way, rely on the moral authority of society and conscience of its members, and are

---

[44] E. Durkheim, *The Division of Labor in Society*, trans. G. Simpson, New York (1964), 108.

[45] W. Moberly, *The Ethics of Punishment*, London (1968).

[46] See N. MacCormick, *H. L. A. Hart*, London (1981), 66, 136–7, 141–3.

[47] Hart, *Law, Liberty, and Morality*, 65 (emphasis added).

used as criteria of moral judgement by any and all of its members without any special authorization or qualification. Thus whether a certain kind of action is seen as morally wrong in a society, whether a society adheres to a standard prohibiting that kind of action, can be established by finding out whether ordinary members of that society condemn actions of that sort. Their condemnation vindicates the standard, and demonstrates that its violations are held to be morally wrong. Criminal laws are similar to moral rules in that they also express standards of behaviour. But they express the standards of society organized into a state with its legal order; these standards rely on the authority of the state and its legal order, and are authoritatively formulated and applied solely through formalized procedures in appropriate institutions. Legislative institutions of the state pass criminal laws which determine some of our most important legal rights, and make their violations into offences. It is then up to criminal courts and institutions which carry out sentences passed to condemn actions that violate such laws and infringe the rights defined by them. This condemnation is expressed by punishment. By giving expression to it, punishment vindicates the law broken, reaffirms the right violated, and demonstrates that its violation was indeed an offence. This means that if there are to be rights sanctioned by the criminal law, if some acts are to be offences, if there is to be criminal law at all—there has to be punishment. And the other way round: if there is no punishment, there are no offences, no criminal law, no rights determined and sanctioned by such law.

This, of course, does not mean to say that if, for instance, a thief who has stolen from me manages to escape the police and the court, that shows that his theft was not an offence, and that I actually had no right sanctioned by the criminal law to the piece of property stolen. But if the state and the legal order did not even try to punish him and other thieves, if thieves *as a rule* were not prosecuted and punished, the conclusion would have to be drawn that theft is not really an offence, and that property rights do not really obtain, at least in the sense of rights established and guaranteed by the criminal law.

There is a standard objection that arises at this point. Hart puts it in the following way:

What is meant by the claim that the punishment of offenders is an appropriate way of expressing emphatic moral condemnation? The normal way in which moral condemnation is expressed is by *words*, and it is not clear, if denunciation is really what is required, why a solemn public statement of disapproval would not be the most 'appropriate' or 'emphatic' means of expressing this. Why should a denunciation take the form of punishment?[48]

Now this, I should say, is not quite accurate even of moral condemnation pure and simple. We do express moral condemnation verbally most of the time, but this is not the only normal way of expressing it. We also give it expression by cooling down and otherwise reducing our relations with the person who has committed a serious moral misdeed, sometimes by breaking off all contact and communication. Ostracism is the ultimate moral sanction available to a community when it has to deal with an individual who has put himself beyond the moral pale. But this is a minor point.[49] The main point concerns the denunciation of violations of criminal laws and rights such as those to life, bodily integrity or property, guaranteed by these laws. What would we think if the state and its legal order really reacted to such actions only by issuing 'solemn public statements of disapproval?' The state, which proclaimed the law giving validity and binding character to these rights, would desist from making use of its apparatus of coercion and force, which is one of its essential, defining features, in the face of their violations. And there would be a pronounced dissimilarity and disproportion between those violations which affect their victims very palpably, and the merely verbal reaction to them to which the state and the legal order would limit itself, which might not affect the person to whom it is addressed in the least. In view of all this, I think that both those whose rights were being violated, and those who were violating them—and everyone else, for that matter—would be sure to conclude that those rights were not valid after all, were not really recognized, at least as rights defined and guaranteed by the criminal law, and in any serious manner. For the notion of 'taking X seriously' seems to preclude radical dissimilarity and disproportion between X and whatever one does by way of responding to it. A misdeed cannot be shown to be an offence, the right infringed and the law violated by it cannot be reasserted and vindicated, if the act supposed to do this is by its nature so dissimilar to the deed, and so disproportionate to it in its weight, as a mere verbal condemnation, however solemn, would be. The necessary seriousness and weight can be secured only by punishment.

In order to avoid a possible misunderstanding at this point, let me emphasize that this connection between the expression of condemna-

---

[48] Ibid., 66.

[49] It is noted by Hart himself in *Concept*, 175–6; see also *Law, Liberty, and Morality*, 76–7.

tion of the offence through punishment, and the notions of an offence, a right defined by the criminal law, and the criminal law itself, is not predicated upon the function of this condemnation as a means of prevention of future offences. The thesis is entirely backward-looking. If by punishing we manage to prevent the commission of offences, infringements of rights and violations of the law in the future, so much the better; but neither such effects, nor the intention to attain them, are inherent in the enterprise. We shall have demonstrated that an action was an offence, and reaffirmed the right violated and the law broken by it, even if the condemnation expressed by punishment proves completely inefficient in preventing future offences of the same kind. And we ought to punish so as to do this, for our failure to punish would be incompatible with our adherence to the law and respect for the right in question, and our belief that their violation is an offence.

Still, it might be objected, to interpret and defend punishment as the condemnation of the offence in these purely retrospective terms is to put the cart before the horse. 'We do not live in society in order to condemn,' says Hart, 'though we may condemn in order to live.'[50] But what kind of life in society would it be, if we could find it in ourselves to condemn, appropriately and seriously, only those wrongdoings—including the most reprehensible ones—whose condemnation could be justified in terms of *its* expediency?[51]

[50] Hart, *Punishment and Responsibility*, 172.

[51] The last two sections of this paper are meant merely to suggest the background of my objections to Hart's theory of punishment, advanced at the end of section IV, 2. I have discussed some aspects of retributivism in some detail in 'On Some Arguments against the Retributive Theory of Punishment', *Rivista Internazionale di Filosofia del Diritto*, vol. 56 (1979), 'On Retributivism and the *lex talionis*', ibid., vol. 61 (1984), and *Banquos Geist: Hegels Theorie der Strafe*, Hegel-Studien, Beiheft 29, Bonn (forthcoming).

5.2 Comment

THOMAS MORAWETZ*

My comments will make evident the debt we all owe to Herbert Hart. Hart's account of the justification and explanation of punishment is, as Primoratz shows, more persuasive than most theories and has been widely influential. My own questions will be methodological as well as substantive. They will draw upon a remark made by Hart in a context having nothing to do with the theory of punishment.[52] In his recent criticism of Dworkin, Hart says that 'a satisfactory foundation for a theory . . . will not be found as long as the search is conducted in the shadow of utilitarianism'.[53] Debates about punishment continue to be conducted in this shadow whether they involve its acceptance, its rejection, or the quest for a middle way between utilitarianism and retributivism. My critique has two parts. I shall first show why the idea of a middle way is unstable and how theoreticians gravitate to one or the other pole as long as they take the opposition seriously. I shall then question the very idea of an opposition between two polar modes of justification and give reasons for thinking it a myth.

I

The apparent opposition between two modes of moral justification could hardly be more familiar and deep-seated. To the so-called forward-looking or utilitarian theorist only anticipations of desirable states of affairs are the sorts of things that can count as justification. To the theorist who invokes justice, any recommendation that does not entail just treatment is morally groundless. The very idea of a middle way is, therefore, suspect to the extent that these methodological standpoints seem irreconcilable.

One can, of course, try to shrug the problem away. One can move to the level of intuitions about acceptable results in particular cases and

* © Thomas Morawetz 1987.
[52] H. L. A. Hart, 'Between Utility and Rights', reprinted in Hart, *Essays in Jurisprudence and Philosophy*, Oxford (1983).
[53] Ibid., 62.

embrace a kind of eclecticism in method, a middle way by default.[54] This consists in middle-level generalizations from particular intuitions. But it is the nature of theoretical investigation to view eclecticism with suspicion, to view it as capitulation in the face of difficulty. Eclecticism *is* the theorist's admission of failure unless the theorist's job is reconceived not as the job of finding a theory but of finding out whether it is possible to find a theory.[55]

The merits of eclecticism are peripheral to my main concern in this section. A second look at the writers discussed by Primoratz shows the extent to which they are captives of one or the other pole of methodological debate once the opposition is taken for granted. Let us see how and why they fail to describe a middle way, whether they are writers who would defend the utilitarian mode of justification or oppose it because its recommendations flout justice.

I

Anthony Quinton's theory confuses description of the conditions of punishment with justification of punishment.[56] It is correct to say by way of description that guilt is a condition of punishment. The institution or practice of punishing has this as a pervasive and unexceptionable feature. But this is not the retributivist's point. The retributivist claims that the practice *must* have this feature to be justified morally. He identifies justice with this feature and says that any practice that lacks it *a fortiori* lacks justification.

The same point can be made somewhat differently. Quinton writes as if it were merely a feature internal to the practice of punishment that punishment is restricted to the guilty. He says that the utilitarian challenge is not answered by this because the challenge is made from outside the practice and has the form, 'Why this practice and not another? Why adhere to this limitation on the practice of punishing?' The retributivist, Quinton notwithstanding, claims to be speaking from outside as well.

Quinton cannot succeed in defusing the retributivist challenge since the retributivist's purpose cannot be to describe a contingent internal feature of systems of punishment. This can be seen in terms of the

---

[54] See for example Bernard Williams, 'Conflicts of Values' and 'The Truth in Relativism', reprinted in Williams, *Moral Luck*, Cambridge (1981); Thomas Nagel, 'The Fragmentation of Value', in Nagel, *Mortal Questions*, Cambridge (1979).

[55] See note 54; Nagel is especially illuminating on this point.

[56] Anthony Quinton, 'On Punishment', in H. B. Acton (ed.), *The Philosophy of Punishment*, London (1969).

linkage between retribution and justice. *If* the retributivist merely identified retribution with punishment conditional on guilt, he could be interpreted as offering a description without normative intent. He could be uncommitted on whether retribution in this sense is desirable. But to describe the connection between punishment and guilt as a requirement of *justice* is to make a normative claim. If the connection is an essential feature of justice, then a system that lacks this feature is unjust. For the retributivist, the aspirations of justificatory theory framed in non-retributive terms are incoherent. Taken seriously, the retributivist leaves us not with the task of finding a justification other than justice, but with the task of understanding what it could possibly mean to justify a system while conceding the irrelevance of justice.

Thus, Quinton avoids the choice between two modes of justification only by declining to identify the retributivist claim as one of justice.[57] Once the retributivist claim is so identified the abyss between the two modes seems unbridgeable. Quinton defends utilitarianism only by interpreting retributivism as a noncompetitor.

2

Rawls's position in 'Two Concepts of Rules' shares some features with Quinton's.[58] Rawls, like Quinton, offers two levels of analysis, internal and external. Unlike Quinton however he does not confuse this with the distinction between description and normative justification.[59] Rawls distinguishes the internal move of justifying a particular action within a practice (a particular application of a rule) from justifying the practice itself as a system of rules. The effect of this bifurcation is to allocate the different modes of justification to different domains. Justice becomes a characteristic and virtue of the application of rules and forward-looking (utilitarian) considerations justify the choice of rules.

It is imporatnt to see just how this theory fails.[60] The theory makes the existence of just treatment a provisional consideration of a fully justified practice. At best just treatment is a feature of a system that, *qua* system,

---

[57] Obviously the contention that *justice* is a logical and not a moral matter is plainly wrong.

[58] John Rawls, 'Two Concepts of Rules', in Michael Bayles (ed.), *Contemporary Utilitarianism*, New York (1968).

[59] Rawls's distinction is between two compatible kinds of justification. He concedes the normative force of each kind.

[60] The inapplicability of Rawls's model to justification as it occurs in 'open' practices like law (as opposed to 'closed' practices likes games) is the main subject of my paper, 'The Concept of a Practice', *Philosophical Studies*, vol. 24, no. 4 (July 1973).

is justified by considerations other than justice, and these other (forward-looking) considerations have conceptual priority. This is unconvincing. As Rawls sees by the time he comes to write *A Theory of Justice*,[61] justice cannot be purely an intra-systemic criterion of normative criticism. If it makes sense to assess an application of a rule as just, it also makes sense to refer to the rule itself as just (in its general application). If there are just rules, there are also just systems of rules. The notion of moral justification is not severable, and the moral standpoints of intra-systemic participant and extra-systemic observer (or rule-maker) are not distinct.[62] Justice makes the same claim on both.

Primoratz offers a different criticism; to my mind a less convincing one. He says the rule-utilitarian could countenance punishing the innocent. This is a different claim because it says that Rawls might obtain counter-intuitive results, not that he gives an unconvincing explanation for the intuitions on which all are likely to agree. The utilitarian could defuse Primoratz's claim in several ways. As a preliminary matter he might say that proferred examples are far-fetched and unpersuasive and that bad examples make bad theory.[63] He may go further and reject the suggestion (that he would countenance a system in which the innocent are officially sanctioned and the public is kept in ignorance of this) in three ways. He may first attack the example on its facts. He may say there is an ineradicable risk that such a policy would become known and that public confidence and obedience would be dramatically threatened. This is a pragmatic rather than a principled reply, and seems to concede the objection. In principle, the rule-utilitarian approves the situation *if* the risk can be eliminated, as in practice it cannot.

But the utilitarian has two responses that are more interesting. One response is that the weight that must be assigned to harming the innocent—the subjective disappointment, the pain of unfair treatment—is such that it *necessarily* outweighs whatever benefits there may

---

[61] Cambridge, Mass. (1971). By this time, Rawls has explicitly rejected utilitarian forms of justification and puts forth an account of justice as a term to be deployed in criticism from an external standpoint.

[62] The distinction here is illustrated by the roles of judge and legislator respectively. The legislator, according to Rawls's model, stands outside the system and makes the rules for it, as a baseball commission would for baseball. The judge is like an umpire and acts inside the game. In my article (note 60) and in *The Philosophy of Law*, New York (1980), chap. 2, I criticize this use of the distinction.

[63] See G. E. M. Anscombe, 'Modern Moral Philosophy', *Philosophy*, vol. 33 (1958), 9–12.

be. The suggestion here is that even if the utilitarian adheres to the criteria of evaluation most often associated with utilitarianism, and speaks of maximizing happiness or satisfaction,[64] it is open to him to make interpersonal comparisons in various ways. It is open, that is, to say that the disappointment of the punished innocents has such intensity and such qualities that it has overwhelming, decisive weight.[65]

The third response is for the utilitarian to adopt non-standard criteria of evaluation and to speak not of happiness and subjective satisfaction but of well-being and the common good. He is then in a position to conclude that a regime of injustice cannot serve the common good. (I shall have more to say about such a theory in part II.)

The second and third responses need elaboration and defence. The second, it will be objected, throws justice out the front door only to admit it through the back by saying that special and decisive weight should be assigned by the utilitarian to the sense of justice outraged. The third response merely raises doubt about what mode of utility determination would be satisfactory.

3

If Quinton and Rawls offer two utilitarian strategies which fail to accommodate the sense of justice, can we do better by taking retributivism more seriously? You will recall that Primoratz distinguishes Hart's views from Rawls's and develops his own suggestions as corrections of Hart. Hart's theory is an attempt at a 'middle way', one that makes use of what Nozick calls 'side constraints'.[66] On this view, utilitarian goals cannot be pursued in ways that violate justice, not because rules of justice are provisionally or contingently the best rules for pursuing utility, but because they represent an independent value that limits such pursuit. The system is 'a compromise between partly discrepant principles'.[67]

Primoratz presents his suggestions about justice not as a compromise

---

[64] Utilitarianism, as propounded by Mill and Bentham, speaks of the greatest happiness for the greatest number. In the twentieth century, utilitarians have frequently refined these references to ones about 'want satisfaction' and 'preference satisfaction'. See, for example, Harlan Miller and William Williams (ed.), *The Limits of Utilitarianism*, Minneapolis (1982).

[65] See my *Philosophy of Law*, 101–6.

[66] Robert Nozick, *Anarchy State and Utopia*, New York (1974) chap. 3, especially pp. 28–33: 'The side-constraint view forbids you to violate . . . moral constraints in the pursuit of your goals', 29.

[67] H. L. A. Hart, *Punishment and Responsibility*, Oxford (1968), 10.

but as a vindication of retribution. Hart clearly invokes justice to safeguard the rights of potential subjects of punishment. Primoratz on the other hand invokes retributivism to emphasize the right of 'society' that offenders be punished with a suitable degree of severity.[68] Hart sees guilt as a threshold condition for punishment, a necessary but not sufficient condition. The application of punishment must not only be justly deserved (that is, only the guilty may be punished and only with severity no greater than the seriousness of the offence), but it also serves the 'general justifying aim' of furthering common ends.[69] Primoratz demands a more encompassing role for the notion of retribution.

In order to evaluate Primoratz's response to Hart, we must try to separate the principle of retribution from the principle of justice. There is no need to do so if we are considering only Hart's requirement (*a*) that punishment be limited to the guilty; this may be called a requirement of retribution or one of justice. Primoratz however finds additional requirements in the notion of retribution, (*b*) that the state be seen as having a duty to punish the guilty and (*c*) that intuitions of proportionality set a lower limit as well as an upper limit to the severity of punishment. While conceding that these are requirements implicit in the notion of retribution, I shall shortly give reasons for questioning whether they are requirements of justice.

Three aspects of Primoratz's scheme are immediately apparent.

1. As Primoratz acknowledges and explains, this is not a mixed scheme, 'middle way'. It is a purely retributive scheme, one that makes no appeal whatever to forward-looking considerations. Such a scheme may have benefits from a forward-looking standpoint, but it is not justified in terms of those benefits.

2. Primoratz's suggestions are echoed in statutory schemes of sentencing, in the announced aims of sentencers, and in the expectations of lay persons.[70] It is often said virtually as a truism that the guilty should be

---

[68] Many political philosophers suggest that rights belong to individuals rather than social groups. See, generally, Alan Gewirth, *Human Rights*, Chicago (1982), and Ronald Dworkin, *Taking Rights Seriously*, Cambridge, Mass. (1978).

[69] Hart does not clearly endorse a utilitarian interpretation of the general justifying aim.

[70] Consider, for example, Section 1170 of the California Penal Code (1976 amendment): 'The Legislature finds and declares that the purpose of imprisonment for crime is punishment. This purpose is best served by terms proportionate to the seriousness of the offense with provision for uniformity in the sentences of offenders committing the same offense under similar circumstances.'

punished and punished with sentences they deserve. Utilitarian modes of justification generally are offered in opposition to this received wisdom, offered as the rationalized suggestions of reformers.[71]

3. Primoratz's suggestions do not fit legal practice, where many principles flout these retributive guidelines. Defendants may buy immunity from prosecution by choosing to incriminate their associates. Under prevailing American law, prosecutions are dropped and convictions overturned when the state violates the statutory or constitutional rights of 'guilty' defendants.[72] The first of these practices may be justified only by expediency, but the latter is typical of a large class of practices sometimes justified by principle.

We can now try to evaluate Primoratz's principles, which carry a long tail of controversy. While the processes of pleading and trial are designed to classify implicated actors as guilty or innocent, other aspects of criminal law make clear the artificiality and idealization involved in this separation. Criminal law everywhere recognizes a range of excusing and mitigating conditions, and it recognizes that each condition expresses a heterogeneous mix of situations and dispositions.[73] Most defendants, unlike Eichmann, do not carry out long-term campaigns of intentional, atrocious conduct. The awareness that many are at the cusp of excusability should make us wary of claiming that there is a duty to punish the guilty as a discrete and isolable class. The same awareness of heterogeneity should make us see how unclear it is to claim that the punishment should fit the seriousness of the offence. Is seriousness measured by the amount of harm caused, the amount of harm intended, the atrocious character of the offence as opposed to the degree of harm,[74] or the degree of commitment, ambivalence, or remorse displayed by the offender?[75]

These problems of a retributivist view are not fatal. We all do in fact rank instances of offensive conduct using the language of comparative seriousness.[76] We sympathize with the duty to punish the guilty as long

[71] See, for example, Ted Honderich, *Punishment: The Supposed Justifications*, Harmondsworth (1971), 52–9.

[72] The development of this practice under the US Constitution is documented and explained in Yale Kamisar, *et al.* (eds.) *Modern Criminal Procedure*, 5th edn., St. Paul (1980), chaps. 5, 10 and 11.

[73] See, for example, Glanville Williams, *Criminal Law: The General Part*, 2nd. edn., London (1961), chaps. 8, 10, 11, 17 and 18.

[74] See John Kleinig, *Punishment and Desert*, The Hague (1973), chap. 7.

[75] Ibid., chaps. 3–5.

[76] Ibid., chap. 7.

as we understand it to refer to those who are morally as well as legally guilty. A decision for or against retributivism as represented by Primoratz's principles will not occur on these grounds alone. Jeffrie Murphy has argued that both utilitarianism and retributivism are based on evident principles and not merely disputable intuitions or emotions. 'That the maximization of social utility is important is no more obviously true than that a man should not unfairly profit from his own moral wrongdoing.'[77] Murphy goes on to remark that retributivism draws its theoretical underpinnings from that aspect of justice that deals with reciprocity. For Kant, criminal law exists to prevent those who disobey the rules of conduct from gaining an unfair advantage over those who obey.[78]

The Kantian view has not stood unchallenged, and major difficulties with it are predictably similar to points already made. We have seen that retributivism, and the underlying theory of reciprocity, underestimate the mix of offenders. Not all seek to profit as from an unfair bargain, and some who seek to do so do not achieve any gain (even before punishment). The notion of reciprocity between the criminal and society *or* between the criminal and his victim is a metaphor drawn from a kind of relationship that is both simpler and importantly different.[79] While justice requires reciprocity in the case of an actual compact or within a small group with voluntary and mutual undertakings, it is much less clear what justice requires under the conditions of actual criminal offence.

Let me summarize. In this section I have indicated the gravitational force of the two modes of moral justification, and of the difficulty of imagining and defending a middle way. Quinton and Rawls exemplify the utilitarian or forward-looking mode while Primoratz presents a form of retributivism. Each writer adopts one or the other mode without in the end bridging the gap between them or offering a convincing accommodation. Quinton and Rawls give insufficient attention to the *extra-systemic* role of justice while Primoratz offers a traditional defence of retributivism that is not obviously in accord with justice. While justice is congruent with a weak retributivism, with the conviction that only the

[77] Jeffrie Murphy, *Retribution, Justice, and Therapy*, Dordrecht (1979), 77.
[78] Immanuel Kant, *Metaphysical Elements of Justice*, trans. John Ladd, Indianapolis (1965) (translation of *Metaphysische Anfangsgründe der Rechtslehre*, 1797).
[79] The use of such metaphors and of this style of reasoning is criticized persuasively by M. B. E. Smith, 'Is There a Prima Facie Obligation to Obey the Law?', *Yale Law Journal*, vol. 82 (1973), 950.

guilty should be eligible for punishment, it is not congruent with a stronger form of retributivism, the notion that there is a duty to punish the guilty with fitting severity.

In the next section I shall discuss Ewing's 'educative' theory[80] and, once more, Hart's theory to consider whether they offer a middle way between the two modes of moral reasoning and more importantly whether the notion of the existence of such an opposition between two modes is an illusion.

II

The utilitarian or forward-looking mode of moral justification requires analysis. In section I, I distinguished elements of the retributive mode and assessed their relationship to justice. In this section I shall argue for a reconception of forward-looking justification which implies that there is no putative opposition between two modes. In this way reasoning about punishment must emerge from 'the shadow of utilitarianism', from a context in which familiar forms of utilitarianism are swallowed whole, rejected, or adopted with demarcated constraints.

The simplest and most inadequate forward-looking theory is met in the law student's first brush with criminal law. It says that criminal punishment serves four goals: to incapacitate offenders (special deterrence), to give a general disincentive for crime (general deterrence), to rehabilitate, and to achieve retribution.[81] The first three are identified as forward-looking in contrast with the problematic fourth. Primoratz claims to find such a forward-looking theory in Hart when he says that Hart could not justify punishing Eichmann unless it served the purpose of deterring other potential Eichmanns. The assumption is that general deterrence is the only possible justification when special deterrence and rehabilitation are so clearly not at issue.

This formulation from the catechism of law texts is plainly inadequate. A forward-looking theory by its nature takes into account every effect of a practice on the common good. The effects of criminal adjudication and punishment on the incidence of crime are the first effects that come to mind but there are others. Although he is critical of the so-called denunciatory theory of criminal law, Hart reminds us that

[80] See Section III of Primoratz's paper and A. C. Ewing, *The Morality of Punishment*, London (1929).

[81] See, for example, Wayne LaFave and Austin Scott, *Criminal Law*, St. Paul (1972), 21–5.

the visible public process of trial and conviction affirm values that bind society.[82] A society in which stable standards of punishment generally reflect and reinforce moral values is one in which persons rest secure in their capacity to act and plan and in which they experience little discontinuity between public events and private expectations. The notion of the common good is not severable from the notion of a society with these characteristics.

It is important to see how this theory goes beyond Ewing's. For Ewing, the deterrent (more generally, preventive) effect of punishment is achieved only in part by threat. It is realized most effectively when fear of punishment is buttressed by the reinforcement of personal moral constraints on conduct. As Primoratz observes, this account assigns a distinctive but clearly subordinate role to the principle that only the guilty be punished. But it is defective in its explanation of why and how a system must include this aspect of justice. It says that such a system will prevent crime more effectively but it ignores the more widespread and immediate benefits of a just system.

A useful discussion of these benefits is in Joel Feinberg's essays, 'The Expressive Function of Punishment' and 'Justice and Personal Desert'.[83] Feinberg draws attention to what he calls 'natural responsive attitudes' to the actions of others, to the congruity—logical as well as emotive—between gratitude and kindness, resentment and intentional injury. There is a fittingness between 'one person's actions or qualities and another person's responsive attitudes'.[84] These attitudes are the foundations of a shared sense of what treatment persons deserve and they owe nothing to forward-looking goals. But, Feinberg notes, consideration of the common good 'gives reasons (in addition to natural inclination) for expressing our attitudes and appraisals' in such institutions as criminal adjudication and punishment.[85] There are reciprocal effects of reinforcement and conditioning between individual responsive attitudes and institutional criteria for decision. Feinberg notes that whether or not symbolic public disapproval helps or hinders deterrence and reform, it serves other functions that are inherent in such expression.[86] Among these are authoritative disavowal of certain kinds of harmful conduct, vindication of the law as rooted in moral values, and

---

[82] Hart, *Punishment and Responsibility*, chap. 7.
[83] Joel Feinberg, *Doing and Deserving*, Princeton (1970), chaps. 4 and 5.
[84] Ibid., 82.
[85] Ibid., 83.
[86] Ibid., 101.

formal absolution of those who are free of blameworthy conduct.[87] It is easy to think of these functions as Ewing does, as means to an end and as needing vindication in the light of some aspect of the common good.[88] Let us consider the steps of the argument and see why that is not so.

First, there is an important distinction between resenting and justified disapproval.[89] Unlike resentment, justified disapproval carries with it the claim of a demonstration that the disapproved conduct violates shared norms of mutual respect and dignity. In other words, resentment is a personal responsive attitude toward actions affecting oneself, while disapproval is a judgement backed by reasons about actions affecting oneself *or* others. They are different categories of response—one

---

[87] Ibid., 101–4.

[88] The point here is elusive and controversial. Consider two controversies.

(1) Hart among others is critical of a denunciatory or expressive theory of punishment. Does Feinberg's account escape these criticisms? The brunt of Hart's argument is that it is a mistake to use public opinion (deep-seated widely shared moral indignation) as the criterion for what to punish, whether to punish, and how severely to punish. (*Punishment and Responsibility*, 170–2.) To defer to public opinion is to ignore that law should not 'passively reflect uninstructed opinion but actively help to shape moral sentiments to rational common ends'. (171) Further, it flies in the face of pluralism and assumes that there is a 'single homogeneous social morality whose mouthpiece the judge can be'. (171)

In fact Feinberg does not make these mistakes. He is talking not about criteria for what to punish but the effects of punishing. The decision to punish and the decision how much to punish shall be made by other criteria (by identifying 'rational common ends') but the effects of such decisions will inevitably reinforce or affront public sentiment and wise decisions take that effect into account. Hart himself observes that 'it is indeed important that the law should not in its scale of punishment gratuitously flout any well-marked common moral distinctions'. (172)

(2) Primoratz raises the question of whether denunciation is a forward or backward-looking consideration, whether the fact that it is denunciation has justificatory force apart from such forward-looking considerations as reinforcement of values. He says that his 'thesis is entirely backward-looking. If by punishing we manage to prevent the commission of offences, infringements of rights and violations of law, so much the better; but neither such effects, nor the intention to attain them are inherent in the enterprise.'

It is hard to fathom what this means. Surely it cannot mean that any act of denunciation is justified because it is an act of denunciation. Surely whether the act is justified depends on what is denounced, and not everything denounced by public opinion is *a fortiori* justifiably denounced. Any justification must come in the form of reasons why the act denounced contravenes an established system of shared values. The nature of such values is such that to honour them in the present is to demonstrate a conviction that they are to be honoured in the future. That is what it means for them to be values. It seems sophistical therefore to say that denunciation, when it is justified, can be backward-looking and not forward-looking at the same time.

[89] The best treatment of this distinction and of its significance for moral philosophy is P. F. Strawson, 'Freedom and Resentment', in Strawson, *Freedom and Resentment and Other Essays*, London (1976).

emotive, one cognitive—but they are responses to the same kind of action. Secondly, there is a logical relationship between resentment or disapproval on the one hand and certain kinds of conduct on the other. What we blame and praise is not always arbitrary or a matter of idiosyncratic preference, but is sometimes a matter of shared standards, a shared sense of the common good. This is what John Rawls taps when he finds and describes the 'sense of justice'.[90] Thirdly, any forward-looking characterization of the common good will describe social institutions in which the sense of justice is realized and reinforced, not as a means to some other end but as an indispensable aspect of living well with others. Fourthly, the requirement that a system of punishment be just (that punishment be allocated to the guilty and that moral blameworthiness play some role in determining the severity of punishment) is an inherent requirement of any characterization of the common good.

If all this is true, Primoratz's 'most telling' criticism of Ewing and of forward-looking theories in general misses the mark. Repeatedly Primoratz tells us that such theories fail because a system, justified in forward-looking terms, could encompass conviction and punishment of the innocent if it was generally believed that those punished were guilty. In this way deterrence could be maximized while the psychological benefits of a just system could be achieved most efficiently though institutionalized hypocrisy.

This counter-example is irrelevant because a forward-looking theory is an attempt to describe a situation in which the common good *is* best secured not one in which persons *happen to believe* that the common good is secured. The counter-example would suggest itself only to someone who thought that there was no difference, but the difference could hardly be greater. One would not confuse (Primoratz surely would not) a situation in which persons believed wrongly that they were safe from crime from one in which potential offenders were really prevented from committing crimes. If so, one should keep distinct a situation in which persons believed they lived in a just society from one in which they were in fact treated justly.

The point here is methodological. To understand this we must distinguish conceptual relationships from contingent ones.[91] For ex-

---

[90] Rawls, *Theory of Justice*, chap. 8.

[91] I am drawing on the familiar and highly problematic distinction between analytic (conceptual) truths and synthetic (contingent, empirical) truths. Very roughly, the distinction is between propositions whose truth is apprehended through one's under-

ample, the relationship between the common good and security from harm is conceptual, not contingent. It is part of the notion of the common good that persons be safe and secure, and the question of why deterrence is a desirable goal is not meaningful.[92] But the relationship between the common good and just treatment is also conceptual and not contingent. If this is so, the question why punishment should be limited to the guilty requires no answer. The attempt to refute Primoratz's counter-example on its own terms, to answer it by showing that systematic injustice would not (as a contingent matter) be balanced by gains from enhanced deterrence, is misconceived *ab initio*. It is misconceived not because the empirical question is close or undecidable, but because gains in added safety are in principle not the sorts of things that can justify systematic injustice.[93]

What relationship do these remarks have to Hart's theory? In one sense we have strayed hardly at all, since Hart himself says that punishment of the innocent is not the sort of thing that may be justified by social expediency. The unwillingness to punish 'would still remain even if we were certain that . . . the fact of innocence would not get out or would not cause great alarm if it did'.[94] He generalizes this by saying that 'the pursuit of a single social aim has its restrictive qualifier' and that 'our main social institutions always possess a plurality of features which can only be understood as a compromise between partly discrepant principles'.[95] Most simply, this means that the *distinctive* aim of criminal law, the control and minimization of crime, is pursued in the context of other values, ones that are affected by what we do with criminal law but are not unique or distinctive to the institution of judging and punishing.

It would be a mistake to take this as an example of a general conflict

standing of the meanings and uses of the terms as opposed to propositions whose truth is determined by inspection of empirical situations. 'Ethics is a branch of philosophy' is a proposition of the first kind while 'Harold Stassen is the Republican nominee for president' is an example of the second. The distinction has spawned endless debate among philosophers. Among the most influential discussions are W. V. Quine, 'Two dogmas of Empiricism', in Quine, *From a Logical Point of View*, 1961, and H. P. Grice and P. F. Strawson, 'In Defense of a Dogma', *The Philosophical Review*, vol. 65, no. 2 (1956).

[92] One can describe the ways in which persons benefit from safety and security, but these descriptions do not have explanatory value. If the value of safety and freedom from harm are not self-evident, there is little to be said to demonstrate their value. Compare Hart's discussion of the minimal content of natural law in *Concept*, chap. 9.

[93] The distinction between what is true 'as a rule' and what may be true as an exception is crucial here.

[94] Hart, *Punishment and Responsibility*, 77–8.

[95] Ibid., 10.

between forward-looking values and justice, or, as Hart puts it, between utility and justice. Hart has in mind, of course, the familiar opposition with which we began between maximizing the sum of happiness or satisfaction in the population and satisfying justice.[96] My suggestion has been that the first of these is a chimera. Happiness and satisfaction are understandable and realizable not *in vacuo* but in a social context. The kind of happiness or satisfaction realizable in a just context is not comparable or commensurable with happiness or satisfaction realizable in an unjust context. The kind of happiness that is relevant to forward-looking anticipations of the common good is necessarily the first.

I use the term 'forward-looking theory of the common good' in preference to the term 'utilitarianism' because the latter is tainted in ways I have already suggested. Throughout its tangled history utilitarianism has been associated with the notion that happiness or satisfaction are only contingently or accidentally related to the moral features of a social context. A context in which the greatest happiness is gained by the greatest number may or may not be a just society; its justice remains to be demonstrated.[97] In Hart's most recent work he sees, I think, the vulnerability of traditional utilitarianism. He says that a satisfactory theory (of rights) will not be found in the shadow of utilitarianism[98] and that we must move away from debate about 'the ways in which utilitarianism has ignored certain values taken to be uncontroversial'.[99] At the same time, he calls for 'a more radical and detailed consideration of the ways in which rights relate to other values'.[100] My remarks are intended to be in the spirit of these observations.

Two points need clarification.

1. It will be said that any attempt to integrate justice into a forward-looking theory must fail. He who takes justice seriously is oblivious to consequences and affirms that justice will be done even if the heavens fall.[101] This objection fails in two ways. First, appearances notwith-

---

[96] Hart, *Essays in Jurisprudence and Philosophy*, 116.

[97] This position, as we have seen, is held by rule-utilitarians as well as other utilitarians. It is compatible with this position that intuitions of what is just may be clearer than intuitions of what is best in utilitarian terms. If that is true, the measure of just intuitions by utilitarian criteria may never be made.

[98] Hart, *Essays in Jurisprudence and Philosophy*, 195.

[99] Ibid., 195.

[100] Ibid.

[101] 'Fiat justitia ruat coelum', proverb, attributed to Lucius Calpurnius Piso Caesoninus.

standing, the objection does not itself set justice in opposition to future consequences, but rather sets in opposition two different sets of consequences, the effects of just treatment and the effects of unjust treatment. In this sense, it is itself forward-looking. Secondly, the continuing debate about justice and forward-looking theories is concerned with established systems of rules (practices) not particular cases of injustice. The objection would have to be rewritten to refer not to justice in the particular case but to just rules. That said, one who holds the view I have defended may concede that individual cases of injustice may occur and need to be excused, but in principle they must remain exceptions within a system of justice. If the objector's suggestion is that the heavens would fall were justice done systematically, that is, were just rules adopted, then he purveys a pessimism to which there is no reasonable response.

2. It will also be said that by integrating justice into a forward-looking theory I have absorbed Primoratz's own suggestions that there is a duty to punish the guilty and to do so proportionately. This is to forget the caveats laid out above. Justice, on my view, speaks uncertainly to Primoratz's issues. It may counsel us to distinguish among the guilty in the light of circumstances, to weigh ameliorating or aggravating situational factors in deciding when and how to punish.

This disagreement can be put more formally. Let us distinguish four propositions.

(a) A forward-looking theory of the common good will prescribe a system of just rather than unjust treatment.
This, I have argued, is a conceptual matter.

(b) A just system of punishment will restrict punishment to the guilty.
This too is a conceptual matter and not an empirical question.

(c1) A just system of punishment will always punish the guilty and will punish them with severity proportionate to the seriousness of their offences.
This proposition is treated as conceptual by Primoratz. Compare it with the following.

(c2) In a just system of punishment there are ordinarily good reasons to punish the guilty and to do so with severity proportionate to the seriousness of their offences.

I have suggested that c2 and not c1 best describes the requirements of justice and that this is not incompatible with Hart's position. It would follow from c2 that whether and how an offender should be punished in a particular case is a matter to be decided on the basis of all good reasons that are relevant, not only those prescribed by Primoratz's version of retributivism.

III

This paper has one unexplained premiss. It is that the most familiar way of defining a forward-looking theory, identified over the decades with utilitarianism, is incoherent. To defend this premiss would bring us far afield, into the epistemology of moral reasoning. The premiss can and must at least be described, however briefly and roughly. It is shared by both most utilitarians[102] and anti-utilitarians.[103] By its terms, individuals are seen as entertaining life plans (plans for maximizing happiness or satisfaction) atomistically, life plans involving identifiable ends.[104] The ends reflect personal choices or dispositions and may have any content. The point of moral reasoning for the utilitarian is to ascribe moral justification to the co-ordination of such plans to maximize collective and cumulative satisfaction. This is identified with the common good. For the anti-utilitarian the point of moral reasoning is to uncover the appropriate constraints on the pursuit of these ends so that each individual is accorded the protection of respectful treatment. This is expressed (at least in part) in the constraint of justice. For the anti-utilitarian moral justification lies in satisfaction of the conditions set by such constraints.

To begin to see the incoherence of the premiss one must challenge the underlying picture of human experience and aspiration. One must sketch an alternative picture, one in which the genealogy of personal awareness of the good lies *ab initio* in social interaction and is describable essentially in interpersonal terms of reciprocity. It would follow that the notion of a personal good is best seen as derived from participation in the common good and that the common good inherently involves, as I

---

[102] See, for example, the work of J. S. Mill and Jeremy Bentham, Richard Brandt and David Lyons.

[103] See, for example, the work of Ronald Dworkin and John Rawls.

[104] In other words, each person is seen as determining what shall count as her/his personal goals and as going about maximizing the satisfaction of those goals. One individual's goals may or may not include the empathetic realization of the goals of others to whom she/ he has affective ties.

have argued, a system of just rather than unjust treatment. I take it that a move away from the atomistic epistemological premiss is a move away from the utilitarian dialogue, a move out of the shadow of utilitarianism. Its elaboration is a project for another time.

5.3 Comment

YORAM SHACHAR*

In this short comment I propose to discuss Primoratz's plea for reinstating retribution as an independent positive justification for punishment, based on what he terms a fundamental non-deductive moral principle. I shall mainly question his insistence on the legitimacy of the use of, in his words, 'intuitions, feelings and attitudes' in justifying the infliction of suffering on those who behave immorally.

Primoratz sets out towards the end of his paper first to elucidate his fundamental moral principle and then to 'support it in a non-deductive way'. Both elucidation and support require further scrutiny.

As to the meaning of the proposed principle—not much is made clear, except that it is of the 'just desert' type. For instance, he argues that 'punishment is just when it is deserved by the commission of an offence'. Though he seems to be clear about the identity of the punishment-giver as the state, he is less clear about the nature of the offence which justifies the punishment. Saying that a person deserves to suffer for a moral offence seems different from saying so in relation to an offence in the legal sense. More importantly, the idea of inflicting pain on a person for the reason that he or she deserves it does have a distinct intuitive appeal when it is inflicted 'in exchange' for pain inflicted by the person punished *on another person*. The idea of deserving to suffer seems much less sensible where gross immoralities are committed without upsetting any balance of human suffering. Primoratz's allusion to an 'offence' in this connection, thus, remains vague, and so does the principle built around the term.

As to supporting the principle, Primoratz first suggests the unsupported assumption that 'some punishments are legitimate and called for', and then goes on to state that both pure utilitarianism and Hart's 'middle way' can achieve unjust results by either punishing the innocent or failing to punish (or punish adequately) the guilty.

It is difficult to conceive how either the assumption or the statement or their combination add anything by way of 'arguing in favour of his theory'. Primoratz admits as much by intimating that they would certainly fail to convince anyone who is not previously and intuitively committed to his particular brand of retribution.

Surprisingly enough, however, Primoratz does revert shortly afterwards to a more conventional, perhaps even deductive method of arguing from a general theory when he feels compelled to 'account for the difference in our moral judgement [between serious and petty crime] in terms of a general theory of the gravity of offences which would justify the different treatment . . .' Yet Primoratz deduces too much from the theory of the gravity of offences when he uses it to explain his willingness to abandon the urge to punish altogether when reaching below a certain level in the seriousness of crime. A simple statement of the theory of gravity of offences would only entail the insistence that punishment matches the gravity of offence, that serious offences be met with great suffering and light offences with moderate suffering. It is a scheme of proportions between blameworthiness and punishment which is not directly relevant to the question of the strength of the link between them. It explains, for instance, why many small criminals should each deserve a small amount of punishment, not why the retributivist should remain indifferent as to whether they are all punished or not. The same problem remains, of course, if we think of the 'just desert' version of retribution in terms of settling some cosmic account of sufferings and equity.

In fact, despite this accidental slip into argument from general theory, Primoratz probably remains here as ardently intuitive as he claims earlier to be. The fluctuations he detects in willingness or demand to mete out totally ineffectual punishment seem more directly related to the ebb and flow of emotional reaction to harmdoing than to any 'general theory of justice into which the retributive view of punishment could be fitted'.

INTUITIVISM AND THE CRIMINAL LAW

Contrary to Primoratz's assertion, one can question his conclusions without 'tak[ing] exception to the method of appealing to our particular moral conviction [intuitions, feeling, attitudes] in moral philosophy'. The issue in question is not the soundness of the intuitive method in moral philosophy in general, but its usefulness in justifying the behaviour of the law, or more particularly, the infliction of pain by organs of the law on persons who break some of its rules. My main objection to using the intuitive method in arguing about the criminal law stems from the strong suspicion that criminal law in modern society is itself a powerful, perhaps the most powerful, creator of attitude, and that there is something methodically wrong in justifying the perpetuation of its practices merely on the basis of attitudes which it created or helped critically to create.

There would not have been much wrong in the dependence between law and moral attitude if external observation of the behaviour of law acted as a source of experience and a catalyst of reflective constructive processes leading to coherent and internally-created moral attitudes. It is, of course, highly improbable that the law acts in any way remotely resembling such processes.

Jerome Frank's description of the law acting as a misplaced and pathetically inadequate parent-figure, replacing in the modern secular adult mind all previous sources of security and moral authority,[105] combined with Jean Piaget's description of the ways in which the moral attitude of the child is shaped, while still under parental domination,[106] rather supports the proposition that the law routinely creates attitudes which are of little intrinsic value and are certainly useless as an authoritative justification for the law itself. It is not easy to prove empirically that the criminal law indeed creates attitudes in such a manner, but I suggest the following synthesis of findings, sketched very broadly, as prima-facie evidence.

Piaget shows that the moral attitude of the smaller child is a collection of shallow impressions gathered from the way he or she conceives parent reaction to domestic wrongdoing.[107] So, for instance, an angry instinctive reaction based on the amount of harm produced by the child breeds in small children a predominantly harm-oriented attitude to questions of responsibility for wrongdoing. Later, children develop the mental ability to create moral attitudes themselves, on the basis of a multitude of experiences, mainly through play and peer co-operation. The most noticeable clue in Piaget's work to the achievement of such mature, internally-created, and relatively well-worked-out moral attitudes is the child's ability to reduce drastically the importance of actual harm in the judgement of wrongdoing and replace it by motives, intentions, and knowledge of circumstances. Later research among groups of adults did not show any significant sign of change in this particular attitude to

[105] J. Frank, *Law and the Modern Mind*, London (1949).
[106] J. Piaget, *The Moral Judgment of the Child*, New York (1965), 113–20, 134–9.
[107] Ibid., and D. C. Gutkin, 'The Effect of Systematic Story Changes on Intentionality in Children's Moral Judgments', *Child Development*, vol. 43 (1972), 187.

wrongdoing in the private domain.[108] Young adults still ignored the amount of actual harm done and judged by motive, when hypothetical wrongdoing was confined to house or family. However, when Leslie Sebba picked the minds of very similar groups of adults, he discovered amounts of judgement-by-harm comparable only to the amount found in the most infantile of Piaget's small children.[109] What could be the reason for such a regression? Sebba's adults were asked to react to situations of 'real' crime borrowed from the Criminal Code of Pennsylvania. A very plausible explanation of their primitive harm-oriented attitude to guilt and punishment is that it is merely a distorted reflection of the criminal law's attitude to crime. The way criminal law *actually* sends out the messages and the way they are ordinarily perceived, resembles the message-perception relationship between parent and infant. Both produce a kind of subservient morality which does supply the subject with a host of ready-made attitudes, but which can hardly be claimed as a legitimate justification for the perpetuation of the message-producing practice by the dominant agent, be it the parent or the law.

The law is in the business of punishing wrongdoing for a long time. In Judaeo-Christian civilization it seems to have been obsessed with doing so more than in other civilizations, clearly as a reflection of our particular religious heritage. In the triangle of religion, law, and personal moral attitude, religion no doubt played the dominant role. Basic attitudes to sin and punishment were shaped by religion and in turn shaped the law. As religion fades away as a major source of moral attitude for the majority of western society, leaving law and opinion in a scene devoid of much critical and disciplined reflection, the danger arises that law and our attitude to it be locked in a spiral of mutual reinforcement, perpetuating anachronistic dogma.

It is imperative that this thoughtless spiral be checked by an effort on our part to think critically rather than complacently rely on established attitudes. The very ease with which we relate punishment to crime in our minds should serve as a reason for constantly questioning it and

[108] C. F. Surber, 'Developmental Processes in Social Influence: Averaging of Intentions and Consequences in Moral Judgment'. *Developmental Psychology*, vol. 13 (1977), 674; D. C. Gutkin, 'Maternal Discipline and Children's Judgements of Moral Intentionality', *Journal of Genetic Psychology*, vol. 127 (1957), 55.

[109] L. Sebba, 'Is Mens Rea a Component of Perceived Offense Seriousness', *Journal of Criminal Law and Criminology*, vol. 71 (1980) 124. Also M. Riedel, 'Perceived Circumstances, Inferences of Intent and Judgments of Offense Seriousness', *Journal of Criminal Law and Criminology*, vol. 66 (1975), 201.

testing its justification by reliance on principles outside the belief itself; in other words, for searching for a general justifying theory.

I shall state no opinion as to the most desirable theory. Hart's predominantly utilitarian approach, along with other combinations of utility and retribution have stood well against onslaught. Alan Gewirth's recent heroic efforts to devise an all-embracing principle of morality have also made it possible to deduce, test, and discuss notions of punishment as part of a whole system of morality.[110] Whether totally successful or not, all these efforts seem more appealing than Primoratz's suggestion that we start the process of justification from the *assumption* that some punishment is justified. Quite clearly, if we cannot come up with good moral reasons for punishment, we must stop punishing.

THE EICHMANN TRIAL AND THE ABUSE OF EXAMPLES

No single act of punishment deters all potential offenders, and all acts of punishment probably deter some others or deter them some of the time. Of all *single* acts of punishment, that of Eichmann may well have deterred the most. Perhaps uniquely in the history of mankind, the threat of man-made punishment has been extended by that single act beyond the conventional limit of time, place, and sovereignty, thus upsetting some previously existing balances in the calculus of deterrence for official murderers. It is wrong to show that some official murderers have not been deterred, for no single act of punishment deters all others. The question of onus of proof still remains of course but it is not different here from areas of more conventional criminality.

Primoratz is entitled to assume hypothetically non-deterrence in the Eichmann case as he does for the sake of argument but I suggest it would have been more interesting to hypothesize on an anonymous and much broader scale. What, it could be asked, if it transpires after all that no punishment ever produces any grain of good in terms of deterrence? that those inclined to behave immorally go on doing so whatever the threat? In short that no punishment achieves anything in terms of bettering humanity? Would punishment still exist?

What examples of the Eichmann type do achieve is an instant reproduction in the mind of the otherwise more detached and reflective thinker of the same urge to lash out, inflict pain and kill, perhaps more often experienced by others. As claimed earlier, this should act as a

[110] A. Gewirth, *Reason and Morality*, Chicago (1978).

powerful reason for doubling the efforts to justify rather than as a direct reason to punish.

DENUNCIATION

The denunciatory justification for punishment is a familiar meeting ground for the various groups of theorists. Agreeable to many classical retributivists for self-evident reasons, it can also seem attractive to the utilitarian for its attitude to punishment as a medium, a means of expression. Yet the controversy is inevitably resumed when each side examines denunciation more carefully in terms of their own basic theory. Doubt from the utilitarian side typically takes some form of the proposition that, while punishment may well communicate a message, it does so in a very clumsy and costly manner, and that other means of communication can be more suitable if communicating a message is all we mean directly to achieve.

Primoratz retorts that punishment is the only means serious and weighty enough to achieve the ultimate goal of reinforcing in the minds of message-receivers the belief in the validity of criminal laws. In the most succinct formulation of the argument he proposes that '. . . if some acts are to be offences, if there is to be criminal law at all—there has to be punishment.' This, of course, is tautological for it merely repeats the definition of criminal law as the branch of law which commends by threat of punishment. But I believe that he does not escape the same error when he expands the argument to include the concept of rights guaranteed by criminal law, and claims that if breaches of such rights were only condemned verbally then all 'would be sure to conclude that those rights were not valid after all, were not really recognized, at least as rights defined and, guaranteed by the criminal law, in any serious manner'.

The deliberate infliction of suffering on a human being is indeed a serious matter. But the belief that it is the only proper reaction to the violation of a rule of conduct, and therefore its only test of validity, stems from habit and convention rather than any logical necessity. Primoratz refers to such conventional thinking in his frequent allusions to common opinion (for example, the 'what would we think if . . .' type of argument), but he fails to justify it on any other acceptable grounds.

Whether or not, and in what circumstances, we are justified in backing rules of conduct with threat of punishment is the subject of enquiry. If indeed we find a justification for the protection of rights by way of rules backed by threat of punishment, then we must certainly carry out the threat as long as it serves that purpose. But where punishment cannot achieve the original justifying purpose, it can only communicate a message of frustrated anger or vain pride, and as such it becomes far too costly to be tolerated.

Now the cost of punishment, the horror of deliberately inflicting pain on another, can perhaps be tolerated when weighed against the pain inflicted on the victim by the person punished (as the classical retributivists profess) or against the good that can be achieved in the future (as utilitarians prefer), but support for the pure[111] denunciatory justification can allow neither past pain nor future advantages to count directly in the calculus of justification, and it therefore brings the question of cost into painfully sharper focus.

What, finally, of Eichmann? Was his punishment meaningful as an expressive act of reinforcing the validity of rights protected by criminal law? The Eichmann trial did have an overwhelming communicative effect, but it all radiated from the well-staged court proceedings and their surroundings, through words, images, and gestures. The act of punishment itself was universally felt to be a sordid affair, devoid of any significant meaning either in terms of reinforcing values or, for that matter, true retribution. Taking Eichmann's life was only justified because of its unique deterrent effect. But if we abide by Primoratz's suggestion to ignore that effect, then even the existence of Eichmann's empty human shell was too precious to be exchanged for an empty message.

---

[111] It is not always possible to ascertain the degree of purity (in the sense of independence from other arguable theories) of Primoratz's argument for the denunciatory justification. At one stage, for example, he relates the seriousness of the message-by-punishment to the seriousness of the victims' suffering in a way which seems to rely heavily on the 'just desert' version of classical retribution which he propagates earlier in the paper.

6.1 Intentions and *Mens Rea**

MICHAEL MOORE

I HART AND THE DEBATE ABOUT DIRECT AND OBLIQUE INTENTIONS

We are indebted to H. L. A. Hart for a series of articles illuminating the various ways in which culpability is graded by those states of mind lawyers lump together as *mens rea*.[1] One of the questions that here interested Hart was whether the most serious culpability with which a harm could be caused was marked by intention (in the sense of purpose), or whether some other mental state or set of mental states should be used as the marker of most serious culpability. Children commonly distinguish harm caused 'on purpose' from harm caused in other ways, and the question Hart pursued was whether such a focus on purpose is correct when culpability is being assessed.

As Hart perceived, one can get at this question—of the role of purpose in assessing culpability—only if one is clear about the concept of purpose, or what Bentham called direct intention.[2] Specifically, purpose is to be distinguished from mere belief or foresight that a harm is likely to occur (Bentham called such belief states 'oblique intentions'). The distinction between purpose and knowledge is a distinction based on the agent's reasons: there are those consequences that are part of one's chain of reasons for acting; whether desired as means or as ends, they are directly intended. On the other hand, there are those consequences that are believed by the actor to be substantially certain to occur that are not part of his chain of reasons for acting. These he knows will follow on states of affairs for which he acts, but he does not act in order to bring them about.

---

* © Michael Moore 1987.

[1] Hart discussed *mens rea* in 'The Ascription of Responsibility and Rights', *Proceedings of the Aristotelian Society*, vol. 49 (1949), 171–94; again in 'Legal Responsibility and Excuses', in S. Hook (ed.) *Determinism and Freedom*, New York (1958); and in 'Negligence, *Mens Rea* and Criminal Responsibility', in A. Guest (ed.), *Oxford Essays in Jurisprudence*, Oxford (1961). More specifically focused on intention is 'Decision, Intention and Certainty' (with Stuart Hampshire), *Mind*, vol. 67 (1958), 1–12; and 'Intention and Punishment', *Oxford Review*, vol. 4 (1967), 5–22, all but the first are reprinted in Hart, *Punishment and Responsibility*.

[2] Jeremy Bentham, *An Introduction to the Principles of Morals and Legislation*, New York (1948), 200–21.

This distinction is sometimes put in terms of 'desire': an agent directly intends those consequences he desires to bring about, he only obliquely intends those he expects to come about but does not desire to bring about. In fact, 'desire' marks the wrong distinction here. One might directly intend some consequence yet not desire it (in a very popular sense of that word, at least); as where one intends to escape prison, and must kill the prison guard in order to do so. In such a case the death of the guard is one's chosen means and thus is directly intended, no matter how great may be the regret with which the action is done. Alternatively, one might cause some harm, desire that it occur, and yet not directly intend that harm; as where one desires the death of the prison guard because one hates him, does an act knowing that it will kill him, but does the act for an entirely different reason, namely, to escape. In such a case a known consequence is desired, but the desire is not among the actor's chain of reasons for acting; the consequence is thus not directly intended.

The purpose/knowledge distinction is thus based, not on 'desire', but on the concept of reasons for acting. On a causal account of reasons,[3] the distinction will become a causal distinction: if a consequence is the object of a belief/desire set that causes one's behaviour, then that consequence was the object of one's purpose; whereas if that consequence figures only in those belief/desire sets that do not cause the act in question, then that consequence was only within the objects of one's predictive beliefs about what was probable or certain to occur.

To illustrate: imagine two persons, A and B, each of whom has as his purpose the destruction of an airplane in mid-flight. A wants to blow up the plane because he has insured the life of the passengers and has as his ultimate purpose the collection of the money on their lives. B wants to blow up the plane because he has insured the plane and has as his ultimate purpose the collection of the money on the plane. Only A has as his purpose the death of the passengers. B, while he knows that the passengers will surely die if he destroys the plane in mid-flight, does not have as his purpose that they die; their death is not necessary to achieve anything B wants to achieve. Accordingly, for B their death is a known side effect to the achievement of B's purposes, whereas for A their death is a necessary means that form part of the chain of reasons (purposes) for which A acts.

---

[3] I defend the causal account of reasons for action in Moore, *Law and Psychiatry: Rethinking the Relationship*, Cambridge (1984), Chap. 1.

Hart argued that the culpability of persons such as A and B was the same and, accordingly, that no distinction should be drawn in the criminal law between knowing and purposeful killers: both were deserving of the most severe punishment reserved for the most serious category of homicide, murder. Hart's argument here was quite straightforward and persuasive. Even the actor who only knows that some harm will come about as a result of his activities still has *control* over whether that harm will occur or not.[4] Given his knowledge, he has as much control over causing the harm as the actor who has that harm as his purpose: both have *chosen* to bring it about. Accordingly, for either a utilitarian or a retributivist, Hart concluded, the criminal law should punish those who act knowingly equally with those who act with a prohibited harm as their purpose.

Others have disagreed. Anthony Kenny, for example, has urged that the criminal law should mark the difference between purpose and knowledge so that a directly intended death is murder but an obliquely intended death is only manslaughter.[5] Others, such as G. E. M. Anscombe, have found more moral merit in the use of the distinction by the Catholic doctrine of 'double effect' than did Hart.[6] According to the latter doctrine, an evil knowingly brought about might be justified (depending on the circumstances) but an evil that it was the actor's purpose to bring about can never be justified. In the airplane case, for example, if A and B each have good reason for needing their respective insurance monies—to prevent an unjust war, for example—only B could raise the question of justification.

---

[4] Also finding the control issue determinative of culpability are Eric D'Arcy, *Human Acts*, Oxford (1963), 170–4, and Hans Oberdick, 'Intention and Foresight in Criminal Law', *Mind*, vol. 81 (1972), 389–400.

[5] Anthony Kenny, 'Intention and Purpose', *Journal of Philosophy*, vol. 63 (1966), 642ff., revised and reprinted as 'Intention and Purpose in Law', in R. Summers (ed.), *Essays in Legal Philosophy*, Berkeley (1968). Kenny's later views on the moral and legal importance of the distinction between purpose and knowledge are set forth in his *Will, Freedom and Power*, Oxford (1976), and 'Intention and *Mens Rea* in Murder', in P. M. S. Hacker and J. Raz (eds.), *Law, Morality, and Society*, Oxford (1977).

[6] G. E. M. Anscombe, 'Modern Moral Philosophy', *Philosophy*, vol. 33 (1958), 1–10; also Anscombe, reply to Bennett, in *Analysis*, vol. 26 (1966), 208; also Anscombe, 'War and Murder', in R. A. Wasserstrom (ed.), *War and Morality*, Belmont, California (1970). Anscombe's essential argument—that any deontological ethic requires that some moral distinction be drawn between results that are directly intended and those that are only obliquely intended on pain of incoherence in its 'absolute' moral prohibitions—has been seconded by a number of philosophers. *See*, e.g., J. L. Mackie, *Ethics*, New York (1977), 159–68; Charles Fried, 'Right and Wrong—Preliminary Considerations', *Journal of Legal Studies*, vol. 5 (1975), 165–200.

It is not my purpose in this essay to take a position in this debate between Hart and his critics. Rather, I wish to examine what I would characterize as the metaphysical presuppositions of the debate itself. My target, in other words, is neither Hart nor his critics but rather the sceptic who would deny significance to the debate itself.

Both Hart and his critics presupposed that there is some correct way in which to fix the object of one's purposes. Without such an objective mode of saying *what* an actor's purposes might be, neither Hart nor his critics could meaningfully categorize cases as being instances of purpose or of knowledge. Take A and B, the earlier hypothesized plane-destroyers. Suppose we identified the blowing up of the plane with the passengers on it as the very same event as the killing of those passengers;[7] suppose further that we think that the identity of events implies the identity of the purposes that have those events as their objects. On both such suppositions we should classify B as well as A as someone who has the killing of the passengers as his purpose: for B by hypothesis had as his purpose the blowing up of the plane; because that event *was* the killing of the passengers, B's purpose also was to kill the passengers.

To prevent this collapse of knowledge into purpose in every case, we need some theory that tells us how to individuate intentions, that is, that tells us when we have two different intentions and when there is in reality only one. One can use the distinction between purpose and knowledge only if one has some such theory of individuation. Without such a theory, one would have no way to prevent the collapsing of every supposed case of knowledge into a case of purpose.

This problem has not gone unnoticed in the literature on intentions. Hart himself gave two examples as he briefly noted the difficulty: (1) G strikes a glass violently with a hammer because he wants the noise of the hammer making contact with the glass to attract the attention of someone else—did G necessarily intend to break the glass, given that he did intend to strike the glass hard enough to make some noise? Hart believed in such a case, that 'when a foreseen outcome is so immediately and invariably connected with the action done that the suggestion that the action might not have that outcome would by ordinary standards be regarded as absurd, or such as only a mentally abnormal person would seriously entertain: the connection between action and outcome seems therefore [in such cases] to be not merely contingent but rather to be

---

[7] The identity thesis here is discussed in Alvin Goldman, *A Theory of Human Action*, Englewood Cliffs, New Jersey (1970), 1–10.

conceptual.'[8] (2) Arguably different, Hart thought, was the case in which a doctor crushes the skull of a foetus in order to save the life of its mother. Here, Hart found it plausible to distinguish the crushing of the skull from the death of the foetus, so that an intention to do the former need not be identified as an intention to cause the latter as well.[9]

Other examples from the more recent literature include: (3) The eccentric surgeon, D, who 'wishes to remove P's heart completely from P's body in order to experiment upon it. D does not desire P's death (being perfectly content that P shall go on living if he can do so without his heart), but recognizes that in fact his death is inevitable from the operation to be performed'.[10] Anthony Kenny concludes of this case that because of the 'immediacy' of death upon removal of a heart, the directly intended heart removal is also a directly intended death. (4) If Espinoza intends to appoint Garcia, and Garcia is fifty years old, does Espinoza intend to appoint a fifty-year old man?[11] In his book on intention J. W. Meiland concludes that the answer is 'yes'; the second intention is 'inseparable' from the first, and so should be identified with it. (5) Lord Hailsham recently posed the earlier given airplane hypothetical example for himself, concluding that an intention to blow up the plane would be conceptually 'inseparable' from an intention to kill the passengers, so that both A and B should be said to have directly intended the death of the passengers.[12]

Lastly, consider the following four examples of R. A. Duff's:[13] (6) X intends to get drunk, does so, knowing full well that he will be hungover the next day; does X intend to be hungover? Duff thinks not: 'being

---

[8] Hart, 'Intention and Punishment', 120.

[9] Ibid., 123–4. This Papal example is also discussed by Philippa Foot, 'The Problem of Abortion and the Doctrine of Double Effect', *Oxford Review*, vol. 5 (1967), 5–15. Foot's intuitions here differed from Hart's: 'A certain event may be desired under one of its descriptions, unwanted under another, but we cannot treat these as two different events, one of which is aimed at and the other not. And even if it be argued that there are here two different events—the crushing of the child's skull and its death—the two are obviously much too close for an application of the doctrine of double effect.' Ibid., 6–7.

[10] Kenny, 'Intention and Purpose in Law', 149. The example is originally from Glanville Williams, *Criminal Law—The General Part*, 2nd edn. London (1961), 39.

[11] J. W. Meiland, *The Nature of Intention*, London (1970), 13. This example is much like that of Robert Audi, 'Intending', *Journal of Philosophy*, vol. 70 (1973), 387–403, 396. 'Suppose that at a restaurant X intends to order lobster tails and believes that in ordering them he will be ordering the most expensive item on the menu, though he is not concerned with their price. Must X also intend to order the most expensive item on the menu?'

[12] *Hyam* v. *Director of Public Prosecutions*, [1975] A. C., 55, [1974] 2 All Eng. Rep. 41, 51–2.

[13] R. A. Duff, 'Mens Rea and the Law Commission Report', [1980] *Crim. Law Review*, 147–60.

drunk and being hung over are distinct, though causally related, states of affairs', and therefore X 'can intend the former without intending the latter'.[14] (7) I retain Brown's car, thereby depriving him of his own use of it; do I thereby intend to deprive Brown of the use of his car? Duff thinks so: 'my retaining Brown's car for my own use is not distinct from his being deprived of it, since these are aspects of the same state of affairs';[15] in such a case, if I intend the first state of affairs I intend the second as well. (8) Likewise, if I intend to decapitate Brown, wanting only his head to show to another, and not caring a fig about his living or dying, do I intend Brown's death? According to Duff, there is a 'logical connection' between decapitation and killing: '"Brown is decapitated but survives" does not specify an intelligible possibility, since it is part of the logic of our concept of "human beings" that decapitation kills them: if we could imagine a being who was not killed by decapitation, that would not be a human being'.[16] Since decapitation logically entails death for Duff, to intend to decapitate *is* to intend to kill. (9) A, a man, intends to remain unmarried. According to Duff, because 'unmarried male' is synonymous with 'bachelor', A must also intend to remain a bachelor. To intend the first *is* to intend the second.

Despite the attention to this problem in the literature, however, there is no agreement as to how we should individuate intentions. Hart in one breath gave us two quite different tests—immediate and invariant causal connection, and conceptual connectedness. Kenny adopts the first of these, Lord Hailsham the second. Meiland would appear to think that the identity of intentions is governed by the identity of the events that form the objects of such intentions. Duff in the first two of his examples would appear to agree with Meiland's event-identity test, but in Duff's last two examples he substitutes the stronger relations of entailment or synonymy for his earlier extensional test of identity. In brief, we face a variety of theories of individuation that are not the same nor is any argument given as to why we should prefer one to another.

Given this state of affairs it is not surprising to find metaphysical positions being gerrymandered so as to fit one's moral positions, and vice versa. Indeed, it is easy to see how one's metaphysics here may correlate naturally with certain moral or legal views about the relevance of purpose versus knowledge in marking most serious culpability. A fine-grained theory of individuation will refuse to classify many more

---

[14] Ibid., 153.
[15] Ibid.
[16] Ibid.

states of affairs as directly intended than will a coarse-grained theory. A fine-grained theorist, accordingly, will have every incentive to consider knowledge no less than purpose as sufficient for most serious culpability. A coarse-grained theorist, on the other hand, has a much lessened incentive to allow knowledge to be sufficient for serious culpability; for he can say that such states of affairs were directly intended without regard to the knowledge of the subject.

Consider as an example of this Glanville Williams's and Anthony Kenny's views on the case of the eccentric surgeon mentioned earlier.[17] Kenny's coarse-grained theory defines such a case as one of direct intention, so he has no need to allow knowledge to suffice in order to punish the doctor as a murderer. Kenny thus is free to argue, as indeed he does, that only direct intentions should be punishable as murder, for he can do so and yet capture cases like that of the eccentric surgeon anyway. Williams also finds it intuitive to punish the eccentric surgeon as a murderer, but Williams holds a more fine-grained theory of individuation, whereby one refuses to say that the intention to cut out the heart just is an intention to kill; Williams, accordingly, must argue (as he does) that knowledge should count equally with purpose when one gives legal meaning to the 'malice' required for murder, for this is the only way Williams can punish severely cases such as the eccentric surgeon.

Scepticism about the meaningfulness of such a moral/legal debate arises the moment one becomes sceptical that there is any correct theory of individuation of intentions. Mark Kelman, for example, tells us that we use coarse or fine-grained theories pretty much arbitrarily, whenever it suits us.[18] The result of such scepticism is to cast doubt on the existence of any distinction between harm directly intended and harm only foreseen as substantially certain to occur. For one can manipulate what is considered to be directly intended, and what only obliquely so, by simply shifting one's view of the metaphysics on which the distinction depends.

[17] Williams, *Criminal Law*; Kenny, 'Intention and Purpose'. Hans Oberdick is quite explicit about this trade-off, rejecting Kenny's notion that any harm 'invariably connected' with one's intentional act will itself be intended because Oberdick's moral position about knowledge does not require any coarse-grained metaphysics about intentions. See 'Intention and Foresight', 391.

[18] Kelman, 'Interpretive Construction in the Substantive Criminal Law', *Stanford Law Review*, vol. 33 (1981), 591–673. See particularly 595–6, 620–33. Kelman does not see the issue as one of fine- or coarse-grained theories of individuation of intention, but talks instead of 'broad' and 'narrow' views of intentions. Despite the differing language, the problem Kelman is adverting to is how one individuates intentions by their objects.

One of my purposes in this paper is to examine whether such scepticism is warranted. This I shall do by seeing what can be done about developing a consistent theory of how we individuate intentions. Although my focus is on the theory of individuation presupposed by the direct/oblique distinction, it is worth noting how pervasive is the legal need to have such a theory. In the law of criminal attempts, for example, one must have such a theory to render intelligible the question, 'If the accused did all he intended to do, would it have been criminal?'[19] Similarly, a theory of individuation of intentions is needed to give teeth to the constitutional prohibition against being twice put in jeopardy for 'the same offence', for sometimes that question will turn on whether the defendant had the same intention or two distinct intentions as he performed various acts.[20] Similarly, in the law of conspiracy one must decide that there is the 'common purpose to attain an objective' required for there to be a conspiracy. Finally, even if one rejects the moral and legal significance of the distinction between purpose and knowledge, one will still need a theory of individuation of mental states, in this case states of belief; one will need such a theory in order to distinguish those things one actually believes from those things an actor *should* believe if he were non-negligent.

Despite the general need throughout criminal law for a theory of individuation of mental states by their objects, I shall focus on the context discussed above. Is there some principled basis to choose between Kenny's coarse-grained theory, or Williams's fine-grained theory? Or is it, as Kelman suggests, an essentially arbitrary decision that reduces the debate about the moral and legal relevance of the distinction between direct and oblique intentions, to so much ado about nothing?

[19] The dependence of this test on some theory of individuating intentions is discussed in H. L. A. Hart, 'The House of Lords on Attempting the Impossible', *Oxford Journal of Legal Studies*, vol. I (1981), 149–66.
[20] See, e.g., *Irby* v. *United States*, 390 F. 2d 432 (D. C. Cir. 1967), in which a defendant who broke into a house had an intention that may have been conditional and disjunctive: to take whatever property he found if the house were unoccupied (which constitutes housebreaking with intent to steal), or to take property by force from the owner of the house if the house were occupied (which if done, constitutes robbery). The defendant in *Irby* not only entered the house arguably with such an intention, but found the occupant therein and proceeded to rob him. Having pleaded guilty to one count of housebreaking and to one count of robbery, the issue as the court conceived it was whether the defendant had one intention or two. The majority of the court held that these were two distinct intentions, and therefore allowed consecutive sentencing for the two offences of house-breaking and robbery. See generally *People* v. *Neal*, 55 Cal. 2d 11, 9 Cal. Rptr. 607, 357 P. 2d 839 (1960), for the California Supreme Court's 'single intent or objective' test for double jeopardy.

II   THE METAPHYSICS OF INTENT-INDIVIDUATION

Perhaps the place to start is by asking the ontological question, what are objects of intentions? Very generally, three possibilities suggest themselves: that they are sentences that do not refer to real objects in the world; that they are real objects in the world; and that they are propositions that are only 'indirectly' about real objects in the world. An example may help to make these possibilities intelligible. Suppose someone, Jones, intends to enter room no. 6. The object of his intention can in this case be divided into two parts: the subject, which is he, Jones; an action, his entering; and an (accusatory) object of the action verb, the room to be entered. The object of the intention is not any one of these, but all three together.

The three possibilities are: (1) that the object of Jones's intention is the *sentence*, 'He (Jones) enters room no. 6'. So construing intentional objects uses a special sense of 'sentence' here, namely, the words are said to lack reference and extension (and hence a truth value). The sentence is a sentence only in the limited sense that it is a string of symbols that is syntactically well-formed, but devoid of the semantic interpretations that normally attach to these symbols in more ordinary contexts. This construing of intentional objects as sentence-like entities means that a mental state such as an intention should be viewed as a relation between a person X, and a (syntactic) sentence. There is no relation, on this view, between X and real world things, like actions or rooms, because these real-world things are not (quite literally) talked about in such contexts.

On this view, one might analogize the words that appear in the objects of intentions to the word 'dint' as used in expressions 'by dint of'. Grammatically, 'dint' may look like a noun that has as its role the naming of something, but in reality there are no dints in the world. The expression 'by dint of' is what Quine called a fused idiom, one that contains parts (words) that *look* as if they refer to things, but which in reality play non-referential roles in language.[21] Analogously, one might suggest, one should view the objects of intentions as fused idioms, which look syntactically as if they were meaningful sentences, some parts of which referred to things; in reality, however, objects of intentions are strings of symbols, and to say that Jones

---

[21] W. V. Quine, *Word and Object*, Cambridge, Mass. (1960), 244. Dan Dennett explicitly analogizes the objects of mental states to fused idioms in Dennett, *Content and Consciousness*, New York (1969), Chap. 1.

intends S, expresses only a relation between Jones and the sentence S.

This view gains some plausibility, perhaps, when one recalls Brentano's observation that many of the 'things' people want, wish for, hope for, or intend, do not exist in the real world. In such cases, one might say that they enjoy a special form of existence called 'Intentional inexistence'; or, if one wants to avoid that road to modern phenomenology, one can say with Quine that we need not bother about the existence of such 'things' because the words that seem to refer to them do not refer at all.

(2) The second possibility takes the opposite tack. It is committed to the view that words appearing in the sentence fragment, 'he enters room no. 6' have their normal reference and extension. 'He' refers to that person holding the intention; 'enters room no. 6' has as its extension those actions that constitute an entering of that room; and 'room no. 6' has its normal reference to that room.

Unlike the first view, this view of objects as real world objects has the advantage of maintaining the ordinary semantics of the words that describe those objects. It does not suffer from the seeming implausibility of saying, as does the first view, that 'he' does not refer to the holder of the intention, or that 'room no. 6' does not refer to room no. 6. The second view, unfortunately, has some difficulty accommodating itself to Brentano's insight that the objects of intentions or other mental states may not exist as real world objects. What, one may ask, is the reference of the sailboat hoped for by Jones when that sailboat does not exist except as the object of a hope by Jones?

With intentions in particular, it will not do to think that the verbs of action, such as 'enter', refer to a particular action of entering; for that particular action has not yet occurred. Intentions, like beliefs about future occurrences (predictions), but unlike perceptual beliefs, inherently have to do with actions or states of affairs that have not yet occurred. Indeed, there is no guarantee that such intended or predicted actions will ever occur. Accordingly, the view being here considered must be modified so as to avoid saying that there is reference to such future actions or states of affairs that have not yet occurred and may not ever occur.[22]

---

[22] Our ordinary way of talking about intentions can be very misleading in this respect, for we speak as if we formed intentions about *particular* actions or states of affairs (rather than about types of actions or states of affairs). E.g.: 'He intended the harm' where 'the harm' seems to refer to the particular event that occurred. I want to say that one never intends *the* harm; rather, one intends that there be *some* event-token that will instantiate some event-type. One forms intentions, in other words, over types of acts or states, not over particulars.

Each of these two positions on the nature of intentional objects has a name in the philosophical literature, for each of them was distinguished by Quine. The first view is that mental state verbs create contexts that are *referentially opaque*; the second view is that such verbs create contexts that are *referentially transparent*.[23] Quine himself straddled the two views, urging that mental state verbs ('belief' was Quine's usual example) are inherently ambiguous, sometimes creating opaque contexts and sometimes transparent ones.

If one adopts an opaque view of the matter, so that objects of intentions are sentence-like entities, one adopts with it a very fine-grained mode of individuating intentions. For it matters, on the opaque view, exactly how the words are strung together as to whether two nominally distinct intentions are one and the same. Jones's intention to enter room no. 6 would, for example, be different from Jones's intention to enter room no. 6 (by the front door), different from Jones's intention to go into room no. 6, and yet distinct from Jones's intention that room no. 6 be entered by him. This view counts these as different intentions because the words used, or their syntax, are different, even if their (normal) meanings might be the same.

The transparent view, by way of contrast, implies a very coarse-grained theory of individuation. This view would imply that it does not matter how one describes or names room no. 6, nor how one refers to the action of entering; any intention whose object is the entering of that room is but one intention. An intention to enter room no. 6, for example, is (identical with) an intention to enter a room in which marijuana is being smoked, so long as room no. 6 is such a room.

I am going against ordinary usage here because I can see no sense to the alternative. What would an intention be about if its object referred to a particular event, and yet that event never occurred? In such cases one has to say the reference is to a type and not to a particular. Yet surely nothing changes about what the intention was when the event *does* occur; surely one does not have an intention about a type that becomes an intention about a particular event, depending on subsequent events. Better to say: the intention is always about a type of event which, if the intent succeeds, will be instantiated by some event-token.

Probability theorists make this same move about predictive beliefs when they deny any sense to the question, 'what was the probability of a particular event occurring?' Predictive beliefs also only make sense when construed to be about *types* of events of which the actual events that occur may be instances.

[23] My explication of the referentially opaque sense is something of a caricature of Quine's actual views. Quine never actually said what the reference or extension was for opaque contexts, other than that it was unclear ('opaque'). I have accordingly re-characterized the opaque sense in what is to me a clearer, if more far-fetched way: treat the objects of belief just like quoted sentences (rather than the *indirect* discourse favoured by Quine as the analogy to the propositional attitudes).

Neither of these theories of individuation seems to conform to our intuitions about when intentions (or other mental states, for that matter) are the same. The opaque view is too fine-grained,[24] and the transparent view is too coarse-grained. An example showing the former is one where the only shift is a syntactic one (Jones intends that he enter room no. 6, versus Jones intends that room no. 6 be entered by him). Surely these are the same intentions, despite the differing syntax of the intentional objects. An example showing the latter is provided by Keedy in discussing the impossibility doctrine in the law of criminal attempts: 'If A takes an umbrella which he believes to belong to B, but which in fact is his own, he does not have the intent to steal, his intent being to take the umbrella he grasps in his hand, which is his own umbrella . . .'[25] Unpacked, the hypothetical asserts that from: (1) A intends (takes the umbrella in his hand), and the true identity, (2) the umbrella in A's hand = A's own umbrella, it follows that: (3) A intends (takes A's own umbrella). Surely this conclusion is to be resisted, denying as it does any importance to A's beliefs about *whose* umbrella he was taking.

In addition, neither of the ontological views that generate these theories of individuation are themselves very plausible (independently of their generating implausible theories of individuation). It is wildly counter-intuitive to think that the 'he' and the 'room no. 6' in the earlier example in no way refer to the person who holds the intention or to room no. 6 as Quine's opaque sense of 'intend' requires. On the other hand, it is strange to say that 'enters' in the example refers to some particular action that has not yet occurred and may never occur, as Quine's transparent sense of 'intend' seemingly requires. And there are more technical objections to each of these views. Plainly needed is some third view.

(3) Enter, propositions. A view which construes the objects of intentions as being propositions has a number of virtues. To begin with, it implies a theory of individuation that need not be so fine-grained as the opaque view, nor as coarse-grained as the transparent view. One need not resist, for example, the identification of Jones's intention that he enter room no. 6, with Jones's intention that room no. 6 be entered by

---

[24] On occasion the opaque view will not be fine-grained enough. Suppose two contracting parties utter identical sentences to one another about the shipping terms for goods sold by one to the other: 'Ex Peerless, Bombay'. Suppose further that each referred to a different ship by the word, 'Peerless'. Their intentions differed (as the court held in this famous case) despite the identity of the sentences uttered by each.

[25] E. Keedy, 'Criminal Attempts at Common Law', *University of Pennsylvania Law Review*, vol. 102 (1954), 464–7.

him; although the syntax of these sentences differs, the proposition expressed by them does not (or at least need not). On the other hand, one may resist identifications such as Keedy's: A's intention to take the umbrella in his hand (which A believes belongs to B) differs from an intention to take A's own umbrella—even if the umbrella taken *is* A's own umbrella—because the propositions are different for the two intentions. True, the proposition that is the object of the first intention is about A's umbrella, as is the proposition that is the object of the second intention hypothesized; yet (as Frege asserted) *how* one refers to that umbrella matters.[26] A, if he has the first intention, refers to that umbrella under the description, 'B's umbrella'; if A had the second intention, he would refer to that umbrella under the description, 'my own umbrella'. Since there are different *senses* to these singular terms (even though for A having the same *reference*), these are two different propositions; and, with different propositions as their objects, these are two different intentions, contrary to Keedy's conclusion.

Viewing intentions as 'propositional attitudes' has additional virtues, independently of better conforming to our intuitions of when intentions are the same. With propositions one may thread the narrow channel between the opaque view that words in intentional objects have no reference or extension, and the transparent view that words in such contexts have (only) their normal reference and extension. A believer in propositions such as Frege will urge that words used in intentional contexts refer ultimately to real world things, but do so 'indirectly'; the immediate reference of such words is to their sense. (Thus, to have the same proposition one must have not only the same ultimate reference, as in the Keedy example, but also the same sense.) With regard to Brentano's worry about non-existent things, this view would maintain that the *only* reference in such cases is to the sense (or properties) that would characterize such an object if it existed. To say that Jones intends that he enter room no. 6 would accordingly be construed so that: 'room no. 6' refers indirectly but ultimately to room no. 6, and directly to the sense of 'room no. 6', and 'enters' does not refer (even ultimately) to any particular action on Jones's part, even if pursuant to his intention he should enter room no. 6; 'enters' rather refers only to a *type* of action of which Jones's later action would be an instance.

---

[26] G. Frege, 'The Thought: A Logical Inquiry', in P. F. Strawson (ed.), *Philosophical Logic*, Oxford (1967), 17–38; Frege, 'On Sense and Reference', in P. Geach and Max Black (eds.), *Translations from the Philosophical Writings of Gottlob Frege*, Oxford (1977), 56–78.

Despite all of these virtues, this third view about intentional objects runs into some thorny problems about propositions. One of these problems is perhaps not as bad as it appears. This is the 'queerness' objection, an objection that finds abstract entities such as propositions to be suspicious characters with which to populate the mind. That problem may be less serious than it appears if one can ultimately cash out propositions to functional states of mind and, ultimately, to physiology.[27] At least in their use as objects of mental states, there is nothing that demands that propositions be irreducibly abstract entities with no correlations in the functional organization of mind and in the structure of the brain.

More serious is the kind of post-Quinean scepticism about synonymy or sameness of sense. If one doubts that there is in natural languages any such relation, that seems to doom any Fregean theory of propositional identity, dependent as is the latter on a notion of sameness of sense. Such philosophical scepticism about synonymy and analytic relations leads some contemporary philosophers, such as Geach, to 'doubt whether there is such a concept as propositional identity'.[28] Geach's conclusion is 'that nobody really has the faintest idea what he means when he says, 'The proposition that p is the same as the proposition that q'.[29]

Despite such deep and widespread philosophical scepticism about synonymy and analytic entailments generally, we each employ some common sense measure of when two words, phrases, or sentences 'mean the same thing'. Even Quine implicitly recognized as much, given his 'method of paraphrase' as one of the steps necessary to ascertain our true ontological commitments. However much the sophisticated philosophical arguments convince us that there can be no acceptable acocunt of synonymy, we each employ some notion of sameness of meaning in everyday life.

This fact is not raised in order to elevate common sense over philosophical insight. Rather, it is to say that we each have beliefs about the correct ways to pick out and name an individual or a class of individuals. We each, that is, have some ideas about the sense (in the Fregean sense of the word) of our singular terms and of our predicates. Some ways of picking out particulars and universals are preferred by us and dubbed the 'meaning' of such words. These need not be (and will

---

[27] For one such attempt, see Brian Loar, *Mind and Meaning*, Cambridge (1982).

[28] P. T. Geach, *Logic Matters*, Berkeley (1980), 176.

[29] Ibid., 170. For similar scepticism by Quine, see *Word and Object*, 200–21.

not be) the actual senses of the words; rather, they will include all the images, names, and partial descriptions which each person employs to bring something before his own mind, what David Kaplan terms 'vivid' names.[30] Use of any of such vivid names or descriptions should, to the person involved, seem like the use of a synonym. He should say that 'bachelor' and 'unmarried male person', for example, are just different ways of picking out the same class of individuals and that both descriptions 'mean the same thing'.

These beliefs allow us to make sense of the idea of 'same sense' in a way that is not subject to Quinean objections. In the context of mental state individuation, we should say that two propositions are the same when the senses (meanings) of the words expressing them are believed to be the same by the holder of the mental states in question.[31] This subjective test does not give a criterion of propositional identity generally; it only does so for the limited context of individuating propositions when they are the objects of mental states.

Not only does this subjectivist criterion of sameness of meaning avoid Quinean problems, but on reflection one should seek such a criterion here anyway. As Kaplan notes, 'the notion of a vivid name is intended to go to the purely internal aspects of individuation'.[32] Actual synonymy, if it existed, would be a relation within a language but about some particular person only in so far as his mental states made no mistakes about that language. In individuating mental states, however, what is wanted is some principle that is internal to the individual person whose mental states they are. The subjectivist criterion of 'same sense' satisfies this legitimate demand in a way that no purely language-based criterion could.

Assuming such a subjectivist move gets one around Quinean objections, the theory of individuation that results will have two requirements.

---

[30] David Kaplan, 'Quantifying In', in L. Linsky (ed.), *Reference and Modality*, Oxford (1971), 112–144.

[31] It may seem that this subjectivist idea of synonymy is open to the kind of circularity objections that Butler advanced against Locke's memory criterion of personal identity: consciousness of personal identity cannot constitute a criterion of personal identity because 'the former presupposes the idea of personal identity'. Yet the circularity charge is warranted here no more than against Locke: I do not use our sense of the inter-substitutability of various ways of referring to the same thing as constituting a criterion of synonymy; whether there really is any relation in a natural language properly called synonymy I leave open. 'Believed synonymy' is for my purposes enough (just as 'believed self-identity' was enough for Locke). See, on the circularity problem, David Wiggins, *Sameness and Substance*, Cambridge, Mass. (1980), chap. 6.

[32] Kaplan, 'Quantifying In', 135. See also Quine, *Word and Object*, 201–2.

Two nominally distinct intentions will be the same when the language used to describe their objects: (1) has the same reference and extension; and (2) where that language means the same to the holder of the intention(s) in question.

Application of each of these aspects of propositional identity reveals a fine-grained theory of individuating intentions quite at odds with Hart's and other legal philosophers' examples and assumptions. Take the first requirement, that there be reference to the same type of state of affairs or type of action. Hart was right to distinguish a crushing of the skull of an infant from a death of that infant, but wrong to identify the breaking of glasses with the striking of glasses. In each of these pairs of cases, there are distinct types of events (and thus, distinct types of intentions with regard to these types of events).

One necessary condition to identifying particular events is if they have the same causes and the same effects.[33] One necessary condition to identifying types of events is if they have the same causal powers.[34] A particular skull-crushing may properly be said to cause the death of the foetus whose skull is crushed, but the death of the foetus does not cause its skull to be crushed; skull-crushings have the power to cause death, but deaths do not have the power to cause skull-crushings. Likewise, striking a particular glass may cause it to be broken, but the breaking of the glass does not cause the glass to be struck; and glass-strikings have the power to cause glass-breakings, but glass-breakings do not have the power to cause glass-strikings. In short, there are asymmetrical causal relations between each of these pairs of events, and between each of these pairs of types of events, that prevents identifying one as the other.

The same holds true for most of the examples quoted earlier in part I. Asymmetrical causal relations exist between: heart-removals, and deaths; blowing up a plane in flight, and the deaths of any passengers on it; getting drunk, and being hung over; retaining another's car, and depriving him of his use of it; decapitation, and death. In each of such cases, there are distinct types of events, and an intent to bring about the first is *not*, accordingly, an intent to bring about the second. The test the courts and commentators have used here—about how 'invariant', 'immediate' or 'certain' are the causal sequences between the two types of events—is just the opposite of what one should be saying. That there is a causal connection at all between the pairs of event-types should lead

---

[33] D. Davidson, 'The Individuation of Events', in N. Rescher (ed.), *Essays in Honor of Carl G. Hempel*, Dordrecht (1969).

[34] D. M. Armstrong, *A Theory of Universals*, Cambridge (1978), Chap. 16.

courts exactly the other way, namely, to conclude that these are distinct types of events.

A few of the examples earlier examined are not of this sort. More plausibly one might identify the appointment of Garcia, and the appointment of a fifty-year-old man, as the same event, if Garcia is indeed fifty; likewise, one might identify remaining unmarried and remaining a bachelor as the same types of states of affairs. For such examples one must invoke the second aspect of propositional identity, that having to do with identity of meaning.

For most persons we know, 'bachelor' and 'unmarried male' are synonymous ways of picking out the same class of individuals. For such persons an intention to remain unmarried and an intention to remain a bachelor are one and the same intention. By contrast, an intention to appoint Garcia may be the same as an intention to appoint a fifty-year-old man, but only if the description, 'the fifty-eyear-old man', is the way in which the holder of the intention(s) calls Garcia to mind in this context. If Garcia's being fifty years old is not that imporatnt ('vivid') to the holder of the intention, then one cannot substitute, 'fifty-year-old man' for 'Garcia' in the object of the intention; for such intentions are distinct, and one is not necessarily the other.

The upshot of all this is that our metaphysics of intent individuation yield a theory quite at odds with that assumed by courts and commentators when they talk of 'the same intention'. It is not that we have no theory of intent-individuation, as sceptics such as Kelman believe. Thus, one cannot argue that the distinction between direct and oblique intentions is manipulable at will. Still, the terms of the debate about direct and oblique intentions should change considerably when placed on its proper metaphysical foundations. Those such as Kenny who wish to argue for the primacy of purpose in explicating intention have much more of a job cut out for them than they acknowledge, as do those who would make moral sense of the doctrine of double effect.[35]

Those in Kenny's position have but two options here. First, they can accept the fine-grained theory of individuation, and argue that none the less there is a significant difference in culpability between one who intends a harm and one who only knows that harm will result from his

---

[35] Philippa Foot recognizes as much about the doctrine of double effect, when she acknowledges that a fine-grained theory of individuation would 'make nonsense of it from the beginning'. 'Abortion and Double Effect', 6. The 'nonsense' such a fine-grained theory makes of the doctrine is that of a morally unjustifiable distinction, not some kind of literally nonsensical statements.

activities. In such a case Kenny must argue that there is a moral difference between the killer who blows up a plane in order to collect life insurance on the passengers and the killer who blows up a passenger-laden plane in order to collect insurance on the plane. Here, Hart's moral argument seems difficult to get around: both killers deliberately chose money over human life. That one needed the passengers to die in order to get the money, whereas the other only knew that they would die from the acts necessary to get the money, seems morally insignificant.

Alternatively, those favouring the moral significance of the purpose/knowledge distinction could attempt to work out some basis for a more coarse-grained theory of individuating intentions; given what has been said about the metaphysical correctness of a very fine-grained theory, the basis for their more coarse-grained theory must be some policy argument for equating two admittedly distinct intentions. In the context of criminal punishment, such policies should have to do with moral culpability. Needed here is some moral theory that would justify saying that intentions that are really quite distinct should none the less be treated as the same for purposes of determining culpability.[36] It is to the possibility of there being such a moral theory of intent individuation that the next section is devoted.

III MORALLY EQUIVALENT INTENTIONS

In *Hyam v. Director of Public Prosecutions*[37] Lord Hailsham hinted at such an alternative moral basis for a coarse-grained theory of intent-

---

[36] The discussion that follows in section III is directed only at situations where there is no justification at issue, so that a doctrine of morally equivalent intentions deals only with the relative culpabilities of two quite culpable intentions. For (what I would take to be) a discussion of a moral theory of equivalent intentions in the context of the doctrine of double effect, see Jonathan Bennett, 'Whatever the Consequences', *Analysis*, vol. 26 (1966), 83–102, and John Finnis, 'The Rights and Wrongs of Abortion', *Philosophy and Public Affairs*, vol. 2 (1973), 117–45. The jumble of factors that Bennett and Finnis identify as determining when an effect is intended as a means, or only known to be brought about as a side consequence, are each of them factors for which independent moral argument must be given. One should say of all of them, what Judith Thomson says of one of them, that 'it is hard to see how anyone could think that this question has any bearing at all on the question whether a given death is, on the one hand, an agent's ends or means, or on the other hand, a mere foreseen consequence of what he does to save his life'. Thomson, 'Rights and Deaths', *Philosophy and Public Affairs*, vol. 2 (1973), 146–59, at 151. Put my way: what good is the distinction between direct and oblique intentions if to give the distinction any bite at all one must import into it a whole range of independent moral considerations. that themselves require explication and defence? The direct/oblique distinction in such a case does no moral work and should be dropped from the discussion.

[37] [1974] 2 All Eng. Rep. 41.

individuation. In *Hyam* the defendant had had a relationship with a man who subsequently became engaged to be married to a Mrs Booth. In an effort to scare Mrs Booth into leaving town and breaking off the engagement, the defendant set fire to the front entranceway of Mrs Booth's house, resulting in the deaths of Mrs Booth's two daughters. In affirming the defendant's conviction for murder, Lord Hailsham required that the defendant have a direct intention—mere knowledge, or oblique intention, could not suffice for murder. The question as Hailsham therefore framed it was whether the defendant's mediate but direct intention to expose Mrs Booth to the serious risk of death was sufficiently like an intention actually to cause death or grievous bodily injury, that the one should be said to *be* the other so that the defendant could be punished as a murderer. Lord Hailsham assumed the intention that defendant had—to expose Mrs Booth to risk in order to scare her— was logically distinct from an intention to cause either grievous bodily harm or death. None the less:

[T]he moral truth [is] that if a man, in full knowledge of the danger involved, and without lawful excuse, deliberately does that which exposes a victim to the risk of probable grievous bodily harm . . . or death, and the victim dies, the perpetrator of the crime is guilty of murder and not manslaughter to the same extent as if he had actually intended the consequences to follow. . . . This is because *the two types of intention are morally indistinguishable, although factually and logically distinct*, and because it is therefore just that they should bear the same consequences for the perpetrator. . .[38]

Lord Hailsham assumed that there is a significant difference in the culpability of those who directly intend a death and those who only obliquely do so. None the less, he assumes there is some moral theory that justifies him in treating as an intention to kill or inflict grievous bodily harm, an intention that is admittedly not an intention to kill or inflict grievous bodily harm. Clearly this moral theory cannot be based on the *knowledge* of someone like Hyam that imposing a risk of death on Mrs Booth might well in fact kill her. If Hailsham thought that, he would have had no business in distinguishing direct from oblique intentions; either, in such a case, should suffice for murder. What is needed by Hailsham is a moral theory that does not depend on the knowledge of the acting subject as its basis for equating one intention with another.

A glimpse of such a theory may perhaps be found in the legal doctrine of transferred intent which holds that an intention to harm A is

[38] Ibid., 55.

equivalent in legal effect to an intention to harm B, where B is the person the defendant actually harms. The defendant did not intend to harm B, but if he did intend to harm A and in trying to do so harmed B, the intent to harm A will be sufficient *mens rea* for the completed offence.

One way to account for the doctrine of transferred intent is through a moral theory that says that the identity of a victim is a morally insignificant aspect of a defendant's intention; that, accordingly, the intention the defendant had (to harm A) will be treated as if it were the intention prohibited (to harm B), even though they are in reality different intentions. The harm intended is just as bad as the harm caused, so the intention is 'transferred' from one harm to the other.

Such a moral theory (of the substitutability of morally equivalent intentions) may also find expression in the legal docrine of implied malice. These are the cases in which the defendant intends to kill someone but does not intend to kill any particular person; as where he shoots into a crowd indiscriminately. One might say in such cases that the intention the defendant had (to shoot anyone) is sufficiently bad that it will be 'transferred' to the harm the defendant actually caused, the death of some one particular person.

One might also glimpse outcroppings of such a moral theory in the legal doctrines surrounding felony-murder, grievous bodily harm murder, mayhem, and also in torts. For felony-murder, for example, one might think that although the harm intended (say, arson) is different from the harm caused (death), morally both are so bad that the intent to do the one should be identified as the intent to do the other. Likewise, for the doctrine of grievous-bodily-harm murder: even though the harm intended (grievous bodily harm) is different from the harm caused (death), the intent to do the former is so bad that it will be treated like the intent to do the latter as well. Similarly in mayhem: to be mayhem there must be disfigurement, yet American criminal law makes clear that an intent to hit will suffice as an intent to disfigure if disfigurement is caused by that hitting.[39] Tort law can be similarly construed: an intent to hit will suffice for the harm caused by the hitting even if there was no intent to harm; an intent to hit may be thought culpable enough to classify the harm as intentionally accomplished rather than negligently so, giving rise to the more severe sanctions reserved for the intentional torts.[40]

[39] *State* v. *Hatley*, 72 N.M. 377, 384 P. 2d 252 (1963). See generally Wayne R. LaFave and Austin W. Scott, *Criminal Law*, St. Paul, Minn. (1972), 616.

[40] *Vosburg* v. *Putney*, 80 Wis. 523, 50 N.W. 403 (1891).

There are two problems with the sort of moral theory just sketched. One is a query about the coherence of the theory, the other, about its correctness. The coherence point first: most of the cases where one is tempted to say the intention the defendant had is 'close enough' to the one prohibited to be identified as the same, are cases where the intended harm is not bad (or bad enough) by itself; it is only bad because it will probably cause a further harm, which is really bad. Consider the decapitation, heart-removal, and skull-crushing examples. On the theory here considered, an intent to do any of these things is as bad as the intent to kill, and therefore these two admittedly different intentions will be in law be said to be the same. The problem lies in how the culpability of the intent to decapitate, for example, is fixed. If the intent to decapitate is bad only because decapitations always cause deaths, and deaths are bad, then this alleged moral theory about morally equivalent intentions is in reality a back-door way to the objective theory of intention. What one is really saying in such a case is that this defendant, because he intended to decapitate (crush the skull, cut out the heart), should have known that what he was doing would cause a death, and this makes him as culpable as one who intends to cause a death.[41] If *this* is one's theory of individuating morally equivalent intentions, then the supposed moral theory here is no more and no different from the moral theory that says that negligence is as culpable as purpose when a harm is caused. Better to assert such a theory openly when it can be assessed for its (im)plausibility and not hide it by the language of morally equivalent intentions and the like.

These same remarks apply to *Hyam* itself. One might think that risking harm to another, when that other knows of the risk and fears it, is an independently bad thing to do. If so, then an intended risking of death can be equated to an intended killing without trivializing the theory of morally equivalent intentions. More plausibly, however, one might think that risking death to another is bad because you just might kill them. If this is so, then the intent to risk death is morally equivalent to an intent to cause death only in the trivial sense just mentioned (namely, where the badness of the intent to risk just is the negligence with respect to death that accompanies that intent).

---

[41] The high degree of negligence here is undoubtedly what courts and commentators are getting at when they speak of the 'moral certainty' (Lord Hailsham) or the 'immediate and invariant connection' (Hart and Kenny) of the harm occurring if the defendant achieves what he is aiming at. One would indeed be very negligent not to have foreseen, e.g., death of passengers on a plane one plans to blow up in mid-air.

Consider also Lord Hailsham's hypothetical example of the plane destroyed in mid-air with passengers aboard. Blowing up a plane without passengers in it is a bad thing to do. Yet I doubt that it is this badness that outrages us enough to equate an intent to blow up the plane with the intent to kill the passengers. Rather, what outrages us enough to equate the two is the *knowledge* of the defendant that his greedy act will kill many innocent people. It is his knowledge of the certainty of death, not his intent to destroy the plane, that inclines us so strongly to classifying him as a murderer. In which case there is no moral theory that identifies the one intention as the other, save the very same moral theory that Lord Hailsham was trying to avoid by his requirement of a direct intention for murder.

Not all instances of a supposedly independent moral theory will collapse in this way. Rape is bad independently of the risk of death to the victim; inflicting grievous bodily harm on another is bad independently of its risking death to the person so harmed; hitting is bad independently of the likelihood of disfiguring the person hit. In such cases, when one classifies, for example, an intent to rape or to inflict grievous bodily harm as enough for murder when death ensues, or when one classifies an intent to hit as enough for mayhem when disfigurement results, one is holding two intentions to be close enough in culpability to be treated as the same for punishment purposes. The problem in these cases, however, is that the moral theory that sanctions these identities seems wrong. An intentional rapist may be very culpable, but he is not as culpable as an intentional killer. Someone who intentionally strikes another and puts out an eye because the other moved his head at the last second is culpable, but surely not as culpable as one who not only hits but intends to put out an eye with the blow.

Equating these cases is to operate with a kind of crude forfeiture theory, whereby once a defendant has crossed some threshold of culpability we should not care about making any further discriminations in the degree of culpability. Yet it is just this kind of forfeiture theory which was rejected by the courts of England over a century ago when they worked out the no substitution of *mens rea* rule in criminal law.[42] Even if the intent to do one thing is *more* culpable than the intent to do

---

[42] *Regina* v. *Pembliton*, 2 Cox Crim. Cas. 607 (1874) (intent to hit a person with a stone not substituted for the intent to damage property required for a conviction of malicious damage to property); *Regina* v. *Faulkner*, 13 Cox Crim. Cas. 550 (1877) (intent to steal which, when acted upon, led to the firing of a ship, not substituted for the intent to fire the ship required for a conviction of arson).

another,[43] if a defendant causes the second harm but not the first he should be liable only for the attempt to do the first; he should not be held liable for the second crime (unless knowledge or recklessness is enough—in which event he should be held for *those* mental states, not the other intention). The important moral principle that underlies these cases is one requiring the concurrence of act, intent, and causation before one is fully culpable. One needs a 'guilty mind' (here, direct intention) *with respect to the harm prohibited*, not with respect to some other type of harm, if one is fairly to be held responsible for causing that harm.

It may seem that the implied malice and the transferred intent cases are not subject to either of these objections. That is, in these cases, the harm intended may be thought to be bad independently of its risking the harm caused; and intuitively, it may seem more appealing to say that an intent to hit A or to hit anyone, where B is hit instead, will suffice for guilt at intentionally hitting B. The moral theory that would equate the two intentions seems neither incoherent nor incorrect.

Yet the implied malice and the transferred intent cases need not be accounted for by some moral theory as to when we may substitute intentions. An alternative way to account for such cases is to say that the intention some defendant actually had is an instance of just the type of intention the statute prohibits. We need not say of such cases that we are 'transferring' or substituting intentions, nor need we seek moral grounds with which to justify treating as the same two in fact distinct intention-types.

The trick is to examine statutes that prohibit act-types such as intentional killings. For obvious reasons statutes are not formulated to prohibit the killing of particular, named persons. They rather prohibit the intentional killing of 'a human being'.[44] As is well known to logicians,[45] the indefinite article is ambiguous here: the unlawful intent may be either an intent to kill someone, in the sense of some one particular person; or the prohibited intention may be an intention to kill someone in the sense of anyone. The ambiguity is in the scope of the existential quantifier. The first statement should be symbolized as:

---

[43] Consider in this regard the facts of *Pembliton* (note 42 above): the defendant threw a stone, intending to hit another person. The stone instead broke a window. The defendant's conviction for malicious property damage was quashed because the intent to harm persons would not be substituted for the intent to damage property; this, despite the greater evil in what the defendant intended to do than what he in fact did.

[44] See, e.g., California Penal Code §188.

[45] Quine, *Word and Object*, 146–51.

1. ∃x[yI(Kyx)]

(There is some person x such that y intends that he kills x.)

The second statement, on the other hand, does not require quantification into the intend operator:

2. yI[∃x(Kyx)]

(y intends that there be someone he kills.)

A reasonable construction of criminal statutes is to say that they make unlawful intentions of either type. If this is so then the transferred intent and implied malice cases quite literally instantiate one of the types of intentions prohibited by law. An intent to kill A, where B is killed instead, is an intent to kill someone in the sense of (1) above; an intent to kill anyone within a crowd is an intent to kill someone in the sense of (2) above. These being unproblematic instances of the types of intentions prohibited by law, there is no need for a moral theory of equivalent intentions in order to account for our intuitions that these cases merit the severe punishment reserved for *intentional* killers.[46]

The upshot of all this is that there is no plausible moral theory that can urge us to identify two distinct intentions as the same. Whenever a legal theorist urges us to treat two distinct intentions as the same, one of two things is true: (*a*) either he is using knowledge or recklessness or negligence as the touchstone of culpability, despite his supposed concern with purpose; or (*b*) he is urging some crude forfeiture theory of culpability that is inconsistent with the basic moral requirement that

---

[46] There are problems about the transferred intent cases but these are not problems connected with the insufficiency of the defendant's intention. Rather, they are proximate cause problems about the concurrence of the causation and *mens rea* elements. The concurrence principle holds that the defendant must have caused a particular harm that instantiates the type of harm intended. The question in such cases is whether we individuate types of harm by the persons who suffffer them or not. The transferred intent doctrine says that we do not take into account the identity of the victim; the problem is that we do take the identity of the victim into account in negligence cases (at least in jurisdictions following the Cardozo's opinion in *Palsgraf* disallowing that there can be negligence 'in the air, so to speak'). However one comes out here will not affect the fact that the defendant's intention in these cases quite literally is an instance of the type of intention prohibited by statutes.

Imagine an analogous case, where the charge is mayhem: the defendant strikes the victim, intending to put out the victim's left eye; the victim turns his head at the last moment, and the right eye is put out instead. It does not require a doctrine of transferred intent to hold the defendant guilty of mayhem: he quite literally intended to put out 'an eye'. If there is a problem here, it is again one of proximate causation: do we individuate the types of harm so finely that we should say there are distinct types? I think not. *The* type of harm prohibited by the mayhem statute is disfigurement, so that if a defendant intended *a* disfigurement of someone and he caused a disfigurement of someone, then he satisfies the statute and the concurrence principle.

there be proportionality between punishment and culpability. In the first case he does not have a theory of morally equivalent *intentions*; in the second case, while he has such a theory, it is not a very plausible one.[47]

IV CONCLUSIONS

1 Contrary to the scepticism mentioned in the introduction, there is an answer to the question of what an individual directly intends and an answer to the question of whether his direct intention is the same as some type of intention prohibited by law and morality. The distinction between direct and oblique intentions, accordingly, is not an illusory one based on an arbitrary metaphysical posit. Those moral and legal philosophers who wish to debate the relative culpability of direct and oblique intentions have, accordingly, something to argue about.

2 The distinction is, however, a distinction that classifies cases quite differently from the way most legal theorists suppose. If one individuates intentions by their propositional objects, as I have here urged that we do in ordinary explanatory contexts, one will separate intentions that most theorists wish to hold the same. The result is to shift the debate about the moral relevance of the distinction considerably. Properly individuated, many of the mental states that are counted as direct intentions of a prohibited sort are in reality at best oblique intentions only. Since these

[47] This last point is implicitly recognized by those many courts that have sought to ameliorate the harshness of the felony–murder rule by requiring that the underlying felony be one 'inherently dangerous to human life'. By restricting in this way the kinds of intentions that can be substituted for an intention to kill, courts in effect have recognized that having a very bad intention by itself does not merit the sanctions attached to murder; rather, that bad intention (to do the underlying felony) must be one whereby the defendant manifests his recklessness (or extreme negligence) with regard to life. The felony–murder rule thus approaches a reckless/negligent homicide doctrine having nothing to do with substituting one bad intention the defendant had for the intention to kill, which he did not have. The next logical step is that taken by the Model Penal Code (Proposed Official Draft, 1962, sec. 210.2), which reduces the felony–murder doctrine to no more than a presumption of recklessness manifesting extreme indifference to human life.

A similar development has taken place with the grievous-bodily-harm-murder doctrine. Many states have reduced the harshness of the rule by defining 'grievous bodily harm' to be an injury 'likely to be attended with dangerous or fatal consequences'. *People* v. *Crenshaw*, 298 Ill. 412, 416, 131 N.E. 576, 577 (1921). By so limiting the intentions that can be substituted for an intention to kill, the courts have in effect required some recklessness with respect to death before they will substitute a grievous bodily harm intention for an intention to kill. Again, the Model Penal Code has taken the next logical step of eliminating the substituted intention entirely as a ground for murder, replacing it with an explicit question about the actor's recklessness in bringing about a death. See American Law Institute, *Model Penal Code and Commentaries*, Part II, Comment to section 210.2 at 28–9 (1980).

are often cases where severe punishment seems warranted, the moral case for allowing knowledge (oblique intention) to suffice along with purpose as the marker of most serious culpability, is stronger than many have thought. All of which is to say that H. L. A. Hart may have been more correct than he knew on this issue.[48]

3   There is no moral theory that is both coherent and correct and that allows one to identify admittedly distinct intentions as the same for criminal law purposes. Because legal theorists and judges have believed that there is such a theory, however, we have a criminal law that abuses the concept of intention and abuses the significant degree of culpability that that concept marks. Crude forfeiture doctrines abound in criminal law, where an intention to do one thing (for example, inflict grievous bodily harm) is treated as an intention to do something else (that is, to kill). Disabused of the idea that there is some moral justification for equating such distinct intentions, we can see such doctrines for what they are: a dilution of purpose and knowledge as the touchstones of most serious culpability and the substitution of negligence. Whether such substitution is a good idea is a matter that can be debated. One sees the right issue here, however, only by being clear about how one fixes the objects of intentions. An intention to inflict grievous bodily harm is *not* an intention to kill, and there is no good reason to pretend otherwise.

[48] Taking 'know' contrary to Hart's apparent view quoted earlier, that to know some proposition p is also to know all the conceptual implications of p. On the latter conception of 'know', Hart already knew all the foregoing to the extent that it is presupposed by what he said about the direct/oblique distinction.

6.2 Comment

DAVID HEYD*

The general programme underlying Michael Moore's paper seems to be both necessary and important. The legal discourse of intentions (not only in the context of *mens rea*) calls for clarification for which metaphysical, logical, and epistemological arguments must be deployed. The legal theorist cannot just claim that the ontological status of intentions, their individuation, and the ways by which they are recognized are irrelevant to their use in the lega context. Success in Moore's programme may serve well in establishing traditional legal distinctions. Failure would mean a more relativistic approach, or even hint at the undesirability of using intentions as grounds for legal judgement.

As a commentator I will exercise my right to point to some difficulties in Moore's attempt and to cast some doubts without feeling obliged to offer solutions of my own or alternative theses. It is certainly easier to play the role of the uncommitted sceptic, but as the sceptic has been granted prima-facie legitimacy in Moore's paper, I would like to join him in his critical stance. I will address myself mainly to the metaphysical, logical, and epistemological aspects of Moore's presentation.

My principal concern is with the possibility of individuating intentions and with Moore's thesis that intentions can be fully individuated (in the metaphysical sense) through their objects which are propositions. The gist of my argument will be that the individuation of mental entities such as intentions by their propositional objects is hopelessly *circular* and hence of little theoretical (or indeed legal) value.

Moore considers three candidates for the status of the object of an intention: a sentence, a real object, and a proposition. These three candidates serve as the three respective methods for the identification of intentions. Moore forcibly argues against the first two and tries to justify the third. Yet, to start near the end of his argument, how are we to individuate propositions? Moore's Fregean answer is: both by their reference and by their sense. Assuming that sameness of reference does not give rise to any special problems, how are we to establish sameness of sense? Can we circumvent Quine's warnings about synonymy? Moore

* © David Heyd 1987.

believes that he can, by offering a weaker concept of the agent's subjective beliefs. But by that move Moore shifts the criterion of individuation back to the problematic and mysterious arena of mental states! That is to say, in trying to individuate subjective mental events or attitudes in terms of objective propositions Moore is willy nilly led back to the realm of belief. The propositional attitude of intention is analysed in terms of propositions which are themselves considered as relative to other propositional attitudes, namely beliefs. This is a typical circular trap. Moore is aware that this principle of individuation of propositions applies only to those propositions which are the objects of mental states, and not to propositions in general, but by that he cannot avoid conceding the circularity of his principle of individuation *when applied to intentions*.

To put it more succinctly: in the context of intention, the meaning (or sense) of what I do (or as I will argue in a moment, of the description under which my action is intentional) is not just a matter of cognitive belief but a matter of intention. Thus, the fact that two senses are the same for me is a matter of what I intend in my action. The circularity is now quite obvious: my intention is individuated through its object, a proposition, which in turn is individuated through my intention. The threat of circularity seems to be more damaging to Moore's proposed solution than the vagueness of his notion of sameness of sense, which in itself is not logically fatal.

The flaw of a circular method of individuation of intentions may explain why Moore must complement his method by suggesting a functional criterion: For the functionalist two intentions are the same if they have the same functional role in the explanation of the agent's behaviour. For example, the intention to remain a bachelor is identical with the intention to remain unmarried (on the condition that 'bachelor' and 'unmarried' mean the same to the intention-holder). So far so good; but if we choose such an easy, behaviouristic criterion of individuation of intentions, why bother in the first place with propositions whose ontological status is problematic and whose individuation can only be achieved by reverting to the intentions in question? Furthermore, the functionalist criterion does not seem to me to yield Moore's very fine-grained theory of individuation which is the product of the subjective criterion of sameness of sense. For although 'striking a glass with a hammer' and 'breaking a glass with a hammer' do not have the same sense, they *usually* have the same functional role in explaining behaviour. And the same would apply to 'decapitation' and 'killing'. This divergence of the allegedly overlapping criteria casts doubt on the chance of integrating behaviouristic and mentalistic strategies of intention-individuation.

Having shown some of the difficulties in identifying intentions through propositions (and keeping in mind the widely-held suspicions regarding the very existence of propositions), let us turn now to an old, though not uncontroversial, picture of the matter. The objects of intention are neither sentences, nor real objects, nor propositions—but simply actions. This might be a promising line for the theorists interested in individuation. For the individuation of actions can be achieved, according to Davidson, for instance, by treating them as events and then subjecting them to a causal criterion which objectively and uniquely identifies them.[49] Moore claims that actions cannot serve as objects of intentions because intentions refer by definition to actions which have not yet occurred and which might never occur. However, I see no problem in admitting *possible* (rather than actual) actions as objects of intention. Possible actions or future events can be easily individuated along Davidsonian lines.

Secondly, Moore is critical of the causal theory of action-individuation because of what he refers to as the asymmetrical causal relations between pairs of actions and events such as the following: heart removals cause deaths, but deaths do not cause heart removals; hitting causes disfigurement, but disfigurement does not cause hitting. Yet I think Moore reaches a wrong conclusion in this matter because of a conceptual confusion of two types of entities—actions and the events which are their results. In a Davidsonian theory of action-individuation the pairs to be compared are heart removals and *killings* (not deaths), hitting and *disfiguring* (not disfigurement). Thus we can say that heart removals *are* killings and that hitting is disfiguring (at least in certain circumstances).

So far we stand on the solid ground of a coarse-grained extensional theory of individuation of actions. But can this be our clue to the individuation of intentions? Not really; for as *objects* of intentions actions must come under some description. We can never intend a bare action. Human actions (so far as they are intentional) can only be identified through their descriptions. But as we know, any action can be given an indefinite number of descriptions. How can we hope to select the relevant description which makes the action the object of an intention? Again we are confronted with the disturbing circularity: there is no other

---

[49] Cf. D. Davidson, 'Agency' and 'The Individuation of Events', both in D. Davidson (ed.), *Essays on Actions and Events*, Oxford (1980), particularly pp. 52, 61, 179.

way to fix the relevant description but through the examination of what the agent intended in doing the act in question.

Circularity also characterizes the attempt to individuate desires: I want *this*, let us say a physical object which can be individuated in extensional language. But *qua* an object of my desire 'this' can be individuated only in intentional terms, that is to say through certain descriptions of the object which make it desired to me (for example redness or sweetness).

To summarize this point: my scepticism concerning the individuating criteria of intentions emerges from the logical gap between the Anscombe/Davidson ontology of actions and Moore's ontology of intentions. The ontology of actions is economic and based on coarse-grained criteria of individuation. It is extensional and objective and seems to me superior to other ontologies of actions. The realm of intentions is linked to that of action, but, alas, only through the description of the action (or in Moore's terms through the notion of sense-as-it-is-understood-by-the-agent). This makes the solid theory of action-individuation quite useless for the theory of intention-individuation which is consequently trapped in circularity. Propositions, although usually considered to be mind-independent entities, do not fare better than real actions as a means of identifying intentions. It is hard to see how the transparent view of an event—or object-individuation—can serve to individuate intentions which appear in typically opaque contexts. An alternative attempt would consist of the individuation of intentions as mental events or as neurophysiological occurrences, but that is surely beyond Moore's programme of individuating intentions through their *objects*.

My scepticism is reinforced by the vagueness of Moore's ontology of intentions: his world of intentions can be anything between the relatively economic, coarse-grained picture yielded by a functional theory and the very prolific, fine-grained theory of the subjective notion of sameness of sense.

The scepticism concerning intention-individuation naturally affects the direct/oblique distinction. I would like to raise a few points in this context, the first relating to the doctrine of double effect. Consider the act sometimes called 'euthanasia': This act can be described as 'relieving of pain' but it can also be described as 'killing'. The moral justification of the act is sometimes based on the identification of the intention behind the act as relating to the first description rather than the second (even though we assume that the agent *knows* that pain relief *is* killing in that particular case). But there are alternative ways of viewing the case: we could for example say that the agent intends the action under the description 'relieving pain by killing' (where the killing becomes *part* of the direct intention), or even under the description 'killing in order to relieve pain' (where the killing is directly intended as a *means*). The doctrine of double effect seems to me a desperate attempt to justify a preference for one description as the individuating factor of the intentional action. But it is a purely *ad hoc* solution, at least from the point of view of a metaphysically-based principle of individuation such as that sought by Moore.

The same doubt is cast on the attempts to distinguish oblique from direct intentions in other pairs of examples. Take Moore's case of the man causing a plane to explode in order to collect the insurance. We can say that his intention was to blow up the plane knowing that many passengers will die. We can no less aptly say that his intention was to explode a fully-loaded plane (thus making the death of the passengers part of his direct intention). The test of desire (whether he would have been glad if he could achieve his goal without killing the passengers) is of no use here, because relative to a third description of the same action namely 'he made an attempt to collect one million dollars' even the description 'he exploded the plane' (which was initially treated as direct) becomes oblique.

An even clearer example is the prisoner who, trying to escape from prison, kills the guard. Now, according to a coarse-grained theory of action-individuation there is here just one action but it can be given a wide variety of descriptions. If 'escaping from prison' is the description under which the action is directly intended then the description 'killing the guard' is only obliquely intended. But why not describe the action as 'setting oneself free' (making both former descriptions the object of his oblique intention)? An answer in terms of the prisoner's desires is again unhelpful, since although we can say that he would prefer escaping without killing, we can no less sincerely say that he would prefer becoming free without escaping (perhaps gain legal pardon).

So although I believe there is some logical structure governing the variety of descriptions of a given action (as is shown by Anscombe), I find it hard to tell *what* was the agent's intention in a specific action. Can introspection solve the problem? Not necessarily; for although we can lie about our intentions (thus proving that we know what they are *not*), we cannot always tell the whole truth about them (thus proving that we do not exactly know what they *are*).

I should also add that when Moore says that a coarse-grained theory is inclined to assimilate oblique intentions with direct ones thus assigning knowledge a much lesser role, he ignores the fact that one of the main motives for such an assimilation of intentions is indeed the very knowledge or certainty of the agent that the action under one description is identical to the action under the other description (as for example in the case of the eccentric surgeon). However, knowledge is just one reason for assimilation (or differentiation) of intentions. Moral reasons play an important role in the individuation of intentions. Moore has presented strong arguments against this view but I cannot discuss them here. I would only add that a sceptical attitude leads one to believe that in the absence of metaphysical principles the individuation of intentions is guided by pragmatic moral and epistemological considerations which may often yield conflicting results.

So to sum up my argument: as intentions cannot be individuated like objects of events, that is independently of other entities, they must be individuated through their objects. So far I share Moore's views. There are two possible candidates for such objects: actions and propositions. But actions can function as an individuating criterion only under descriptions which are themselves intentional in nature. And propositions, which like actions look promising for the task of individuation (being objectively identifiable) are also of little use because according to Moore they are in the context of intention identified relative to the agent's subjective belief (and intentions). Circularity breeds scepticism. But of course scepticism is never the last word; it is just a challenge for further refinements and new solutions.

6.3 Comment

MORDECHAI KREMNITZER*

The argument put forward in this comment is complex. We believe the relevance of Moore's analysis to criminal responsibility is limited, for two reasons: firstly, the central concept in criminal law is *mens rea*, not intention; secondly, Moore's analysis does not deal with the moral grounds for differentiating between kinds of intention. Since Moore himself does not discuss the first point, we shall base our own discussion on Hart's analysis of *mens rea*. We will conclude with some general comments on Moore's approach.

I INTENTION AND *MENS REA*

In discussing the mental element in the criminal law Hart says that '. . . the most prominent of these mental elements and in many ways the most important is a man's intention'.[50]

I Intention

In our view, if 'intention' is given its *normal* meaning, then the statement is incorrect. We would suggest that this view is not in contradiction with that of Hart himself, since he pointed out that the legal concept of intention differs from its common meaning.[51] In order to justify the above-cited statement, Hart refers to 'intention or something like it'[52] in a single phrase, whereas we are speaking of intention in the strict sense, the volitional relationship of a person to a future event, on the assumption that a cognitive relationship to that event exists, namely, that there is foreknowledge of it.[53] The event is an objective from the point of view of the perpetrator, whose aim is to bring it about.

---

* © Mordechai Kremnitzer 1987.
[50] H. L. A. Hart, *Punishment and Responsibility*, 114.
[51] Ibid.
[52] Ibid., 116.
[53] In the context of criminal law a future event is generally a consequence, sometimes an objective whose attainment is not necessary for commission of the crime, and sometimes future conduct, as in the offence of breaking and entering.

2 Mens rea

The accepted definition of *mens rea* is awareness by the perpetrator of the *actus reus* of the crime, of the nature of the conduct, the relevant circumstances according to the definition of the crime, and of the consequence on which it depends, if any. In special cases, where the offence depends upon a purpose whose achievement is not required, or a motive, the purpose or the motive are included in the definition.

3 The limited function of 'intention'

If we consider intention—and it is not clear why 'intention or something like it' should be considered—in its normal meaning, we find that it is not generally required as a condition for criminal liability, except in special cases or in certain cases as an aggravating factor. Its function is therefore limited both with regard to its importance (not usually ranking as a minimum condition for criminal liability) and to its scope. As regards the latter, of the three components of the *actus reus*, intention is likely to be relevant to only one future, and uncertain matter, mainly the consequence. Even in consequence-based crimes, the rule for *mens rea* offences is that foresight is sufficient;[54] criminal liability does not depend on an intention that the consequence occur.[55]

The fact that intention is included in *mens rea* is not decisive,[56] since the lower threshold for criminal liability is more important than its upper limit. In practice, for reasons of evidence, the law's *minimum* requirement only will generally be reflected by what was proved in court or found by it.

In legal systems such as the English and Israeli, which do not, as a rule, have minimum or mandatory sentences, where the sentences laid down for offences frequently fail to reflect any rational progression in severity, and where the connection between punishment in law and practice is often incidental, it is difficult to understand why an element whose primary significance is in creating an aggravated form of the offence should receive so much attention, while at the same time so little attention is paid to questions such as whether the *mens rea* should include advertent negligence. Furthermore, if consistency is sought in a

---

[54] Hart, *Punishment and Responsibility*, 117; G. Williams, *The Mental Element in Crime*, Jerusalem (1965), 73.

[55] The intention required in attempts is one of the exceptions to this rule.

[56] Although Hart mentions it several times. See *Punishment and Responsibility*, 117, 119, 121.

legal system, one is obliged to ask whether there is any justification in the offence being aggravated by intention in one case (causing death, for example) and not in others (personal injury or damage to property).

Some of the cases in which the legislator uses the term 'intention'—essentially crimes of specific intent—are relics from the time when a general theory of punishment of attempts had not yet been formulated. Punishment of attempts ensures a general, systematic, and consistent set of rules instead of the casuistic approach that characterized earlier practice.

In some cases although the text uses terms of purpose, what is really required is motive. When what is defined as purpose refers to the objective elements of the offence and not to a future objective, we face a motive and not a purpose. One does not strive to achieve existing reality, but one may be motivated to action by it.

4   *The use of intention in the strict sense*

When the term 'intention' is interpreted to include situations of recklessness it exposes the law to criticism for misleading use of language, and to suspicion and lack of respect.

The concept is made ambiguous, and is thus deprived of its clear message when one wishes to use it in the narrow sense, since there is no assurance that it will be understood and interpreted in that sense. It cannot, therefore, be said that there is no importance in the distinction between intention in the narrow and in the broad sense as stated by Hart.[57] It is necessary to distinguish between two separate questions: (*a*) what constitutes a sufficient mental element for criminal liability? and (*b*) what is the meaning of the element of intention?

It seems that the broadening of the concept 'intention' has its origins in a failure to distinguish between these two questions or, to be more exact, in a routine answer to the first question, under the influence of the past, namely: the general mental element, usually both necessary and sufficient, is intention. When the first step is taken, then a second follows: broadening the concept of 'intention' to include indifference and advertent negligence.

II   FORESIGHT OF A CONSEQUENCE AND INTENTION

I   Conceptual considerations

Where the foresight of a consequence or an object as a certainty or high

---

[57] See Hart, *Punishment and Responsibility*, 117.

probability is treated as a case of intention or substitute for intention (even when the consequence is not desired), it is the perpetrator's assessment that the result or the objective will certainly be realized—an assessment which is personal and subjective. It is not sufficient that the result be foreseen by the perpetrator and that the objective probability of the result occurring is one of certainty or nearly so. Nor is it suffficient that a certain situation is nothing but the side-effect of the aim intended by the perpetrator since the perpetrator himself is not always aware of the fact. The perpetrator must himself have assessed the level of probability as certain or nearly so.

Hart wrote:

The exceptions to this usage of 'intentionality' are cases where a foreseen outcome is so immediately and invariably connected with the action done that the suggestion that the action might not have that outcome would by ordinary standards be regarded as absurd, or such as only a mentally abnormal person would seriously entertain: the connection between action and outcome seems therefore to be not merely contingent but rather to be conceptual.[58]

If the objective expressions of the level of probability given in the passage cited serve as evidence of the existence of such an assessment, all well and good, but this element is in substance subjective. The passages in Moore's article where he tries to deal with the approach that describes as negligence the lethal consequences in cases such as blowing up an aeroplane or cutting off a head, must be viewed in the same critical light. If all that can be attributed to the perpetrator is negligence, that is potential awareness only, then this is an entirely different matter which does not imply intention or a substitute for intention.

There is a distinction between foresight of the consequence as a certainty or near-certainty and foresight of the consequence in general. In our discussion of foreseeing the consequence with certainty or near-certainty, the phrase 'near-certainty' may be understood in the narrow sense as the maximum certainty with which future events can be regarded, or in the broader sense of slightly lower certainty, recognizing the possibility of doubt existing. The doubt, however, must be entirely theoretical, based, in the words of Williams, on a 'miracle', a 'wholly extraordinary chance', so that the perpetrator does not rely on it or

---

[58] Ibid., 120.

entertain any hope that the consequence or goal will thereby not be realized; just as a doubt of this nature does not prevent the judge in a criminal case from making a finding of fact that contradicts such doubt. It is important to distinguish between foresight of this kind and foresight of the possibility of the consequence occurring at a lower level, which satisfies the normal requirements of *mens rea*, but is not intention or a substitute for it. This distinction has not received sufficient emphasis, in the writings of both Hart and Moore.[59]

2   Awareness as a substitute for intention

On the assumption that awareness at its highest level is different from intention, it is, perhaps, justified to recognize it as a substitute for intention, that is, to state in the Criminal Code that where intention is required, this requirement may also be satisfied by awareness at its highest level. Note that we are not seeking here a justification for the imposition of criminal liability but for the imposition of liability—in the normative sense—to the same degree. The justification for this is that when the perpetrator acts with total assurance of the consequence occurring, or without hope of it not occurring, he may be regarded as having made a choice in the fullest sense of the word. From this point of view there is no difference between him and a person acting with intent.[60] He has shown an extreme anti-social attitude in not being deterred from doing the deed in spite of his awareness of the certainty of the consequence. It cannot be said of him—as it may be said of the person guilty of advertent negligence, and possibly of the person guilty of indifference—that if he had seen the consequence as certain, he would have avoided acting as he did. Considerations of retribution, deterrence of the offender and general deterrence justify this substitution of intention for awareness at its highest level.

We may now challenge Moore's thesis. If we conclude that it is

[59] When Hart examines the Steane case he uses the terminology of foresight and not of foresight at its highest level (125, 126). In contrast, dealing with the mental element in attempt, he uses G. Williams's example—pushing somebody off a cliff, describing the perpetrator as 'believing that this will in all probability lead to his death' (126). Moore uses Bentham's term 'oblique intention' to describe awareness at its highest degree, although Bentham was not using it in the same sense but for a consequence that 'was in contemplation, and appeared likely to ensue in case of the act being performed, yet the prospect of producing such consequence did not constitute a link in the aforesaid chain' (J. Bentham, *The Principles of Morals and Legislation*, New York (1948), 84).

[60] See also Feller's line of argument: S. Z. Feller, 'The "Knowledge" Rule', *Israel Law Review*, vol. 5 (1970), 352, 359, 360.

justified to give equal weight to oblique intention and direct intention on the basis of considerations which are mainly moral, why is it important whether these intentions are the same or equal? Or, more generally, if our discussion and its results are valid and right, does it not show that the way to cope with such questions is *moral comparison*, and not an examination which seeks total equality (or sameness), as suggested by Moore?

3 Application of the substitute

There is support for the view that in Anglo-American law the scope of application of the substitute is limited to crimes of general intent and does not apply to crimes of specific intent, which are characterized by a striving to achieve an objective whose attainment is not necessary under the definition of the offence.[61] A different view is taken by Hart and Glanville Williams who support full application of the substitute.[62] Israeli law also applies the broad approach.[63]

In our view, if the considerations upon which recognition of a substitute is based are valid, then they are in principle valid in all cases in which intention is required, and the failure to apply the substitute requires special grounds. It could even be argued that the substitute is more justified in cases of specific intent, where intention as a rule constitutes an element whose absence makes the conduct permissible, than in cases of general intent, where in the absence of intent the crime as a rule is reduced to a lesser offence for which indifference or advertent negligence are sufficient. In the first case there is considerable distinction between conduct with awareness at its highest level and the alternative of permissible conduct, as against the lesser distinction between conduct with awareness at its highest level and conduct not at the highest level of awareness. The same should also apply to attempt, subject to a distinction between cases where the attempt requires a further act by the perpetrator himself in order to complete the offence and where it does not. The further act required of the perpetrator is

---

[61] Hart, *Punishment and Responsibility*, 125, 126; Williams, *The Mental Element in Crime*, 23, 24.

[62] Hart, *Punishment and Responsibility*, 127; Williams, *The Mental Element in Crime*, 24, 15.

[63] *Kahanovitz* v. *A.G.* (1949) 2 *P.D.* 890; *Ajami and others* v. *A.G.* (1959) 13 *P.D.* 421; *A.G.* v. *Grünwald* (1958) 32 Psakim 3; *A.B.* v *A.G* (1960) 14 *P.D.* 310; *Kurt Sita* v. *A.G.* (1961) 15 *P.D.* 1373; *A.B.* v *A.G.* (1962) 16 *P.D.* 2397. P.D. stands for *Piskei Din*, opinions of the Israeli Supreme Court and *Psakim*, the same.

entirely within his control and his decision. It can be maintained that the minimum required of the person making the attempt is a decision to do what depends on his own actions, in order to complete the crime. As long as this decision is inchoate in him, the perpetrator has not crossed the Rubicon even in terms of the *mens rea*. Therefore, in considering the relation of the perpetrator to his future conduct, his own assessment of the likelihood of his future actions should not be regarded as sufficient, even if it is very high. This distinction may be applied in other cases of specific intent.

III CONCLUSION

From the relatively limited question of the law's treatment of cases where the act was accompanied by a high degree of awareness Moore digresses into a discussion first of the theory of equality between types of intention and then of other cases such as transferred intention and felony-murder. Consequently, it is difficult to obtain a clear picture of the author's view on the question which forms the starting-point of his article. The lack of clarity is all the greater because in several places the impression is given that the author considers equal legal treatment justified in cases of direct intention and in cases of a high degree of awareness (in his terminology: 'oblique intention') because there is no significant moral difference between them. On the other hand, he states elsewhere that there is no reasonable moral theory that would permit equal treatment of different types of intention. Does this apply also to the author's own moral theory?[64] Does it mean that the case of 'oblique intention' should be treated differently from a case of direct intention? If the answer is affirmative (because there is no reasonable moral theory that would permit equal treatment of different types of intention), then two cases between which there is no significant moral difference would not be treated equally. If the answer is negative (they should be treated alike) then Moore himself admits a moral theory that permits equal treatment of different types of intention.

The author perhaps attributes too much importance to identity of intention, at times creating the impression that equitable legal treatment of two types of intention depends on that identity of intention. I maintain that Moore's theory is, at most, the first step in the examination and after

[64] And his analysis of 'transferred intent'.

this step must come the second and crucial step of moral evaluation of the different types of intention. The fact that two types of intention are equal or the same requires that they would be treated alike, but the fact that they are different does not necessarily entail a differentiated treatment. This is especially so because according to Moore 'Sameness of intention ... will involve one in determining each of these two questions: first, whether the same type of state of affairs is being referred to: and second, whether the sense or meaning of the expression used to refer to such types of states of affairs is the same'. This theory is very fine-grained and leads in every problematic case to a conclusion of 'non-sameness'. For instance, the crime of murder in Israeli law includes both killing to facilitate the commission of an offence and killing in order to secure escape or avoidance of punishment; robbery includes the use or threat to use actual violence 'in order to obtain or retain the thing stolen or to prevent or overcome resistance to its being stolen or retained': criminal trespass is committed when someone enters the property of another with intent 'to intimidate, insult *or* annoy' the possessor. According to Moore's theory, in all these examples, each of the offences covers different types of intentions, and should not therefore be treated alike. In our view, while each of the offences doubtlessly covers different types of intentions, the question of how to treat them is an open question, to be answered mainly on moral considerations. It might be argued, from this point of view, that they deserve the same treatment, although they are not the same. When Moore criticizes the felony-murder doctrine and says that 'An intentional rapist may be very culpable, but he is not as culpable as an intentional killer', he is right because there is a major difference in culpability between the two cases. At times, however, there is no significant difference in culpability between different types of intention. Is there a significant difference between the intention to kill one's mother and the intention to kill one's father or between an intention to insult a possessor or an intention to annoy a possessor?

It should also be remembered that the categories in criminal law are relatively broad, regularly including widely divergent acts or intentions, (for example, petty theft and theft of the Crown Jewels, theft from poverty and theft by the affluent, are all included in the definition of theft). Therefore, the guidelines for punishment are also relatively broad, allowing room for manœuvre to fit the perpetrator and his act. A striking example is the inclusion of intention, indifference, and advertent negligence in the single category of *mens rea* in Anglo-

American law. Let us assume that intending a consequence and fore-seeing it in a high degree of probability are *different* mental states. Ascription of liability should be a matter of the relative proximity or similarity, on moral grounds, of the mental states; and on the alterna-tives the law permits. If the law imposes liability for both intentional and reckless conduct, the classification should turn on relative moral similarity to either the one or the other. If the law imposes liability *only* for intentional conduct, classification of high probability foresight should turn on whether its similarity to intention justifies liability as against permissibility. The interesting point is that in dealing with Kenny and (inaccurately) with Hart,[65] Moore states: 'Here Hart's moral argument seems difficult to get around: both killers deliberately chose money over human life. That one needed the passengers to die in order to get the money, whereas the other only knew that they would die from the acts necessary to get the money, seems morally insignificant.'

It therefore appears that the 'problem does go away', and without the need in this connection for a theory of comparing types of intention. We take the view that Moore's theory on comparison of types of intention is 'too fine-grained'. The maximum that he is prepared to accept is a recognition of functional equality, when 'senses (meanings) of the words expressing them are believed to be the same by the *holder* of the mental states in question'. The result is that an intention to kill with a knife, by stages or with particular cruelty is not equivalent to intention to kill (since it can be assumed that in the eyes of the intender these two types of intention might be distinguished). Not to mention the difficulty of knowing or proving the holder's belief. Is an agreement between A who intends to kill C (his enemy), and B who intends to kill C (not his enemy) something less than a conspiracy? Can such a theory be of real use to the criminal law?

On the other hand, it is *possible* that in the area of moral comparison the author takes an approach which is 'too coarse-grained'. He adopts an argument used by Hart to justify *imposing* criminal liability on awareness (not necessarily of a high degree) in order to justify the attribution of *equal* criminality to awareness of the highest degree and intention. If it is a question of transferring the whole of Hart's argument

[65] Hart's argument was not restricted to the case of awareness at its highest level but referred to cases in which the mental element is foresight (even at a lesser, 'normal' level) of the possible consequence, while not wanting it to happen. On the other hand, Hart argued only for a justification of imposing criminal liability in such cases (121, 122), while Moore describes Hart's argument as an argument for equal treatment (treating these cases in the same way in which intention is treated).

from justification of the liability itself to the question of its degree, the result is moral equality between one who was aware of the possible consequence (even at a low level) with one who desired that consequence. This is far too sweeping a comparison. It is easy to illustrate this with the case of advertent negligence, where the perpetrator is aware of the danger of the possible consequence, but does not wish it to happen, and hopes or even believes that it will not happen or that he will be able to avoid it, like the circus marksman who shoots at an apple on his son's head and causes his death. Can it be said of him that he chose the fatal consequence in the same sense as one who intends to kill or is convinced that the fatal consequence will occur has a choice, or that from a moral point of view there is no difference between them? The difference between the two cases has led Continental law to treat the former as attracting criminal liability by way of exception, together with negligence, and to require an express provision rather than be derived from the general rule. The case of indifference is different from advertent negligence and closer to intention, but the agent's indifference to the *possibility* of its occurring, while there is also a possibility of its not occurring, does not necessarily prove that he would not be deterred from acting if the consequence were *certain*. Indifference to a harmful consequence is a state of mind worthy of severe condemnation, but, surely, actually to desire the harmful consequence is even worse.

Two final remarks. First, from the point of view of the normal meaning of intention, 'oblique intention' is not at all an intention. Therefore, what was needed from the start was not a theory of individuation of intentions according to their objects, but a theory of comparison between different mental states (intention and foresight of an object as a certainty or high probability while not wanting it to happen).

Secondly, intentions may differ not only according to their objects, but also according to the mode or process of their creation. We are referring to the difference between *dolus deliberatus* which is characterized by premeditation and *dolus repentinus* which is characterized by spontaneity. Here although there is sameness in objects, moral evaluation might lead us to differentiated treatment.

In our view, the main effort should be directed towards identifying criteria for the moral evaluation and comparison of different mental states, so that for these purposes we may be able to rely on more than our intuition.

7.1 A Theory of Complicity* [1]

SANFORD KADISH

My subject is the criminal law doctrine of complicity, the body of rules determining when one person becomes responsible for crimes committed by another. The question I ask is how the doctrine of complicity can best be interpreted as a coherent concept. This entails articulating the relationships between different parts of the doctrine, that are related to it, particularly causation; identifying the general propositions that afford logical and conceptual unity to the rules of liability; in short, developing the analytical framework that gives the doctrine of complicity its distinctive character.

My primary concern is with the interpretation of existing doctrine, not with judging it or proposing ways of improving it. Therefore I had better make two observations at the outset lest it be thought that I regard doctrine as some disembodied thing that exists wholly independently of social purposes or moral constraints.

Doctrine does tend to have some sort of life of its own. Considerations of consistency and coherence tend to attract certain conclusions and to repel others, quite apart from judgements of the social desirability of holding the defendant liable in particular cases. At the same time, no doctrine could long survive if it worked at cross-purposes with the social objectives of the system of law in which it functioned. It would soon be replaced, unless the system were static and unresponsive, with new doctrine, with new starting points. In the long run such independent life as criminal doctrine enjoys, by virtue of the claims that consistency and coherence make upon the law, is dependent on the doctrine serving the purposes of the criminal law.

There is a further and deeper relationship between doctrinal and normative considerations that should be emphasized at the outset, because it helps explain why doctrines of criminal liability are worth taking seriously despite the traditional American scepticism of doctrine.

* © Sanford H. Kadish 1987.
[1] Editor's note: This paper is an abridged version of the first part of a longer study, which appears in its entirety and in revised form in *California Law Review*, vol. 73 (1985), 329–410, under the title 'Complicity, Cause and Blame: A Study in the Interpretation of Doctrine.'

The decision to impose criminal liability is not governed solely by the social purposes of the practice of punishment. It is also governed by the moral justification of punishing persons for their conduct and for the results of their conduct. Indeed, criminal liability is best understood as responding primarily to considerations of the latter kind, the attainment of social purposes through punishment being confined, at least in most cases, to punishment for actions for which the defendant can be blamed. It follows that doctrines of criminal liability, being generalizations of the conditions in which punishment is proper, are primarily statements of moral import. Therefore, the kind of doctrinal interpretation attempted in this study necessarily entails an attempt to identify the nature of the pervasive intuitive judgements that make criminal liability morally acceptable in some circumstances, but not in others.

I   THE CONCEPT OF BLAME

An attempt to account for the doctrine of complicity must begin with the concept of blame, a concept that reaches so deeply into the jurisprudence of the criminal law that no account of the law can succeed without explicating its meaning and its role.

Blame represents a judgement of disapproval of an action in violation of some norm, but it is appropriate only where it can be said that the person to be blamed is responsible for that action. The concept of responsibility that underlies blame is elusive and controversial, but fundamental to it on any account is the notion of choice.

We perceive human actions as differing from natural events in the world. Things happen and events occur. They do not occur anarchically and haphazardly, but in sequences and associations that have an inevitable quality about them, which we express in terms of causation and understand in terms of laws of nature. Human actions stand on a different footing. While man is a mere subject under the laws of the natural world, he is total sovereign over his own actions. Except in special circumstances, he possesses volition through which he is free to choose his actions. He may be influenced in his choices, but influences do not work upon him like wind upon a straw, but rather as considerations on the basis of which he chooses to act. He may also be the object of influence in the larger sense that he is the product of all the forces that shaped him. But his actions are his and his alone, not those of his genes or his rearing, because if he wished he could have chosen to do otherwise.

The justification of this view of human action is the subject of the controversy over free will and determinism. I need not enter that controversy, for however it is resolved, it is enough for purposes of this study that the view of human actions I described is a central feature of the concept of blaming and that without that concept moral responsibility would lose its essential character. The questions we must address are what blame entails and how far it helps account for the doctrines of the criminal law.

Blaming, both in common usage and in the criminal law, has a variety of senses. One sense of blame has to do with whether the act is one that should be disapproved of. We can not be blamed for an action we should do. A different sense of blame has to do not with justification, but with excuse. Even if what the person did cannot be justified, he still may not be blameable if his action, for a variety of possible reasons, was not a product of that freedom to do otherwise that the notion of blame imports. The law responds to this sense of blame with a variety of defences, including absence of a voluntary act, duress, infancy, insanity, as well as a mistake or accident for which the person cannot be faulted.

A third sense of blame entails not just blaming for the action, but blaming for something that occurs as a consequence of the action, that is, fixing blame for a result. If I insult my guest who leaves in high anger and, distracted by the incident, walks into the path of an oncoming car, whether I may be blamed for his injury will not turn on whether I should be excused for the injury. It would not make sense to speak of being excused for something that happens; we may be excused only for what we do. The question here is whether the injury may be attributed to my action, whether it can fairly be regarded as belonging to the action I chose to do. In common usage, as well, therefore, as in the law, the question of whether we may be blamed for a consequence of our action turns on whether we may be said to have caused that result or to be blameable for it on some related ground.

A consequence of a person's action may be of two general kinds. It may consist of things happening. If I light a match in an area containing explosive vapours, which ignite and start a fire that spreads and burns down a building, I may be blamed for the burning of the building because I can be said to have caused it. I started a chain of events which led to the burning of the building through cause- and effect-relationships governed by laws of nature. The other kind of consequence consists of the actions of other persons. I may have persuaded another responsible person to light the match or I might have helped him by giving him a match for the purpose. Here the other person caused the burning of the house. But whether I am to be blamed for the other person's action would not normally be assessed by asking whe her I caused his action, but by asking whether my persuading or helping him made me accountable for wrongs he committed. The criminal law, responding to these common perceptions of the relationship between actions and consequences, has developed two separate doctrines for fixing blame. The doctrine of causation deals with fixing blame for natural events; the doctrine of complicity with fixing blame for the criminal action of another person. In comparing these doctrines I shall draw heavily on the classic treatment of legal causation by Hart and Honoré.[2]

Let us now consider further the reasons for the distinction between these two kinds of consequences, and how they give rise to two separate doctrines for determining responsibility for consequences. As I have just said, we regard a person's acts as the products of his choice, not of regularities of nature which require that certain happenings will occur whenever certain conditions are present. Therefore, antecedent events do not cause a person to act in the same way they cause things to happen, and neither do the antecedent acts of others. To treat the acts of others as causing a person's actions would be inconsistent with the premiss on which we hold a person responsible. (I may say parenthetically that one class of actions constitutes an exception to this proposition: actions that are not fully volitional are often treated as caused and made subject to causation doctrine. I have dealt with actions of this kind in an omitted part of this paper, as part of an examination of the fit between complicity and causation doctrine.)

I do not mean to say that the language of causation is inappropriate to describe the influence one person has on the actions of another, even when the latter's actions are entirely volitional. We commonly speak of one person occasioning the actions of another, or of one person's acts as the result or consequence of what another person says or does. This is appropriate because causation broadly conceived concerns the relationship between successive phenomena, whether they have the character of events or happenings or of another person's volitional actions. The point I mean to stress is that in dealing with the influence of one person upon the actions of another we refer to a different kind of causal concept than

---

[2] Hart and Honoré, *Causation in the Law*, Oxford (1959) (hereafter *Causation*).

that involved in physical causation. However philosophers may dispute the point, so far as the law is concerned the way in which a person's acts produce results in the natural world is significantly different from the way in which a person's acts produce results in the form of the volitional actions of others.

The view of a volitional human action as freely chosen has two important implications, both of which were pointed out by Hart and Honoré in *Causation in the Law*. The first is that when we examine a sequence of events that follows upon a person's action, the presence of a human action in the sequence precludes assigning causal responsibility to the first actor. What follows upon the second actor's action is something the second actor causes, and no one else can be said to have caused it through him.

The other (and related) implication is that when we seek to determine the responsibility of one person for the volitional actions of another the concept of physical cause is not available to determine the answer, for whatever the relation of one person's acts to those of another, it cannot be described in terms of that sense of cause and effect appropriate to the occurrence of natural events without doing violence to our concept of a human action as freely chosen.

These implications of the way we conceive of human actions give rise to the doctrine of complicity in the following way. Criminal prohibitions take two principal forms. Most threaten punishment for defined kinds of actions, sometimes only when some harm eventuates, but sometimes whether or not it does. Examples include appropriating another's property, receiving stolen goods, breaking and entering defined structures, obtaining property by false pretenses, having sexual relations with another against her will, killing a person in the course of operating a motor vehicle. The other form threatens punishment for causing some defined harm, with no further description of the action prohibited: causing the death of another (killing) is the most common example. To be guilty of the first kind of crime (action crimes, we may call them) the person charged must engage in the particular kind of activity prohibited. To be guilty of the second kind (result crimes), he must be found to have caused the result by any action that suffices to do so.

How, then, can the law reach those whose conduct makes it appropriate to punish them for the criminal actions of others—a person, for example, who persuades or helps another to commit a crime? Action crimes are not committed by such persons, since the person does not engage in the prohibited action. Some general doctrine is required through which such persons may be found liable. But what appropriate form should the doctrine take? If it were not for the very special way in which we conceive of human actions, causation doctrine might serve this purpose, on the view that one who intentionally causes another to commit certain actions falls under the prohibition against committing those actions. But our conception of human actions as controlled by choice will not allow that to work. Volitional actions cannot be said to be caused, since we do not regard a human action as subject to generalized laws of cause and effect which make it necessary that a person act in a certain way because of another person's action. Some alternative doctrine is needed, therefore, which imposes liability on the first actor who is to blame for the conduct of another, but which does so upon principles that comport with our perception of human actions. This is the office of the doctrine of complicity.

What, then, of result crimes? It follows from what was said about human actions that causation doctrine itself cannot make the first actor liable for the prohibited result where it is the volitional action of the second actor that causes the result. As Hart and Honoré put it, the latter's action serves as a barrier through which the causal enquiry cannot penetrate to hold the first actor liable.[3] If the first actor is to be held responsible for the crime it must be accomplished through an alternative doctrine that is consistent with our conception of human actions. The doctrine of complicity serves the same function for result crimes that it serves for action crimes.

II THE THEORY OF COMPLICITY

For these reasons, then, the doctrine of complicity, sometimes referred to as the law of aiding and abetting, or accessorial liability, emerges to serve the purpose of defining the circumstances in which one person (whom I will refer to as the secondary party or actor, accomplice or accessory) becomes liable for the criminal actions of another (the primary party or actor, or the principal). In exploring the theory of this doctrine I will consider in turn four issues: the nature of the liability imposed on the secondary party, the kinds of actions which create this liability, the intention with which those actions must be committed; and the relevance of the success of those actions in achieving their objective.

---

[3] Ibid., 338.

1 The nature of the liability.[4]

The basic premiss of complicity liability is that the secondary party, when he participates in the actions of the primary party in prescribed ways, which will hereafter be discussed, partakes of the liability of the primary party. Therefore without a principal who is criminally liable there can be no accomplice, for there is no criminal liability in which he can share. In a word, the liability of the secondary party is dependent or derivative. This stands in contrast to causation liability where the liability of the actor rests entirely on his own actions and is independent of the liability of anyone else.

It should be emphasized that the secondary party's liability derives from the imposition on him of the liability of the principal and not from attributing to him the actions of the principal. This follows from the concept of a volitional human action. Volitional actions are the choices of the primary party. Therefore they are his acts and his alone. One who 'aids and abets' him to do those acts, in the traditional language of the common law, can be liable for doing so, but not because he thereby caused the actions of the principal or because they are his acts in any sense. His liability rests on the liability of the principal, which, because of the secondary party's own actions, he is made to share.

A variety of outcomes in the law of complicity exhibit the derivative character of complicity liability. It is well accepted that a secondary party is liable as an accomplice for influencing or aiding a crime committed by another which the secondary party is not himself capable of committing. An unmarried man, for example, cannot himself commit bigamy, because that crime extends only to those who, being already married, marry again. But he can be convicted of bigamy as an accomplice by aiding or influencing a married person to commit the crime. Where a husband is incapable of raping his own wife, he may nonetheless be liable for her rape by another if he helps or encourages him to do the act. Liability in these cases is consistent only with the premiss that the liability of the secondary party is based on the liability of the primary party, in which he partakes, since he could not be held for violating the law himself.

---

[4] Editor's note: This part of the paper belongs to an earlier version, and it is published here so that Gur-Arye's comments will be intelligible. For the modified version, based among other things on these comments, see 'Complicity, Cause and Blame', especially pp. 337–42.

2   *The action*

Two kinds of actions of the secondary party render him liable for the criminal actions of the primary party: intentionally influencing the decision of the primary party to commit a crime, and intentionally helping the primary actor to commit the crime where the helping actions themselves constitute no part of the actions prohibited by the crime. These commonly overlap because knowledge that aid will be given encourages the principal's decision to go forward. None the less, analytically there remains the difference that in one case the secondary actor's liability is based on his contribution to the primary actor's decision to commit the crime; in the other, his liability is based on the assistance he gives the primary actor in executing the crime. In one case he may be thought of as acting upon the primary actor; in the other, of acting with him.

Holding a secondary party liable for influencing the principal's decision to act does not run afoul of the premiss that the latter's acts are determined by his own choice and not by antecedent circumstances or by the actions of others. To deny that a person's volitional actions are caused, in the sense that natural occurrences are caused, is not to deny that people are influenced in their decisions to act by what other people say and do, as they are influenced by all their experiences. As Hart and Honoré have pointed out,[5] the characteristic form of influencing another is the giving of reasons for an action, which differs from causal influence in that the influence operates not as a determining condition, but as a consideration that renders a particular course of action more desirable to the primary actor.

Liability for helping another commit a crime is likewise compatible with the prevailing concept of volitional action. To say that a person may be assisted in carrying out his intended actions is, of course, not to imply that his actions were caused, for the acts he does toward commission of the crime represent his own choices.

3   *The intention*

Whether the mode of involvement in the criminal act of another is influence or assistance, the law of complicity is generally taken to require that the secondary actor act intentionally; that is, he must act with the intention of influencing the primary actor to commit the

[5] Hart and Honoré, *Causation*, 39, 41, 69.

criminal acts with the *mens rea* required by the crime, or of assisting him to do so. So, for example, if a person spontaneously shouts approval to one committing an assault without really intending to encourage him he cannot be held as an accomplice in the assault no matter how influential the encouragement was in fact. This stands in contrast to causation doctrine, which permits a person to be held liable for a result even where he did not intend it.

The requirement of intention, however, does not preclude holding a person for complicity in a crime for which recklessness or negligence suffices for liability. When a person does an act which recklessly causes the death of a person, he is liable for manslaughter as a principal offender. That he did not intend the death is irrelevant. Likewise when another person intentionally helps or influence the principal to do that very action he shares the criminal liability of the principal. Thus, one who knows a boiler is defective but none the less encourages another to fire it is an accomplice to the other's crime of manslaughter if the boiler explodes and kills someone. The requirement of intention for complicity liability is satisfied by the intention of the secondary party to help or influence the primary party to commit the act that resulted in the harm. These cases, therefore, mark no exception to the principle that a secondary actor must act intentionally in influencing or assisting the primary party.

It is important to distinguish these cases from those in which the criminal liability of the principal arises not from the actions the secondary party intended him to do, but from further actions that the secondary did not intend. The latter may have been reckless as to those further actions, they may have been probable and foreseeable, but the fact that they result in death makes only the primary party guilty of manslaughter, and not the secondary party, because he did not intend them.

So, for example, a defendant who lends his car keys to an inebriated driver is an accomplice to the driver's crime of driving under the influence of alcohol. But he would not be liable for manslaughter as an accomplice of the drive where the driver's liability arises out of particular acts of reckless driving—for example, driving in the wrong direction on an expressway and colliding with an oncoming vehicle—that the defendant could not be said to have intended.

One finds in the law a number of instances where courts, and sometimes legislators, blur or even reject the intention requirement in favour of a probable consequences rule that permits holding a person liable as an accomplice where the fault of his action is that it leads another to commit a crime, even though it was not intended to do so. The explanation is to be found in the faulty fit between complicity and causation doctrines, so that without some bending in one or the other of these doctrines there could be no liability at all. I am obliged to omit a discussion of these issues in the interest of time. At all events, we may take the requirement of intention to be an integral part of the concept of complicity. Indeed, the fact that these exceptional cases give trouble to courts and commentators is precisely because this is so.

The theory of the intentionality requirement is not obvious. One possible explanation is that it would be undesirable to draw the circle of criminal liability any wider because of the pall that would be cast on our ordinary actions if we had to fear criminal liability for what others might do on the ground that our action made their acts more probable. But these considerations cannot be the explanation, since we are actually prepared to rest liability on the probable action of others whenever causation doctrine is applicable, as in the case where an irresponsible person takes advantage of the opportunity our actions provided to commit a criminal harm. The policy against restricting freedom of conduct solely because of fears of what another may do cannot explain why we require intention for complicity, but not for causation.

The explanation of the requirement of intentionality for complicity liability (and of the absence of that requirement for causation liability) must be found elsewhere. It may reside in the notion of agreement as the paradigm mode by which a principal (he would be the secondary party in the terminology of the criminal law) becomes liable for the acts of another person. This appears to be the rationale of the legal doctrine primarily concerned with the creation of liability for another's action, the civil law of agency. The liability of the principal in civil law rests essentially on his consent to be bound by the actions of his agent, whom he vests with authority for this purpose. To be sure, under the prevailing objective approach of the law of contracts, it is the principal's manifestation of consent, rather than his subjective state of mind, that determines the authority of the agent and the rights of third parties, but this is attributable to the policy of facilitating business transactions by protecting persons who reasonably rely on the appearances the principal creates. Thus, in so far as manifesting consent to be bound by the acts of another is a general requirement for holding one person liable for the actions of another, the requirement of intention for complicity liability becomes more readily explicable. Obviously, in the context of the criminal law literal consent to be criminally liable is irrelevant. But by intentionally acting to further the criminal actions of another, the secondary party is voluntarily placing himself in the same status as the principal party. The intention to further the acts of another that create liability under the criminal law is the equivalent to manifesting consent to accountability for them under the civil law.

This theory would also explain why intention is not required where the grounds of responsibility for some result is causation. In these cases the liability of the person does not derive from the criminal acts of another. Either there is no other person intervening between the actor's action and the result, or the other person's actions are not regarded as volitional actions at all, but, in view of the irresponsibility of the intervening actor, as events that the person causes. His liability does not at all depend on the actions of another, but on his own actions, as a primary party, and intention is therefore not necessary to establish criminal liability.

There remains the deeper question, assuming this account is correct, of why consent should be a general requirement for becoming liable for another's actions. The reason may again involve the characteristic way we view the actions of persons in contrast to the happening of events. Persons are autonomous agents, governed by their self-determined choices. We are responsible for ourselves and what our actions cause in the physical world, and we may cause things to happen unintentionally as well as intentionally. However, what other people choose to do as a consequence of what we have done is their action and not ours. Our actions do not cause what they do in the sense that our actions cause events. Only when we have voluntarily joined in the action of others by intentionally helping or inducing them to act do notions of autonomy permit making us responsible for their actions. I am not suggesting that this is a good and sufficient reason for not holding a person responsible for the voluntary acts of another which the actions of the first person may recklessly or negligently occasion, (although whether this is more suitably accomplished through a causation analysis is another question.) I am only proposing that the strong pull toward consent as the necessary condition of accomplice liability may be explained by the law's adherence to the premiss of the autonomy of human action.

4 The result

Like causation, the doctrine of complicity by its nature requires a result. It is not a doctrine of inchoate liability. The acts of the secondary party must have contributed in some way to the criminal action of the principal. If they have not, he is not liable for the principal's crime. This is because the doctrine of complicity, like that of causation, functions to fix blame upon a person for a result. Causation determines when a person is responsible for a subsequent event; complicity determines when he is responsible for the subsequent criminal action of another. The doctrines of causation and complicity are to this extent cognate.

This is not to suggest that it would be incongruous to apply the concept of attempt to complicity, converting it thereby into a doctrine of inchoate liability, as some jurisdictions have done. To do this is equivalent to expanding liability for a result-crime to reach those who attempt to cause the result. But the fact that a person may be liable for attempting to cause a result does not mean that he may be found liable for causing the result on a finding that he tried. The same is true of complicity and attempted complicity. It is a central feature of complicity doctrine, then, that liability cannot arise if the acts of the secondary actor were unsuccessful in influencing or assisting the principal to commit the crime. To this extent the secondary party's liability depends on his succeeding.

If these claims are to hold, however, it is necessary to account for some well-established propositions of complicity doctrine that at first blush seem to undercut the requirement of a successful contribution.

The common notion of success is captured in the ordinary expression of something having 'mattered', of it 'having made a difference'. In causation, the requirement of a condition *sine qua non* assures this sense of success, since the requirement means that without the act the result would not have happened as it did. In complicity, however, a *sine qua non* relationship in this sense need not be established. It s not required that the prosecution prove, as it must in causation cases, that the result would not have occurred without the action of the secondary party. The commonly accepted formulation is that to establish complicity, any influence or help suffices for liability.

These propositions are illustrated in two familiar cases. In *State* v. *Tally*[6] Tally's responsibility for the killing of the deceased by two others turned on his having sent a telegram to a telegraph operator instructing him not to deliver a warning telegram earlier sent to the victim by his relatives. The warning telegram was not delivered and the killers were

---

[6] 102 Ala. 25, 15 So. 722 (1894).

unaware of Tally's attempt to help them. The court found these facts sufficient to establish Tally's liability as an accomplice, stating:

The assistance given . . . need not contribute to the criminal result in the sense that but for it the result would not have ensued. It is quite sufficient if it facilitated a result that would have transpired without it. It is quite enough if the aid merely renders it easier for the principal actor to accomplish the end intended by him and the aider and abetter, though in all human probability the end would have been attained without it. If the aid in homicide can be shown to have put the deceased at a disadvantage, to have deprived him of a single chance of life, which but for it he would have had, he who furnished such aid is guilty though it can not be known or shown that the dead man, in the absence thereof, would have availed himself of that chance. As where one counsels murder he is guilty as an accessory before the fact, though it appears to be probable that murder would have been done without his counsel.

In *Wilcox* v. *Jeffery*[7] the publisher of a jazz magazine was held guilty of aiding and abetting an illegal public performance by an American saxophonist by buying a ticket and attending the concert in order to report on it in his magazine. The court upheld the conviction, stating: 'The appellant clearly knew it was an unlawful act for [the saxophonist] to play. He had gone there to hear him, and his presence and his payment to go there was an encouragement.'

The doctrine illustrated in these cases raises a question of what it means for the secondary actor's contribution to have made a difference. For in what sense can the contribution be said to have mattered if it was not a necessary condition of the primary party's decision to commit the crime or of his committing it as he did? Should we conclude, after all, that complicity does not require a successful contribution? I think not, for the following reasons.

In at least one class of cases the same requirement of a *sine qua non* that prevails in causation also prevails in complicity. There is no accomplice liability where it can be established that the attempted contribution failed to achieve its purpose because it never reached its target. So, for example, one who shouts encouragement to another to attack a third person where the other is deaf and otherwise unaware of his presence or encouragement could hardly be held liable for the assault as a secondary party. The same conclusion applies to the demonstrably futile attempt to aid another. The secondary party may be liable if the principal is aware of the proferred aid, since knowledge of

the efforts of another to give help may constitute sufficient encouragement to hold the secondary actor liable. But it is not doubted that the
secondary actor may not be held liable where his demonstrably ineffec-
tive effort to aid is unknown to the primary actor. So, for example, if a
person unlocks the door of a building in order to facilitate a burglar's
entrance, but the burglar, unaware of this effort to help him, breaks and
enters through a window, the secondary actor could not be held as an
accomplice to the burglary. He has not helped the burglar commit the
burglary, despite his best efforts to do so.

In these cases the absence of a *sine qua non* relation between the acts of
the primary and secondary actors precludes liability, just as the absence
of that relation between the act and a subsequent event precludes
liability in causation. We may not conclude, therefore, that successful
contribution is unnecessary for complicity. What is wanted is an
interpretation of the notion of success that accounts for this aspect of the
doctrine as well as that reflected in the *Tally* and *Wilcox* v. *Jeffrey* cases. I
propose the following. A successful contribution to the action of the
principal means that the influence or aid given by the secondary party
could have made some contribution to the criminal action of the
principal; in other words that without the influence it is possible that the
principal would not have acted as he did. Unlike causation cases the
prosecution need not prove a but-for relationship. But that does not
mean complicity liability can be imposed if the secondary party fails to
influence the principal—as we saw, when it is shown that he could not
have been successful there is no liability—only that it suffices that the
facts establish a possibility of success.

But we are still left with a puzzle. In causation, proof of a but-for
relationship is required; in complicity, a possibility suffices. How should
we account for this?

On one level, the answer to the puzzle follows from the fact that the
concept of a *sine qua non* condition belongs to the natural world of cause
and effect and has no place in accounting for human actions. Compare
physical causation and complicity. Physical causation deals with natural
events in the physical world. Experience teaches us that an event occurs
in consequence of some antecedent events, whether the conduct of a
person or of other natural events. Barring miracles, we can speak with
certainty. This permits of the concept of sufficient conditions, enabling
us to conclude that if those conditions are present a certain result has to
occur; and of the concept of necessary conditions, enabling us to
conclude that if some conditions are absent, the result cannot occur. In

cases of causation, therefore, once the facts are established we can determine with certainty whether a condition was a *sine qua non* of a subsequent event. We can say in every instance either that the event would not have happened if that condition were not present, or that it would have even if the condition were absent. Of course, the facts may be in dispute or be unascertainable, and so we may have to find them on the level of probability. But the future is latent in the past in the sense that if we knew all the facts we could determine with certainty what would happen.

Cases of influencing another to commit an act are different. We do not view relationships that include volitional human actions as governed by laws of nature. The result at issue in complicity is another volitional human action and, as we have seen, those are perceived as controlled ultimately by the actor's choice, not by natural forces. No matter how well or fully we learned the antecedent facts we could never say that it had to be the case that the other person would choose to act in a given way.

In a word, every volitional actor is a wild card; he need never act in a certain way. He responds as he chooses to influences and appeals, such as the influence of another. An influence may have been a necessary condition for his action, in the sense that without it he would not have acted. But this cannot be established with certainty the way we can establish the certainty of certain physical effects having to occur when specified prior events (but-for conditions) take place. Since the actor could have chosen to act without it, it is always possible that he might have. No laws of nature can settle the issue. *Sine qua non* in the physical causation sense, therefore, does not exist in accounting for human actions, because, on the view of human action we have been postulating, there are no necessary conditions for an act of will.

In dealing with the meaning of a successful contribution, I have thus far dwelt mainly on the situation where the secondary party's contribution takes the form of aid—lending a hand, supplying the tools or information, or driving the car. Where the principal is aware of the aid, as he is in most cases of complicity, the possibility of influence (through reliance and encouragement) is always present. Apart from this, in most cases where aid has been successfully given, it can be said that without the aid the crime would not have been committed as it was; in this sense the secondary party's aid is but-for condition of the crime. That is what successful aid means, in contrast to attempted aid. So, for example, if I provide the jemmy that the principal uses to gain illegal entry, my assistance was a but-for condition of the entry he made. To be sure, he might have entered anyway—with his own jemmy or by other means. But he did not. For what actually eventuated, my aid was a necessary condition, and demonstrably so.

The one case where this is otherwise is where the aid is unknown to the principal and takes the form of influencing a third person to do (or not to do) an action designed to aid the principal. The *Tally* case is an example. It could not be demonstrated that if *Tally* had not instructed the telegraph operator not to deliver the warning telegram the deceased's life would have been spared. The reason is that human actions intervened, and hence all one could demonstrate is that the aid might have made a difference. These cases of aid, therefore, are subject to the same analysis as all cases of influence.

There are several other aspects of the requirement of a result that I have time only to allude to:

1 It is commonly said that any aid or influence no matter how slight, suffices for complicity. This is best understood to mean that any possibility that the contribution was a *sine qua non* is enough, no matter how unlikely the possibility. The effect is to allow criminal liability to be imposed on those whose actions were virtually inconsequential. Nothing in the theory of complicity would preclude a requirement of a showing of substantial aid or influence.

2 Since aid or influence may be effectively contributed even to an unwitting principal, it is no part of complicity doctrine that the principal must be aware he is being influenced or aided.

3 Causation doctrine requires more than a *sine qua non* relationship to establish liability; the added requirement is expressed as the requirement of legal or proximate cause. The provenance of complicity as a cognate doctrine of causation is shown in its requirement of analogous elements in addition to the possibility of a *sine qua non* relationship.

I conclude with a challenge that could be made to the basic feature of my interpretation of the doctrine of complicity. There is a strong case to be made that in some situations it is both sound in policy and conformable to our intuitions of just blaming to hold a person liable for recklessly facilitating the wholly voluntary criminal action of another. Some courts have made that case and some legislation rests on it, the judgement being expressed either by a doctrine of reckless complicity or by one that accepts the principle that voluntary actions can be caused. This is an important challenge to the doctrinal interpretation I have offered, particularly when expressed in the latter way. But it is not necessarily a serious one for the following reasons.

First, there is strong resistance to the case for extending liability in these situations and much law is the other way. It is not the case, therefore, that it is clear that voluntary actions can be caused, but that there is an ambivalence on this issue in some situations. Secondly, that we are sometimes prepared to treat another's voluntary action as having been caused is not inconsistent with a general reluctance to do so, or with the view that that reluctance is reflected in the provenance and shape of complicity doctrine. Thirdly, the strong evidence in support of that premiss, to be found in its power to explain many features of complicity doctrine, is not seriously undermined by evidence that we sometimes find it acceptable to blame a person for unintentionally causing another's voluntary action. There is reason to expect that our social experience in blaming for results should be broadly responsive to several fundamental propositions. There is no reason to expect that anything so human and subjective should exist without some tension and even contradiction.

7.2 Comment

MIRIAM GUR-ARYE* [8]

The purpose of Kadish's paper is to show 'how the doctrine of complicity can best be interpreted as a coherent concept'. Regarding coherence as the main purpose leads Kadish to the conclusion that there are certain propositions which ought to characterize complicity whether or not the courts in common law jurisdiction so hold.

In his own words: 'Since my thesis is that the concept of complicity, if it is to be principled and logically consistent, in short, coherent, necessarily entails certain conclusions and forecloses others, I have felt free to conclude that certain propositions *'must' represent the law . . .'* (emphasis added).

In this comment I wish to show that the propositions considered by Kadish as the 'basic premiss of complicity' are not propositions that *'must* represent the law of complicity'. Before elaborating on my own arguments, let me remind you briefly of Kadish's main points, concerning the role of complicity and its basic premiss.

Kadish's whole study (not only the shortened version we have just heard) is based, in fact, on two main assumptions. First, one can be said to cause another's actions only where those actions are not fully volitional; while volitional actions, based on the choice of the actor to act, are not caused by another in the same sense. Therefore, to hold one person liable for the volitional actions of another, we need an additional doctrine to that of causation; namely, the doctrine of complicity.

Secondly, to hold the secondary party liable, under the doctrine of complicity, for the volitional actions of the principal 'His liability must rest on the liability of the principal, which, because of the secondary party's own actions, he is made to share'. The liability of the secondary party 'derives from the liability of the principal, and not . . . from the actions of the principal which may be attributed to him. Without a principal who is criminally liable there can be no accomplice, for there is

---

* © Miriam Gur-Arye 1987.

[8] Editor's note: Dr Gur-Ayre commented on an earlier and fuller version of Kadish's paper. Her contribution is reprinted here as originally delivered.

no criminal liability in which he can share'. Thus, the basic premiss of complicity, according to Kadish is that 'the secondary party *partakes* of the liability of the primary party'.

My argument which relates to both assumptions is the following.

First, we may need the doctrine of complicity, and not that of causation, even where the actions of the principal are not fully volitional; that is, even where the principal is not criminally liable. Secondly, to hold one person liable, under the doctrine of complicity, for the *volitional* actions of another who is criminally liable, does not require that 'his liability must rest on the liability of the other'.

To clarify the last point first I shall use the case of co-principals as an example. In his paper Kadish maintains, and rightly so, that where two parties commit an offence together, both are liable as primary parties, even where neither of them commits all the acts constituting the offence; as where in order to rob, one holds a victim at gunpoint while the other, unarmed, takes his wallet. In that case both are co-principals committing robbery. Their liability—as Kadish emphasizes in another context—is *direct*, rather than derivative. Yet, in a sense, each principal is held liable not only for his own acts but also for the acts of the other: both are liable for committing the *whole* offence although neither of them commits *all* the acts constituting it. What, then, is the basis to hold one principal liable for the acts of the other principal as well as for his own? The acts of each principal may not, to use Kadish's terms, 'be attributed to' the other principal, since he cannot be said 'to *cause* them'. Nor does the liability of each principal, which is direct rather than derivative, 'rest on the liability of' the other principal. An alternative, or at least an additional, basis is, therefore, needed to hold both principals liable for the whole offence.

The alternative basis which I wish to offer as the 'basic premiss' of complicity is that *all* parties, both the secondary (the accomplice) and the primary (the principal) are parties to the *commission* of the offence: each takes part in a different stage required for the commission of the offence, which in fact has been committed.

To clarify this, one should visualize the different stages towards the commission of an intentional offence committed by one person. The actor first *intends* to commit the offence, he may then do *preparatory* acts designed to help him in the commission, after that he *begins* to commit the offence and then *completes* its commission. In that case, the actor will not be held liable *separately* for his preparatory acts, even in the exceptional cases where those acts are punishable under a specific offence of preparation. Nor will he be held separately liable for an attempt to commit the offence. Rather, he will be liable for the complete offence, in the commission of which all the previous stages are merged. The legal situation is, and should be, the same where several persons are involved in the different stages required for the commission of the offence: the *instigator*, who intends that the offence be committed, persuades the principal to commit it; the *aider* does the preparatory acts designed to help the principal to commit the offence; and the *co-principals* begin to commit the offence together and complete its commission. Here too, all the stages toward the commission of the offence are being merged in the complete commission, and each party is liable for the complete offence, the commission of which stems from the collaboration between them. Yet, since only the principals take part in the stage of commission itself, their liability for the commission of the offence is direct. By contrast, the liability of the secondary parties— both the instigator and the aider—derives from the commission of the offence: they take part only in the stages previous to the commission.

Viewing the liability of the secondary parties as liability which derives from the commission of the offence, does not necessarily contradict Kadish's main thesis, that the liability of the secondary parties derives from the *liability* of the principal, in the sense that 'without a principal who is criminally liable there can be no accomplice'. Yet, this thesis is not a proposition that '*must* represent the law' of complicity, as Kadish takes it to be; rather, it depends on one's understanding of the concept of 'commission' in the context of complicity. Nor is it a proposition which represents the law of complicity in jurisdictions other than the common law. Under the German law for example, the liability of the secondary parties derives from the wrongful conduct of the principal, not from his liability. There is, therefore, complicity in a wrongful conduct, although the principal may be excused. The basis of that is not that the wrongful conduct of the principal is attributed to the secondary parties; the basis is rather, that the secondary parties take part in the stages required for the commission of the wrongful conduct. To describe the German law in this context goes beyond my limited purpose at this point. I may only mention that the concept of 'wrong-doing' in this connection is not identical with that of the '*actus reus*'; it includes, *inter alia*, all elements specified in the definition of the offence: both the *actus reus* and the mental element. However, the actor whose conduct fits the definition of the offence may be excused for his wrongful conduct, where it will be unjust and unfair to blame him for his intentional or negligent conduct.

Leaving German law aside, the point I would like to emphasize in this context concerns the other argument mentioned above; namely, that we may need the doctrine of complicity even where the actions of the principal are not wholly volitional. Kadish, in fact, assumes that whenever the principal is not criminally liable the 'secondary party' can be said to *cause* the principal's actions, and thus the proper ground of liability is causation and not complicity. There might, however, be cases where although the actions of the principal are not wholly volitional, the secondary party *cannot* be said to cause those actions; rather he can only be said to help the principal in committing them. In such cases, causation is not the proper ground for liability. Whether liability under the doctrine of complicity should be imposed (in such cases), is a question of policy rather than coherence.

To clarify this point take the following example: *B* coerced *A* to kill *V* by threatening *A*'s life. A passer-by—*C*, moved by *A*'s plight, gave him his gun. *A* killed *V* by using *C*'s gun. *A*'s conduct in killing *V* was not wholly volitional (he was coerced to do so by the threat to his life). In many legal systems *A* will be excused on the ground of duress. *B*, who coerced *A* to kill *V*, can indeed be said to cause *A*'s actions. Thus, *B* will be held liable for killing *V* through the actions of *A*, on the basis of causation. What about *C* who gave his gun to *A*? *C*, I believe, cannot really be said to cause *A*'s actions. He may only be said to provide *A* with the means in fact used in killing *V*. This is exactly the essence of aiding. Therefore, whether *C* will be held liable or not may depend on the doctrine of complicity and not on that of causation.

One may contend that, in helping *A*, *C* in fact helped *B* (the coercer) to kill *V* through the actions of *A*. But should the conclusion be different where the coercer himself is not criminally liable (he is insane for example); or where the danger to *A*'s life stems from a natural event rather than from a threat of a human-being (namely, necessity rather than duress)?

Under German law *C* might be held liable as an accomplice in the wrongful though excused conduct of *A*: by offering him his gun he helped *A* in the commission of the wrongdoing (the sacrifice of *V*'s life to save *A*'s). Under Kadish's thesis, which reflects the prevalent view in common law jurisdictions, *C* will not be held criminally liable, since there is no complicity where the principal is not criminally liable. Both conclusions are logically consistent with the doctrine of complicity as a coherent concept. Which conclusion is preferable depends mainly on questions of policy. On the one hand, it may be argued that personal excuses granted in cognizance of the actor's special situation ought to influence only his own liability and not that of his accomplices: only he should not be blamed for his wrongful conduct. On the other hand, it can be argued that the culpability of the accomplice is influenced by that of the principal: by helping the principal he is moved by his special situation. Therefore, both should not be blamed for either committing the wrongful conduct or helping in its commission.

Thus, in the case we are dealing with, one may argue that only *A*, whose life had been in danger, may be excused for the wrong he had done by sacrificing *V*'s life. In recognition of the instinct of self-preservation it would be unfair to demand that he avoid saving his own life even where the only way to do so entails the sacrifice of *V*'s life. By contrast, we may, and even should, require that a third party—*C* in our case—whose life is not in danger, should avoid taking a stand in a conflict between the lives of other people. If this argument is sound, than the conclusion reached by German law, that *C*, in our case, should be liable under the law of complicity for helping *A* to save his life, is sound as well.

On the other hand, it may be argued that we are not dealing with cases where one sits back and considers which life is preferable. We are talking about cases of 'necessity' where there is a grave and immediate danger to life. Precisely because life is at stake, people might, almost instinctively, step into the situation without thinking twice. In doing so they are primarily moved by the pressure to save life. This pressure should negate the culpability of both: the one who saved his own life by sacrificing another's and the one who helped him in doing so. If this argument is sound, than the conclusion would indeed be that *C* in our example should not be held liable under the law of complicity, as Kadish maintains.

However, the conclusion that the liability of the secondary parties derives from the liability of the principal, does not imply the further conclusion that—to use Kadish's terms—'the liability of the secondary party must rest on the liability of the principal that he is made to share'. This leads me to the last point I wish to put forward in this comment.

The proposition that the liability of the secondary party rests on the liability of the principal has led Kadish to conclude that the liability of the secondary party cannot be greater than that of the principal. According to Kadish, only where some features of the primary party's actions are not volitional in the full sense, can the liability of the secondary actor, which is based on causation rather than complicity, be greater.

This approach might, unfortunately, lead to undesirable implications. To illustrate this, let us consider the case of aggravating or mitigating circumstances. In various legal systems personal circumstances either aggravate or mitigate the offence. Thus, patricide (killing one's parents) is, in many legal systems, an aggravated form of murder, while infanticide (where a mother kills her new-born baby) is a mitigated form of murder. Similarly, stealing by clerk or servant is an aggravated form of theft.

At least where the aggravating circumstances obtain only in the secondary party, the propositions laid down by Kadish must lead him to the conclusion that those circumstances ought to be ignored. To show this let us assume that a son instigates another to kill the instigator's father, or a servant helps another to steal from the servant's employer. In both cases, Kadish will be bound to conclude that the secondary parties are liable only for the basic offence: simple murder rather than patricide in the first case, and simple theft rather than stealing by servant in the other case. The reason will be that, since the principal is only liable for the basic offence of either murder or theft, under the doctrine of complicity the liability of the secondary parties cannot exceed that of the principal. On the other hand, liability on the basis of causation is improper, since neither the son nor the servant can be said to have caused the principal's actions which were fully volitional (at least where the principal knew that he was killing the instigator's father, or that he was stealing from the servant's employer).

Yet, the reasons for the aggravation of the offence clearly exist where the aggravating circumstances obtain in the secondary parties as well as in the principal. To ignore them only because the son, in the first case, did not himself kill his father but instigated another to do so, or because the servant in the other case just helped another to steal from his employer, would frustrate the purpose which justifies the aggravation of the offence.

If this conclusion follows logically from the 'basic premiss' of complicity, one should question the premiss itself: is it indeed a premiss that the doctrine of complicity *must* be based on? I believe that it is not. This brings me back to the previous points in my argument.

1   The basis of complicity is *not* that 'the secondary party partakes of the liability of the primary party'; the basis is rather that all parties—both

the secondary and the primary—are parties to the *commission* of the offence.

2 The liability of the secondary party does not 'rest on the liability of the principal'; rather, all parties, including the principal, are liable for taking part in the different stages required for the commission of the offence, which in fact has been committed.

3 The liability of the secondary parties is indeed derivative, since they only take part in the stages previous to the stage of commission. Whether their liability should derive from the liability of the principal or from the wrongfulness of his conduct, depends on whether the culpability of the principal influences the nature of the commission.

4 Even where one is to conclude that the liability of the secondary parties derives from the liability of the principal, this conclusion only requires that the offence be committed by a principal who is criminally liable. The liability of either party is, however, independent: it rests only on his contribution to the commission of the offence, rather than on the other party's (the principal's) liability.

The implications of these propositions on the issue of aggravating or mitigating circumstances would be as follows. Aggravating or mitigating circumstances do not constitute an independent offence; they merely influence the severity of the penalty by constituting the aggravated or mitigated form of the basic offence. Where the basic offence has been committed, each party will be held liable for taking part in one of the stages required for its commission. However, where the *liability* for the commission is either aggravated or mitigated by personal circumstances, the liability of the secondary party for whom such a circumstance obtains, should be either aggravated or mitigated as well. Thus, the liability of a son, who has contributed to the commission of murder by instigating to kill his (the instigator's) father, should be aggravated: he should be held liable for patricide which is no more than an aggravated form of murder.

PART III
ENFORCEMENT OF MORALS

8.1 Autonomy, Toleration, and the Harm Principle*

JOSEPH RAZ

This is an article about the relation between two ideas, autonomy and toleration. Both are deeply rooted in liberal culture, and I shall rely on this fact. I shall say very little to explain the liberal concepts of personal autonomy and of toleration, just enough to make the points on which the argument of this article depends. I shall say even less on the reasons for valuing personal autonomy. My purpose is to show that a powerful argument in favour of toleration is derivable from the value of personal autonomy. This is not a surprising conclusion. I hope some interest lies in the details of the argument; but the main interest is in what it does *not* establish, in the limits of the autonomy-based principle of toleration.

There are, of course, other powerful arguments for toleration. Their conclusions overlap those of the argument from autonomy, being narrower in some areas and wider in others. This is exactly what one would expect. It shows the strength of the commitment in our culture to toleration that it is supported by different arguments from different points of view. Nor need a single individual be too parsimonious in the arguments on which his faith in toleration rests. Many of them can be subsumed under one moral umbrella. There is, however, a special interest in closely examining the argument from autonomy. It is sometimes thought to be the specifically liberal argument for toleration: the one argument which is not shared by non-liberals, and which displays the spirit of the liberal approach to politics. This article contributes to an exploration of this view. It does so in two ways.

First, it is sometimes assumed that respect for autonomy requires governments to avoid pursuing any conception of the good life. In other words the ideal of autonomy is used to support a principle of toleration reflecting anti-perfectionism, the exclusion of ideals from politics. I shall argue that no such conclusion follows from a concern for personal autonomy. Therefore, if liberalism, or any liberal tradition is wedded to anti-perfectionism then it must find some other roots.

* © Joseph Raz 1987.

Another well-known liberal argument for toleration is based on the harm principle. This principle, first formulated by J. S. Mill, has found a powerful champion in H. L. A. Hart. The principle asserts that the only purpose for which the law may use its coercive power is to prevent harm. In the last section of this paper I shall argue that the autonomy-based principle of toleration is best regarded as providing the moral foundation for the harm principle. It explains why liberals are sometimes willing to employ coercion to prevent harm, as well as why they refuse to use coercion for other purposes. Thus viewed the principle helps assess the relative seriousness of various harms, as well as to answer potentially damaging criticisms of the harm principle which claim that it reflects the ideology of the night watchman state.

I AUTONOMY AND PLURALISM

The ruling idea behind the ideal of personal autonomy is that people should make their own lives. The autonomous person is a (part) author of his own life. The ideal of personal autonomy is the vision of people controlling, to some degree, their own destiny, fashioning it through successive decisions throughout their lives. Once stated in this way the problems involved in working out a plausible conception of autonomy become only too evident. No one can control all aspects of his life. How much control is required for the life to be autonomous, and what counts as an adequate exercise of control (as opposed to being forced by circumstances, or deceived by one's own ignorance, or governed by one's weaknesses) is an enormously difficult problem. Fortunately for us, although its solution is required in order to formulate policies to implement the autonomy-based principle of toleration, it is not required in order to appreciate the structure of the argument for toleration, which is our sole concern. All that has to be accepted is that to be autonomous a person must not only be given a choice but that he must be given an adequate range of choices. A person whose every decision is extracted from him by coercion is not an autonomous person. Nor is a person autonomous if he is paralysed and therefore cannot take advantage of the options which are offered to him. We will need to examine some of the criteria of adequacy for available options. But, for the purposes of the present argument, we do not require a general doctrine of the adequacy of options.

One other aspect of the problem of adequacy of options has to be noted here in order to avoid a common misunderstanding. People usually control their lives not by deciding once and for all what to do for the rest of their lives. Rather they take successive decisions, with the later ones sometimes reversing earlier decisions, sometimes further implementing them, and often dealing with matters unaffected by the earlier decisions. The question arises, to what extent does autonomy require the continuous possibility of choice throughout one's life. Given that every decision, at least once implemented, closes options previously open to one (it may also open up new options) the question of whether, and when, one's own decisions may limit one's autonomy raises tricky issues.

Autonomy is often confused with self-realization. But the two are distinct moral ideals. Self-realization consists in the development to their full extent of all the valuable capacities a person possesses. The autonomous person is the one who makes his own life and he may choose the path of self-realization or reject it. Nor is autonomy a precondition of self-realization for one can stumble into a life of self-realization or be manipulated into it or reach it in some other way which is inconsistent with autonomy. One cannot deny this last claim on the ground that one of the capacities one has to develop is that of choosing one's own life. For this and any other capacity can be developed by simulation and deceit, that is, by misleading the person to believe that he controls his destiny. In any case autonomy is at best one of many elements which contribute to self-realization and it does not enjoy any special importance compared with many of the others.

It follows that the autonomous person must have options which will enable him to develop all his abilities, as well as to concentrate on some of them. One is not autonomous if one cannot choose a life of self-realization, nor is one autonomous if one cannot reject this ideal. Here lies one clue to a proper understanding of what counts as 'an adequate range of options' necessary to make a person autonomous. Our concern is not to develop this idea but to bring out the point which it illustrates, that is, that a commitment to autonomy entails commitment to moral pluralism.

Let us approach this problem in two stages. Given that it requires an opportunity to concentrate on some and neglect others of one's capacities, it requires that incompatible forms and styles of life be available. Developing this idea will be the subject of the second line of argument. But first let it be noted that autonomy requires that many morally acceptable, though incompatible, forms of life be available to a person. This is an additional aspect of the test of adequacy of the available options. It is of great importance to the connection between autonomy and toleration.

I shall use a rather artificial and extreme example to bring out the point. Imagine a person who can pursue an occupation of his choice but at the price of committing murder for each option he rejects. First he has to choose whether to become an electrician. He can refuse provided he kills one person. Then he is offered a career in dentistry, which again he is free to refuse if he kills another person, and so on. Like the person facing the proverbial gunman demanding 'your money or your life', who is acting freely if he defies the threat and risks his life, the person in our dilemma is acting freely if he agrees to murder in order to become a dentist, rather than an electrician. If he does so then his choice does not tend to show that his life is not autonomous. But if he chooses the right way and agrees to be an electrician in order to avoid becoming a murderer then his choice is forced.

I think it will be generally agreed that in this case the life of the person in my example is not autonomous and that his choice and the nature of his options are enough to show that he is not. That is, our judgement that he is not autonomous is unaffected even if the example is developed to show that his predicament is a result of a series of bizarre accidents and coincidences resulting from the breakdown and freak behaviour of several computers in some futuristic society. Autonomy requires a choice of goods. A choice between good and evil is not enough. (Remember that it is personal, not moral, autonomy we are concerned with. No doubt is cast on the fact that the person in the example is a moral agent and fully responsible for his actions. So are the inmates of concentration camps. But they do not have personal autonomy.)

Autonomy cannot be achieved by a person whose every action and thought must be bent to the task of survival, a person who will die if ever he puts a foot wrong. Similarly, it cannot be obtained by a person who is constantly fighting for moral survival. If he is to be moral then he has no choice, just as the person struggling for physical survival has no choice if he is to stay alive.

Given this conclusion, how is autonomy related to moral, or value pluralism? Moral pluralism is the view that there are various forms and styles of life which exemplify different virtues and which are incompatible. Forms or styles of life are incompatible if, given reasonable assumptions about human nature, they cannot normally be exemplified in the same life. There is nothing to stop a person from being both an ideal teacher and an ideal family person. But a person cannot normally lead both the life of action and of contemplation, to use one of the traditionally recognized contrasts, nor can one person possess all the virtues of a nun and of a mother.

To establish moral or value pluralism, however, the existence of a plurality of incompatible but morally acceptable forms of life is not enough. Moral pluralism claims not merely that incompatible forms of life are morally acceptable but that they display distinct virtues, each capable of being pursued for its own sake. If the active and contemplative lives are not merely incompatible but also display distinctive virtues then complete moral perfection is unattainable. Whichever form of life one is pursuing there are virtues which elude one because they are available only to people pursuing alternative and incompatible forms of life.

Such descriptions of moral pluralism are often viewed with suspicion, at least in part because of the elusiveness of the notion of a form of life. How much must one life differ from another in order to be an instance of a different form of life? The question seems unanswerable because we lack a suitable test of relevance. Indeed there is no test of relevance which would be suitable for all the purposes for which the expression 'a form of life' was or may be used. But this does not matter as the test of relevance we require is plain. For the purpose of understanding moral or value pluralism forms of life differ in their moral features.

Two lives must differ in the virtues they display, or in the degree that they display them, if they are to count as belonging to different forms of life. A form of life is maximal if, under normal circumstances, a person whose life is of that kind cannot improve it by acquiring additional virtues, nor by enhancing the degree to which he possesses any virtue, without sacrificing another virtue he possesses or the degree to which it is present in his life. Belief in value pluralism is the belief that there are several maximal forms of life.

Moral pluralism thus defined is weak moral pluralism. It can be strengthened by the addition of one or more of the following three claims (and there are further ways of refining and subdividing them). First, the incompatible virtues are not completely ranked relative to each individual. That is, it is not the case that for each person all the incompatible virtues can be strictly ordered according to their moral worth, so that he ought to pursue the one which for him has the highest worth, and his failure to do so tars him with a moral blemish, regardless of his success in pursuing other, incompatible, moral virtues.

Second, the incompatible virtues are not completely ranked by some impersonal criteria of moral worth. Even if the first condition obtains it is still possible to claim that, although there is no moral blemish on me if I am a soldier and excel in courage because I am made of bronze, excellence in dialectics, which is incompatible with courage and is open only to those made of gold, is a superior excellence by some moral standards which are not relative to the character or conditions of life of individuals. The second thesis denies that such impersonal strict ordering of incompatible virtues is possible.

Thirdly, the incompatible virtues exemplify diverse fundamental concerns. They do not derive from a common source, or from common ultimate principles. Some forms of two-level and indirect utilitarianism are morally pluralistic in the weak sense, and may also accept the first two strong forms of moral pluralism. But they are incompatible with the third.

There is yet another sense in which the value pluralism explained above is weak. 'Moral' is here employed in a wide sense in which it encompasses the complete art of the good life, as Mill might have said. It is in fact used in a sense which encompasses all values. The point of keeping the expression 'moral value', rather than talking simply of values, is to avoid two possible misunderstandings. First, 'value' is sometimes used in a relativized sense, to indicate not what is of value but what is held to be so by some person, group, or culture. Secondly, some people hold that some kinds of values, for example aesthetic ones, provide no reasons for action: that they are relevant merely to appreciation. In this article 'value' is non-relativized and is understood to constitute or imply the existence of reasons for action.

Whatever the truth in any of the strong varieties of moral pluralism, valuing autonomy is compatible with their rejection. It does commit one, however, to weak moral pluralism (and henceforth by 'moral pluralism' I will refer to the weak variety). Autonomy is exercised through choice, and choice requires a variety of options to choose from. To satisfy the conditions of the adequacy of the range of options the options available must differ in respects which may rationally affect choice. If all the choices in a life are like the choice between two identical-looking cherries from a fruit bowl, then that life is not autonomous. Choices are guided by reasons and to present the chooser with an adequate variety there must be a difference between the reasons for the different options.

Furthermore, as was argued above, the options must include a variety of morally acceptable options. So the morally acceptable options must themselves vary in the reasons which speak in favour of each of them.

Plainly the reasons for an option may, but need not, pertain to the object to be realized through its pursuit. They can, for example, pertain to the manner of its pursuit: is it pursued vigorously, carefully, or determinedly; is its object sought through a high risk policy, in a carefully planned way, spontaneously, and so on. There often are reasons to prefer an option because of the manner in which it pursues its object. It seems plausible to assume that autonomy requires a variety in the choices which reflects both kinds of considerations, a variety regarding both what to do and how to do it. Be that as it may, my only assumption is that reliable ability to act for reasons of a particular kind requires a certain disposition. This is true both where the reasons concern the object (for example, generosity) and where they affect the manner of its pursuit (for example, spontaneity). Finally, I am assuming that such dispositions, being dispositions to pursue valuable options, are virtuous, that they constitute so many virtues.

The upshot of the above is that autonomy presupposes a variety of conflicting considerations. It presupposes choices involving trade-offs, requiring relinquishing one good for the sake of another. Since excellence in the pursuit of goods involves possession of the appropriate virtues, the existence of these conflicts speaks of the existence of incompatible virtues, that is of moral pluralism. A person may have an autonomous life without attaining any virtue to any high degree. However, he inhabits a world where the pursuit of many virtues was open to him, but where he would not have been able to achieve them all, at least not to their highest degree. To put it more precisely, if autonomy is an ideal then we are committed to such a view of morality: valuing autonomy leads to the endorsement of moral pluralism.

II PLURALISM AND TOLERATION

It is sometimes supposed that moral pluralism by itself establishes the value of toleration. However, refraining from persecuting or harassing people who possess moral virtues which we lack is not in itself toleration. I do not tolerate people whom I admire and respect because they are generous, kind, or courageous, whereas I am not. Toleration implies the suppression or containment of an inclination or desire to persecute, harass, harm, or react in an unwelcome way to a person. But even this does not yet capture the essence of toleration. I do not tolerate the courageous, the generous, and the kind even if I am inclined to persecute them and restrain myself because I realize that my desires are entirely evil.

Toleration is a distinctive moral virtue only if it curbs desires, inclinations, and convictions which are thought by the tolerant person to be in themselves desirable. Typically a person is tolerant if and only if he suppresses a desire to cause to another a harm or hurt which he thinks the other deserves. The clearest case of toleration, whether justified or not, is where a person restrains his indignation at the sight of injustice or some other moral evil, or rather at the sight of behaviour which he takes to be of this character. Whether a person is tolerant or not depends on his reasons for action. Himmler did not tolerate Hitler when he did not kill him. But an anti-Nazi may have spared his life out of a misconceived sense of duty to let people carry on even when they are in the wrong.

I emphasized the tolerant person's view that in being tolerant he is restraining an inclination which is in itself desirable. The typical cases referred to are cases in which the intolerant inclination is in itself desirable because it is a reaction to wrongful behaviour. Is it then part of our notion of toleration that only the wrongful or bad can be tolerated? Many writers on the subject assume so. But this view is unwarranted. To be sure one cannot tolerate other people because of their virtues. But one can tolerate their limitations. A person can tolerate another's very deliberate manner of speech, or his slow and methodical way of considering every issue, and so on. In all such cases what is tolerated is neither wrong nor necessarily bad. It is the absence of a certain accomplishment. This is not an attempt at hair-splitting. The reason people lack certain virtues or accomplishments may be, and often is that they possess other and incompatible virtues and accomplishments. When we tolerate the limitations of others we may be aware that these are but the other side of their virtues and personal strengths. This may indeed be the reason why we tolerate them.

Toleration, then, is the curbing of an activity likely to be unwelcome to its recipient or of an inclination so to act which is in itself morally valuable and which is based on a dislike or an antagonism of that person or of a feature of his life, reflecting a judgement that these represent limitations or deficiencies in him, in order to let that person have his way or in order for him to gain or keep some advantage. (As was pointed out to me by P. M. S Hacker, mercy is sometimes a special case of toleration. One can tolerate out of mercy.)

This characterization of toleration deviates from the view which is most common in writings on political theory in two respects. My explanation relies on four features. First, only behaviour which is either unwelcome to the person towards whom it is addressed or behaviour which is normally seen as unwelcome is intolerant behaviour. Secondly, one is tolerant only if one inclines or is tempted not to be. Thirdly, that inclination is based on dislike or antagonism to the behaviour, character, or some feature of the existence of its object. Finally, the intolerant inclination is in itself worthwhile or desirable.

Political theorists tend to concentrate on one hostile reaction as the only possible manifestation of intolerance: the use of coercion. They are resistant to the thought that an expression of a hostile view, for example, may be intolerant behaviour. Secondly, as was observed above, it is often thought that only if a person judges another or his behaviour to be wrong or evil can he be tolerant of that person or of his behaviour.

I shall say little about the first point. If there is a concept of intolerance according to which only coercive interventions are intolerant then this is not the ordinary notion of intolerance but one developed by political theorists to express a particular point of view. I know of no reason for sharing that point of view. The ideas of toleration and of intolerance identify modes of behaviour by their grounds and object. They do not identify them by the means employed. Saying this is not saying that all the manifestations of intolerance are either equally acceptable or equally unacceptable. It is merely to point out that here are concepts that identify actions by their motives and not by the means those motives lead to.

I have already explained the reasons for rejecting the view that only the bad or the wrong can be tolerated. The fact that intolerance can be directed at people's limitations and that those can be aspects of some other virtues which those people possess acquires special significance for those who believe in moral pluralism. It provides the link between pluralism and toleration.

At the end of this article I shall argue that, within bounds, respect for personal autonomy requires tolerating bad or evil actions. But toleration can also be of the good and valuable when it curbs inclinations which though valuable in themselves are intolerant of other people's morally acceptable tastes and pursuits. While pluralism as such need not give rise to occasions where toleration is called for, some very common kinds of pluralistic moralities do. Let us call them competitive pluralistic moralities (there are competitive moralities which are not pluralistic but they do not concern us).

Competitive pluralism not only admits the validity of distinct and incompatible moral virtues, but also of virtues which tend, given human nature, to encourage intolerance of other virtues. That is, competitive pluralism admits the value of virtues possession of which normally leads to a tendency not to suffer certain limitations in other people which are themselves inevitable if those people possess certain other, equally valid, virtues. The very traits of character which make for excellence in chairing committees and getting things done, when this involves reconciling points of view and overcoming personal differences, those very traits of character also tend to make people intolerant of single-minded dedication to a cause. And there are many other examples, the prevalance of which suggests that most common forms of pluralism are of the competitive kind.

It is possible that all viable forms of pluralism are competitive. Failing that it is likely that the variety of valuable options which is required by the ideal of autonomy can only be satisfied by competitive moral pluralism. This view is plausible given the range of abilities many people have. We assume that moral life will be possible only within human communities, and that means that the range of capacities development of which is to be made possible in order for all members of the community to be autonomous is greater than the range necessary to assure an individual of autonomy. That is a consequence of the fact that both the genetic differences between people and the social needs for variety and for a division of labour lead to a diversity of abilities among people. The moral virtues associated with the diverse forms of life allowed by a morality which enables all normal persons to attain autonomy by moral means are very likely to depend on character traits many of which lead to intolerance of other acceptable forms of life. All those forms of life are not only morally legitimate but also ones which need to be available if all persons are to have autonomy. Therefore respect for autonomy by requiring competitive moral pluralism also establishes the necessity for toleration.

Even if one rejects my supposition that given human nature autonomy can only be realized within a community which endorses a competitive pluralistic morality, even if one thinks that that supposition is based on a misguided view of human nature, that it is perhaps too pessimistic, even if one believes that autonomy and pluralism are possible without conflict, the above conclusion is not undermined. Even on these optimistic assumptions it is still the case that competitive pluralism contributes, where it exists, to the realization of autonomy. Therefore, competitive pluralism provides an argument for a principle of toleration. The only modification is that on the more optimistic assumptions there may be circumstances in which there will be no need to rely on the principle, circumstances in which the conflicts which activate it do not arise. This does not invalidate the principle of toleration. And, of course, in our world it is not merely idly valid; the circumstances for its invocation are very much with us.

III THE SCOPE AND LIMITS OF AUTONOMY-BASED TOLERATION

The previous section argued that competitive moral pluralism of the kind which is required by respect for autonomy generates conflicts between people pursuing valuable but incompatible forms of life. Given the necessity to make those forms of life available in order to secure autonomy there is a need to curb people's actions and their attitudes in those conflicts by principles of toleration. The duty of toleration is an aspect of the duty of respect for autonomy. To judge its scope and its limits we need to look at the extent of our autonomy-based duties generally.

Since autonomy is morally valuable there is reason for everyone to make himself and everyone else autonomous. But it is the special character of autonomy that one cannot make another person autonomous. One can bring the horse to the water but one cannot make him drink. One is autonomous if one determines the course of one's life by oneself. This is not to say that others cannot help, but their help is by and large confined to securing the background conditions which enable a person to be autonomous. This is why moral philosophers who regard morality as essentially other-regarding tend to concentrate on autonomy as a capacity for an autonomous life. Our duties towards our fellows are for the most part to secure for them autonomy in its capacity sense. Where some of these writers are wrong is in overlooking the reason for the value of autonomy as a capacity, which is in the use its possessor can make of it, that is, in the autonomous life it enables him to have.

There is more one can do to help another person have an autonomous life than stand-off and refrain from coercing or manipulating him. There are two other categories of autonomy-based duties towards another person. One is helping in creating the inner capacities required for the conduct of an autonomous life. Some of these concern cognitive capacities, such as the power to absorb, remember and use information, reasoning abilities, and the like. Others concern one's emotional and imaginative make-up. Still others concern health, and physical abilities and skills. Finally, there are character traits essential or helpful for a life of autonomy. They include stability, loyalty, and the ability to form personal attachments and to maintain intimate relationships. The third type of autonomy-based duties towards another concern the creation of an adequate range of options for him to choose from.

As anticipated all these duties, although based on the value of the autonomous life, are aimed at securing autonomy as a capacity. Apart from cultivating a general awareness of the value of autonomy there is little more one can do. It is not surprising, however, that the principle of autonomy, as I shall call the principle requiring people to secure the conditions of autonomy to all people, yields duties which go far beyond the negative duties of non-interference, which are the only ones recognized by some defenders of autonomy. If the duties of non-interference are autonomy-based then the principle of autonomy provides reasons for holding that there are other autonomy-based duties as well. Every reason of autonomy which leads to the duties of non-interference would lead to other duties as well, unless, of course, it is counteracted by conflicting reasons. Such countervailing reasons are likely to be sometimes present, but they are most unlikely to confine the duties of autonomy to non-interference only.

So far I have emphasized the far-reaching political implications of the ideal of autonomy. But autonomy-based principles of toleration have clear limits to which we must turn.

First, while autonomy requires the availability of an adequate range of options it does not require the presence of any particular option among them. A person or a government can take action eventually to eliminate soccer and substitute for it American football, for example. The degree to which one would wish to tolerate such action will be affected by pragmatic considerations which can normally be expected to favour erring on the side of caution where governmental action or action by big organizations is concerned. But it has to be remembered that social, economic, and technological processes are constantly changing the opportunities available in our society. Occupations and careers are being created while others disappear all the time. The acceptable shapes of personal relationships are equally in constant flux, and so is the public culture which colours much of what we can and cannot do. Not everyone would agree that such processes are unobjectionable so long as the government does not take a hand in shaping them. The requirements of autonomy as well as other considerations may well call for governmental intervention in directing or initiating such processes.

It is important in this context to distinguish between the effect of the elimination of an option on those already committed to it, and its effect on others. The longer and the more deeply one is committed to one's projects the less able is one to abandon them (before completion) and pick up some others as substitutes. But even if such a change is possible, denying a person the possibility of carrying on with his projects, commitments, and relationships is preventing him from having the life he chose. A person who may but has not yet chosen the eliminated option is much less seriously affected. Since all he is entitled to is an adequate range of options the elimininated option can, from his point of view, be replaced by another without loss of autonomy. This accounts for the importance of changes being gradual so that they will not affect committed persons.

The second main limitation of autonomy-based toleration has already been mentioned. It does not extend to the morally bad and repugnant. This point raises an issue of great importance to the understanding of the relation between autonomy and other moral values. No one would deny that autonomy should be used for the good. The question is has autonomy any value *qua* autonomy when it is abused? Is the autonomous wrongdoer a morally better person than the non-autonomous wrong-doer? Our intuitions rebel against such a view. It is surely the other way round. The wrongdoing casts a darker shadow on its perpetrator if it is autonomously done by him. A murderer who was led to his deed by the foreseen inner logic of his autonomously chosen career is morally worse than one who murders because he momentarily succumbs to the prospect of an easy gain. Nor are these considerations confined to gross breaches of duties. Demeaning, or narrow-minded, or ungenerous, or insensitive behaviour is worse when autonomously chosen and indulged in.

A second question presents itself now. Could it be that it is valuable to make evil and repugnant options available so that people should freely avoid them? Is the person who rejected a life of mindless idleness, for example, better than one who never had the chance of choosing it? Three reasons are often produced in support of this view. First, people must be tested and prove themselves by choosing good rather than evil. Second, the need to choose refines one's moral judgement and dis-crimination. Third, the presence of evil provides the occasion for developing certain moral virtues. Whatever sound sense there is in all three considerations derives from the thought that the morally good not only manages his life morally, but would have done so even if circumstances were less favourable or presented more temptations or pressures for evil.

Opportunities for the immoral and the repugnant cannot be eliminated from our world. It may be possible to develop a new form of tape that will make the copying of music from tape in breach of copyright impossible. One opportunity for immorality, let us assume, would thereby disappear. But the vice that it displayed, the vice of, let us say, dishonest dealing, will still have lots of opportunities to be practised. It may, in principle, be possible to eliminate the opportunities for practising some specialized vices. But then, in a world from which they were well and truly eradicated, the corresponding specialist moral ability, that of being good in avoiding that vice, would not be one the absence of which is a moral weakness or blemish. The morally good, in other words, are those who would have led a moral life even if the circumstances of their life were less favourable, but only in the sense of being able to cope with the temptations and pressures normal in their society.

For the most part the opportunities for dishonesty, indolence, insensitivity to the feelings of others, cruelty, pettiness, and the other vices and moral weaknesses are logically inseparable from the conditions of a human life which can have any moral merit. Given their prevalence one cannot object to the elimination of opportunities for evil on the three grounds cited above. The same kind of considerations show that only very rarely will the non-availability of morally repugnant options reduce a person's choice sufficiently to affect his autonomy. Therefore, the availability of such options is not a requirement of respect for autonomy.

Autonomy is valuable only if exercised in pursuit of the good. The ideal of autonomy requires only the availability of morally acceptable options. This may sound a very rigoristic moral view, which it is not. A moral theory which recognizes the value of autonomy inevitably upholds a pluralistic view. It admits the value of a large number of greatly differing pursuits which individuals are free to choose. But is the principle of autonomy consistent with the legal enforcement of morality? To the examination of this question we must now turn.

IV AUTONOMY AND THE HARM PRINCIPLE

Mill's harm principle states that the only justification for coercively interfering with a person is to prevent him from harming others. My discussion will revolve round the somewhat wider principle which regards the prevention of harm to anyone (himself included) as the only justifiable ground for coercive interference with a person. The harm principle is a principle of toleration. The common way of stating its point is to regard it as excluding considerations of private morality from politics. It restrains both individuals and the state from coercing people to refrain from certain activities or to undertake others on the ground that those activities are morally either repugnant or desirable. My purpose is to compare the scope and justification of the harm principle with those of autonomy-based toleration.

That there may be at least some connection between the autonomy and the harm principles is evident. Respect for the autonomy of others largely consists in securing for them adequate options, that is, opportunities and the ability to use them. Depriving a person of opportunities or of the ability to use them is a way of causing him harm. Both the use-value and the exchange-value of property represent opportunities for their owner. Any harm to a person by denying him the use of the value of his property is a harm to him precisely because it diminishes his opportunities. Similarly injury to the person reduces his ability to act in ways which he may desire. Needless to say, a harm to a person may consist not in depriving him of options but in frustrating his pursuit of the projects and relationships he has set upon.

Between them these cases cover most types of harm. Several forms of injury are, however, left out. Severe and persistent pain is incapacitating. But not all pain falls into this class and even pain which does incapacitate may be objected to as pain independently of its incapacitating results. The same is true of offence. Serious and persistent offence may well reduce a person's opportunities. It may even affect his ability to use the opportunities he has or frustrate his pursuit of his goals. But many cases of causing offence fall short of this. All offensive behaviour may be reprehensible as offensive, independently of its consequences to the affected person's options or projects. Similar considerations apply to other forms of injury such as hurting people's feeling.

It is of interest to note that pain and offence, hurt and the like are harmful only when they do affect options or projects. For 'harm' in its ordinary use has a forward-looking aspect. To harm a person is to diminish his prospects, to affect his possibilities adversely. It is clear that supporters of the harm principle are also concerned with the prevention of offence and pain. It is not clear whether they extend it to encompass all forms of hurting or adversely affecting people. For clarity's sake we could distinguish between the narrow harm principle which allows coercion only for the prevention of harm in the strict sense of the word and the somewhat open-ended broad harm principle which allows coercion for the prevention of pain, offence, and perhaps some other injuries to a person as well.

I hope that these observations are as uncontroversial as they are intended to be. I have tried to follow the common understanding of harm, but to describe it in terms which bring out the connection between harm and autonomy. They reinterpret the principle from the point of view of a morality which values autonomy. That is, they are not an account of the meaning of 'harm' (only the point about the forward-looking aspect of harm belongs to an account of its meaning). People who deny the moral value of autonomy will not be committed to denying that there are harms, nor that harming people is, as such, wrong. But they would have to provide a different understanding of what behaviour harms others. Since 'causing harm' by its very meaning demands that the action is prima facie wrong it is a normative concept acquiring its specific meaning from the moral theory within which it is embedded.

This way of thinking of the harm principle may help resolve our response to two potentially decisive objections to it. First, the principle seems to forbid the redistribution of wealth through taxation, and the provision of public goods out of public funds on a non-voluntary basis, as well as to proscribe such familiar schemes as a tax-financed educational and national health systems, or the subsidization of public transport. Secondly, the only reason for coercively interfering with a person in order to prevent harm is that it is wrong to cause such harm. But if coercive interventions are justified on this ground then they are used to enforce morality. If so why stop with the prevention of harm? Why not enforce the rest of morality?

Let us assume that we accept the second objection and maintain that it is the function of governments to promote morality. That means that governments should promote the moral quality of the life of those whose lives and actions they can affect. Does not this concession amount to a rejection of the harm principle? It does, according to the common conception which regards the aim and function of the principle as to curtail the freedom of governments to enforce morality. I wish to propose a different understanding of it, according to which it is a principle about the proper way to enforce morality. In other words I would suggest that the principle is derivable from a morality which assigns high value to individual autonomy and regards the principle of autonomy, which imposes duties on people to secure for all the conditions of autonomy, as one of the most important moral principles.

To derive the harm principle from the principle of autonomy one has to establish that the autonomy-based duties never justify coercion where there was no harm. This brings us immediately to the first objection. Governments are subject to autonomy-based duties to provide the conditions of autonomy to people who lack them. These extend beyond the duty to prevent loss of autonomy. This may seem as an endorsement of the first objection to the harm principle. But is it? It is a mistake to think that the harm principle recognizes only the duty of governments to prevent loss of autonomy. Sometimes failing to improve the situation of another is harming him.

One can harm another by denying him what is due to him. This is obscured by the common misconception which confines harming a person to acting in a way which results in that person being worse off after the action than he was before. While such actions do indeed harm, so do acts or omissions the result of which is that a person is worse off after them than he should then be. One harms another by failing in one's duty to him, even though this is a duty to improve his situation and the failure does not leave him worse off than he was before. Consider a disabled person who has a legal right to be employed by any employer to whom he applies and who has fewer than four per cent disabled employees in his work force. If such an employer turns him down he harms him although he does not worsen his situation. If you owe me five pounds you harm me by delaying its repayment by a month.

So if the government has a duty to promote the autonomy of people the harm principle allows it to use coercion both in order to stop people from actions which would diminish people's autonomy and in order to force them to take actions which are required to improve peoples' options and opportunities. It is true that an action harms a particular person only if it affects him directly and significantly by itself. It does not count as harming him if its undesirable consequences are indirect and depend on the intervention of other actions. I do not, for example, harm Johnson by failing to pay my income tax, nor does the government harm him by failing to impose a tax which it has a moral obligation to impose, even if it can be established that Johnson suffered as a result of such failures. In each case the culprit can claim that the fact that Johnson is the one who suffered was decided not by the guilty action but by other intervening actions (which may not have been guilty at all).

But even though I or the government did not harm Johnson we caused harm. If you like, call it harm to unassignable individuals. The point is that one causes harm if one fails in one's duty to a person or a class of persons and that person or a member of that class suffers as a result. That is so even when one cannot be blamed for harming the person who suffered because the allocation of the loss was determined by other hands. A government which has a moral duty to increase old age pensions harms old age pensioners if it fails to do so, even though it does not harm any particular pensioner.

The upshot of this discussion is that the first objection fails, for the harm principle allows full scope to autonomy-based duties. A person who fails to discharge his autonomy-based obligations towards others is harming them, even if those obligations are designed to promote the others' autonomy rather than to prevent its deterioration. It follows that a government whose responsibility is to promote the autonomy of its citizens is entitled to redistribute resources, to provide public goods and to engage in the provision of other services on a compulsory basis, provided its laws merely reflect and concretize autonomy-based duties of its citizens. Coercion is used to ensure compliance with the law. If the law reflects autonomy-based duties then failure to comply harms others and the harm principle is satisfied.

But the autonomy principle is a perfectionist principle. Autonomous life is valuable only if it is spent in the pursuit of acceptable and valuable projects and relationships. The autonomy principle permits and even requires governments to create morally valuable opportunities, and to eliminate repugnant ones. Does not that show that it is incompatible with the harm principle? The impression of incompatibility is encouraged by the prevalent anti-perfectionist reading of the harm principle. That reading is at odds with the fact that the principle merely restricts the use of coercion. Perfectionist goals need not be pursued by the use of coercion. A government which subsidizes certain activities, rewards their pursuit, and advertises their availability encourages those activities without using coercion.

It is no objection to point out that the funds necessary for all these policies are raised by compulsory taxation. I assume that tax is raised to provide adequate opportunities, and is justified by the principle of autonomy in a way consistent with the harm principle in the way described a couple of paragraphs above. It is in deciding which options to encourage more than others that perfectionist considerations dominate. Here they are limited by the availability of resources mobilized in the above mentioned way. The harm principle is consistent with many perfectionist policies of the kind required by any moral theory which values autonomy highly. It does, however, exclude the use of coercion to discourage non-harmful opportunities. Can that exclusion be derived from the principle of autonomy?

If the argument of section three is sound, then pursuit of the morally repugnant cannot be defended from coercive interference on the ground that being an autonomous choice endows it with any value. It does not (except in special circumstances where it is therapeutic or educational). And yet the harm principle is defensible in light of the principle of autonomy for one simple reason. The means used, coercive interferences, violate the autonomy of their victim. The coercion of criminal penalties is a global and indiscriminate invasion of autonomy. Imprisoning a person prevents him from almost all autonomous pursuits. Other forms of coercion may be less severe, but they all invade autonomy, and they all, at least in this world, do it in a fairly indiscriminate way. That is, there is no practical way of ensuring that the coercion will restrict the victims' choice of repugnant options but will not interfere with their other choices. A moral theory which values autonomy highly can justify restricting the autonomy of one person for the sake of the greater autonomy of others or even of himself in the future. That is why it can justify coercion to prevent harm, for harm interferes with autonomy. But it will not tolerate coercion for other reasons. The availability of repugnant options, and even their free pursuit by individuals does not detract from their autonomy. Undesirable as those conditions are they may not be curbed by coercion.

V THE HARM PRINCIPLE: WIDE OR NARROW?

Our enquiry is almost complete. We set out to explore the limits of toleration required by a perfectionist political morality, one which not only holds that individuals have moral duties towards others, but that they may use political means in trying to discharge their duties. The required limits of toleration may be wider than this enquiry suggests. There may be other independent arguments for toleration and in some ways the boundaries they dictate may differ from those here indicated. But some alternative arguments are not acceptable if the argument of this essay is sound. Anti-perfectionist arguments are alternatives rather than complementary to ours. The morality whose implications were explored is one which places a very high value on personal autonomy. We saw that such a morality presupposes competitive pluralism. That is, it presupposes that people should have available to them many forms and styles of life incorporating incompatible virtues, which not only cannot be all realized in one life but tend to generate mutual intolerance.

Such an autonomy-valuing pluralistic morality requires a principle of autonomy which will protect people pursuing different styles of life and assure the survival of the options to pursue different forms of life. The principle of autonomy itself generates such a principle of toleration. We explored the limits of the principle which are two. First, it does not protect nor does it require any individual option. It merely requires the availability of an adequate range of options. We saw that this lends the principle a somewhat conservative aspect. No specific new options have a claim to be admitted. The adequacy of the range is all that matters, and any change should be gradual in order to protect 'vested interests'. Secondly, the principle does not protect morally repugnant activities or forms of life. In other respects the principle is a strong one. It requires positively encouraging the flourishing of a plurality of incompatible and competing pursuits, projects and relationships.

It turns out that the boundaries of the autonomy-based toleration are those stated by the harm principle. It allows perfectionist policies so long as they do not require a resort to coercion. Both coercion and manipulation invade autonomy. A morality which values autonomy highly will shun either except where they are required to protect autonomy. The harm principle deserves its place as the liberal principle of toleration not because it is anti-perfectionist. For it is not. But because, as J. S. Mill, its original advocate, and H. L. A. Hart, its leading protagonist in recent times, clearly saw, it sets a limit on the means allowed in pursuit of moral ideals. While such ideals may indeed be pursued by political means, they may not be pursued by the use of coercion (or, as I have mentioned above, manipulation) except in exceptional cases. Those are cases which involve harm and they are exceptional because they typically involve a violation of the autonomy principle. The principle sets a necessary condition only. It does not justify all uses of coercion to prevent harm. But it puts an end to the use of coercion for other purposes.

One last, but crucial ambiguity remains to be resolved. Do these considerations vindicate the wide or the narrow harm principle? The drift of the argument so far shows that if coercion may only be used to protect people's autonomy then the narrow principle is the right one. For 'harm' in the narrow sense is confined to infringement of the conditions of autonomy. But commitment to this conclusion can be justified only if no other moral offence or breach of duty could justify infringement of autonomy. This is tantamount to assigning to autonomy lexical priority in the moral scheme of things. Nothing in this essay justifies this conclusion. Nor has it been the classical liberal position. It has allowed that the prevention of pain may sometimes justify invasion of personal autonomy. If so then the principle to endorse is the wide one.

8.2 Comment

C. L. TEN*

Raz's argument is complex and important. I shall concentrate on my disagreements with him. He presents an autonomy-based defence of the principle of toleration. This principle of toleration is perfectionist and it in turn provides the moral foundation for a harm principle similar to that advocated by J. S. Mill and H. L. A. Hart. The argument for toleration proceeds to show that autonomy requires a variety of valuable options which can only be satisfied by competitive moral pluralism. But competitive moral pluralism generates conflicts between people pursuing incompatible forms of life, and so a principle of toleration is needed in order to curb intolerant actions and thereby to allow diverse forms of life to flourish.

Raz's argument for toleration depends on the relationship between autonomy and moral pluralism. The ideal of autonomy is that people should control their own lives at least to some degree. This can only be realized if they have an adequate range of choices and options, including a variety of morally acceptable options. This variety is reflected in the different kinds of reasons for choosing various options. Some of the reasons relate to the nature of the object to be pursued, while others relate to the manner in which the object is to be pursued. The ability to respond to reasons favouring valuable options depends on the existence in human beings of an appropriately virtuous disposition. Faced with a choice between the cultivation of many different virtues, a person is unable to attain all the virtues to their highest degree. Moral pluralism is the view that different and incompatible forms of life have distinctive virtues which cannot all be attained by a person who pursues any one form of life. Moral pluralism is thus presupposed by the ideal of personal autonomy. But the version of moral pluralism that is presupposed is only what Raz calls weak moral pluralism which maintains that there are several maximal forms of life. 'A form of life is maximal if, under normal circumstances, a person whose life is of that kind cannot improve it by acquiring additional virtues, not by enhancing the degree to which he possesses any virtue, without sacrificing another virtue he possesses or the degree to which it is present in his life.'

The argument so far establishes a connection between autonomy and moral pluralism, but the case for toleration has yet to be made. This relies on one crucial step invoking the notion of competitive moral pluralism which is the form that pluralism commonly takes. Competitive moral pluralism recognizes the value of incompatible moral virtues which tend to encourage intolerance of other virtues. Raz's argument then is that if all normal persons are to be allowed to be autonomous, there is a need for diverse forms of life. But the moral virtues associated with these diverse forms of life are likely, given human nature, to depend on character traits many of which lead to intolerance of other acceptable and valuable forms of life. There will therefore be conflicts between mutually intolerant people all of whom are pursuing valuable but incompatible forms of life. Toleration, by regulating these conflicts, allows diverse forms of life to develop.

Raz's argument for toleration is now complete, and he goes on to show how the autonomy-based defence of toleration provides a foundation for the harm principle. But I should like to concentrate on his case for toleration.

It might at first seem odd that Raz should insist that respect for autonomy *requires* competitive moral pluralism, or that it *presupposes* competitive moral pluralism, or even that 'autonomy can only be realized within a community which endorses a competitive pluralistic morality'. For if his argument succeeds it seems to show that respect for autonomy requires not competitive moral pluralism but just moral pluralism. No doubt Raz believes that competitive pluralistic moralities are very common forms of pluralism, and he even suggests that perhaps all viable forms of pluralism are competitive. But this does not show that autonomy presupposes or requires competitive moral pluralism. The distinctive feature of moral pluralism is its acceptance of virtues which encourage intolerance of other virtues, and this, taken on its own, is a feature which threatens the realization of personal autonomy, and cannot therefore be something presupposed or required by it.

But perhaps Raz's argument is that, given the quirks of human nature, autonomy can only be realized for all if allowance is made for different and incompatible forms of life many of which display virtues leading to intolerance of other forms of life and their corresponding virtues. Unless the validity of such diverse forms of life is accepted, there will be no scope for the development of the ideal of autonomy. But any doctrine which recognizes the validity of distinct, incompatible, and mutually intolerant virtues is a form of competitive moral pluralism. So perhaps Raz is right in claiming, on the basis of the correctness of his assumptions, that competitive moral pluralism is required by the ideal of personal autonomy.

But now a problem arises as to why it is that moral pluralism should be competitive. If people accept the fact that there are valuable forms of life other than their own, what is the basis of their attitude of intolerance? We are normally intolerant of those forms of life which we reject or disapprove of. Raz suggests that intolerance is directed at people's limitations. A person with one virtue may lack other incompatible virtues. But this does not seem to be a sufficient basis for intolerance, for people will be aware that the missing virtues are missing precisely because they are incompatible with the virtue that is present. Surely the recognition of the value of the latter will generate acceptance or resignation rather than hostility or dislike. Indeed the acceptance of moral pluralism, with its recognition of several maximal forms of life, involves an acknowledgement that the 'deficiency' of a maximal form of life cannot be removed without lowering the quality of that form of life. The result is likely to be tolerance rather than intolerance of the necessary limitations of others.

Raz's account of the relations between autonomy, competitive moral pluralism, and toleration makes his case for toleration inapplicable to some of the central areas in which liberals have pleaded for toleration, namely in the areas of religion and sexual behaviour. In the case of religion, conflicts are generated because one group does not recognize the value of the religious practices and beliefs of the others. There is no acceptance here of several maximal forms of life. If religious pluralism were accepted, then conflicts would disappear, and along with them, the need for toleration. Similarly in the area of sexual conduct, the hostility of the moral majority to certain forms of sexual conduct is based on the rejection of the value of those forms of conduct. Where a minority's sexual conduct is accepted by a majority as displaying certain virtues which are incompatible with the virtues of the majority, we do not find mutual or unilateral hostility. Thus some members of the moral majority, who are dedicated parents, recognize that whatever virtues they have are incompatible with the different virtues displayed in the lives of celibate priests and nuns. And it is perhaps fair to add that this recognition is reciprocated. There may be an acknowledgement of one another's limitations, but there is no resulting intolerance.

Within a relatively narrow range of sexual conduct and religious practices where moral pluralism is accepted, and there is a recognition of several maximal forms of life, we do not find any need for a principle of toleration because the conflicts and hostilities which such a principle seeks to regulate are absent. Toleration becomes necessary only when one moves outside this narrow range into areas where moral pluralism is rejected. Raz is aware that in the clearest cases toleration is needed to restrain one's indignation at moral evil. But this is the kind of toleration that is cherished by liberals in the religious and sexual areas, and it is not amenable to the autonomy-based defence that Raz provides. Does this suggest some weaknesses in Raz's account of autonomy? I think that it does.

Raz maintains that a commitment to autonomy entails a commitment to moral pluralism. By moral pluralism he means the view that incompatible forms of life are morally acceptable and that they display distinct moral virtues. But I doubt that autonomy commits one to moral pluralism in this sense. For if an autonomous person is one who shapes his or her own life, then what autonomy requires is that people should be allowed to choose from different and incompatible forms of life. There is no one form of life which should be imposed on all against their will. But although autonomy requires the toleration of different forms of life, it does not require that each form of life has its distinct moral virtues. It is possible, although not necessary, that only one form of life is virtuous.

Raz denies this because he argues that if this were the case agents would not have a proper choice. 'Autonomy requires a choice of goods. A choice between good and evil is not enough.' But the example used to illustrate this point does not quite succeed. We are asked to consider the case of a person deciding whether to be an electrician. He is free not to be an electrician if he murders one person. Raz points out that if the person chooses rightly and agrees to be an electrician in order to avoid murdering, then he is not autonomous. Raz is of course right here. However, the lack of autonomy does not depend on the fact that the person is presented with a choice between good and evil, but rather on the different fact that one option, the commission of murder, is totally unacceptable to him, and is therefore not a live option. The rejection of the option need not be based on moral grounds.

I have argued that our endorsement of the value of autonomy does not involve an acknowledgement that different and incompatible forms of life have distinct virtues. If this is correct, then an autonomy-based defence of toleration is relevant after all to the religious and sexual cases mentioned earlier. For the reason why toleration is necessary in order to promote autonomy is because the realization of the autonomy of different individuals will lead them to the pursuit of different and incompatible forms of life. Since it is often the case that they each regard only one of these forms of life as valuable, the ideal of autonomy leads to conflicts generated by the disapproval of the forms of life chosen by others. Toleration is necessary to prevent the expression of disapproval from being directed into coercive conduct which prevents others from realizing their autonomy.

Raz argues that, contrary to the views of political theorists who concentrate on intolerance in the form of coercive acts, the expression of a hostile view can be a form of intolerance. He may be right here, but criticisms of the conduct of others and of their choice of life plans often include reasons for them to act or choose differently. These reasons may actually help others in the effective and rational exercise of their autonomy. In any case, if one regards another person's form of life as intrinsically inferior to one's own, it would be difficult to refrain from hostile criticism. Such expressions of hostility are not in many cases incompatible with the recognition of the value of autonomy because, unlike coercive acts, they still leave others as the final arbiters of the value of the hostile views and of the chosen way of life. It is only when people's lives are inextricably bound together, or when they are living in very close and unavoidable proximity, that the expression of hostile views can usefully be treated as a form of intolerance that is incompatible with the endorsement of the value of autonomy.

Raz argues that the autonomy-based account of toleration is perfectionist. But if the sketch of autonomy given above is correct, then there is an important sense in which the autonomy-based defence of toleration is anti-perfectionist. I have argued that respect for autonomy presupposes only that people be allowed to choose for themselves different and incompatible forms of life. There is no presupposition that each form of life carries with it distinct virtues, although of course this may in fact be the case compatibly with the endorsement of the value of autonomy. However, it is likely that, whatever the objective truth may be about the virtues of different forms of life, many of those participating in a form of life will regard, from the subjective point of view, their own chosen way of life as the only virtuous one, and will see no moral merit in forms of life incompatible with it. The autonomy-based case for toleration will constrain them from imposing their views on others.

The principle of toleration is anti-pefectionist in the sense that it is neutral between different forms of life, and does not presuppose the correctness of any of them. However, the basis of its neutrality is not scepticism about morality, but rather a commitment to the value of autonomy. So the principle of toleration cannot be neutral between all moral values, for it itself is an embodiment of one set of values against others. But it is a principle of political morality concerned with the regulation of the relationships between different individuals or groups, and different forms of life. Such a principle of political morality naturally cannot be neutral between principles of political morality for it must reject all other principles, for example legal moralism and paternalism, which are incompatible with it. But it can be, and indeed must be, neutral between competing moralities about the best form of life for individuals. It is therefore at the level of what constitutes the good life for individuals or groups, and not that of political morality, that the autonomy-based principle of toleration is anti-perfectionist.

Perfectionism, on the other hand, is a principle of political morality that seeks to maximize the value endorsed by a favoured morality of the good life. An autonomy-based principle of toleration, because it is a competing principle of political morality, is incompatible with perfectionism. But it does not have to dispute the presupposition of perfectionism at the level of the good life. Thus it does not have to deny that there is one form of life that is objectively better than all others. Its neutrality at that level means that it takes no sides on this particular issue.

Raz thinks that because the autonomy principle is perfectionist, it requires governments to create morally valuable opportunities and to eliminate repugnant ones. But he sees a government's pursuit of such perfectionist goals as achievable not through the use of coercion but rather through the encouragement it gives to worthwhile activities. The refusal to use coercion to eliminate morally repugnant, but non-harmful, opportunities is justifed on the ground that coercion is a blunt instrument that invades the autonomy of the individual in an indiscriminate manner. There is in practice no effective way of using coercion only to limit people's morally repugnant choices without also interfering with their other choices.

This point is surely arguable. It is not clear why, for example, a law which prohibits certain morally repugnant but harmless sexual activities will also interfere with people's choices in other areas. It is therefore not obvious that Raz's autonomy-based account of toleration is wholly consistent with the harm principle. Raz points out that, 'the availability of repugnant options, and even their free pursuit by individuals does not detract from their autonomy'. This is true, but it does not provide a sufficient defence of the harm principle. On Raz's account, 'Autonomous life is valuable only if it is spent in the pursuit of acceptable and valuable projects and relationships.' So even when autonomy is violated through the use of coercion to curb a person's activity, this in itself is quite consistent with a perfectionist account of autonomy. If the person's activity is repugnant, then, on this view, nothing valuable is lost by interference with it.

Furthermore, Raz seems to adopt an aggregative notion of autonomy when he argues that, 'a moral theory which values autonomy highly can justify restricting the autonomy of one person for the sake of the greater autonomy of others or even of himself in the future'. This provides a basis for an interpretation of the harm principle which would not, I think, he endorsed by liberals like Mill. For example, on Raz's view it is justifiable to sacrifice the autonomy of one person completely if this would thereby increase the greater autonomy of others. The sacrifice would still be justified even when the increase in autonomy of each of the others is very small but there are many others. This account of autonomy therefore runs into the same kinds of distributive problems which have featured in critiques of utilitarianism. Raz's notion of autonomy is also consistent with a substantial degree of paternalism.

I doubt that the importance of autonomy is adequately illustrated in Raz's claim that the autonomous life is valuable only when it is spent in the pursuit of acceptable and valuable projects. I think that the importance of autonomy rests at least in part on the resulting constraint on what may be done to individuals in order to make them pursue desirable goals. This is not to say that any form of life, so long as it is autonomously chosen, is valuable. Raz convincingly argues against this claim. But there are a variety of alternatives to this mistaken view. One alternative is to treat autonomy as an essential ingredient of any good or morally acceptable form of life. On this view, autonomy is a necessary but not a sufficient condition of the good life. This no doubt captures some of the spirit of the liberal defence of autonomy.

But there is also another liberal view that regards autonomy not as an ingredient of the good life, but as a requirement of what is right in political morality. Respect for autonomy is the basis on which a person's choices are protected from interference by others, even when the interference is designed to promote the good life. As an element of political morality, respect for autonomy prohibits us from interfering with a person's choices simply on the ground that we disapprove of the content of those choices. It circumscribes the type of reasons which may be used to justify state regulation of the activities of our fellow citizens.

If the harm principle is to be supported by the principle of autonomy, then the harm principle is a principle of political morality. The fact that it involves the enforcement of political morality does not therefore place it on the same level as those perfectionist theories which seek to enforce various moralities of the good life.

8.3 Comment

LEON SHELEFF*

The inescapable dilemma of liberal philosophy is that its weaknesses are deeply embedded in its underlying premisses; its key ideas carry—in the very attractiveness that they offer—the seeds of their own distortion. In a sense this may be true of all philosophies and ideologies—that they suffer inherently from the consequences of contradictions which often become only too apparent in the course of their consummation. Perhaps that is why one of the founders of sociology, Max Weber, was so insistent on the usage of ideal-types as a methodological tool—allowing theorists to set out the full range of their basic ideas in elaborate detail, without the necessity to base it on empirical reality.

In contrast, of course, Marxists have stressed that praxis is an essential part of their theory; yet here pragmatic realization of communist ideology has done much to undermine the power of pure theory. At the other end of the ideological spectrum, conservative thought in the form of the sociology of structural-functionalism, has been declared by Rolf Dahrendorf[1] to be basically utopian, and therefore not representative of any real society, since it describes a static model which, by the very nature of things, cannot be.

Similar considerations—of a gap between ideal and reality—apply to liberal thought; yet more so, because the very fundamentals of a liberal ethos, even at the theoretical stage, portend potential failure. This is seen, for instance, when liberalism is analysed in terms of its relations with other competing philosophies. For, whereas liberalism declares its willingness to share the societal stage with other ideologies, some of these other ideologies withhold similar rights and recognition from liberalism (as well as from other competing ideologies).

To adopt a well-worn cliché from the geo-political reality of the Middle East, liberalism must win all its battles, for the first battle it loses might be its last. In contrast, in all its own victories, intellectual, political,

---

[1] Rolf Dahrendorf, 'Out of Utopia: Toward a Reorientation of Sociological Analysis', *American Journal of Sociology*, vol. 64, 115–27.

whatever, liberalism, by definition, must leave all its vanquished foes to challenge again and to fight another day.

I once heard, as a student, a lecture espousing the cause and the concept of a liberal university, in which the lecturer ended his convincing presentation of the advantages of such a university over any alternative approaches—for example, of religious or ideologically-oriented academic education—with the haunting phrase, 'But I may be wrong'. It is just such qualifications and riders, indicating so much of what is beautiful, powerful, attractive, meaningful, and unique in liberalism, which also disclose its potential vulnerability.

The concepts that Raz has stressed in his paper, toleration and autonomy, epitomize these essential dilemmas in the liberal position. Thus, the liberal willingness to tolerate non-liberal ideas may be exploited for the purpose of subverting liberalism. The liberal idea of an autonomous human being becomes empty phraseology when people fear freedom and independence, and wish to evade the burdens of liberalism's plentiful possibilities, or the challenges which its varied and enticing options offer. And, of course, people cannot be forced, against their will, to become fully autonomous beings, as required by the liberal model. Indeed, the most acute dilemma confronting liberalism is its attitude toward coercion, its unwillingness to utilize power to enforce any particular pattern of behaviour.

It is here that the harm principle provides a partial solution, for through its judicious use, intervention may be justified in certain defined circumstances. Thus, while traditional liberalism does not generally allow for coercive measures to ensure desirable ends, it does allow for coercion in order to prevent certain defined undesirable consequences. The limits of personal autonomy and of societal toleration are thus generally drawn at the point of harm to others. The harm principle is a neutral non-normative rule, which has served as the lodestar for measuring the nature of liberal concession to coercive interference.

The converse of the harm principle is the refusal to allow coercion for the promotion of social betterment. Far better—so goes the liberal thesis—that people should suffer from their inability to handle the benefits that ensue from autonomy than that their liberty should be diminished in order to impose on them the benefits that others might desire for them. Yet for all its importance there are exceptions to the harm principle in its pure form.

Firstly, some liberals, most notably Jeremy Bentham and John Stuart

Mill,[2] allow for coercion in the pursuit of virtue in certain defined circumstances—where they concede the need for a legal obligation to rescue a fellow being in danger or dire distress. This latter aspect has been a major lacuna in recent liberal writings, as Anthony Honoré[3] has pointed out. Raz too has ignored this aspect.

Secondly, coercive measures may also be used where paternalistic considerations so require. Here certain groups of people, generally including such examples as the young and the mentally-handicapped, are considered to be inherently incapable of a rational and responsible utilization of the options that a liberal framework provides.

Raz has little to say about paternalism, but in passing adopts what he acknowledges as being a 'somewhat wider principle', which would allow coercion to prevent not only harm being done to others but also to oneself. This seems to me a dubious extension of the harm principle, allowing for extensive paternalistic intervention, which can only infringe on the capacity for autonomous behaviour. However, Raz does not develop this point so I shall not deal with it here, beyond the comment that the prevention of self-harm, if this is indeed the position adopted by Raz, seems a serious deviation from traditional liberalism.

Far more important—as well as innovative and, in my opinion, welcome—are two other contributions that Raz makes to traditional thought. Firstly, Raz argues indirectly for a possible connection between law and morality; secondly, he argues for the possibility of using coercive means for the purpose of pursuing an improvement in the situation of another. As to the first point he is ranging himself against one of the most accepted positions of liberal thought, argued most strongly by Hart; as to the second he is touching on a point generally ignored by liberals today, but which was the concern of Mill in some of his writings on economic themes.

Dealing with the harm principle, Raz claims that it is not activated in a moral vacuum, but may actually be an outcome of the expression of moral values. Whereas most liberals see the harm principle as being designed specifically to limit government interference in questions of morality, Raz sees the harm principle as being an expression of a morality that stems from individual autonomy, that is, the harm

---

[2] Jeremy Bentham, *An Introduction to the Principles of Morals and Legislation*, London (1970); John Stuart Mill, *On Liberty*, New York (1947).

[3] Anthony M. Honoré, 'Law, Morals and Rescue' in James J. Ratcliffe (ed.), *The Good Samaritan and the Law*, New York (1966); see also Leon S. Sheleff, *The Bystander: Behavior, Law, Ethics*, Lexington, Mass. (1978), 174–5.

principle is really a technical means of ensuring the moral values of individual autonomy; what is happening in essence is not a negative blocking of coercive interference (for instance in the cases of private morality, as described by Hart) but *a positive assertion of the morality of autonomy* that allows, if you will, for 'private morality'.

In adopting this approach Raz is claiming that liberalism is no different from other ideologies; it too must insist on a moral basis for its position, its toleration must not be seen as some weak and vacillating submission to 'anti-perfectionism which leads to the exclusion of ideals from politics'. On the contrary, it must proclaim and espouse the advantages of individual autonomy, as an expression of a moral value.

This is a major statement. If the moral principle of autonomy is a key aspect of liberalism, and if morality is intertwined with politics, then in contrast to Hart, Raz is acknowledging, even if indirectly, a connection between law and morality; for, as I have argued elsewhere,[4] politics is the channel through which law is linked to morality. Simply put, the implication of this line of thinking is: we should allow behaviour that Hart terms 'private morality', not because the law should not intervene in questions of morality, but because of a 'public morality' which favours individual autonomy.

However, once the relevance of morality for liberal thought is acknowledged, further possibilities emerge. Often the issue is not just that of ensuring a person's autonomy; what is often at stake is the *moral basis for defining what constitutes harm*. From this perspective moral pluralism involves not only the possibility of allowing others to practise undesirable patterns of behaviour as long as no harm is done to others (the minimum liberal position), but the willingness to concede that the definitions of harm may be different. There are indeed situations in which neither the concept of private morality nor of individual autonomy will provide a suitable framework for determining the limits of coercion.

Often liberal approaches assume that there is agreement as to the existence and nature of harm. This is noted for instance in Edwin Schur's work on 'crime without victims',[5] where since there is no victim, there is no need for coercive means. This is a presumably non-normative approach, very akin, both in its underlying liberal assumption, and in its ultimate outcomes, to the traditional liberal position. Yet,

[4] Leon S. Sheleff, 'Morality, Criminal Law and Politics', *Tel Aviv University Studies in Law*, vol. 2 (1976), 190.
[5] Edwin M. Schur, *Crime Without Victims: Deviant Behavior and Public Policy*, New Jersey (1965).

often, a deep *moral* issue is at stake as to whether or not there is a victim; whether or not coercion should be used is dependant on a prior decision, which may be controversial, as to whether or not there is a victim, or, in Raz's terminology, whether or not there is harm, caused by someone. The situation is seen in its most acute form when there are two conflicting harms, and the question becomes which should be considered the more serious.

Thus one of the examples provided by Schur is of abortion, ignoring the fact that the foetus may be considered by some as a victim. The issue then becomes whether the harm to the foetus (an emerging being) is to be considered as greater than the harm of forcing a woman to bear and give birth to a baby she does not want. Generally, those who see a moral conflict here, base it on the question of which has the greater right—the unborn child with a right to be born, or the woman's right to control over her own body. But the issue could equally be presented in opposite terms, as to which is the harm which is to be averted. Since, for liberals, coercion is dependent on the harm principle, this latter test might be more meaningful than that of an analysis of human rights. Indeed, in those countries which do allow limited abortion, this is the approach adopted. Possible negative psychological or sociological consequences are a prerequisite for allowing abortion, which is not seen as being the woman's automatic right. Similar considerations could be applied in other areas of private morality and autonomy. It may well be that in some instances the moral value of autonomy will suffice to determine the limits of coercion. In others, a moral measurement of possible harms might be more pertinent. Raz has recognized this possibility by writing that the harm principle helps assess the 'relative seriousness of various harms'.

To sum up then, I would suggest that when Raz talks of a connection between morality and politics, he is opening up the possibility of a reassessment of liberal thought which would lead to an acceptance of a connection between law and morality; and that the issue of morality might be not just one of positively asserting the need for individual autonomy, but of examining the moral basis for defining harm.

On the other hand, Raz attempts to provide the harm principle with a wider definition than is generally accepted, or, as I shall argue, than is warranted. Through the harm principle, Raz attempts to incorporate the possibility of acting to improve the situation of another. Harm, in his opinion, may be caused not just by actual damage, but also by 'failing to improve the position of another' and by 'denying him what is due to him'. Raz claims then that 'one harms another by failing in one's duty to him, even though this is a duty to improve his situation and the failure does not leave him worse off than he was before'.

Now it seems to me that such an approach is in direct conflict with the adamant stand taken by Mill, in his book *On Liberty*, on the need to prevent the use of coercion to make mandatory any action which will be to the betterment of the other person. (Parenthetically it should be noted that in his quote Raz certainly does not seem to be suggesting the exception of the bystander, for Mill's willingness to concede intervention in such a situation, in contrast to Raz, is based specifically on the need to ensure that the person is not left worse off than before.)

What then is Raz hinting at? I would suggest that the implications of what Raz has written may involve encroaching on the economic sphere. Now that *would* be a continuation of Mill's work. Unfortunately Raz does not spell this out in full, although the one example that he gives—of the rights of a disabled worker seeking employment—certainly hints at this intention. For Mill, the exceptions to his pure liberal theory of non-involvement, are found outside his classic on liberty, and may indicate later developments in his thought.[6] While his economic work is an extension of his own ideas as expressed in *On Liberty*, and is linked to the pure liberal approach of Adam Smith, it also contains his reservations on the possibilities of socialism. The fact is that Mill allowed for some degree of coercive involvement in economic matters.

Most of the liberals writing in jurisprudence tend to steer clear of such issues. (However, an interesting jurisprudential approach is developing which seeks to apply economic perspectives to legal problems.) Closely linked to liberalism is libertarianism, a concept being developed mainly in the United States to argue (particularly in direct contrast to American-style liberalism in politics such as the New Deal and the Great Society programmes with their extensive provisions for state intervention) that the rules of non-intervention in the realm of personal behaviour and private morality should be equally applied in the economic sphere.[7] *Laissez faire* economics becomes the parallel of individual autonomy. While such a position would perhaps have been perfectly acceptable to Adam Smith, it seems to me that Mill would have had many reservations. For in his work on economics, the position adopted by Mill was, in certain limited areas, to allow for state intervention. This

---

[6] John Stuart Mill, *Principles of Political Economy*, London (1909). See also 'Chapter on Socialism', *Works*, vol. 5.

[7] See for instance, *Journal of Libertarian Studies*.

is in conflict with libertarianism, but seems close to the position adopted by most liberals in American politics. The question is, what is the position of liberals writing academic treatises in jurisprudence?

John Rawls has referred to this issue in his *Theory of Justice*.[8] For him there are two key rules constituting the essence of justice—one relating to the need for liberty, the other for equality. However, whereas his only reservation about liberty is similar to the traditional liberal approach of not causing harm to others, his reservations about equality are far more extensive, allowing deviations from equality since, according to him, the 'less' equal will reap benefits from the total advantages that accrue to society by virtue of the talents and efforts of the 'more' equal. Now, while Rawls is insistent that such a position is non-normative, and is a logical conclusion which anyone working behind a 'veil of ignorance' would adopt, the fact of the matter is that it seems to be a position taken by someone who aspires to liberty more than equality, someone who is more of a liberal, let us say, than a socialist. One doubts whether there is indeed a real veil of ignorance and the preference that Rawls expresses for liberty over equality is, I would suggest, a consequence of his own basically liberal philosophy. A socialist would, perhaps, have placed different kinds of restrictions on the two key values of liberty and equality, in such a way that equality would be preserved even at the expense of some curtailment of liberty.

It may well be that this is what Mill himself was working toward, despite his many severe strictures on the dangers of socialism. Indeed, the statements which most clearly reveal his evolving position here are to be found not in his academic treaties, but in his autobiography, where he warmly acknowledges his wife's influence on his thinking in this regard. He indicates clearly that from a position of total negation of socialism, based on his belief in democracy, he and his wife attempted to merge the best of both these ideas. He writes: '. . . our ideal of ultimate improvement went far beyond Democracy, and would class us decidedly under the general designation of Socialists'.[9] In fact what Mill was apparently seeking was a means of ensuring the liberty of democracy (or liberalism) in the realm of ideas with the means of ensuring fairness in the field of economics. One thing is clear. Unlike Rawls, Mill did not see the economic issue as one of equality but rather as one of overall social justice; in order to achieve the improvement of mankind, he was prepared to consider and condone certain deviations from the principles

---

[8] John Rawls, *Theory of Justice*, Cambridge, Mass. (1971).
[9] John Stuart Mill, *Autobiography*, New York (1924), 162.

of pure liberalism. He was prepared to allow coercive measures in order to ensure a more just and fair allocation of resources—and coercive interference in this area involved *inter alia* restrictions on inheritance and landed property, the taxation of wealth, and the existence, finally, of a static economy. While this latter would come about largely through voluntary means as peoples' needs became satisfied, one wonders whether Mill would not, in modern times, allow far greater interference, given the nature of ecological issues in the modern world.

In any event it seems to me that much liberal writing in jurisprudence has ignored the fact that the issue of determining the limits of liberty relates not only to the question of social behaviour, but must also deal with the degree of coercion and control which a state is willing to impose in order to ensure that desirable standards of justice are maintained in the economic sphere. The crucial issues are not just whether liberalism allows tolerance of problematic and controversial patterns of behaviour, such as homosexuality, prostitution, drugs, or abortion, but whether it is willing to be tolerant of injustice in sharing the achievements of a society, or whether it wishes to use coercive measures to eradicate the effects of such injustice.

In a thoughtful and comprehensive analysis of individualism, the British philosopher Steven Lukes has dealt with what he calls the Basic Ideas of Individualism, which include, *inter alia*, autonomy, privacy, and the political economic, ethical and methodological aspects of individualism.[10] His final chapter is entitled 'Taking Equality and Liberty Seriously', and he concludes his analysis by suggesting that 'the only way to realize the values of individualism is through a humane form of socialism'.

I would argue that it is specifically toward such an end that Mill, whatever his criticisms of socialism, was moving. Modern day liberals—especially jurists—have ignored this issue; while many of those who have handled it, have preferred to pursue the libertarian approach, of applying the values of liberty in the field of general human behaviour to the specific area of economics.

Raz hints at the possible need for greater involvement in economics, and acknowledges the theoretical possibility of coercive intervention for the betterment of mankind. His reference here is in the context of the harm principle. What is needed, however, is not some recognition that harm may be caused by not contributing to the betterment of another,

[10] Steven Lukes, *Individualism*, Oxford (1973).

but a positive assertion of the potential good to be gained from an active search for economic justice; as Raz says, in pursuing a concept of the good life.

Finally, then, I suggest slight amendments to two of the innovative aspects related to the harm principle as presented by Raz:

1   In asserting the moral value of autonomy, he does not go far enough; it is harm itself which must be subjected to moral searching.

2   On the other hand, and somewhat paradoxically; in asserting the duty to improve the situation of another, Raz has linked it—and limited it—to the harm principle; he again has not gone far enough. It is the benefit itself which must be seen as the moral principle which is being expressed. What emerges from this latter point is that the full meaning of liberty—of toleration and autonomy—can only be gauged when we have answers not only to the limits of liberty in the realm of the traditional freedoms, of speech, movement, and belief, but when liberals have confronted the question of the degree of coercion they are prepared to countenance in order to ensure a just distribution of goods, services, and rewards. Here is the great difference between liberalism and libertarianism. Here is the great challenge confronting those who carry the liberal mantle. These are the questions which must be posed. What are the limits of toleration that a liberal is prepared to accept in considering economic justice? How precious is individual autonomy when it is used to gain advantage at the expense of other autonomous beings, who happen to be less endowed with human abilities?

Liberalism must be tested not only in its capacity to draw the limits of the criminal sanction,[11] or to define the overreach of the criminal law,[12] or to protect private morality. It must also meet the test of ensuring the maximum amount of liberty compatible with the maximum amount of economic justice. Having laid down fairly extensively and clearly the minimum limitations on liberty compatible with the liberty of others, its new task is to seek similar minimum limitations of liberty, compatible with the minimum deviations from economic justice.

[11]   Herbert Packer, The Limits of the Criminal Sanction, Berkeley, California (1968).
[12]   Norval Morris, 'The Overreach of the Criminal Law', *Acta Juridica* (1977), 40.

Bibliography of H. L. A. Hart*

1. 'The Ascription of Responsibility and Rights', *Proceedings of the Aristotelian Society* 49 (1948–9), 171–94.
2. 'Is There Knowledge by Acquaintance?', *Proceedings of the Aristotelian Society*, Supplementary Volume 23 (1949), 69–90.
3. Book review of Jerome Frank's *Law and the Modern Mind* in *Mind* 60 (1951), 268–70.
4. 'A Logician's Fairy Tale', *Philosophical Review* 60 (1951), 198–212.
5. 'Signs and Words' (on J. Holloway, *Language and Intelligence*), *Philosophical Quarterly* 2 (1952), 59–62.
6. *Definition and Theory in Jurisprudence*: an inaugural lecture delivered before the University of Oxford on 30 May 1953, Clarendon Press, Oxford, 1953.
7. 'Philosophy of Law and Jurisprudence in Britain (1945–52)', *American Journal of Comparative Law* 2 (1953), 355–64.
8. 'Justice', *Philosophy* 28 (1953), 348–52 (on G. del Vecchio, *Justice*).
9. Introduction to *John Austin, The Province of Jurisprudence Determined etc.*, Weidenfeld & Nicolson, London (1954), vii–xxi.
10. 'Are there any Natural Rights?', *Philosophical Review* 64 (1955), 175–91.
11. 'Theory and Definition in Jurisprudence', *Proceedings of the Aristotelian Society*, Supplementary Volume 29 (1955), 239–64.
12. Book review of Axel Hägerström's, *Inquiries into the Nature of Law and Morals* in *Philosophy* 30 (1955), 369–73.
13. 'Blackstone's Use of the Law of Nature', *Butterworths South African Law Review* (1956), 169–74.
14. Book review of Hans Kelsen's *Communist Theory of Law* in *Harvard Law Review* 69 (1956) 772 ff.
15. 'Murder and the Principles of Punishment: England and the United States', *Northwestern University Law Review* 52 (1957), 433 ff.
16. 'Analytic Jurisprudence in Mid-twentieth Century; a reply to Professor Bodenheimer', *University of Pennsylvania Law Review* 105 (1957), 953–75.
17. 'Legal and Moral Obligation', *Essays in Moral Philosophy*, ed. A. I. Melden, University of Washington Press, Seattle (1958), pp. 82–107.
18. 'Legal Responsibility and Excuses', *Determinism and Freedom*; Proceedings of the First Annual New York University Institute of Philosophy, ed. S. Hook, New York (1958).
19. 'Positivism and the Separation of Law and Morals', *Harvard Law Review* 71 (1958), 593–629.
20. with S. Hampshire: 'Decision, Intention and Certainty', *Mind* 67 (1958), 1–12.

* Excluding translations and reprints of Hart's work, as well as further minor items.

21. 'Dias and Hughes on Jurisprudence', *Journal of the Society of Public Teachers of Law* NS4 (1958), 143–9.

22. 'Immorality and Treason', *Listener* (30 July 1959), 162 ff.

23. 'Scandinavian Realism', *Cambridge Law Journal* 17 (1959), 233–40 (on Alf Ross's *On Law and Justice*).

24. with A. M. Honoré: *Causation in the Law*, Clarendon Press, Oxford (1959). Second edn. Clarendon Press, Oxford (1985).

25. 'Prolegomenon to the Principles of Punishment', *Proceedings of the Aristotelian Society* 60 (1959–60), 1–26.

26. *The Concept of Law*, Clarendon Press, Oxford (1961).

27. 'Negligence, *Mens Rea* and Criminal Responsibility', *Oxford Essays in Jurisprudence*, ed. A. Guest, Clarendon Press, Oxford (1961), 29–49.

28. 'The Use and Abuse of the Criminal Law', *Oxford Lawyer* 4 No. 1 (1961), 7–12.

29. Book review of Dennis Lloyd's *Introduction to Jurisprudence; with selected texts* in *Law Quarterly Review* 77 (1961), 123 ff.

30. 'Acts of Will and Responsibility', *The Jubilee Lectures of the Faculty, Sheffield University Faculty of Law*, ed. O. R. Marshall, London (1961).

31. 'Bentham' (Lecture on a Mastermind), *Proceedings of the British Academy* 48 (1962), 297–320.

32. *Punishment and the Elimination of Responsibility* (Hobhouse Memorial Trust Lecture, 16 May 1961), Athlone Press, London (1962), 32 pp.

33. Book review of Richard A. Wasserström's *The Judicial Decision* in *Stanford Law Review* 14 (1962), 919–26.

34. 'Acts of Will and Legal Responsibility', *Freedom of the Will*, ed. D. F. Pears, Macmillan, London (1963), 387–47.

35. Introduction to C. G. Perelman: *The Idea of Justice and the Problem of Argument*; tr. J. Petrie, Routledge & Kegan Paul, London (1963), vii–xi.

36. Book review of Oliver Wendell Holmes: *The Common Law* in *The New York Review of Books* 1 (1963–4), 15–16 (No. 4, 17 October 1963).

37. 'Kelsen Visited', *UCLA Law Review* 10 (1963), 709–28.

38. *Law, Liberty, and Morality* (The Harry Camp Lectures), Oxford University Press (London), 1963.

39. 'Self Referring Laws', *Festkrift tillägnad Professor, Juris Doktor Karl Olivecrona* vid hans Avgäng frän professorsämbetet den 30 Juni 1964 av kolleger, larjungär och vänner. Kungl. Bocktryckeriet P. A. Norstedt & Söner, Stockholm (1964), 307–16.

40. *The Morality of the Criminal Law*, two lectures (Lionel Cohen Lectures, 1964), Magnes Press, Hebrew University, Jerusalem; Oxford University Press, London (1965), 54 pp. (a. Changing Conceptions of Responsibility; b. The Enforcement of Morality).

41. Book review of Lon L. Fuller's *The Morality of Law* in *Harvard Law Review* 78 (1965), 1281–96.

42. 'Il Concetto di obbligo', trad. di G. Gavazzi, *Rivista di Filosofia* 57 (1966), 125–40.

43. 'Beccaria and Bentham', *Atti del convegno internazionale su Cesare Beccaria*, Academia delle Scienze di Torino, Memorials of the Academy Series 4a no. 9, Turin (1966).

44. 'Bentham on Sovereignty', *The Irsh Jurist* NS 2 (1967), 327–35.

45. 'Intention and Punishment', *Oxford Review* 4 (1967), 5–22.

46. 'Varieties of Responsibility, *Law Quarterly Review* 83 (1967), 346–64.

47. 'Legal Positivism', *Encyclopedia of Philosophy*, ed. P. Edwards, vol. 4, Macmillan and Free Press, New York (1967), 418–20.

48. 'Problems of Philosophy of Law', *Encyclopedia of Philosophy*, ed. P. Edwards, vol. 6, Macmillan and Free Press, New York (1967), 264–76.

49. 'Social Solidarity and the Enforcement of Morality', *University of Chicago Law Review* 35 (1967–8), 1–13.

50. *Punishment and Responsibility: Essays in the Philosophy of Law*, Clarendon Press, Oxford (1968) (including items no. 15, 18, 25, 27, 30, 32, 36, 40a, 45, and 46 of this bibliography).

51. 'Kelsen's Doctrine of the Unity of Law', *Ethics and Social Justice*, ed. M. K. Munitz and H. E. Kiefer, 171–99. vol. 4 of Contemporary Philosophic Thought: The International Philosophy Year Conferences at Brockport; State University of New York Press, Albany (1968–70).

52. 'Duty', *International Encyclopedia of Social Sciences*, ed. David L. Sills, vol. 4, 320–3, Macmillan and Free Press, New York (1968).

53. with J. H. Burns, Introduction, critical notes, and index to Jeremy Bentham: *An Introduction to the Principles of Morals and Legislation*, ed. J. H. Burns and H. L. A. Hart, Athlone Press, London (1970). (Collected Works of Jeremy Bentham.)

54. Introduction, critical notes and index to Jeremy Bentham: *Of Laws in General*, ed. H. L. A. Hart, Athlone Press, London (1970). (Collected Works of Jeremy Bentham.)

55. 'Jhering's Heaven of Concepts and Modern Analytic Jurisprudence', Jhering's Erbe; *Göttinger Symposium zur 150 Wiederkehr des Geburtstags von Rudolph von Jhering*, 68–78; hrsg. von F. Wieaker und Chr. Wollschläger, Vandenhoeck & Ruprecht, Göttingen (1970).

56. 'Bentham's "Of Laws in General"', *Rechstheorie* 2 (1971), 55–66.

57. 'Bentham on Legal Powers', *Yale Law Journal* 81 (1972), 799–822.

58. 'Abortion Law Reform; the English Experience', *Melbourne University Law Review* 8 (1972), 388–411.

59. 'Bentham on Legal Rights', *Oxford Essays in Jurisprudence* (2nd series), ed. A. W. B. Simpson, 171–201, Clarendon Press, Oxford (1973).

60. 'Bentham and the Demystification of the Law', *Modern Law Review* 36 (1973), 2–17.

61. 'Rawls on Liberty and Its Priority', *University of Chicago Law Review* 40 (1973), 543–55.
62. 'Law in the Perspective of Philosophy: 1776–1976', *New York University Law Review* 51 (1976), 538–51.
62. 'Bentham and the United States of America', *Journal of Law and Economics* 19 (1976), 547–67.
64. 'American Jurisprudence through English Eyes: The Nightmare and the Noble Dream', *Georgie Law Review* 11 (1977), 969.
65. With J. H. Burns: Introduction, critical notes and index to Jeremy Bentham: *Comment on the Commentaries and A Fragment on Government* ed. J. H. Burns and H. L. A. Hart, Athlone Press London (1977), (Collected Works of Jeremy Bentham.)
66. Book Review of *Morality: an Introduction to Ethics* by Gilbert Harman, and *Ethics: Inventing Right and Wrong* by J. L. Mackie, *New York Review of Books* XXV, no 3 (1978).
67. 'Utilitarianism and Natural Rights', *Tulane Law Review* 53 (1979), 663–80.
68. 'Between Utility and Rights', *Columbia Law Review* 79 (1979), 828–46.
69. 'Death and Utility' review article on *Practical Ethics* by Pete Singer, *New York Review of Books* XXVII, no. 8 (1980).
70. 'El Nuevo desafio al positivismo juridico', *Sistema* 36, Madrid (1980), 3–18.
71. 'The House of Lords on Attempting the Impossible', in ed. C. Tappe *Crime, Proof and Punishment: Essays in Memory of Sir Rupert Cross*, Butterworth (1981); reprinted in *Oxford Journal of Legal Studies* 1 (1981), 149–66.
72. *Essays on Bentham: Studies in Jurisprudence and Political Theory*, Clarendon Press, Oxford 1982, 272 pp. including items no. 42, 43, 44, 57, 59, 60, 63 and 69 of this bibliography.
73. Introduction to paperback edition of Jeremy Bentham: *An Introduction to the Principles of Morals and Legislation*, ed. J. H. Burns and H. L. A. Hart (XXIII–LXX) Methuen, London and New York (1982).
74. *Essays in Jurisprudence and Philosophy*, Clarendon Press, Oxford (1983), 396 pp. (including items no. 6, 19, 23, 36, 37, 39, 41, 48, 49, 51, 55, 61, 62, 64, 67, 68 and 71 of this bibliography).
75. 'A. R. N. Cross, 1912–1980', Proceedings of the British Academy, London, Vol. lxx (1984) 705–34.
76. Review of *Bentham* by Ross Harrison in *Mind* 90 (1985), 153–8.

Index

DATE DUE